Our current understanding of children with disruptive behavior disorders owes much to the work of these authors, whose influential research has shown us that disorders of child behavior are also disorders of emotional development. In this landmark publication, they unpack what practitioners need to know about the science of prosocial emotions and callous–unemotional traits. No practitioner should be without the evidence-based knowledge and tools now available to help recognize children with limited prosocial emotions and respond to their unique needs.

—**David J. Hawes, PhD,** Professor of Clinical Psychology, School of Psychology, University of Sydney, Sydney, Australia

Bringing together decades of theoretically driven research with a wealth of clinical experience, this book will be a valuable tool for practitioners working with children and adolescents with early onset conduct disorders. Highly recommended.

—Mark Dadds, PhD, Professor of Child Psychology, University of Sydney, Sydney, Australia; Director, Growing Minds Australia

This will be *the* book for clinicians and other practitioners caring for children and adolescents with conduct problems and limited prosocial emotions.

—Robert James Blair, PhD, Professor and Director of Child and Adolescent Psychiatry Research, Department of Psychiatry, Virginia Commonwealth University, Richmond, VA, United States

Drs. Paul Frick and Eva Kimonis, pioneering leaders in the study of youth conduct disorders and limited prosocial emotions, have produced an indispensable book that offers a clear, integrative framework for understanding these complex conditions. Importantly, they also provide concrete, practice-ready guidance for diagnosis, treatment, and future policy. This book will be essential reading for researchers, clinicians, and trainees alike, filling a critical gap in the child mental health literature.

—Rebecca Waller, PhD, Associate Professor of Psychology; Director, Emotion Development Environment & Neurogenetics (EDEN) Lab, Department of Psychology, University of Pennsylvania, Philadelphia, PA, United States

This book is a real game changer and will ensure that limited prosocial emotions will be appropriately assessed and considered in interventions for disruptive behavior disorders. I have lost count of the number of parents, teachers, and clinicians who have reached out to me, asking what to do with a child whose behavior is aggressive and dangerous but appears to have limited capacity for empathy and guilt. It has been heartbreaking to tell them that much of what we know is in academic journals and has not yet reached clinical and educational services. This book by Drs. Frick and Kimonis will change that—for the benefit of children, young people, and their families.

—Essi Viding, PhD, FBA, FMedSci, Professor of Developmental Psychopathology, University College London, London, United Kingdom

This is an essential book for those assessing and treating youth and families with mental illness, particularly young people with behavior problems and antisocial and aggressive behavior. The book is written by two of the foremost leaders in the field—Paul Frick, who essentially founded this area of research, and Eva Kimonis, who has done the most extensive and cutting-edge research in the treatment of limited prosocial emotions. The book is easy to follow and provides an expert, pioneering description of research in the field, along with practical advice and guidance on assessing and treating youth with limited prosocial emotions. This book should be compulsory in courses on child interventions, in clinical and forensic graduate programs, and is an ideal guide for practicing clinicians looking to become more adept in this challenging practice area.

—Luke W. Hyde, PhD, Professor, Department of Psychology, University of Michigan, Ann Arbor, MI, United States

A CLINICAL GUIDE TO WORKING WITH YOUTH WITH CONDUCT DISORDERS AND LIMITED PROSOCIAL EMOTIONS

A CLINICAL GUIDE TO WORKING WITH YOUTH WITH CONDUCT DISORDERS AND LIMITED PROSOCIAL EMOTIONS

PAUL J. FRICK
EVA R. KIMONIS

AMERICAN PSYCHOLOGICAL ASSOCIATION

Published by
American Psychological Association
750 First Street, NE
Washington, DC 20002
https://www.apa.org

Order Department
https://www.apa.org/pubs/books
order@apa.org

Typeset in Meridien and Ortodoxa by Circle Graphics, Inc., Reisterstown, MD

Printer: Gasch Printing, Odenton, MD
Cover Designer: Anthony Paular Design, Newbury Park, CA

Library of Congress Cataloging-in-Publication Data

CIP data has been applied for.
Library of Congress Control Number: 2026000656

ISBN 9781433843808 (paperback)
ISBN 9781433843815 (epub)
ISBN 9781433850196 (pdf)

https://doi.org/10.1037/0000500-000

Printed in the United States of America

10 9 8 7 6 5 4 3 2 1

This book is dedicated to all of the amazing students and colleagues who have contributed to the work presented in this book and made my academic journey rewarding and fun. It is also dedicated to my family, who always loved and supported me and pushed me to always be at least "moderately successful," especially my love and constant support, Vicki.

—PAUL J. FRICK

This book is dedicated to the many incredible students I've worked with over the years who have become like family to me throughout their research journeys. Their curiosity, dedication, and hard work have contributed to the knowledge shared in these pages and made this work deeply fulfilling. I am also grateful to the inspiring colleagues whose work has sparked new ideas and deepened my thinking.

To my formidable mentors—especially the one I'm so fortunate to write this book with—whose unwavering support and championship have guided me at every stage. And to the loves of my life, Elle, Theo, and Ken, who remind me of what truly matters and keep me grounded in all the best ways.

—EVA R. KIMONIS

CONTENTS

Introduction: Assessing and Treating Children and Adolescents With Disruptive Behavior Disorders Who Lack Empathy and Guilt 3

I. OVERVIEW OF THE LIMITED PROSOCIAL EMOTIONS SPECIFIER AND ITS SIGNIFICANCE 11

1. An Overview of Research on Diagnosing Limited Prosocial Emotions in Children and Adolescents 13
2. Clinically Important Differences Between Children With Limited Prosocial Emotions and Other Children With Conduct Problems 25
3. Distinct Emotional, Cognitive, and Social Characteristics of Children and Adolescents With Limited Prosocial Emotions 37

II. CLINICAL ASSESSMENT AND DIAGNOSIS OF CHILDREN AND ADOLESCENTS WITH LIMITED PROSOCIAL EMOTIONS 57

4. General Considerations in the Assessment of Children and Adolescents With Limited Prosocial Emotions 59
5. Using the Inventory of Callous-Unemotional Traits in Clinical Assessments of the Limited Prosocial Emotions Specifier 79
6. Using the Clinical Assessment of Prosocial Emotions (CAPE) in Clinical Assessments of the Limited Prosocial Emotions Specifier 91

III. TREATING CHILDREN AND ADOLESCENTS WITH LIMITED PROSOCIAL EMOTIONS **113**

7. An Overview of Treatments That Work for Children and Adolescents With Limited Prosocial Emotions **115**

8. Parent–Child Interaction Therapy Adapted for Callous-Unemotional Traits **141**

9. Illustrative Clinical Case Study Involving Parent–Child Interaction Therapy Adapted for Callous-Unemotional Traits **191**

10. Expanding the Reach of Treatments for Children and Adolescents With Limited Prosocial Emotions **239**

IV. FUTURE DIRECTIONS FOR RESEARCH AND PRACTICE **261**

11. A Road Map for the Future of Assessing and Treating Children and Adolescents With Limited Prosocial Emotions **263**

Appendix: QR Codes for Accessing Various Assessment Tools, Treatment Manuals, and Other Resources 273

References 277

Index 311

About the Authors 319

A CLINICAL GUIDE TO WORKING WITH YOUTH WITH CONDUCT DISORDERS AND LIMITED PROSOCIAL EMOTIONS

Introduction

Assessing and Treating Children and Adolescents With Disruptive Behavior Disorders Who Lack Empathy and Guilt

Conduct problems in children refer to behaviors that hurt or violate the rights of others (e.g., fighting, bullying, stealing, vandalism) or violate major societal norms (e.g., lying, truancy, running away from home). As evident from these examples, conduct problems can range from fairly minor problematic behaviors like lying and skipping school that do not lead to substantial harm to others to serious assaults that lead to significant injury and trauma. Some children and adolescents who show conduct problems lack empathy and guilt, and this group often shows a particularly severe pattern of conduct problems that involves serious aggressive behavior and substantial harm toward others. Recent research on youth who lack many prosocial emotions has suggested that, in addition to showing more severe behavior problems, they may have different causes to their conduct problems compared with other children and adolescents with behavioral difficulties. These unique causes are often not adequately addressed by many of the most common mental health interventions used to treat youth with conduct problems, which may explain why existing treatments may not be as effective for youth with limited prosocial emotions (Perlstein et al., 2023). As a result, these children and adolescents present an important challenge to mental health professionals. The goal of this book is to provide a clear and evidence-based guide to mental health providers to help them meet this challenge.

The research guiding the recommendations in this book builds on decades of work showing that children and adolescents with conduct problems are a

https://doi.org/10.1037/0000500-001
A Clinical Guide to Working With Youth With Conduct Disorders and Limited Prosocial Emotions, by P. J. Frick and E. R. Kimonis

serious mental health concern. Although some level of acting out is not unusual in children and adolescents, less than 10% of youth worldwide show conduct problems serious enough to cause problems for themselves, such as being suspended from school or getting in trouble with law enforcement, or serious enough to cause problems for others, such as injuring others in a fight or damaging others' property in very costly ways (Canino et al., 2010; Rivenbark et al., 2018). Furthermore, children with conduct problems are at risk for a host of mental health problems later in adolescence and into adulthood, including being at higher risk for substance abuse, anxiety, depression, and suicidal behavior. They are also at risk for legal problems (e.g., arrest), reduced educational attainment (e.g., dropping out of school), social difficulties (e.g., poor marital adjustment), limited occupational success (e.g., poor job performance), and physical health problems (e.g., poor respiratory function) throughout their life (Odgers et al., 2007, 2008). Thus, the presence of conduct problems in childhood can be an early indicator of difficulties that can lead to a host of problems for the child later in life.

In addition to these personal costs, serious conduct problems also have tremendous social costs. In a study conducted in New Zealand in which all children born in single year were tracked through childhood and adolescence and into adulthood, those who showed serious conduct problems in childhood represented only 9% of the sample. However, they accounted for 50% of all criminal convictions, 15% of all hospital bed night stays, 16% of all emergency department visits, 21% of all prescriptions filled, 13% of all injury claims, and 25% of all welfare benefit months in the sample (Rivenbark et al., 2018). Similar results have been reported in other countries as well. For example, in the United Kingdom, estimates have suggested that, by age 28, children with serious conduct problems have utilized 10 times the amount of government assistance compared with people who did not have serious conduct problems in childhood or adolescence (Scott et al., 2001).

It is quite clear from this research that conduct problems represent a significant mental health concern. But the news is not all grim. Research on children and adolescents with conduct problems also suggests that there are several effective treatments that can reduce conduct problems and, in doing so, lessen the risk for many of the problematic long-term outcomes (McMahon & Frick, 2019). Unfortunately, the vast majority of children who could benefit from these treatments do not receive them. This failure to receive effective treatment can be due to a number of reasons, ranging from parents hoping their child will "just outgrow" their behavior problems, to misconceptions that conduct problems are simply "bad behavior" that should be punished rather than treated with mental health interventions, to logistical barriers such as transportation issues or long waitlists. In addition, many mental health professionals are not trained to provide the types of treatment that are most effective for reducing serious conduct problems in children and adolescents. As a result, even when children with conduct problems access treatment, they often do not get the types of treatment that have proven to be most effective. Finally, even when a child with conduct problems receives research-supported interventions, those with the most severe behavior problems, such as those with limited prosocial emotions, often still leave treatment with significant problems (Perlstein et al., 2023). We argue that this limited effectiveness is due to the frequent use of a "one-size-fits-all" approach to treatment that ignores the fact that the causes of serious conduct problems can vary greatly from child to child. As a result of these differing causal processes, treatments should also vary across children and adolescents with conduct problems and be tailored to their unique needs.

To help tailor treatments, this book aims to provide clear guidance for the identification and treatment of one group of children and adolescents with serious conduct problems—those who show limited prosocial emotions. Our approach to treatment is a culmination of over 3 decades of research in which we have investigated the various causes of serious conduct problems, with a specific focus on children and adolescents with lower levels of prosocial emotions. Our early research clearly showed that this group of youth with serious conduct problems seemed to have distinct causes to their behavior problems. We then focused our research on how to identify and diagnose this important group of youth with conduct problems. Finally, most recently, we conducted research on how to modify mental health treatments to be more effective for these children and adolescents. This book attempts to summarize this work and make its implications for clinical treatment clear for mental health professionals across a range of disciplines who treat children and adolescents with conduct problems.

This approach to treatment can be illustrated by two cases that were seen in our clinical practice several decades ago. Two boys were referred for treatment around the same time and were about the same age. Both were referred due to cruelty to animals. One boy had used a gun to "shoot a cat out of a tree." The other had been caught using a knife to cut a cat's tail. In treatment, the first boy explained that he had been trying to get the cat down from the tree. He first tried throwing rocks to "scare it down," but when that did not work, he went inside, got his father's gun, and tried to "shoot around the cat" in hopes it would come down. Instead, he accidentally shot the cat. He teared up while recounting the story and expressed deep regret over what had happened to the cat. In treatment, the second boy described an extended history of doing "experiments" with cats and other animals. He would study how the different cats responded as he cut more and more of their tail off. He described himself very unemotionally as "being a scientist doing research on animals' emotional responses to pain."

Despite being referred for treatment for the same problem behavior, the boys' emotions and motivations leading to the animal cruelty were quite different. As a result, their treatment had to be individualized. For the first boy, he seemed to have problems thinking through the potential consequences of his actions in a way that allowed him to evaluate their potential outcomes. He had a history of acting in ways that got him into trouble because he acted impulsively and did not think about the potential harm that could result from his actions.

He typically felt bad about his behavior but needed help in learning how to "think before he acted." Several evidence-based treatments focus on helping a child to develop these skills in behavioral regulation (McMahon & Frick, 2019).

In contrast, the second child clearly could think through his actions and their consequences. Teaching him these skills was not needed. In contrast with the first boy, he did not feel bad about the harm he was causing the animals. He focused instead on what he was getting out of the action (i.e., satisfying his curiosity) and not on the pain and harm it was causing the animal. It fit a pattern he had of hurting people, both physically and verbally, usually with some justification for doing so (e.g., "They deserved it," "They were bugging me," "I wanted something"). Unfortunately, most available mental health treatments for children and adolescents with serious conduct problems did not focus on addressing this callous lack of empathy and the other interpersonal deficits (e.g., lack of guilt and remorse over misdeeds) that often accompanied them. Something different was needed.

So, what does one do for this second child? When we were being trained, we were often taught that most children and adolescents with conduct problems lacked empathy and guilt, like the second child, and that such youth were untreatable. Our research suggests that both of these assumptions are wrong. The vast majority of children and adolescents with conduct problems do not lack prosocial emotions. Further, the minority of youth with behavior problems who do lack prosocial emotions can respond to treatment, if one implements the right treatment. This book guides clinicians on the right approach to treatment for this group of children and adolescents.

The target audience for this book is clinicians from a wide range of mental health professions (e.g., psychologists, counselors, social workers, psychiatrists, developmental–behavioral pediatricians) who are tasked with identifying and treating children and adolescents with behavior problems. Making these diagnoses and providing this treatment take place not only in traditional mental health clinics and hospitals, but also in schools, where students with serious behavior problems often have problems learning and can disrupt the learning and safety of others. They can also take place in criminal justice settings, given that children and adolescents with conduct problems are at risk for engaging in illegal behavior. Thus, the content of this book is relevant for mental health practice in a variety of settings.

Another primary goal of this book was to be evidence-based. We wanted to clearly show how our recommendations for diagnosis and treatment are grounded in both the research that we have conducted and research conducted by others. However, we wanted to describe this research in a way that is useful for practicing clinicians. As a result, we did not attempt to provide an exhaustive review of all of the research that has been conducted on a given topic. Furthermore, our goal was not to provide a critical review of the methodology used in published studies investigating children and adolescents with limited prosocial emotions, nor was a goal to provide an extended discussion of the theoretical implications of this research for causal theory (see De Brito et al., 2021; Frick, 2022; Hyde & Dotterer, 2022; Viding, 2020; Waller & Wagner, 2019, for this type of discussion). Instead, our goal was to provide illustrative examples of studies that formed the empirical basis for the clinical recommendations we make. In doing so, we relied heavily on the research that we have conducted over the past 3 decades, so that we could clearly show how such research directly influenced our clinical recommendations. By providing the research basis for our clinical recommendations, and by illustrating how we integrated our own research and clinical practice, we hope that our book inspires a new generation of clinical researchers who share our passion for improving the mental health care provided to youth with limited prosocial emotions.

When describing this research, we use the term "we" whenever discussing research projects in which at least one of us was directly involved and served as a coauthor in its publication. Our roles in these studies varied widely. More importantly, the research was always done through collaborations with an amazing group of scholars, including students, colleagues, and collaborators from across the world. Also, this work could not have been done without the generous participation of children, caregivers, and teachers who volunteered to take part in the research. Thus, we want to be clear that we do not use the term "we" to take undue credit but instead to recognize the collective effort behind this work and to express our immense gratitude to all who contributed.

To accomplish these goals, we have organized our book into three sections. In Part I, we provide three chapters that focus largely on the research basis for our clinical recommendations. In Chapter 1, we provide a general overview of research on how children typically develop empathy, guilt, and other prosocial emotions, and we describe how this normal developmental process can go awry in some youth. We also provide an overview of past attempts to use this research on conscience development to guide mental health diagnoses of children and adolescents with conduct problems and how limitations identified in these past approaches guided current diagnostic practice. In the next two chapters, we provide summaries of research supporting the clinical importance of identifying children and adolescents with limited prosocial emotions (Chapter 2) and how the causal processes leading to the behavior problems in this group differ in important ways from the causes of conduct problems in other children and adolescents (Chapter 3). This third chapter outlines several distinct causal pathways to conduct problems. It focuses on the differences in these causal processes that we have found to be especially important to successfully tailoring treatment to meet the needs of youth with limited prosocial emotions.

The next two parts of the book include chapters that translate our research into clinical recommendations, first for assessing and diagnosing youth with limited prosocial emotions (Part II) and then for effectively treating this group (Part III). We begin with a broad overview of various methods that have been used to assess the key characteristics used to diagnose youth with limited prosocial emotions and summarize the strengths and limitations of each (Chapter 4). The following two chapters describe methods that we developed to address many of the shortcomings of earlier approaches. One chapter describes a behavior rating scale that can be used as part of the diagnostic process (Chapter 5), and the other outlines a more comprehensive, though time-intensive, method that guides clinicians in making structured professional judgements about whether or not a child or adolescent meets diagnostic criteria for limited prosocial emotions (Chapter 6).

The third section of this book focuses on treatment. In Chapter 7, we provide an overview of treatment research and describe interventions that have proven successful in the treatment of children and adolescents with limited prosocial emotions. In Chapter 8, we comprehensively describe a parent-based intervention for young children we developed, which modifies a highly effective treatment for children with conduct problems to be even more effective for those with limited prosocial emotions. In Chapter 9, we provide an extended case study to illustrate for clinicians how to implement this approach to treatment and address common challenges. This case study describes a child referred to our clinic for treatment. The family consented to our using the description of their treatment in this book. We changed several identifying characteristics to protect the child and his family's identity, but we tried to faithfully present the treatment process as it unfolded for them. Our treatment was developed to be implemented in intensive face-to-face sessions with parents and their young children together, typically in a mental health clinic. In Chapter 10, we discuss how we adapted this treatment to expand its reach, by using videoconferencing technology to implement it within the family home, and by implementing it in schools. Our tests of this intervention have focused on the same age range as those targeted by the original intervention: children in the 2- to 7-year-old range. In Chapter 10, we describe how our treatment approach can guide adaptations to other evidence-based treatments for youth with conduct problems, specifically for older children and adolescents, to be more effective for those showing the limited prosocial emotions (LPE) specifier.

The content and structure of the book was chosen to result in a comprehensive guide to providing evidence-based clinical care for children and adolescents with limited prosocial emotions. It also provides the research bases for our approach to diagnosis and treatment in a way that is accessible to clinicians from many different educational backgrounds with varying degrees of expertise in interpreting social research. We also recognize that the evidence on which we base our recommendations is evolving. Advances in research are critical for continuing to improve assessment and treatment. Thus, we conclude the book with a chapter that focuses on new frontiers in the research, assessment, and treatment of children with limited prosocial emotions. In Chapter 11, we discuss research underway to advance knowledge on children and adolescents with LPE and provide our recommendations for the types of future research we think could be most helpful for advancing diagnosis and treatment for these youth.

In a final note, in this book, we focus on identifying and treating youth who may have victimized others in ways that have led to serious and lasting trauma. We want to be abundantly clear that this focus is not due to a lack of empathy and concern for the immense suffering of these victims. In fact, the driving force of our work throughout our careers has been to reduce the number of victims by preventing victimization. We both entered psychology with a goal to treat victims of violence and crime. However, as one of our instructors in graduate school conveyed to us decades ago, "If you only focus on treating the victim and helping them to cope with the trauma they have experienced, you will always have victims. If you truly want to reduce the number of victims, you have to prevent them from becoming victims" (H. E. Adams, personal communication, n.d.). We believe that such prevention of victimization is best accomplished by effectively treating those who are causing the trauma and thereby preventing or at least limiting their victimization of others. Thus, this book was written to guide clinical practice that will hopefully reduce the number of future victims of crime and violence.

OVERVIEW OF THE LIMITED PROSOCIAL EMOTIONS SPECIFIER AND ITS SIGNIFICANCE

1

An Overview of Research on Diagnosing Limited Prosocial Emotions in Children and Adolescents

Developmental psychologists have long studied how children develop empathetic concern for others and how they learn to experience guilt over their misdeeds. The importance of these "prosocial emotions," which are sometimes referred to as the child's "conscience," was based on evidence that they play a critical role in motivating children to act in prosocial ways that promote healthy social relationships, such as helping others in distress or cooperating with others toward common goals. They also serve as internal regulators, discouraging harmful or rule-breaking actions. In short, a healthy level of prosocial emotions is vital for a child's social development.

Research has revealed key findings about how these prosocial emotions develop. Some children have emotional temperaments that naturally facilitate the development of these prosocial emotions. Research studies have found that these children reacted with empathic concern toward others and with guilt and remorse over misdeeds, even with little external encouragement from others. Other children have emotional temperaments that make it more difficult to develop these prosocial emotions. Research has found that these children showed minimal emotional reactions and little concern for others' distress, or care about the consequences of their behavior, even when caregivers and teachers strongly encouraged and supported them to do so. This research also suggested that certain types of parenting were better than others for encouraging children to develop prosocial emotions. Caregivers who were warm and responsive to their children's needs and emotions seemed to encourage their

https://doi.org/10.1037/0000500-002
A Clinical Guide to Working With Youth With Conduct Disorders and Limited Prosocial Emotions, by P. J. Frick and E. R. Kimonis

children to develop empathic concern for others and to care about the consequences of their actions on others. In contrast, caregivers who were harsh, critical of their children, or who ignored or invalidated their child's feelings were more likely to raise children who struggled to develop these prosocial emotions. Thus, what was abundantly clear from this research was that both the child's temperament and their rearing environment play important roles in shaping healthy prosocial development.

While developmental psychologists were studying how children develop empathy and guilt, clinical and forensic psychologists were investigating individuals who showed problematic behaviors. Such problems can emerge early in development with oppositional and defiant behaviors toward authority and then later in life with antisocial behavior that includes behaviors that violate the rights of others, such as being aggressive and hurting others or stealing from people or destroying their property. Antisocial behavior also includes actions that violate societal norms. In adults, this can involve engaging in criminal behavior or lying and conning others to get what they want. In children and adolescents, such behavior includes skipping school, staying out late at night, or running away from home overnight. Although it seems intuitive that a lack of prosocial emotions would contribute to antisocial behavior, research showed that not all people with serious and persistent antisocial behavior lacked empathy and guilt. Some people engaged in antisocial acts because they were easily angered, leading them to lash out at others in hurtful ways. Some people who did illegal or antisocial acts would get so caught up in the moment that they would act impulsively (e.g., steal things, set a fire) and not think about the consequences of their actions, either for themselves or others. Afterward, they might feel bad or guilty about what they had done, but they often had difficulty anticipating these feelings when confronted with similar situations in the future. However, several clinicians and researchers working with antisocial individuals identified another group of people who acted in antisocial ways because of a pervasive lack of prosocial emotions, who were labeled as showing "psychopathic traits."

RESEARCH ON THE CONSTRUCT OF PSYCHOPATHY

For well over a century, various clinical descriptions of the construct of psychopathy have been proposed (see Patrick, 2022; Skeem et al., 2013, for summaries of this history). One of the clearest and most influential early clinical descriptions of the psychopathy construct was developed by Hervey Cleckley (1941/1976) in his book *The Mask of Sanity*. Cleckley identified key emotional and interpersonal features that distinguished psychopathic adults from others engaged in antisocial or criminal behavior. These characteristics, summarized in Table 1.1, emphasize a distinct pattern of interpersonal (e.g., superficial charm, incapacity for love) and emotional (e.g., lack of remorse or shame, poverty in major affective reactions) characteristics. Importantly, Cleckley did not define

TABLE 1.1. The Construct of Psychopathy in Adults

Cleckley's psychopath	Hare's psychopathy checklist	
Superficial charm	Interpersonal Facet	Affective Facet
Absence of nervousness	Glibness/superficial charm	Lack of remorse or guilt
Untruthfulness and insincerity	Grandiosity	Shallow affect
Lack of remorse or shame	Pathological lying	Callous lack of empathy
Unreliability	Conning/manipulative	Failure to accept responsibility for actions
Pathological egocentricity		
Incapacity for love	Lifestyle Facet	Antisocial Facet
Poverty in major affective reactions	Need for stimulation	Poor behavioral controls
	Parasitic lifestyle	Juvenile delinquency
	Lack of realistic goals	Parole violations
	Impulsivity	Criminal versatility
	Irresponsibility	

Note. The text in the table are not full descriptions of items or symptoms but are abbreviated descriptions provided for illustrative purposes. See Cleckley (1941/1976) and Hare (1999) for actual symptoms and items.

psychopathy by the number or types of antisocial behavior displayed by the individual—although he did note that the antisocial behavior of psychopathic individuals was often considered to be "inadequately motivated" (i.e., without good reason). Rather, he defined it by an apparent failure to develop prosocial emotions that are essential for forming strong social bonds and learning to inhibit behaviors that harm others.

This emphasis on emotional and interpersonal traits delayed the inclusion of psychopathy in major systems for diagnosing mental disorders for decades, as clinicians questioned whether these characteristics could be reliably assessed. Instead, mental health diagnoses such as antisocial personality disorder (ASPD; American Psychiatric Association, 1980) largely focused on classifying individuals according to the number, type, duration, and severity of their antisocial behaviors. However, important research by Dr. Robert Hare challenged this idea by demonstrating that Cleckley's (1941/1976) core interpersonal and affective features of psychopathy could be assessed reliably when using appropriate tools, leading to the development of the Psychopathy Checklist (PCL; Hare, 1980). The items used on the PCL to assess psychopathy, listed in Table 1.1, assess both interpersonal–affective features and antisocial behavior. Importantly, Hare's research showed that definitions of ASPD that primarily focused on antisocial behavior and definitions of psychopathy like Cleckley's (1941/1976) that focused on emotional and interpersonal traits identified a very different set of individuals (Harpur et al., 1989). That is, only a small subset of people with ASPD also showed the callous and unemotional interpersonal features of psychopathy, but this subgroup displayed more severe aggression and violence, were more likely to engage in chronic antisocial behavior over time, were more difficult to treat with traditional mental health interventions, and showed a number of distinct emotional and social deficits, suggesting different underlying causal mechanisms leading to their antisocial behavior. Thus, the use of these interpersonal and affective features of psychopathy was both clinically important for identifying a subgroup of antisocial individuals who were in dire need of intervention for their serious antisocial behavior and etiologically important for identifying a group of individuals whose antisocial behavior seemed to develop from very different causal factors from other people showing similar problematic behaviors.

Research on psychopathy in adults revealed that these affective and interpersonal features were typically longstanding and often emerged early in childhood. However, like ASPD in adults, mental health diagnoses for children and adolescents who showed serious antisocial behavior—such as conduct disorder (CD)—traditionally focused on the type, severity, and duration of the behavioral symptoms rather than on their underlying interpersonal and emotional motivations. Research by Dr. Herb Quay (1987) on delinquent youth paralleled findings in adults, showing that only a small subset of youth who committed crimes showed the affective and interpersonal characteristics used to define psychopathy (e.g., lack of concern for others, untrustworthiness, lack of guilt). Also, like adults showing psychopathic traits, this group of youth engaged in aggressive behavior, their conduct problems seemed to result from different causal processes compared to other delinquent youth, and they were more likely to continue to show antisocial behavior into adulthood (Quay, 1987). In order to reduce the potential stigma associated with calling juveniles "psychopathic," Quay used the term "undersocialized" to describe this pattern of antisocial behavior.

This research prompted the third edition of the *Diagnostic and Statistical Manual of Mental Disorders* (*DSM-III*; American Psychiatric Association, 1980) to introduce the "undersocialized" specifier to designate a subtype of CD (i.e., undersocialized conduct disorder) for the first time in 1980. This subgroup of youth with CD was described as failing to show a normal degree of affection, empathy, or bond with others. Interestingly, unlike most other criteria used to define disorders in the *DSM* in which a person had to show a certain number of symptoms to get the diagnosis, the definition of undersocialized CD provided a number of indicators of social attachment that defined the people *without* the disorder; that is, to qualify for the specifier, the person with CD could only show one or fewer indicators of social attachment to meet the definition.

The inclusion of the undersocialized specifier in the *DSM-III* encouraged a significant amount of research to test its clinical utility. This research found that the undersocialized classification of CD was problematic because it did not produce consistent findings, in contrast to findings from research on adult psychopathy. This inconsistency seemed to be caused by several issues with the diagnostic definition. First, clinicians seemed to have difficulty reliably establishing whether or not the child had too few of the indicators of social attachment to meet the diagnosis, as opposed to determining if the child showed indicators of a callous and unemotional interpersonal style. Second, the diagnostic criteria in the *DSM-III* emphasized the child's inability to form social bonds (e.g., no long-term friendships, does not extend themselves to others, blames or informs on peers) rather than prosocial emotions of empathy and guilt. Thus, this early definition used for youth deviated greatly from both adult definitions of psychopathy and from developmental research on conscience formation. Third, the term "undersocialized" was intended to avoid the potential stigma associated with labeling children and adolescents as being "psychopathic," but this led to confusion about its core and defining features. Clinicians applied the diagnosis inconsistently, using widely varying methods for determining if the child was "undersocialized." Many definitions solely focused on a child's social relationships and did not consider at all whether the child showed a callous and unemotional interpersonal style. For example, the sole description used to make the diagnosis of undersocialized conduct disorder in the 10th revision of the *International Classification of Diseases* (ICD-10; World Health Organization, 1992) was that the child showed significant and pervasive abnormalities in relationships with other children. Because research using this definition was not producing consistent findings, the undersocialized specifier for conduct disorder was removed in the next revision of the *DSM* published just 7 years later in 1987 (*DSM-III-R*; American Psychiatric Association, 1987).

Subsequent *DSM* revisions attempted to refine CD subtypes and moved away from traditional definitions of psychopathy by reverting to using behavioral indicators rather than interpersonal–affective traits to define subgroups of individuals with the disorder. For example, the *DSM-III-R* distinguished between the group type (antisocial acts committed with peers) and the solitary aggressive type (predominantly physical aggression committed alone) within the diagnosis of CD (American Psychiatric Association, 1987). In the next edition of the manual, the *DSM-IV* (American Psychiatric Association, 1994), this classification was replaced by an age-of-onset distinction: childhood onset (CD symptoms present before age 10) and adolescent onset (CD symptoms emerging at age 10 or older). This age-of-onset distinction was based on a large amount of research suggesting that youth who start showing behavior problems earlier in development are more likely to show aggressive behavior (Moffitt et al., 2008), thus capturing the solitary aggressive subtype defined in the *DSM-III-R*.

A wealth of research also showed that children in the childhood-onset group were much more likely to show persistent antisocial behavior into adulthood when compared with those from the adolescent-onset group, who were more likely to desist from problem behavior when they reached adulthood. For example, a large research study conducted in New Zealand followed a whole cohort of children from birth into adulthood and found that children who showed a pattern of serious conduct problems prior to adolescence were more likely to be arrested as adults, especially for violent offenses, compared with those who started showing conduct problems in adolescence (Odgers et al., 2007). In addition, those in the childhood-onset group were more likely to show a host of other problematic mental health (e.g., anxiety, depression, suicide, substance use), medical (e.g., high rates of injury and cardiovascular diseases), social (e.g., higher rates of homelessness), and economic (e.g., unemployment and financial problems) outcomes as adults (Odgers et al., 2008).

Thus, the childhood-onset distinction clearly had important clinical utility by designating a group of youth with CD who were at risk for showing a lifelong pattern of behavior problems and who tended to be more aggressive, which is a key characteristic of adults with psychopathy and of youth who were previously diagnosed with undersocialized CD (Moffitt, 2018). Importantly, our research also suggested that this group was more likely to show a lack of guilt and empathy and other indicators of a callous and unemotional style than children with adolescent-onset CD (Dandreaux & Frick, 2009). However, our research also indicated that, while the childhood-onset CD captured a subgroup with increased callous–unemotional (CU) traits, these traits were not present in all individuals within this category, which raised concerns about whether the classification was specific enough for identifying children who showed limited prosocial emotions (Barry et al., 2000).

ATTEMPTS TO EXTEND THE CONSTRUCT OF PSYCHOPATHY TO YOUTH

Based on these findings, research increasingly focused on how to make distinctions within the childhood-onset group to designate youth exhibiting features similar to those included in definitions of psychopathy used in samples of adults and features similar to those included in developmental research on prosocial emotions in children. One proposed approach was to use a diagnosis that was already in wide use, attention-deficit/hyperactivity disorder (ADHD), to define a subgroup of children with CD (Lynam, 1996). ADHD is defined in part by excess levels of impulsivity that result in a tendency to act without considering potential consequences. As noted in Table 1.1, impulsivity and irresponsibility are included in many definitions of psychopathy as well. Moreover, substantial research showed that children with co-occurring diagnoses of ADHD and CD were more likely to exhibit early onset, as well as show more severe and persistent conduct problems, compared with those with CD without the additional ADHD diagnosis.

However, research identified some limitations in using this subtyping approach. While ADHD was clearly much more common in children with childhood-onset CD than those with adolescent-onset CD, it did not consistently distinguish subgroups within the childhood-onset group. That is, many children with childhood-onset CD also had ADHD, often with a clear developmental pattern of starting to show ADHD symptoms very early in development, followed by increasingly severe conduct problems over time (Waschbusch, 2002). Yet, our research showed that only a minority of these children with comorbid CD and ADHD exhibited the other features of psychopathy, including high levels of CU traits (Barry et al., 2000). Similar findings in adults showed that indicators of the impulsivity and irresponsibility dimension of psychopathy were commonly displayed by people with ASPD, even if they did not show other features of psychopathy (Harpur et al., 1989). In short, while high levels of impulsivity and irresponsibility are commonly found in adults high on other dimensions of psychopathy, these features were not unique to this group. Thus, while ADHD seemed to consistently identify children at risk for childhood-onset forms of CD, it was not specific enough to consistently designate a group that showed a callous and unemotional interpersonal style within this early onset group.

Additionally, impulsive behaviors were not defining features for the indicators of prosocial emotions used in developmental research. While deficits in empathy and guilt may lead a child to disregard the consequences of their actions (e.g., not caring about the effects of their behavior on others), impulsivity can stem from other factors as well (Nigg, 2000). For example, a child could also act impulsively due to being highly emotionally reactive in social situations, and this high level of emotional arousal could lead them to act without thinking of the consequences of their behavior. This example would include the child who gets into fights when angry but then feels remorseful about their behavior when they have calmed down and are no longer mad. A child could also act impulsively because they have trouble anticipating future events, including the potential future consequences of their behavior. This example is often described as problems with the "executive control" of behavior. As a result, the conclusion from this research on problems with impulsivity was similar to what was found in research on psychopathy in adults—namely, the presence of ADHD and the associated elevations in impulsivity were not specific enough to consistently and specifically identify children and adolescents who showed a callous and unemotional style.

Another dimension of psychopathy that was applied to children as a potential way of designating an important subgroup of children with severe conduct problems has been labeled as the interpersonal facet of psychopathy. As shown in Table 1.1, this facet focuses on narcissistic traits, in which the person views themselves as being superior and more important than others, as well as on the manipulative use of others for personal gain. It is important to note that research on this interpersonal dimension is more difficult to interpret and summarize because there has been great variability in how it has been defined in children and adolescents, with some definitions focusing more on the narcissistic traits and other definitions focusing largely on the manipulative use of others (see Frick, 2022, for a summary of this research). However, research using definitions that focused more on the narcissistic traits suggest that these traits overlap a great deal with symptoms of oppositional defiant disorder (ODD) in children (e.g., blames others for their mistakes, becomes angry and annoyed when corrected), which, similar to ADHD, is an extremely common precursor to childhood-onset CD. Thus, like ADHD, use of narcissistic interpersonal traits did not prove specific enough to designate an important subgroup within those showing early onset conduct problems (Frick et al., 2000). Furthermore, the way that the manipulation of others is often defined is by focusing on whether the child lies and cons others to get what they want (Frick, 2022). These behaviors are highly associated with stealing and are considered one of the "covert" or nonconfrontational symptoms that have long been included in the diagnostic criteria for CD (Frick et al., 1993). Thus, the willingness to con and manipulate others appears to be more of a consequence of limited prosocial emotions as one indicator of a person's tendency to show antisocial behavior. Stated another way, conning and manipulative behavior appears to be an indicator of a person's willingness to violate the rights of others rather than a cause of these antisocial behaviors.

Thus, research on several of the dimensions used to define psychopathy in adult samples was not proving useful for designating a distinct subgroup of youth with childhood-onset CD. In contrast, research on the "deficient affective experience" dimension of psychopathy—also called callous and unemotional or "CU" traits—proved to be more useful for this purpose. Like research in adults, this affective dimension appeared to be better at designating a subgroup of antisocial children and adolescents who differed from other youth with behavior problems in ways that have often been associated with psychopathy. Furthermore, these CU traits corresponded much more closely to definitions of prosocial emotions and the affective components of conscience that were the focus of development research. As a result, this distinction could be informed by the decades of research on how these prosocial emotions typically develop in children, and on factors within the child and within their social context (e.g., types of parenting) that can cause this developmental process to go awry in some children and lead to severe and impairing levels of conduct problems.

THE LIMITED PROSOCIAL EMOTIONS SPECIFIER

This evidence supporting the need to focus on prosocial emotions led our research to uncover what were the best indicators of this construct in children and adolescents. In our early research attempting to extend the construct of psychopathy to children and adolescents, we developed a rating scale that could be completed by caregivers or teachers assessing not only CU traits but also the impulsive and interpersonal dimensions of psychopathy (Frick et al., 1994). The items across all of these dimensions are shown in Exhibit 1.1. Six items assessing the affective component of psychopathy loaded on a factor that we labeled the CU factor. Later research, however, suggested that only four of these items consistently assessed the overall construct of CU traits across the various samples in which it was studied (Frick et al., 2000). These include the following CU items:

- Is unconcerned about the feelings of others;
- Does not feel bad or guilty;
- Is unconcerned about performance in important activities such as school or work; and
- Does not show emotions openly.

EXHIBIT 1.1

Items Assessing Multiple Dimensions of Psychopathy in Children

Factor 1

8. Brags excessively about his/her abilities, accomplishments, or possessions.
15. Becomes angered when corrected or punished.
16. Seems to think that he/she is better or more important than other people.
4. Acts without thinking of the consequences.
1. Blames others for his/her mistakes.
11. Teases or makes fun of other people.
13. Engages in risky or dangerous activities.
2. Engages in illegal activities.
20. Keeps the same friends. (I)
9. Gets bored easily.

Factor 2

3. *Is concerned about how well he/she does at school or work.* (I)
12. *Feels bad or guilty when he/she does something wrong.* (I)
5. His/her emotions seem shallow and not genuine.
19. *Does not show feelings or emotions.*
18. *Is concerned about the feelings of others.* (I)
14. Can be charming at times, but in ways that seem insincere or superficial.

Additional Items

6. Lies easily and skillfully.
7. Is good at keeping promises. (I)
10. Uses or "cons" other people to get what he/she wants.
17. Does not plan ahead or leaves things until the "last minute."

Note. Items were rated by caregivers and teachers in sample of 95 clinic-referred children ages 6 to 12 years of age. Results are from a principal-components analysis using an oblique rotation as reported by Frick et al. (1994). Items on the two factors are ordered based on the strength of their factor loadings. Items not included showed inconsistent factor loading or loaded on both factors. (I) refers to items that were inversely scored; items in italics are the four items that seemed to be the best indicators of callous-unemotional traits across samples and formed the basis for the "with limited prosocial emotions" specifier for conduct disorder in the *Diagnostic and Statistical Manual of Mental Disorders, Fifth Edition* (*DSM-5*). Adapted from "Psychopathy and Conduct Problems in Children," by P. J. Frick, B. S. O'Brien, J. M. Wootton, and K. McBurnett, 1994, *Journal of Abnormal Psychology*, *103*, pp. 700–707 (https://doi.org/10.1037/0021-843X.103.4.700). Copyright 1994 by the American Psychological Association.

When the *Diagnostic and Statistical Manual of Mental Disorders, Fifth Edition, Text Revision* (*DSM-5-TR*; American Psychiatric Association, 2022) was considering integrating CU traits into its diagnostic criteria for CD, data using large samples from several different countries supported our findings that these items tended to be the best indicators of CU traits (Kimonis et al., 2015). This research also suggested that when a child with serious conduct problems showed at least two of the four items, they tended to show a more severe, aggressive, and persistent pattern of conduct problems. Thus, the *DSM-5* added a specifier called "with limited prosocial emotions" for those children and adolescents who met the full criteria for CD (i.e., a persistent and impairing pattern of behavior that violates the rights of others or that violates important age-appropriate norms) and who also showed at least two of four CU indicators.

The *DSM-5* also included another important part to their criteria for the limited prosocial emotions (LPE) specifier. That is, the LPE specifier criteria required that two symptoms needed to be displayed persistently (e.g., for at least 12 months) and in multiple relationships or settings. That is, these criteria made explicit that the characteristics of the specifier must be more "trait-like" in reflecting the individual's typical pattern of interpersonal and emotional functioning over an extended period, and not just occasional occurrences in some situations or relationships. This was to ensure that people who only showed these characteristics occasionally (e.g., after a traumatic event) and in certain situations (e.g., only with siblings, only with parole officers) would not meet the LPE criteria. This requirement of being "typical" of a person's emotional style corresponded to how these traits had been measured in research on rating scales but is quite different from how most symptoms of mental health problems are assessed. For example, to diagnose CD itself, one only needs to determine if three or more symptoms have ever been displayed over a 1-year period, with at least one symptom shown in the last 6 months.

The *DSM-5* was published in 2013 by the American Psychiatric Association with this new LPE specifier added to the diagnostic criteria for CD. At the same time, the World Health Organization was working on its revision of the *ICD*, and one of its primary goals was to be as consistent with the *DSM-5* as possible. In 2018, it published the 11th edition of the *ICD* (World Health Organization, 2018) and for its criteria for conduct-dissocial disorder (its version of CD), it also included a "with limited prosocial emotions" specifier. Importantly, the *ICD-11* also includes this specifier for the diagnosis of ODD, given that much of the research showing the importance of CU traits largely used definitions of "serious conduct problems" that included both symptoms of CD and symptoms of ODD. It is also important to note that, unlike the *DSM*, the *ICD* does not specify clear diagnostic thresholds for any of its disorders. So, for the specifier "with limited prosocial emotions," it does not require that a person "must show 2 of the 4 symptoms" like in the *DSM-5*. It simply describes the "typical indicators" needed for the diagnosis. Importantly, its indicators for the LPE specifier included the same four symptoms from the *DSM-5* criteria:

- a lack of empathy or sensitivity to the feelings of others and a lack of concern for others' distress;
- a lack of remorse, shame, or guilt over their own behavior (unless prompted by being apprehended);
- a lack of concern over poor performance in school, work, or other important activities; and

- limited expression of emotions, particularly positive or loving feelings toward others, or only doing so in ways that seem shallow, insincere, or instrumental.

However, the *ICD-11* definition of the LPE specifier also included as a fifth indicator:

- a relative indifference to the probability of punishment.

It is not clear why this additional symptom was added as a primary indicator. As we will discuss in Chapter 3, CU traits have been associated with abnormalities in how a child responds to rewards and punishment. However, how this manifested in children without limited prosocial emotions is not entirely clear from the available research. Furthermore, there does not appear to be research currently supporting that this added symptom enhances the diagnosis of children and adolescents with limited prosocial emotions.

Thus, both the *DSM-5* and *ICD-11* integrated CU traits into their diagnostic criteria as a specifier under the label "with limited prosocial emotions." The criteria used to diagnose the specifier and its name were unchanged in the text revision of the *DSM-5* that was published in 2022 (*DSM-5-TR*; American Psychiatric Association, 2022). It is important to note that the label given when making clinical diagnoses is different from the label used in most research publications. As evident from this chapter, the construct captured by these symptoms of the specifier has been variously called the "affective dimension of psychopathy" or "deficient affective experience facet of psychopathy," "undersocialized," and "callous–unemotional traits" when it has been studied in research. However, when adding the LPE diagnosis to the *DSM-5*, there was great concern about the need to minimize the potential for stigma. Consequently, the *DSM-5* chose a term that would encourage mental health professionals to use the diagnosis to get critically needed treatment to those diagnosed, rather than discourage the use of the diagnosis because of potential pejorative connotations.

Research suggests that this is not an unfounded concern. As we will discuss in more detail in Chapter 4, diagnoses associated with antisocial behavior and psychopathy can lead to stigma by promoting treatment pessimism (i.e., persons with the disorder cannot be treated) or by suggesting that the person with the disorder is "to be blamed" for the condition and should be held accountable by the legal system. Thus, the *DSM* carefully chose the "with limited prosocial emotions" term over "with significant psychopathic traits" or "with significant callous–unemotional traits" in an effort to reduce stigma and to encourage use. However, the *DSM* also wanted to avoid confusion over the research that led to the diagnosis and its key indicators, similar to what had happened with the earlier diagnosis of "undersocialized" CD. That is, both the *DSM-5* and the *DSM-5-TR* make clear in their text description that, despite the different name, the specifier is considered the same construct as what had been studied in research using the term "callous–unemotional traits."

CHAPTER SUMMARY

In conclusion, there is now a specifier for the diagnoses of children and adolescents with conduct problems in the major classification systems for making mental health diagnoses worldwide. This diagnosis designated children and adolescents with behavior problems who are elevated on CU traits and show limited prosocial emotions. Such a change has led to a marked increase in use of this LPE specifier in both applied and research settings and has great potential for enhancing our ability to provide effective and evidence-based treatment to people with this diagnosis. However, to reach this potential, there needs to be a clear guide for mental health professionals on what this diagnosis means and does not mean, how to appropriately make the diagnosis, and then how to effectively treat people once they are diagnosed. The rest of this book provides such a guide.

2

Clinically Important Differences Between Children With Limited Prosocial Emotions and Other Children With Conduct Problems

Now that limited prosocial emotions (LPE) are included as a specifier used in the diagnosis of children with conduct problems, it is critical for clinicians to appreciate what this diagnosis means for clinical practice with children and adolescents who show serious behavior problems. In short, research has documented that this specifier identifies an important subgroup of children and adolescents with conduct problems who differ on several critically important characteristics that make them an especially important group to diagnose and treat (see Table 2.1 for a summary of this work). Furthermore, youth with the LPE specifier show a number of differences in their emotional, cognitive, and social functioning compared with other children and adolescents with conduct problems, which seems to suggest that the causes of the behavior problems are different for the two groups of children. These differences are the focus of the next chapter. However, it is important to note that, if these differences were only important for causal theories, we would not have included a full chapter devoted to this research. We include this chapter because these differences in causal processes between groups of children with behavior problems are critical for guiding our approach to treatment for those with the LPE specifier.

Before discussing this research on the unique characteristics of children and adolescents with the LPE specifier, it is important to note that one of the primary reasons this specifier was added to the diagnostic criteria for conduct disorders was because the LPE symptoms led to important distinctions

https://doi.org/10.1037/0000500-003
A Clinical Guide to Working With Youth With Conduct Disorders and Limited Prosocial Emotions, by P. J. Frick and E. R. Kimonis

TABLE 2.1. Important Clinical Characteristics Associated With Limited Prosocial Emotions

Clinical characteristic	Differences from other youth with conduct problems	Key references
Early onset to conduct problems	• More likely to start their conduct problems prior to adolescence.	Dandreaux & Frick (2009); Silverthorn et al. (2001)
Aggression and violence	• More aggressive behavior that includes both reactive and instrumental forms of aggression, starting as early as preschool. • Aggressive behavior leads to more harm to the victim. • Rated as crueler by caregivers.	Frick et al. (2003); Kahn et al. (2012); Kimonis et al. (2006); Lawing et al. (2010)
Criminal behavior	• More likely to engage in criminal behavior, especially more violent criminal behavior. • More likely to start offending earlier in development, and on average before age 8. • More likely to carry or use a gun when committing crimes. • More likely to nonviolently and violently reoffend after release from a secure facility.	Kimonis, Kennealy, et al. (2016); Neo & Kimonis (2021); Ray et al. (2016a); Robertson et al. (2020)
Bullying	• More likely to bully other children. • More likely to instigate others to bully. • Less likely to help victims of bullying.	Crapanzano et al. (2011); Fanti & Kimonis (2012); Fanti & Kimonis (2013); Thornton et al. (2013)
Risky sexual behavior	• More likely to engage in unprotected and casual sex with partners they do not know well.	McCauley et al. (2016); Thornton et al. (2019)
Poor peer relationships	• Less close, less warm, and less satisfying peer and romantic relationships. • Viewed as colder and meaner by peers. • Associates with more deviant peers and more likely to lead and instigate group criminal activities.	Golmaryami et al. (2021); Haas et al. (2018); Matlasz et al. (2022); Thornton et al. (2015); Vaughan et al. (2023)
Substance use	• More likely to engage in harmful substance use. • More likely to meet diagnostic criteria for a substance use disorder.	Kimonis et al. (2012); Ray et al. (2016a); Sakki et al. (2023); Waller, Baskin-Sommers, et al. (2018)
Suicidal behavior	• Increased lethality of attempts when other risk factors for suicide are present.	Kemp, Picou, et al. (in press)
Adult antisocial behavior	• More adult antisocial behavior, arrests, and antisocial personality disorder traits and diagnosis.	McMahon et al. (2010); Pardini et al. (2018)
Limited response to treatment	• Begins and ends most treatments with more severe conduct problems, despite showing improvement with treatment.	Perlstein et al. (2023)

(i.e., designated important subgroups of children with conduct problems) that were not captured well by existing criteria in mental health classification (see Frick, 2022, for a summary of this research). For example, youth with the LPE specifier often start showing conduct problems early in childhood and so many would also be diagnosed with the childhood-onset specifier for conduct disorder (CD). However, the LPE specifier is only present in a minority of children who would be diagnosed with the childhood-onset type of CD and those with the LPE specifier differ on the clinically important characteristics summarized in Table 2.1. Similarly, children with the LPE specifier show high rates of impulsivity and are often also diagnosed with attention-deficit/hyperactivity disorder (ADHD). However, the LPE specifier is only present in a minority of children with ADHD and those with the LPE specifier differ on the important characteristics summarized in Table 2.1 and in Chapter 4 (see, e.g., Barry et al., 2000). Finally, children with the LPE specifier show more severe conduct problems than other children with either an oppositional defiant disorder (ODD) or CD diagnosis. However, the LPE specifier predicts important characteristics, even when controlling for conduct problem severity (see, e.g., Thornton et al., 2013). Thus, the LPE specifier helps to define an important subgroup of youth with behavior problems that is not adequately captured by other specifiers (i.e., onset or severity specifiers) or comorbid diagnoses (i.e., ADHD) used in the diagnosis of children with disruptive behavior disorders.

A study by the Conduct Problems Prevention Research Group illustrates this added clinical importance of the LPE specifier (McMahon et al., 2010). These researchers reported on a sample of 754 school children who were assessed for indicators of the LPE specifier (i.e., CU traits) in the seventh grade. They studied this sample up until 2 years after they graduated from high school. The students' level of callous–unemotional (CU) traits in seventh grade predicted their antisocial outcomes in early adulthood, even after controlling for the number of ODD symptoms, CD symptoms, and ADHD symptoms, as well as the age of onset of CD. That is, even after accounting for these other diagnostic indicators, the students' level of CU traits in the seventh grade still predicted self-reported criminal behavior, arrests, and the presence of antisocial personality symptoms when the participants were young adults. Thus, the LPE specifier provided critical diagnostic information for identifying a subgroup of children and adolescents with behavior problems who were at risk for problems later in development, which was not being captured by existing criteria for mental health diagnoses. Such findings from research are important to consider when interpreting the research we review later. In this chapter, we focus primarily on clinically important characteristics of youth with the LPE specifier that differentiate them from other children and adolescents with conduct problems. Even more specifically, we focus on differences that would not be captured by other parts of the diagnostic criteria used to diagnose children and adolescents with severe behavior problems.

RISK FOR ANTISOCIAL BEHAVIOR ACROSS THE LIFESPAN

As noted previously, children with conduct problems and the LPE specifier are more likely to start showing behavior problems early in life, well before adolescence and often prior to beginning formal schooling (i.e., before age 5). This early onset of behavior problems is likely due to the core characteristics that define LPE. That is, empathy and concern for others are prosocial emotions that can motivate young children to act in ways that avoid hurting others. A child may want a toy that another child is playing with but refrains from doing things to get the toy that might lead the other child to be hurt and upset. Without appropriate levels of empathy, which serves as an emotional inhibitor (i.e., the child's "emotional brakes"), the child is more likely to act in ways that hurt others to get what they want. Similarly, children often do not break rules or act in ways that might get them in trouble with parents, teachers, babysitters, and other caregivers because they will feel bad or guilty when others are upset. Without appropriate levels of guilt, the child is more likely to act in ways that break rules and defy others because they do not feel badly about upsetting others. Finally, children with the LPE specifier often are more motivated by reward than punishment and, as a result, they tend to pay attention to the positive consequences of their behavior (i.e., getting the toy) and ignore the potential negative consequences of their harmful behaviors (e.g., distressing or hurting the other child).

Thus, the lack of prosocial emotions can make a child more likely to show behavior problems early in life but can also make a person more likely to continue having problems throughout their lifespan. As shown in Table 2.1, research shows that children and adolescents with the LPE specifier are more likely to engage in criminal behavior throughout adolescence and into adulthood. They are also more likely than other youth with serious behavior problems to show antisocial personality disorder and to score high on measures of psychopathy as adults. This latter finding, showing a link between CU traits and later psychopathic traits, led to extensive debate about the stability of the CU traits that form the LPE specifier across development. To begin to address this issue, we conducted a literature review on the stability of CU traits at different developmental periods and over different lengths of time (Frick et al., 2014a). While the stability of CU traits seemed to increase from early to late childhood, even in early childhood there was some degree of stability. That is, we reviewed three studies that provided five stability coefficients from samples of children ages 2 to 8 years of age, showing an average stability coefficient of 0.59 (i.e., moderate stability) over time periods ranging from 6 months to 2 years. On the one hand, this level of stability was similar to the stability found for other forms of mental health problems (e.g., symptoms of ADHD) and more stable than for other personality dimensions in early childhood. On the other hand, this level of stability means that less than 35% of the variance in a measure of CU traits is explained by the child's score on a measure of CU traits at an earlier point in time.

Clearly, this research suggests that a child's level of CU traits can change over time. This is why some have argued for not calling these characteristics "CU traits" in very young children and instead calling them "CU behaviors" (Waller & Hyde, 2017). We recognize the importance of educating clinicians that these traits are changeable and this is particularly important for characteristics like CU traits that many clinicians erroneously assume are entrenched and immutable. However, in our chapters on assessment and diagnosis (Chapters 4 through 6), we also highlight the danger of calling these characteristics "behaviors." That is, some level of these characteristics can be present in typically developing children and they seem to only indicate an impairing clinical condition when they are displayed across settings and relationships. As we highlight in later chapters, this is why the diagnostic criteria for the LPE specifier requires that symptoms be present persistently (i.e., over at least 12 months) and be shown in multiple relationships and settings. This is also why most measures of CU traits do not use ratings of the frequency of the indicators of the LPE specifier to assess them but instead have the person rate "how true" the indicators are of the person being assessed. Thus, it is important to ensure a more trait-like display of the LPE symptoms to avoid misdiagnosing children who show them only occasionally in certain situations. It is also important to note that the symptoms of the LPE specifier focus on emotions that developmental research has shown to motivate prosocial behaviors (e.g., showing sympathy, cooperating with others, helping others). Thus, calling them behaviors could lead to confusion as to the focus of the criteria for the LPE specifier, which is largely on the prosocial emotional motivators and not the prosocial behaviors themselves.

Again, despite these cautions, it is very important for clinicians to recognize that while CU traits are only modestly stable in children and adolescents, they do put the child at risk for problems later in life. So, how should a clinician weigh this risk for problems with the possibility of change? We think this balance is illustrated by a longitudinal study by Don Lynam and colleagues (2007). They reported on a longitudinal study of boys from a high-risk sample who were assessed for CU traits at age 13 and then assessed for psychopathic traits at age 24 using a standardized measure. The correlation between the two measures over this period of time was $r = 0.31$, again suggesting some level of stability but also great potential for change. Furthermore, 21% of the boys who were elevated on the measure of CU traits at age 13 were elevated on the measure of psychopathy at age 24. Again, on the one hand, this suggests that only one in five children with high levels of CU traits went on to show significant psychopathic traits as adults. In short, the majority of those children with elevated CU traits did not show this outcome. On the other hand, children with elevated CU traits at age 13 were over 3.22 times more likely to exceed the clinical cutoff for psychopathy than other children in this high-risk sample. Any indicator of a threefold risk for a very serious mental health condition, like psychopathy, should be viewed as a high-priority target for early intervention. As a result, this is how we view the LPE specifier. We want to be crystal clear that it does not mean that a child will definitely develop psychopathy or even serious antisocial behavior later in life. However, we want to be equally clear that its presence does indicate that the child is at increased risk for these and other problematic outcomes later in life; so early intervention is critical. Furthermore, given that children with the LPE specifier start showing problems very early in life, these early onset behavior problems provide clear targets for such interventions during a time in development when they can be most successful.

VIOLENCE AND SEVERE AGGRESSION

In addition to this increased risk for later problems, there is another reason why children and adolescents with the LPE specifier are a critical clinical concern that warrants an intensive approach to early intervention. That is, they often show high rates of severe aggression and violence. Over the past several decades, we have shown this association in research conducted across the lifespan in several different types of samples. For example, in a sample of children enrolled in a high-risk preschool (*M* age = 3.10 years), CU traits were highly related to the level of aggression displayed by the child, as rated by their teacher (Kimonis et al., 2006). In a sample of older school children (*M* age = 12.43 years), students rated by their caregivers and teachers as showing high conduct problems and CU traits showed higher levels of aggression than children rated as only showing elevated conduct problems (Frick et al., 2003). Interestingly, children with CU traits showed higher rates than other children with conduct problems of both reactive aggression (i.e., aggression that is in response to real or perceived provocation from others) and proactive aggression (i.e., aggression that is premeditated and used for potential gain). In contrast, children rated by caregivers and teachers with conduct problems but without CU traits showed higher rates of reactive aggression than children without conduct problems but they did not differ from other children on their level of proactive aggression. Thus, it appears that children with the LPE specifier show the highest rate of aggression overall and are unique from other children with conduct problems in that they engage in more premeditated and instrumental aggression (i.e., for gain). We replicated this finding using a measure of premeditated aggression in a sample of adolescent boys (*M* age = 15.89 years) who were arrested for committing a sexual offense (Lawing et al., 2010). Consistent with the findings in school children, adolescent boys high on CU traits used more planning when they sexually offended than other boys arrested for committing a sexual offense. Also, boys with elevated CU traits had more victims and were more likely to be violent when they offended than other arrested boys. Together, these findings convincingly show that children and adolescents high on CU traits are more likely than others to be aggressive overall, to show more severe aggression, and to show aggression that is premeditated, planned, and used for gain.

Given this high risk for planned aggression, it is not surprising that another area in which children with CU traits seem to show more aggression is in bullying others. Bullying is a unique form of aggression that takes place between children, which involves the aggressor being in a dominant position (e.g., older, bigger, stronger) and often involves repeated instances of aggression against the same victim who is not able to defend themself. Bullying is a very serious concern for school-aged children because it can lead to a host of mental health problems for the victims of this aggression (Sourander et al., 2007; Storch et al., 2005). In our research, we showed in a number of different samples that children with the LPE specifier were more likely to bully their schoolmates compared with other children with conduct problems (Fanti & Kimonis, 2012, 2013; Thornton et al., 2013). Beyond being more likely to bully other students, we found that students with the LPE specifier were also more likely to assist other students who were engaged in bullying, more likely to encourage others who were bullying, and were less likely to defend the victims of bullying (Crapanzano et al., 2011). Thus, in addition to directly bullying other students, children high on CU traits also contribute to a broader social climate in schools that can encourage and maintain bullying behaviors.

CRIMINAL BEHAVIOR ACROSS THE LIFESPAN

Another type of antisocial behavior that seems to be predicted by CU traits is criminal behaviors. As was the case with aggression and violence, we have found this link in our research studies conducted across several different age groups. In one of our early studies of children ages 6 to 13 referred to a mental health clinic for a psychological evaluation, those children with conduct problems with the LPE specifier were already more likely to have had their first contact with police compared to those who were not elevated on CU traits, despite the mean age of this sample being 9 years old (Christian et al., 1997). We found a similar link between CU traits and criminal behavior in an older sample of school children (Frick et al., 2005) and in a sample of boys who were arrested for the first time in adolescence (Robertson et al., 2021). Finally, we conducted several studies of boys who had been incarcerated for crimes committed in adolescence. In one study of 456 incarcerated boys (*M* age = 16.24 years), we asked them when they first engaged in serious delinquency and we obtained official records documenting their age at first charge for a criminal offense (Neo & Kimonis, 2021). We found that boys with the LPE specifier engaged in serious delinquency 1 year earlier than those low on CU traits. In fact, the average age at first offense for boys high on CU traits was just under 8 years old. In another study of 227 incarcerated boys (*M* age = 15.73), we found that those scoring high on CU traits were quicker to reoffend both violently and nonviolently after they were released from custody (Kimonis, Kennealy, et al., 2016). All of these findings linking CU traits with an early onset of criminal behavior highlight the critical need for early intervention with children with the LPE specifier to prevent a chronic pattern of serious nonviolent and violent criminal behavior.

The association between CU traits and repeated criminal behavior is not surprising, given that a defining feature of these traits is lack of guilt and remorse over misdeeds. However, our research has also pointed to a few clinically important features of the criminal behavior that is displayed by adolescents who show CU traits. We conducted a study of 1,216 adolescents who were arrested for the first time for a moderately severe offense. Those adolescents with the LPE specifier were more likely than other arrested youth to commit their crimes with others, including as part of gang activity (Thornton et al., 2015). When these youth were asked about their role in the crime, those with the LPE specifier were more likely to report that they were "the leader" in the crime and that the crime "was their idea." Similar to what we found for bullying, it appears that youth with CU traits not only commit high rates of criminal behavior, but they are more likely to encourage others to commit illegal behavior. Another finding that we published from the same sample was that youth with the LPE specifier more frequently carried and used a gun in a crime over the 4 years following their first arrest (Robertson et al., 2020). Again, this suggests that adolescents with the LPE specifier were more likely to be involved in more serious and violent types of crimes.

PROBLEMS IN SOCIAL RELATIONSHIPS

From the research reviewed thus far in this chapter, one of the strongest and most consistent findings is that children and adolescents with the LPE specifier are at high risk for showing a stable pattern of antisocial behavior that often involves aggression, bullying, and criminal behavior. These findings alone highlight the clinical importance of identifying children with the LPE specifier early and providing them with effective treatment that can minimize their harm to potential victims. However, research has shown that these outcomes are not the only problems in adjustment that can result from elevated CU traits. That is, children with the LPE specifier have other problems in their social relationships as well. It is not surprising, given their heightened aggression in interpersonal relationships, that our research has also found that children with the LPE specifier are often rejected and disliked by their prosocial peers. In a school-based sample of children in grades 2, 6, and 8, we found that children with CU traits were not only more likely to be rejected by their peers, but they were also frequently described by their peers as being "mean," as someone who "doesn't care who they hurt," and as someone "who always has to get their way" (Matlasz et al., 2022). Children with the LPE specifier were also less likely than other students to be described by their peers as being "easy to make friends with," "someone you can trust," and "someone who is nice." These findings suggest that the behavior of children with the LPE specifier can lead them to have significant difficulties getting along with their peers.

It is important to note, however, that there are also some more positive findings related to the peer relationships of children with the LPE specifier. That is, some findings show that children with the LPE specifier have social skills that are similar to other children (Grieve & Mahar, 2010; Waschbusch, Walsh, et al., 2007) and are able to make friends, with some research showing that they have just as many friends as other children (Muñoz et al., 2008). However, the friendships of children with the LPE specifier are often with other children who get into trouble (Kimonis et al., 2004) and children with the LPE specifier often are very influential in encouraging others to engage in problematic behaviors in the classroom (Kerr et al., 2012). This latter finding is similar to the research we conducted showing that CU traits are related to instigating both bullying and criminal behavior in adolescents. In addition, in our research, we found that while children (Haas et al., 2018) and adolescents (Golmaryami et al., 2021) with the LPE specifier are capable of forming friendships and intimate relationships with others, these relationships are often shorter than the relationships of their peers and are less warm and satisfying. Finally, it seems that people with the LPE specifier do not just show less warmth in their friendships with others, but this perceived lack of warmth extends to other relationships as well, including with caregivers, teachers, and romantic partners later in life (Vaughan et al., 2023). In summary, it appears that children with CU traits have the social skills necessary to make friends, but these children use them to make friends with others who show behavior problems, their social skills are often used to encourage these friends with conduct problems to engage in bullying and other antisocial behavior, and their friendships are often briefer and lacking in emotional closeness.

OTHER PROBLEMS IN ADJUSTMENT

The antisocial and aggressive behavior shown by people with the LPE specifier, their bullying behaviors and aggression toward peers and others, and their willingness to engage in criminal behaviors can all be understood in the context of their limited concern about the effects of their behavior on others. However, our research has also shown that youth with the LPE specifier are at risk for several other potentially problematic outcomes as well. One such problem is substance use. In our study of adolescents who had been arrested for the first time in adolescence, those boys who were high on CU traits were more likely to show a pattern of substance use that included multiple substances, including hard drugs (e.g., hallucinogens, sedatives, cocaine; Ray et al., 2016a). In another study we conducted with 373 incarcerated boys (*M* age = 16.42), we found that those with the LPE specifier were more likely to engage in harmful substance use both before and during incarceration, particularly involving alcohol, and they were more likely than other incarcerated boys to meet criteria for a substance use disorder (Kimonis et al., 2012).

In our studies with justice-involved boys, we found that adolescents with the LPE specifier were more likely to engage in risky sexual behaviors as well.

These risky behaviors included engaging in unprotected sex (i.e., sex without condoms) and in casual sex (i.e., sex with a partner they did not know well; Thornton et al., 2019). Importantly, in Thornton et al. (2019), we showed that this risky sexual behavior was related to the greater substance use in boys with the LPE specifier. That is, their substance use at least partially explained why boys with the LPE specifier were more likely to engage in risky sexual behavior. Taken together, our research with adolescents who had been arrested indicates that adolescents with the LPE specifier appear to be more likely to use more serious substances, and a greater number of them, in adolescence, and this pattern of serious substance use often led them to engage in sex practices that put themselves and others at high risk for sexually transmitted diseases.

In other research, we studied another way that CU traits can increase the clinical impairment of youth in a sample of 396 adolescents (*M* age = 14.5 years) who had been hospitalized for being a danger to themselves or others (Kemp, Picou, et al., in press). Overall, CU traits were related to less suicidal behavior, which was measured by the number of suicide attempts reported by the adolescent, a clinician rating of the severity of suicidal behavior, and the lethality of the suicide attempt. However, in the presence of other risk factors for suicide, such as impulsivity, a family history of suicide, depression, and posttraumatic symptoms, CU traits were related to an increase in the lethality of the suicide attempts. This pattern of findings suggests that the lack of concern over the effects of their behavior may reduce the risk for suicidal behavior in the absence of major risk factors but that CU traits can increase the severity of suicidal behaviors among adolescents with other risk factors for attempting suicide.

CHAPTER SUMMARY

As we noted in Chapter 1, childhood conduct problems are a serious mental health concern because of the many problems they cause for the child throughout development. From the research reviewed in this chapter, it should be clear that those children and adolescents with the LPE specifier are at even higher risk for serious problems in adjustment throughout their life compared with other children and adolescents with serious conduct problems. Those with the LPE specifier show high rates of aggressive, violent, and criminal behavior. As a result, their behavior operates at a high cost to others around them. Youth with the LPE specifier are overrepresented among people who commit violent crimes and also among those who bully others at school. Furthermore, they seem to play a key role in encouraging others to commit crimes and bully others. These problematic behaviors shown by those with the LPE specifier not only lead to problems for others, but they also create problems for the youth with the specifier, making it difficult for them to develop close, long-lasting, and satisfying relationships with others. Youth with the

LPE specifier are also at risk for harmful substance use, risky sexual behavior, and serious suicide attempts. In short, the minority of youth with conduct problems who show the LPE specifier play a role in some of society's most pressing problems. Consequently, they are a critically important group to identify and to intervene with effectively. These clinically important characteristics of people with the LPE specifier, combined with research showing that other parts of diagnostic criteria did not adequately identify this seriously concerning group, were the key reasons why the LPE specifier was added to the diagnostic criteria for conduct problem diagnoses in the *DSM-5* and the *ICD-11*. In short, the research we reviewed in this chapter provides an answer to *why* it is so important to diagnose and intervene with people with the LPE specifier. However, the information in this chapter did not provide clear guidance on *how* to diagnose people with the LPE specifier or how to treat those identified. These topics are the primary focus of the remaining chapters of the book, beginning with the next chapter, which focuses on research uncovering the unique causal processes underlying the behavior problems of this clinically important group of youth. These causal processes provide the basis for our treatment recommendations in later chapters.

3

Distinct Emotional, Cognitive, and Social Characteristics of Children and Adolescents With Limited Prosocial Emotions

The previous chapter focused on differences between children who show serious conduct problems with and without the limited prosocial emotions (LPE) specifier on several characteristics that make it critical to identify them as early as possible and provide them with effective treatment. In this chapter, we focus on how children and adolescents with the LPE specifier differ from other youth with behavior problems on a number of critical emotional, cognitive, and social characteristics. In this selective review, we focus on those characteristics and those causal theories that provide the research basis for our recommendations for treatment. The key findings that we focus on in this chapter are summarized in Table 3.1.

We include this discussion of causal processes in this clinically oriented book because we feel that the reason that children and adolescents with callous–unemotional (CU) traits often leave treatment with significant levels of behavior problems is that the available interventions have failed to consider the unique emotional, cognitive, and social characteristics of those with the LPE specifier (Perlstein et al., 2023). That is, treatments often were designed for treating children with conduct problems more broadly and did not consider the unique needs of those with elevated CU traits. Our modifications of existing treatments that we review in later chapters were specifically designed to take these unique needs into account. Furthermore, we firmly believe and have anecdotal clinical evidence to support that clinicians who understand the basis for our treatment approach are more effective in implementing the treatment, since

https://doi.org/10.1037/0000500-004
A Clinical Guide to Working With Youth With Conduct Disorders and Limited Prosocial Emotions,
by P. J. Frick and E. R. Kimonis

TABLE 3.1. Differences Between the Three Developmental Pathways to Severe Conduct Problems

Developmental pathway	Research findings on primary differences	Theoretical implications on critical developmental mechanisms	Key references
Adolescent-onset	• Tends to show nonaggressive forms of antisocial behavior. • Lower rates of antisocial and criminal behaviors in adulthood than in other pathways. • High levels of peer delinquency. • Families that are poor at monitoring and supervising adolescents. • High levels of rebelliousness and low levels of traditionalism.	Youth in this pathway show an exaggeration of the normal developmental process of identity formation. The normal adolescent rebellion associated with this process is exaggerated due to encouragement of antisocial behavior by delinquent peers and personality traits that lead to rejection of authority and traditional power hierarchies. These youth are more likely to outgrow antisocial behavior problems after adolescence, although they may become "ensnared" in the consequences of their antisocial behavior (e.g., criminal records, school dropout; harmful substance use).	Dandreaux & Frick (2009); Frick & Viding (2009); Moffitt (2018); Odgers et al. (2007, 2008)
Childhood-onset	• High levels of impulsivity. • Heightened emotional reactivity to emotional stimuli. • Highly anxious and distressed by consequences of behavior. • More likely to have cognitive limitations, especially in verbal intellectual abilities and in executive functioning. • Exposed to families that are harsher and more inconsistent in their parenting.	Youth in this pathway have trouble developing the skills needed for appropriate behavioral and emotional regulation due to dispositional vulnerabilities (e.g., emotional hyperreactivity; poor executive control of behavior) that make them more difficult to parent effectively. This interaction between the child's difficult disposition and the harsh and inconsistent parenting they experience leads to conduct problems that are impulsive in nature or that occur during highly emotionally charged situations (i.e., when the child is angry). The child may feel badly about the consequences of their behavior but lacks the skills necessary to control them in the future.	Frick (2022); Frick et al. (2014b); Frick & Viding (2009); Moffitt (2018)

Childhood-onset with limited prosocial emotions	• High levels of impulsivity. • Deficits in attending to, recognizing, and reacting to cues of distress in others starting at an early age. • Abnormalities in response to punishment and punishment learning. • More likely to view aggression and dominance as important social goals and effective means to obtaining desired outcomes. • Associated with less warmth and sensitivity in relationships with caregivers, with evidence of child-driven reductions over time.	Youth in this pathway show deficits in how they respond to emotional displays in others and in their response to and learning from punishment, which lead to problems in the development of empathy and guilt. This lack of prosocial emotions contributes to their persistent aggressive behavior. The lack of prosocial emotions also evokes fewer warm and responsive interactions from their caregivers and in other important social relationships. This process makes naturally occurring corrective environments less likely to occur.	De Brito et al. (2021); Frick (2022); Frick & Kemp (2021); Hyde & Dotterer (2022); Vaughan et al. (2023); Viding & McCrory (2019); Waller & Wagner (2019)

they understand the reasons behind what they are doing in treatment. We also feel that clinicians are more likely to be effective in engaging families in treatment by being able to explain to them why this unique approach is likely to be more effective than any past interventions they may have tried.

Again, the following summary is not meant to be an exhaustive review of the large body of research investigating the correlates to CU traits, nor is it designed to provide novel theoretical insights to guide causal research. Instead, we provide a selective review of the research on a few specific differences between youth with conduct problems who do and do not show the LPE specifier, which were particularly instrumental in guiding our approach to treatment. To illustrate this somewhat selective review of etiology, Viding and colleagues (2005, 2008) in a series of studies from a very large twin study showed that the contributions of genetic and environmental effects were dramatically different in young children depending on their level of CU traits. That is, genetics accounted for about 80% of the variance in conduct problems for those high in CU traits but accounted for only about 30% of the variance in conduct problems for children who were not. These findings are very important for supporting a theory that the causes of conduct problems are very different for young children with and without the LPE specifier. However, these findings do not provide direct guidance in determining the different environmental influences that contribute to the remaining 20% of the variance in conduct problems in those with the LPE specifier, nor do they provide clues as to what predispositions might influence the development of conduct problems in the two groups, so that treatment can be modified to address these distinct causal factors. Thus, in this chapter, we focus instead directly on these potential causal influences that can be targeted in treatment.

DEFICITS IN EMOTIONAL REACTIVITY AND EMOTION RECOGNITION IN YOUTH WITH THE LIMITED PROSOCIAL EMOTIONS SPECIFIER

One of the most consistent findings in terms of differences between children and adolescents with conduct problems who show the LPE specifier compared to those who do not is in how they respond to the emotions of others. That is, youth with conduct problems who show the LPE specifier are less emotionally reactive to the emotional expressions of others, particularly when others are displaying signs of distress, such as being sad or afraid (De Brito et al., 2021). In our research, we have shown this pattern in samples across a wide age range and using multiple ways to measure emotional reactivity, such as showing that images depicting others in distress do not capture the attention of individuals with the LPE specifier (Kimonis et al., 2006, 2019), that they are less likely to mimic others' emotional expressions when watching emotional film clips (Kimonis et al., 2023), and that they do not display the typical reflex of a stronger startle blink response when shown aversive images (Kimonis et al., 2017). Also, in our research, we have found that caregivers notice this lack of attention to others' emotions in their young children, with children with the LPE specifier being rated as less attentive to others' distress by their caregivers (Chan et al., 2023; Levantini et al., 2024). Other researchers have shown this reduced emotional reactivity using brain imaging studies, finding that children with conduct problems with elevated CU traits show lower levels of amygdala activation to fearful facial expressions than other children with conduct problems (Viding et al., 2012).

There are several unanswered questions related to this reduced emotional reactivity in children with elevated CU traits, such as how early it can be detected. That is, emotional deficits have been associated with childhood CU traits in samples with a mean age ranging from 36 months (Wagner et al., 2017) to 11.21 years (Fanti et al., 2016) to 16.8 years (Kimonis et al., 2017). Showing potential deficits even earlier in development, a study by Bedford and colleagues (2015) noted that 5 weeks after birth, infants who preferred to look at objects over human faces were more likely to show CU traits when they were 2.5 years old. Another unanswered question is how broad is this deficit in emotional reactivity—that is, is it specific to facial expressions of sadness and fear or is it broader and encompasses other types of emotions as well? For example, a meta-analysis by Marsh and Blair (2008) showed that persons high on CU traits tended to exhibit reduced responses to a number of different types of emotions, including facial expressions of fear, sadness, and surprise.

Despite these unanswered questions, the consistent finding of reduced emotional responses in children with the LPE specifier is critical because it results in a striking difference from other children with conduct problems. Children with conduct problems who do not show elevated CU traits not only do not show reduced emotional reactivity, but they often show enhanced reactivity to emotional stimuli relative to children without conduct problems. That is, children with conduct problems who are classified into subgroups based on whether they do or do not show the LPE specifier often show opposite patterns of emotional reactivity. These opposing patterns of reactivity have critical implications for conducting and interpreting research on children and adolescents with serious behavior problems (Frick, 2022). Specifically, if one studied the association between emotional reactivity and conduct problems but ignored the differences between those with and without the LPE specifier, the high reactivity in one group would cancel out the low reactivity in the other, and one would conclude that emotional reactivity has very little association with conduct problems. The failure of a significant amount of research to consider these opposing patterns of reactivity is likely why it has failed to find consistent molecular genetic and other biological risk factors for serious conduct problems, many of which may underlie the differences in emotional reactivity between the two groups. In addition to these critical considerations for causal research, this difference in emotional reactivity patterns can have treatment implications as well. That is, different approaches to treatment may be needed if you are trying to teach a child to regulate their intense emotional reactions to others, as opposed to trying to motivate a child to appropriately attend and respond to others' distressed emotions to which they do not experience an emotional reaction.

There is another reason that the reduced emotional reactivity to others' emotions has important theoretical and clinical implications. It is developmentally important for more complex forms of empathy. In a review that we did on the development of empathic concern in children, we summarized research showing that emotional reactivity to others' emotions is present very early in life and helps children learn to take the perspective of others (Frick & Kemp, 2021). One of the earliest examples is contagious crying seen in infants. Later in development, if a child causes another child to cry, this cry is experienced as aversive, even before the child can understand the emotions being displayed in other people. This "emotional contagion" motivates the child to learn what they did to cause the other child to cry, which requires them to learn to recognize emotions in others and their meaning. Children who do not experience this emotional reactivity (i.e., emotional discomfort) to the signs of distress in others will be less motivated to develop their emotional recognition abilities.

Consistent with this contention, research has also shown that CU traits are linked to problems recognizing (i.e., accurately identifying) emotions in facial expressions. In a meta-analysis of caregiver and teacher ratings of how well children recognized emotions in others, CU traits were negatively correlated with these ratings, suggesting that caregivers and teachers rated children with CU traits as being less accurate in recognizing others' emotional states (Waller et al., 2020). Similar findings were seen in a meta-analysis of laboratory measures of emotional recognition that we conducted, which summarized studies using tasks that measured how accurately children and adolescents labeled emotions in human faces. Across 47 studies in children under age 12, and 68 studies of adolescents between the ages of 12 and 18 years, youth with higher CU traits were less accurate in recognizing emotions (Kemp, Miller, et al., 2025).

Similar to research on the association between CU traits and emotional reactivity, it is unclear how specific are the deficits in emotional recognition. That is, they are most consistently found for recognition of fearful and sad facial expressions, but they are sometimes found for other emotions as well. For example, in sample of 214 preschool children (*M* age = 4.7 years), we found that elevated CU traits were related to less accurate recognition of faces depicting anger and happiness, as well as fear and sadness (Kimonis, Fanti et al., 2016). In a sample of 293 middle school children, we found that CU traits were associated with poorer accuracy in recognizing both fearful and angry faces (Ciucci et al., 2024). In addition, some studies have gone beyond simply documenting that children with CU traits are less accurate in recognizing emotions in others by also showing that this tendency is largely explained by the child's reduced attention to the eyes of the facial expression of emotion (Dadds et al., 2007), which can be temporarily overcome by simply instructing the child with the LPE specifier to pay attention to the eyes of others (Dadds et al., 2006). Such findings could be very helpful for guiding interventions to help children overcome their difficulties in recognizing emotions by helping youth learn to pay more attention to others' eyes during expressed emotions. Also, in our study of middle school students, we showed that CU traits were not only related to less accurate recognition of fear in other people's faces, they also related to a tendency (i.e., a bias) to label fearful faces as angry faces (Ciucci et al., 2024). If a child is misinterpreting fear or sadness in others as anger, this could help to explain why signs of distress in others are not leading to empathetic concern and could even be provoking aggressive reactions to perceived threat. Consistent with this possibility, in our study of preschool children, when children were viewing movie depictions of happiness and sadness, those with the LPE specifier were more likely to show incongruent emotions on their own faces, with this emotion most often being anger (Kimonis, Fanti et al., 2016).

As noted previously, the development of emotional recognition skills is somewhat dependent on emotional attention and reactivity, with the emotional reactions motivating a child to learn how to accurately interpret the emotions in others (Frick & Kemp, 2021). Thus, it is not surprising that children with the LPE specifier often show both deficits in their attentional orienting and reactivity to others' emotions and deficits in their ability to accurately identify others' emotions. However, in our meta-analysis of past research (Kemp, Miller, et al., 2025), we found that the negative association between CU traits and emotional reactivity was found in samples throughout the lifespan, including studies we have conducted in various age groups (Kimonis et al., 2006, 2020; Kimonis, Fanti, et al., 2016) That is, deficits in emotional reactivity were associated with CU traits in samples from preschool through adulthood. In contrast, the association between CU traits and problems recognizing emotions decreased in adolescence and adulthood to the point that, sometimes, in older adolescent samples, CU traits were even related to *better* emotional recognition, including in a study we conducted in incarcerated adolescents (Kahn et al., 2017). We interpreted this change across development as suggesting that youth with the LPE specifier initially have trouble learning to recognize others' emotions due to the lack of intrinsic motivation resulting from their deficits in emotional reactivity. However, over time, children with the LPE specifier can learn that there are social advantages to recognizing emotions in others (e.g., being better able to intimidate or manipulate others), and this social motivation helps them to develop better emotional recognition skills. This change in the relationship between CU traits and emotional recognition abilities with increasing child age also has important implications for treatment. That is, they suggest that children can learn to accurately interpret the emotions of others, even if they lack the intrinsic motivation for doing so. However, it requires teaching them the deficient skills needed for emotional recognition, such as paying attention to critical facial features in others during emotional displays. It also requires finding appropriate ways to motivate them to want to learn and become proficient in using these skills. As we discuss in later chapters, teaching these emotional recognition skills is an important component to our tailored intervention for children with the LPE specifier.

PUNISHMENT INSENSITIVITY IN PERSONS WITH LIMITED PROSOCIAL EMOTIONS

Another significant focus of research on how children and adolescents with the LPE specifier differ from other youth with conduct problems is in how they respond to punishment. In a study of children referred to a clinic for a psychological evaluation, we found that children with the LPE specifier, but not other children with behavior problems, played longer on a computer task in which their responding was initially rewarded but was eventually punished (Barry et al., 2000). Specifically, we had children play several computer games for points that could be used to purchase prizes. In each game, the only choice the child had after each trial was to either keep playing or stop. The ratio of rewarded (i.e., winning a point) to punished responses (i.e., losing a point) was set to where the first 10 times the child played, they were rewarded 9 out of 10 times. This established a reward-oriented response set for the child, where they anticipated being rewarded by playing. However, each successive 10 trials, the ratio of rewarded trials decreased (e.g., 8 out of 10 rewarded, 7 out of 10 rewarded) until 9 out of 10 trials were being punished. To maximize the number of points earned, the child had to learn to quit playing as the number of punished trials exceeded the rewarded trials. However, children with the LPE specifier kept playing longer than other children with conduct problems, suggesting that once they learned that a behavior was rewarded, they had difficulty recognizing the shift to that same behavior now being punished.

A number of other studies using other ways of measuring a person's response to punishments also supported that children and adolescents with the LPE specifier show atypical responses to punishment under various conditions (see Byrd et al., 2014, for a review). For example, in a study of adolescents who had been detained for committing a crime, we asked them what they expected to happen in series of situations when they used aggression against a peer to either obtain something or retaliate against them (Pardini et al., 2003). We also asked them how much they would care if certain outcomes happened in these situations. Adolescents with the LPE specifier were more likely than other detained adolescents to expect that their aggression would result in rewards (including social dominance). They also reported that obtaining these rewards was more important to them than avoiding punishment. Thus, one reason why children and adolescents with the LPE specifier may act aggressively is that they expect that their aggression will get them what they want, and this possible outcome is more important to them than avoiding punishment. These deficits in punishment sensitivity contribute to some of the social difficulties seen in children with CU traits. They also help to explain why youth with the LPE specifier show persistent conduct problems, despite being punished for them at home and school or by getting in trouble with the police. Again, while this punishment insensitivity is important for causal theories of how CU traits develop and for explaining some of the problems experienced by persons with the LPE specifier, it also is important in our approach to treatment. As we discuss in later chapters, emphasizing reward-based strategies over exclusively using punishment to change problematic behavior, as well as consistently punishing more serious problematic behaviors, are critical parts to our tailored intervention approach for children and adolescents with the LPE specifier.

THE ROLE OF WARM AND RESPONSIVE PARENTING IN THE DEVELOPMENT OF CALLOUS-UNEMOTIONAL TRAITS

One additional area in which research has suggested that children with the LPE specifier differ from other children with conduct problems is in the parenting they experience and their responses to it. These parenting factors have been critical for causal theories, since many theories place great emphasis on the quality of parenting that the child receives in explaining the development of conduct problems (Frick & Viding, 2009). This research is also critical for treatment of childhood conduct problems, given that most approaches to treatment focus on improving parental responses to the child as a primary goal of the intervention (Frick, 2012).

In one of our early studies, we investigated 166 children between the ages of 6 and 13 who were either referred to our mental health clinic for behavior problems or who were from families in the same community as our clinic referrals (Wootton et al., 1997). We found that a measure of ineffective parenting was associated with conduct problems in children in our sample but only at low levels of CU traits. Ineffective parenting was not associated with conduct problems in children with the LPE specifier. We originally interpreted these findings to suggest that parenting has more of an influence on conduct problems for children lower on CU traits, which would be consistent with the twin studies showing that conduct problems are more influenced by environmental factors in children low on CU traits (Viding et al., 2005, 2008). However, the measure of parenting that we used in our study included a wide range of parenting behaviors, including caregiver involvement with their child, their use of positive reinforcement, inconsistent use of discipline, poor monitoring and supervision of the child, and use of corporal punishment. About a decade after our initial study, Pasalich and colleagues (2012) also investigated the association between parenting and conduct problems in children referred to a mental health clinic for behavior problems. However, they separated harsh and inconsistent parenting from warm and responsive parenting. Their findings closely replicated ours in finding that the measure of harsh and inconsistent parenting was only related to conduct problems at low levels of

CU traits. However, their separation of parenting behaviors offered a new insight. They reported that lower levels of warm and responsive parenting were more strongly related to (greater) conduct problems in children *high* on CU traits. We also found support for the importance of warm and responsive parenting for youth with the LPE specifier in a sample of 227 incarcerated adolescent boys, in which we found that lower levels of maternal warmth and responsiveness were associated with greater aggression when CU traits were high (Kimonis, Cross et al., 2013).

A significant amount of research conducted after these initial studies supported the importance of warm and responsive parenting for children high on CU traits, both in predicting later conduct problems and in their association with CU traits themselves (see Waller et al., 2013, for a review). Furthermore, the importance of warm and responsive parenting is consistent with developmental theories on how empathy, guilt, and other prosocial emotions develop in children. Caregivers model these emotional responses and reinforce their child's use of them in social interactions, beginning with the interactions between caregiver and child (Frick & Kemp, 2021). However, how does one explain the importance of warm parenting in the development of CU traits and on the conduct problems displayed by youth high on CU traits, given the findings from twin studies supporting the strong genetic influence on conduct problems in those with the LPE specifier? One possibility is the presence of a gene × environment interaction. This possibility is best illustrated by Hyde and colleagues (2016), who conducted a study of 561 children who had been adopted early in life. Despite limited or no contact with their children, biological mothers' antisocial behavior predicted CU traits in their children at 27 months of age. This finding clearly supports a genetic contribution to the development of CU traits. However, this link between the biological mothers' antisocial behavior and their children's CU traits was reduced if the child's adoptive mother used reward-oriented approaches to parenting. Thus, for those who may have a biological predisposition for LPE, positive parenting in their adoptive home reduced their risk of developing CU traits. Such findings provide clear support for our focus on improving the quality of parenting a child receives in our tailored intervention for children and adolescents with LPE.

It is also important to note that another reason that warm parenting may be more highly related to conduct problems in those high on CU traits is through a gene × environment correlation. That is, CU traits in the child may lead to decreases in parental warmth and responsiveness over time, what is sometimes labeled as "child effects" on parenting. In a study we conducted testing this possibility in a sample of adolescent boys who had been arrested and assessed multiple times over a 5-year period, CU traits consistently predicted reductions in parental warmth over time, but increasing parental warmth did not predict reductions in CU traits (Vaughan et al., 2023). That is, we found strong evidence for child effects of CU traits leading to reductions in parental warmth in our adolescent sample. These findings have important implications for treatment. While increasing parental warmth may be critical for reducing conduct problems in children with the LPE specifier, this may be quite difficult to do for older children, given that the child's increasing lack of prosocial emotions makes it more difficult for caregivers to be warm and responsive toward the child. Thus, interventions need to break this difficult cycle of CU traits leading to decreases in the warmth of the caregiver–child relationships, which, in turn, can lead to more conduct problems and CU traits.

CAUSAL PATHWAYS TO SERIOUS CONDUCT PROBLEMS

From this review of research, it should be clear that there are a number of differences in the emotional, cognitive, and social characteristics of children with conduct problems, depending on whether or not they show the LPE specifier. While our focus has been largely on the characteristics of those with the LPE specifier and, even more specifically, on those characteristics that play an important role in our approach to treating children with the LPE specifier, it is important to place these findings into a broader understanding of how conduct problems develop. A key assumption to our approach to intervention is that, given that the causes of conduct problems can differ greatly across children and adolescents, the most effective approach to treatment will also differ across subgroups. As a result, a core principle of our approach to treatment is to tailor intervention to the unique needs of children and adolescents with serious conduct problems.

Another reason why we discuss the common causal pathways to conduct problems in this book is to make clear that the group of youth who show the LPE specifier represent only a small subgroup of all children and adolescents with either an oppositional defiant disorder (ODD) or conduct disorder (CD) diagnosis. While this varies depending on the sample studied and the method used to make the LPE specifier diagnosis, our research consistently suggests that between 20% and 55% of children with a conduct problem diagnosis show the LPE specifier (Kahn et al., 2012; Kaouar et al., 2024; Kimonis et al., 2015), with the proportion being about 27% when a comprehensive method is used to make the diagnosis (Goetz et al., 2024). In the previous chapter, we provide clear evidence that, despite being a minority of youth with conduct problems in many samples, those with the LPE specifier are a clinically important group, given the severity and chronicity of their behavior problems. Further, in the next three chapters, we discuss how to identify and diagnose this very important subgroup of children and adolescents with behavior problems. However, this diagnostic process can be enhanced by knowing how those with the LPE specifier differ from other youth with serious conduct problems in terms of the causal process leading to their behavior problems. We have also found that being able to explain these differences in causal processes to families can help motivate them to engage in treatment, even if they have been disappointed with past treatment attempts.

Thus, we conclude this chapter with a brief overview of the different causal mechanisms that lead to conduct problems across children with and without the LPE specifier. Importantly, in our discussion of the different developmental pathways that can lead to these problems, we do not focus on all of the many risk factors that can contribute to children's behavior problems. Research has uncovered an extremely large number of factors in children's neurocognitive abilities (e.g., problems in executive functioning, lower verbal intelligence, differences in the response of certain brain regions to social stimuli), in their response to rewards and punishment (e.g., heightened or reduced sensitivity to punishment and rewards), in their temperament (e.g., heightened or reduced emotional reactivity), and in their personality (e.g., impulsivity; thrill seeking; rebelliousness) that can place them at risk for showing conduct problems (Frick & Viding, 2009). Research has documented just as many risk factors in children's social contexts that can increase their risk for showing conduct problems, ranging from living in certain neighborhoods (e.g., impoverished neighborhoods with high levels of crime and violence), to poor quality childcare and schools, associating with delinquent peers, and having caregivers show use of harsh and inconsistent parenting practices (Frick & Viding, 2009). This extensive body of research is critical to highlight that theories for how conduct problems develop need to consider how these many factors can place a child at risk for developing conduct problems, and that effective treatments for children with conduct problems need to consider how to mitigate these many risk factors. But does this mean we need to have hundreds of different types of interventions that target all of these risk factors to be effective? Also, what about some risk factors that can be prevented but cannot be changed once children have experienced them, such exposure to toxins (e.g., drugs, alcohol, lead) during pregnancy? Clearly, such as research supports early intervention, such as providing quality prenatal care to pregnant women to reduce or eliminate this risk factor, but is there nothing anyone can do to treat the child if such prevention programs are not successful?

In our developmental model, instead of focusing on the risk factors themselves, we focus on what developmental mechanisms may be negatively impacted by these risk factors in children. Rather than focusing on prenatal exposure to toxins, we focus on what such exposure may do to the developing child to put exposed children at risk for conduct problems. With such an approach, treatment can address these more proximal mechanisms, even if it cannot change or undo the risk factor that led to them. Similarly, clinicians working with children who live in neighborhoods in which the child is exposed to high rates of violence often cannot remove the child and their family from these neighborhoods. We want to be clear that we strongly advocate for interventions that attempt to prevent such traumatic exposure in children. However, many clinicians are not in a position to implement such broad policy changes. But does this mean there is nothing that a clinician can do to reduce the behavior problems of children living in high-risk neighborhoods? We feel that intervention can still be effective, if it is tailored to the consequences of living in such neighborhoods, which can vary across subgroups of children with conduct problems. Thus, in the concluding sections of this chapter, we focus on some of the common developmental processes that research has suggested can be disrupted by the many risk factors associated with conduct problems and can lead to conduct problems in children, with a specific focus on how these differ for individuals with and without the LPE specifier.

Adolescent-Onset Conduct Problems

In the first chapter, we discussed the history of the diagnosis of CD in mental health diagnosis and classification. As we noted, since 1994, a distinction has been made between those who start showing serious conduct problems prior to the onset of adolescence (i.e., childhood onset) and those who only start showing conduct problems as they enter adolescence. This distinction identified in the research literature well predated its inclusion in mental health diagnoses. That is, this change in classification followed from research on juvenile delinquency in which a distinction was made between "early starter" versus "later starter" pathways to designate those who start showing criminal behavior prior to or after adolescence (Farrington et al., 1988). Importantly, studies on people referred to mental health treatment for conduct problems or adolescents in juvenile institutions for criminal behavior tend to be about evenly split in terms of this child or adolescent pattern of onset (Moffitt, 2018).

One of the reasons that this age-of-onset distinction has such a long history is that it seems to predict very different outcomes. In terms of delinquency, Farrington et al. (1988) found that boys who were arrested before age 12 showed almost twice as many convictions at two later points in time (between the ages of 16 and 18 and the ages of 22 and 24) than those with a later age at first arrest. In terms of conduct problems, in a New Zealand birth cohort of 539 males followed through age 26, 55% of those whose problem behaviors started before adolescence had a criminal conviction as an adult, with an average rate of 6.9 ($SD = 11.5$) convictions, compared with a conviction rate of 34% and an average rate of 3.5 ($SD = 10.8$) convictions for those whose problem behaviors onset in adolescence (Moffitt et al., 2002). The difference between the two groups was even more dramatic for violent convictions through age 32, in that 32.7% of the men who began showing serious conduct problems before adolescence had been convicted of a violent offense, compared with only 10.2% who started showing serious conduct problems in their adolescent years and only 0.4% who did not show these problems in either childhood or adolescence (Odgers et al., 2008). In short, the adolescent-onset group was less likely to be violent and more likely to outgrow their behavior problems after adolescence.

In addition to these different outcomes, extensive research suggests that both conduct problem groups differ on several dispositional and contextual risk factors as well, which we summarize in Table 3.1. That is, those in the adolescent-onset group seem to show fewer risk factors, both fewer dispositional risk factors (e.g., less impulsivity, less likely to score lower on an intelligence test) and fewer social risk factors (e.g., less family instability, less exposure to harsh parenting). When the adolescent-onset group differs from the control group, the children often show higher levels of rebelliousness and rejection of conventional values and hierarchies, greater exposure to peers who also show conduct problems, and less parental monitoring and supervision (Dandreaux & Frick, 2009; Moffitt, 2018).

The different outcomes and risk factors for children in the adolescent-onset conduct problem group provide clues about the developmental mechanism that may have gone awry for them to develop conduct problems. In other words, the outcomes and risk factors identified from research suggest that the adolescent-onset subgroup of youth with serious behavior problems show an exaggeration of the normative process of adolescent rebellion (Frick & Viding, 2009; Moffitt, 2018). Most adolescents show rebelliousness to authority figures, such as caregivers, teachers, and police. This behavior is actually an adaptive part of adolescents' identity development, whereby they begin to develop their autonomous sense of self and unique identity (i.e., "I am my own self and can make my own decisions") by rejecting traditional status hierarchies (i.e., "I don't have to follow what other people tell me to do"). However, despite some level of rebelliousness being developmentally normative for adolescents, only a very small percentage of adolescents show antisocial behavior that is severe enough to lead to a CD diagnosis or an arrest. So what leads to this "exaggeration" of a normal developmental process resulting in serious behavior problems? The child in the adolescent-onset group may attempt to gain a sense of maturity and adult status in a way that is maladaptive (e.g., breaking societal norms) because it is encouraged by an antisocial peer group, because they have caregivers who do not adequately supervise or monitor the adolescent's behavior, because the adolescent is not connected to their caregiver or to prosocial institutions (e.g., school, church), or because the adolescent has a more rebellious personality (Dandreaux & Frick, 2009; Goetz et al., 2025).

Importantly, the contention that the behavior problems of youth in this group are an exaggeration of a process specific to adolescence, and not due to an enduring vulnerability, can explain why their antisocial behavior is less likely to persist beyond adolescence. However, it is important to note that people in the adolescent-onset group are still more likely to have mental health, occupational, and educational problems in adulthood compared to those who did not show conduct problems in either childhood or adolescence (Odgers et al., 2008). These lingering problems in adjustment could be due to impairments that persist into adulthood due to the consequences of their adolescent antisocial behavior (e.g., a criminal record, dropping out of school, harmful substance use), which are considered "snares" that negatively influence a person's adjustment, even once the primary causes of the antisocial behavior are gone (Moffitt, 2018).

This conceptualization of the adolescent-onset pattern of antisocial behavior illustrates our approach to causal theories of conduct problems by focusing on developmental mechanisms. In our theory, multiple risk factors (e.g., delinquent peer affiliation, poor parental monitoring and supervision, a rebellious personality) are linked to antisocial behavior through their influence on a developmental process (i.e., identity development) that can make this normal developmental process go awry (i.e., the adolescent rebels by acting in an antisocial manner) in some youth and lead to conduct problems.

Childhood-Onset Conduct Problems Without the Limited Prosocial Emotions Specifier

In contrast to this adolescent-onset pattern of antisocial behavior, there is also a childhood-onset pattern in which the behavior problems begin very early in development, as early as the first two to three years of life. These behavior problems begin as oppositional–defiant, angry–irritable, and sometimes aggressive–destructive behaviors that worsen in severity over childhood and into adolescence, when they become more serious antisocial and violent behavior (Rowe et al., 2002). From this research, this group of early starters are more likely to be aggressive and continue to show problems throughout development, including being more likely to persist in their problem behavior into adulthood. Finally, as noted previously, this group of youth with childhood-onset conduct problems tend to present with more dispositional and contextual risk factors than the adolescent-onset group.

As a result of all of these research findings, theories generally suggest that children with a childhood-onset to their behavior problem are more likely to have an enduring vulnerability. Namely, some development process has gone awry that leads to problems across multiple developmental stages, not just a single one. However, from the research we have reviewed throughout this chapter, the developmental process that has gone awry differs between children with and without the LPE specifier. Further, by separating those with CU traits from other youth with serious conduct problems, research has been able to more clearly define the unique risk factors associated with children in the childhood-onset pathway without the LPE specifier, which can provide clues about what developmental processes may be going awry in this group of children that help to explain their antisocial behavior. These factors, how they differ from those for the group with the LPE specifier, and how they relate to potential causal mechanisms are summarized in Table 3.1.

As noted earlier, a key characteristic of youth in the adolescent-onset pathway is that they tend to be less aggressive than those in the childhood-onset pathway. Those children with childhood-onset conduct problems who do not show the LPE specifier tend to be more aggressive than children who show adolescent-onset problems. However, they are less aggressive than children with the LPE specifier and, when they do act aggressively, it tends to be confined to reactive aggression that occurs in the context of high emotional arousal and in response to real or perceived provocation (Frick et al., 2003). This aggression committed when angry is consistent with different patterns of emotional reactivity that have been found between youth with conduct problems with and without LPE. That is, while children with the LPE specifier show reduced reactivity to various emotional stimuli, children with conduct problems and normative levels of CU traits seem to show a heightened level of emotional reactivity across various methods used in research (for examples, see Fanti et al., 2016; Kimonis et al., 2006; Viding et al., 2012).

These emotional processing patterns of children with early onset conduct problems without the LPE specifier suggest that they struggle to develop the skills needed to self-regulate their emotions and behavior (Frick & Morris, 2004; Frick & Viding, 2009). In other words, there are a number of developmental theories for how children develop the capacity to regulate their emotions, defined as the internal and external processes involved in initiating, maintaining, and modulating the occurrence, intensity, and expression of emotions (Grolnick et al., 1996). Important to these theories is that adaptive emotional regulation is not simply a process of learning how to suppress emotional responses, but it also involves the child's ability to respond in an adaptive and flexible manner to stressful demands and emotional experiences (Eisenberg & Morris, 2002). Thus, emotional regulation involves not only the level of a child's emotional reactivity but also the strategies the child uses to regulate this reactivity. These strategies involve processes both within the child, such as attentional shifting, as well as external influences, such as caregivers and other socializing agents who can model appropriate emotional regulation strategies for their child, directly coach a child to respond adaptively to emotional situations, and reinforce the child's use of these strategies.

Thus, children with conduct problems who do not show CU traits seem to show high levels of emotional reactivity, which make it more difficult for them to learn how to regulate their emotions. Further, they often have other risk factors that make it difficult for them to learn how to regulate their emotions, such as showing lower verbal intelligence. For example, in a sample of clinic-referred children with behavior problems, we found that those with conduct problems who were not elevated on CU traits were more likely to have verbal intelligence deficits in comparison with those who showed the LPE specifier (Loney et al., 1998). Expressive language helps young children to better organize and label their thoughts, emotions, and behaviors, allows the child to "self-soothe" through internal dialogue, and these verbal abilities help the child learn to evaluate adaptive responses to emotionally charged events (Gözüm & Aktulun, 2021). Further, developmental research has shown that caregivers who are overly harsh and show high rates of anger do not provide good models to their children for how to adaptively manage intense negative emotions, and they tend to punish their children's emotions and feelings rather than coaching the child in how to effectively regulate big emotions (Spinrad et al., 2020). As noted previously, while parental warmth and responsiveness seem to be particularly important for those high on CU traits, research has suggested that the conduct problems of children without CU traits are more highly associated with harsh and inconsistent parenting.

Thus, those with childhood-onset conduct problems who do not show the LPE specifier often have a number of dispositional (e.g., high emotional reactivity, low levels of intelligence) and contextual (e.g., harsh and inconsistent parenting) factors that can put them at risk for problems regulating emotions, leading to conduct problems in contexts involving high emotional arousal. However, developmental theory also considers other types of self-regulation of behavior that are not directly tied to emotional regulation. Specifically, executive control of behavior refers to the child's ability to regulate their behavior in response to contextual demands or in order to achieve some desired goal. While difficulties in a child's ability to plan, monitor, and alter their behavior can be due to intense emotional arousal, they can also occur in nonemotional situations (Gagne et al., 2021). As was the case with emotional regulation, the development of executive control can also be influenced by lower levels of general intelligence (Engelhardt et al., 2016) and harsh and inconsistent parenting (Valcan et al., 2018). In other words, harsh parenting can make it more difficult for the child to internalize strategies to regulate behavior, resulting in behavioral control through forced compliance to parental demands rather than compliance based on learning rules and strategies for behavioral regulation. Again, all of these risk factors (i.e., problems of inhibition, low intelligence, harsh and inconsistent parenting) have also been associated specifically with conduct problems in children without the LPE specifier.

Thus, a theory to explain how the risk factors associated with childhood-onset conduct problems affect children who do not show the LPE specifier is that they influence the successful development of a child's ability to regulate their emotions and behavior. These problems in self-regulation can result from a diversity of risk factors, not just those we have outlined here. However, the key point is that the developmental processes leading to conduct problems in this group seem to be different from those causing conduct problems in those with the LPE specifier. That is, a child may react angrily and with strong emotions, resulting in conduct problems in highly emotionally charged situations. When the child is able to get their emotions under control, they may feel badly about how their behavior affected others but still continue to have problems controlling their emotions in the future. Conduct problems in this group may involve problems in the executive control of behavior, leading to unplanned impulsive behavior that results from not thinking through the potential consequences of their acts, for which the child may feel remorseful afterward but may still have difficulty inhibiting in the future (Frick & Viding, 2009). Thus, interventions for this group need to focus on helping the child develop skills related to emotional and behavioral regulation and not on deficits in their level of prosocial emotions or emotional processing patterns. Fortunately, there are evidence-based interventions that have proven helpful for this subgroup of youth with conduct problems, which we briefly outline in Chapter 7 (see also Frick, 2012).

Childhood-Onset Conduct Problems With the Limited Prosocial Emotions Specifier

This overview of the various causal pathways to serious conduct problems helps to place the research on children with the LPE specifier into the broader context of how conduct problems develop. Some children can show behavior problems due to difficulties managing the demands of identity development in adolescence that can lead to maladaptive patterns of rebellious behavior, whereas others could show dispositional vulnerabilities in how they regulate their emotions and behaviors that lead to conduct problems that start early in childhood and that can continue into adulthood. These pathways account for most children and adolescents with serious conduct problems. However, the focus of this book is on a smaller but clinically important subgroup of youth who show the LPE specifier. These children and adolescents with elevated CU traits show distinct causal processes from these other subgroups of youth with conduct problems, which lead to a more severe and persistent pattern of behavior that requires a different approach to treatment.

In this chapter, we focused on three key differences between youth with the LPE specifier CU traits compared to other youth with serious conduct problems, which helped guide our approach to tailoring treatment. Children with the LPE specifier often show reduced attention and reactivity to signs of fear, pain, and distress in others, which can make it difficult for them to learn to recognize and respond to these emotions in others in prosocial ways. We have reviewed research that youth with the LPE specifier also show abnormalities in how they process and learn from punishment cues. This body of research shows that they are more likely to view aggression as an acceptable and effective method to obtain their desired goals. We further reviewed research suggesting that youth with and without the LPE specifier differ in their experiences of and their behaviors in response to parenting. Specifically, the conduct problems of children with the LPE specifier seem to be less related to harsh and inconsistent parenting and more strongly related to warm and responsive parenting. These children also seem to evoke fewer warm behaviors from their caregivers over time.

What do these unique risk factors suggest is the critical developmental process that goes awry for youth with the LPE specifier? Deficits in guilt and empathy that define CU traits have long been considered the affective components of conscience (Kochanska & Thompson, 1997). Empathy, defined broadly, is the process by which one attends and reacts to, recognizes, and understands the emotional states of others and it is critical for motivating a child to display prosocial behavior (Frick & Kemp, 2021). The development of empathy is influenced both by dispositional characteristics of the child and by socializing influences of their caregivers and important others in the child's psychosocial context. For example, children who are less emotionally reactive show less physiological arousal to unfamiliar people and circumstances, signs of threat and danger, and punishment cues. They also show fewer strong responses to negative emotional stimuli, such as fear or distress cues, which is the emotional component to empathy. However, caregivers who are warm and highly responsive toward their children can help facilitate improved empathy development for these young emotionally hyporeactive children by modeling empathic concern toward others (see Kochanska, 1995, 1997).

Importantly, a callous lack of empathy is only one defining feature of CU traits, and it is only one aspect of the broader developmental construct of "conscience" that has proven important for the moral regulation of behavior in children. That is, conscience has been defined by developmental psychologists as being the emotional, cognitive, and relational processes by which children learn internal standards to guide their behavior and help them to regulate their behavior in response to the social demands of a situation (Kochanska & Thompson, 1997). The emotional components of conscience refer to the emotions experienced in response to real or imagined consequences of one's behavior, which prominently includes empathic concern for others well-being, but also includes moral emotions resulting from doing something wrong (i.e., guilt). As a result, the desire to modify or regulate one's behavior can be due to its effects on others but also due to a desire to avoid displeasing people who are important to the child, such as their caregivers or teachers. Thus, conscience also includes feelings of remorse and guilt over misdeeds, which help the child learn to follow societal norms related to what is considered appropriate behavior (Kochanska & Thompson, 1997).

There is research indicating that children with the LPE specifier show problems in both parts of conscience development—empathy and guilt. The best evidence for this was provided by a large meta-analysis conducted by Waller and colleagues (2020), who reported that measures of CU traits showed moderate to large associations with measures of both empathy ($\rho = -0.57$) and guilt ($\rho = -0.40$). Furthermore, while developmental research on empathy and guilt has mainly considered their role in motivating prosocial behavior, empathy and guilt could also be important for inhibiting aggressive behavior and other behavior that violates the rights of others. Specifically, the ability to understand pain in others (i.e., cognitive empathy) and to experience emotional discomfort in response to such distress (i.e., affective empathy), as well as the experience of guilt when the child causes the distress in others, can all help a child learn to avoid behaviors that cause these negative emotions in others (i.e., the child hitting someone else; the child taking a toy from another child). Unfortunately, a failure to sufficiently develop these prosocial emotions has often not been considered in many theories that attempt to explain the causes of conduct problems. Even more unfortunately, these deficits in empathic concern for others or in the feelings of guilt and remorse have typically not been the focus of most treatments that have been developed for children and adolescents. However, understanding these deficits in the development of prosocial emotions that seem to be the primary causal mechanism leading to children showing the LPE specifier are essential to our approach to treatment.

CHAPTER SUMMARY

In the previous chapter, we summarized research illustrating why treating children and adolescents with the LPE specifier is so important. Despite being only a subgroup of children with serious behavior problems, their behavior tends to be more severe, aggressive, and persistent across time. In the current chapter, we highlighted research showing how the subgroup with the LPE specifier differs from other youth with serious conduct problems on a number of characteristics that seem to suggest that the causal mechanisms underlying their behavior problems are unique. The severity of the problems displayed by this group makes it abundantly clear why it is so important to diagnose and treat youth with the LPE specifier. The differences in causal processes explain why past treatments have likely not been as effective for this group—because they do not address the risk factors that lead youth with the LPE specifier to develop behavior problems. In the remainder of this book, we focus on guiding clinicians in how they should make the diagnosis of the LPE specifier and how to intervene with children and adolescents who are diagnosed with LPE in ways that recognize their unique characteristics.

II

CLINICAL ASSESSMENT AND DIAGNOSIS OF CHILDREN AND ADOLESCENTS WITH LIMITED PROSOCIAL EMOTIONS

4

General Considerations in the Assessment of Children and Adolescents With Limited Prosocial Emotions

The limited prosocial emotions (LPE) specifier is not an independent diagnosis. That is, it is a specifier for the diagnosis of conduct disorder (CD) in the *Diagnostic and Statistical Manual of Mental Disorders* (5th ed., text rev.; *DSM-5-TR*; American Psychiatric Association, 2022) or for the diagnoses of conduct-dissocial disorder and oppositional defiant disorder (ODD) in the 11th edition of the *International Classification of Diseases* (*ICD-11*; World Health Organization, 2018). As a result, a child or adolescent must first meet the criteria for a conduct problem diagnosis and show the required level of callous–unemotional (CU) traits to be diagnosed with the LPE specifier. Once this is established, the child can be diagnosed with "conduct disorder with limited prosocial emotions" (*DSM-5*), "conduct-dissocial disorder with limited prosocial emotions" (*ICD-11*), and/or "oppositional-defiant disorder with limited prosocial emotions" (*ICD-11*).

What led to the difference in the use of the specifier between the *DSM-5* (used for CD only) and *ICD-11* (used for both ODD and CD)? The research on the ability of CU traits to differentiate between important subgroups of youth with conduct problems largely did not use diagnostic criteria. That is, it typically defined "conduct problems" using measures that included a broad range of conduct problems, including indicators of both ODD and CD, as well as other definitions of antisocial behavior (e.g., criminal behavior) or types of conduct problems (e.g., aggression; Frick et al., 2014b). Thus, it was clear that CU traits were an important specifier for designating subgroups of youth with conduct problems but it was not clear whether this usefulness was dependent

https://doi.org/10.1037/0000500-005
A Clinical Guide to Working With Youth With Conduct Disorders and Limited Prosocial Emotions, by P. J. Frick and E. R. Kimonis

on the type of conduct problems that the child displayed. Given this lack of clarity and that the LPE specifier was a new addition to diagnostic classification, the *DSM-5* chose a more conservative approach by limiting its use to only those persons who showed the more severe antisocial behaviors associated with CD (Frick & Nigg, 2012). This decision would allow more research to accumulate to determine whether the LPE specifier was also useful for and should be expanded for use in other children with conduct problems, such as those diagnosed with ODD. However, the *ICD-11* chose to be more inclusive, given that ODD typically precedes the development of CD (Frick & Viding, 2009), and diagnosing people with LPE could aid in identifying those at greatest risk for this transition so that interventions can be started as soon as possible and be potentially reimbursed by public health systems and/or private insurance.

It is important to note that there is some evidence that elevated levels of CU traits can cause problems for children and adolescents, even in the absence of a diagnosis of CD. For example, Rowe and colleagues (2010) reported results from a very large ($N = 7,977$) community sample of children and adolescents showing that those with elevated CU traits showed a number of problems in adjustment (e.g., problems with peers, elevated mental health problems), even in the absence of CD and even after controlling for their level of conduct problems. Also, CU traits can differentiate subgroups of youth with other disruptive behavior disorders, in addition to CD, who show potentially different risk factors that could help tailor interventions. For example, a study by Musser and colleagues (2013) reported that children with attention-deficit/hyperactivity disorder (ADHD) without a diagnosis of CD but with elevated CU traits showed different responses to emotional stimuli than those with ADHD and neither a diagnosis of CD nor elevated CU traits.

Thus, CU traits may prove over time to be important as a specifier for diagnoses beyond ODD and CD. However, the vast majority of research on CU traits has been conducted in children with serious conduct problems. Currently, the LPE specifier is limited to use with only those children who meet criteria for a conduct problem diagnosis.

As a result of it being a specifier and not an independent diagnosis, the assessment of CU traits to make the diagnosis of the LPE specifier needs to be integrated into a broader assessment of conduct problems. Assessing children with conduct problems requires a comprehensive assessment, and a full description of all of the different areas in need of an assessment is beyond the scope of this book (see Frick et al., 2020; Frick & McMahon, 2018, for such a comprehensive discussion and recommendations for specific methods to use in the assessment). However, in this chapter, we summarize how the research discussed in Chapters 2 and 3 can be used to guide the clinical assessments of youth with serious conduct problems. Importantly, we do not repeat the citations to this research in this chapter to enhance its readability for clinicians. Also, a summary of this research and its implications for assessments is provided in Table 4.1.

TABLE 4.1. General Guidelines for the Assessment of Children and Adolescents With Conduct Problems

Research findings	Implications for assessment	Implications for assessing youth with the LPE specifier
Youth with conduct problems can vary greatly in the types and severity of their behavior problems (Frick et al., 1993).	Assess a wide range of conduct problems and determine if the number of problems and duration meet diagnostic criteria.	Youth with LPE display more conduct problems; they are particularly more likely to show spiteful and vindictive behaviors.
	Assess age of onset of conduct problems using multiple methods.	Youth with LPE commit more illegal acts beginning at an early age.
	Assess whether conduct problems are causing difficulties across multiple situations and settings (e.g., home, school, work, interpersonal relationships), including whether they are causing legal difficulties.	Youth with LPE are more likely to be aggressive, to engage in both reactive and planned/instrumental aggression, and to cause more harm to victims; they are more likely to bully other children or instigate others to bully.
	Assess the level of aggression and the amount of harm to others that the conduct problems cause.	
Youth with conduct problems are at risk for a host of other mental health, social, academic, and occupational problems throughout development (Odgers et al., 2007, 2008).	Assess for the presence of ADHD.	Youth with LPE often have a co-occurring diagnosis of ADHD.
	Assess for the presence of anxiety and depression (including suicidal ideation).	Youth with LPE can show anxiety but they are less distressed by their behavior than other youth with conduct problems.
		Youth with LPE can show more severe suicide attempts if other risk factors for suicide are present.
	Assess for substance use.	Youth with LPE show more harmful substance use.
	Assess for problems in academic or occupational performance.	Youth with LPE do not care about whether they perform well or poorly in school.
	Assess the number and quality of peer relationships.	Youth with LPE can make friends, but it is often with other children who show behavior problems, the friendships are of shorter duration, and the friendships are less warm and satisfying.

(*continues*)

TABLE 4.1. General Guidelines for the Assessment of Children and Adolescents With Conduct Problems (*Continued*)

Research findings	Implications for assessment	Implications for assessing youth with the LPE specifier
Conduct problems are caused by a host of different risk factors that can play a role in the development and maintenance of the conduct problems (Frick & Viding, 2009).	Assess for intellectual deficits. Assess critical temperamental and personality risk factors that are associated with conduct problems, such as problems regulating emotions, rebelliousness, fearfulness, and response to punishment. Assess for associations with a deviant peer group. Assess the family environment, especially the type of parenting used. Assess the broader social ecology (e.g., economic disadvantage, exposure to domestic and community violence).	Youth with LPE are less likely than other youth with conduct problems to show intellectual deficits. Youth with LPE show reduced emotional reactivity to others' emotions, are fearless, and are often unresponsive to punishment. Youth with LPE often associate with a deviant peer group; they are more likely to be the leader in such groups and to instigate antisocial acts, including bullying. Youth with LPE have relationships with caregivers and peers that are lower in warmth and closeness. Youth with LPE are often victims of violence, although they often instigate it.
There are some common causal pathways that can lead to conduct problems, each involving distinct developmental mechanisms that can influence response to treatment (Frick, 2012; Perlstein et al., 2023).	Assess the developmental history of the conduct problem behaviors to determine if they started early in childhood or whether their onset coincided with adolescence. Assess for presence of elevated CU traits.	Youth with LPE often start showing conduct problems early in childhood. Youth with LPE are defined by the presence of persistent CU traits.

Note. ADHD = attention-deficit/hyperactivity disorder; CU = callous-unemotional; LPE = limited prosocial emotions.

ASSESSING FOR A CONDUCT DISORDER

In Chapter 2, we noted that children and adolescents with CD can vary greatly in the number and types of problem behaviors they show, as well as the severity of these conduct problems (e.g., how much harm they cause others). Even within the group of youth who show the LPE specifier, there can be variability in the severity of their conduct problems. In addition, we noted that children with CD are at risk for a host of other problems in adjustment; this is especially true of those with the LPE specifier. In Chapter 3, we discussed some of the common causal processes that can lead to CD, each involving multiple risk factors that could be a target for intervention. Also, the risk factors associated with CD can vary across the different subgroups of youth with CD defined by the age of onset of the conduct problems and the presence of the LPE specifier. As a result of all of this research, assessing for CD involves more than just assessing for the diagnostic criteria for CD and assessing for the symptoms of the LPE specifier. It requires assessing for the frequency and severity of conduct problems, the presence of co-occurring problems in adjustment, the multiple risk factors that could be causing or maintaining the symptoms of CD, and the key indicators that differentiate among the causal pathways (i.e., age of onset of conduct problems, the presence of CU traits). In the following section, we provide guidance on how to conduct such a comprehensive assessment required for adequate assessment of a child or adolescent with CD.

Assessing Number and Severity of Conduct Problems

Because the LPE specifier in the *DSM-5-TR* requires the presence of CD, it is necessary to determine if the child meets the diagnostic criteria for CD. All of the symptoms for CD included in the *DSM-5-TR* involve antisocial behavior that either violates the rights of others or that violates major age-appropriate norms. However, these symptoms can include a wide range of conduct problems of varying severity, ranging from skipping school to rape. The *DSM-5* organizes these symptoms into four categories:

1. aggression to people and animals
2. destruction of property
3. deceitfulness or theft
4. serious violations of rules

As noted previously, the *ICD-11* also allows for the use of the LPE specifier for the diagnosis of ODD. In addition, most children and adolescents who show CD also show ODD symptoms. Thus, it is important to assess the types of conduct problem symptoms for ODD as well, especially in very young children. The symptoms of ODD in both the *DSM-5-TR* and *ICD-11* fall within three categories:

1. angry/irritable mood
2. argumentative/defiant behavior
3. vindictiveness

Thus, to make a conduct problem diagnosis, the clinician must assess a wide range of conduct problems of varying severity. To diagnose CD, at least three symptoms must be present within the last year, with at least one present in the last 6 months. To make the diagnosis of ODD, a person has to show at least four symptoms persistently (i.e., lasting at least 6 months). For both of these diagnoses, not only must the symptoms be present, but they must also cause significant distress for the youth and/or cause problems in the child or adolescent's social, academic, or occupational functioning (i.e., leading to impairment). Further, to make a diagnosis of ODD, it is important to show that the symptoms are more frequent and more severe than would be expected, given the child's age and developmental level. Thus, the assessment of conduct problems requires some type of norm-referenced assessment (e.g., behavior rating scale) that allows one to make the determination of whether the level of behavior is "outside of normal limits" of what would be expected for youth of the same age as the person being assessed.

Children with CD or ODD can vary greatly in the severity of their behavior problems. Thus, their criteria in the *DSM-5-TR* both have ways of designating severity. For ODD, severity is determined by the number of situations in which the child shows conduct problems ranging from mild ODD, in which symptoms are shown in only one setting (typically the home), to severe ODD, in which symptoms are present in three or more settings (e.g., at home, at school, or with peers). For CD, severity is determined by the number of symptoms present and the degree of harm they cause others, with mild CD defined by few conduct problems beyond the three needed to make the diagnosis and that cause relatively minor harm to others (e.g., rule breaking, lying and conning others, truancy) and severe CD defined by many conduct problems in excess of the three required to make the diagnosis and that cause considerable harm to others (e.g., forced sex, physical cruelty, use of a weapon to steal from others). For both diagnoses, a moderate level of severity is defined as a presentation between the mild and severe categories.

While all children with a conduct problem diagnosis would meet the criteria outlined here, research reviewed in earlier chapters highlights several ways that children and adolescents with CU traits may differ from other youth with conduct problems. Specifically, youth with the LPE specifier often show more severe conduct problems. They tend to show more conduct problems in more situations, which are more likely to include aggression that leads to greater levels of harm to others. Thus, it is particularly important to assess the level and type of aggression when assessing children for LPE. It can help to determine what are the worse instances of aggression that the child or adolescent has shown, and to follow-up with questions related to how much harm this aggressive behavior has caused to others. It is also important to assess the context of the aggression shown by the person being assessed. Youth with the LPE specifier show more varied types of aggression, which includes reactive forms of aggression (i.e., in retaliation for real or perceived provocations), instrumental aggression (i.e., aggression to achieve some goal), premeditated aggression (i.e., the aggression is planned), and relational aggression (i.e., aggression that tries to harm the relationships of others, such as telling lies or spreading rumors about someone). The aggression can also take the form of bullying others, which involves repeated instances of aggression against the same person who is not able to defend themselves. In addition to the actual bullying, youth with the LPE specifier often assist others who are bullying, are more likely to encourage others who are bullying someone, and are less likely to defend the victim of bullying.

In short, it is particularly important to carefully assess aggressive behavior when assessing youth suspected of showing the LPE specifier. The importance of this consideration is found across developmental levels, from young children who have not yet started elementary school through to adolescents. In older children and adolescents, it also becomes important to assess their engagement in illegal behaviors. Children with the LPE specifier start engaging in illegal behaviors earlier, engage in more types of illegal behaviors, and take part in more serious illegal behaviors that lead to more harm in others, compared with other youth with conduct problems. Also, youth with the LPE specifier are more likely to be the leader when committing crimes with other youth.

Assessing aggressive and illegal behaviors is important when evaluating both boys and girls suspected of showing the LPE specifier. In our studies of aggression, looking at relational aggression (i.e., harming others through damage to relationships or social status) appears to be especially important for girls because they are more likely to express aggression relationally than physically. In a study we conducted on mixed-sex youth ages 11 to 19, boys and girls showed equal levels of relational aggression (Marsee et al., 2014). Also, boys who showed higher levels of relational aggression typically also showed high levels of physical aggression. However, girls were more likely to show relational aggression without physical aggression, and relational aggression was related to higher levels of CU traits. Thus, failure to assess relational aggression would have missed a number of girls who were harming others but who were not physically aggressive. Research seems to suggest that assessing illegal behaviors may be especially important when assessing girls as well. In a longitudinal study we conducted on school children (in the third through seventh grades), we found that many girls were high on CU traits but were not rated by their caregivers or teachers as having high rates of ODD and CD symptoms (Frick et al., 2003). However, these girls did self-report a significant rate of illegal behaviors. This finding suggests that girls may engage in high rates of covert (or hidden) serious conduct problems that go undetected by the adults around them. Thus, failure to assess both relationally aggressive behaviors and covert delinquent behaviors could underestimate the level of antisocial behavior displayed by girls with the LPE specifier.

Assessing Common Comorbidities

In addition to their antisocial behavior, children and adolescents with conduct problems, both with and without CU traits, are at high risk for showing other problems in adjustment. For those youth who start showing conduct problems in childhood (i.e., the childhood-onset type), one of the most common co-occurring conditions is ADHD. In other words, the vast majority of people with childhood-onset CD also meet diagnostic criteria for ADHD, encompassing those with and without the LPE specifier. Consequently, assessing ADHD should be an important part of any assessment of a child or adolescent with behavior problems, so that treatment can target this diagnosis as well as the child's conduct problems. Given that a primary part of the ADHD diagnosis is impulsivity, it may be surprising that youth with the LPE specifier would also have this diagnosis, given that they are likely to show premeditated or non-impulsive types of aggression. However, as we have noted in our discussion of the types of aggression shown by people with the LPE specifier, they are likely to show both reactive and impulsive types of aggression, as well as premeditated and impulsive aggression. Thus, they can show impulsive behavior like other children with ADHD but can also plan their actions when sufficiently motivated. Generally, people with CU traits can show considerable diversity in the types of conduct problems in which they engage.

Children and adolescents with serious conduct problems can also show comorbid problems with anxiety and depression. This co-occurring emotional distress can be explained for some children with conduct problems as being a sign of a broader problem with emotional regulation. That is, problems in the regulation of emotions can lead to angry and irritable behaviors, including aggression, as well as other forms of negative affect, such as anxiety and depression. However, there is another reason for the frequent co-occurrence between conduct problems and emotional distress. A child or adolescent's conduct problems can lead to a host of problems for the child, such as conflict with caregivers, teachers, and peers; loss of friendships; school disciplinary problems (e.g., detentions, suspensions, exclusion from activities); loss of privileges (e.g., not being allowed to play sports); and legal problems (e.g., arrests). These consequences can lead a child to experience emotional distress, such as anxiety or depression. Given that children with the LPE specifier often show the most severe conduct problems, they often experience the greatest level of impairment associated with them. Thus, they may also show elevated rates of anxiety and depression. However, due to their CU traits, they are often less distressed by the consequences of their problematic behavior than children with the same level of conduct problems without the LPE specifier.

Given the association between anxiety and the severity of the child's behavior problems, anxiety is a critical part of the assessment of children with conduct problems. We have conducted a number of studies finding that some youth with the LPE specifier also show elevated levels of anxiety and when these problems co-occur, the child or adolescent often shows the most severe behavior problems. For example, in our studies of incarcerated adolescents, those elevated on both CU traits and anxiety showed the highest rates of both self-reported and officially recorded institutional violence, as well as other forms of criminal behavior (Kimonis et al., 2011; Kimonis, Fanti, et al., 2013). In addition, those with higher rates of anxiety were also more likely to have a history of sexual abuse and to have engaged in a sexually motivated index offense. In a large community sample of children ($N = 6{,}791$), those high on both CU traits and anxiety had the highest levels of behavior problems, as well as the highest levels of family adversity (Meehan et al., 2017). Similarly, in a study we conducted with 272 adolescents (ages 11 to 18) who had been referred to a community mental health center for treatment, those with the LPE specifier and anxiety were more likely to have histories of both physical and sexual abuse when compared with those with the LPE specifier without anxiety, and this group with anxiety self-reported the highest rate of externalizing behaviors and aggression (Kahn et al., 2013). Thus, the presence of elevated anxiety in those with the LPE specifier is not only a potential indicator of the severity of the child's behavior problems, but comorbid anxiety problems should also alert the clinician of the need to assess the child's history for potential exposure to adverse interpersonal childhood experiences such as maltreatment, overly negative or harsh parenting, domestic violence or other traumatic exposure, and other forms of family adversity. In much of the research done in this area, this subgroup of children with the LPE signifier are described as having "secondary CU traits."

Children with serious conduct problems are also at risk for suicidal behavior, ranging from suicidal thoughts (i.e., ideation), to suicide attempts and completed suicides. This is not surprising given that children with conduct problems often experience many of the risk factors for suicidal behavior, including impulsivity, depression, peer isolation, and exposure to traumatic events. There is not a lot of research testing whether those youth with the LPE specifier may also be at risk for suicidal behaviors. However, in Chapter 2, we described a study we conducted with adolescents who had been hospitalized for being a danger to themselves or others. We found that CU traits were related with less suicidal behavior overall and, in particular, with less suicidal ideation. However, when other risk factors for suicide were present (e.g., a family history of suicide, child depression or posttraumatic symptoms), CU traits were related to an increase in the lethality of the suicide attempts. We interpreted these findings to suggest that the lack of concern over the effects of their behavior in those with the LPE specifier may reduce the risk for suicidal behavior in the absence of major risk factors but that CU traits can increase the severity of suicidal behaviors among adolescents with other risk factors. In short, assessment for suicide-related behaviors should be part of the assessment of all older children and adolescents with serious conduct problems, including those with the LPE specifier.

Impulsivity and negative affect, such as anxiety and depression, are also risk factors for substance use. As a result, it is not surprising that children and adolescents with serious conduct problems are at risk for harmful substance use. Also, it is not surprising that this risk seems to be present for youth with conduct problems, whether or not they also show the LPE specifier, since both groups often show high rates of impulsivity and anxiety and depression. Thus, assessing for potential use of substances should be part of all assessments of children and adolescents with serious conduct problems. However, youth with the LPE specifier seem to be at risk for a more severe pattern of substance use that includes both harder drugs (e.g., hallucinogens, sedatives, cocaine) and alcohol. This substance use can also put adolescents with the LPE specifier at risk for engaging in risky sexual behaviors (e.g., unprotected sex, sex with multiple partners, and with partners they do not know well).

Another common problem for children and adolescents with serious conduct problems is their poor academic performance. Some children and adolescents with serious conduct problems can have problems in school due to their lower levels of intelligence or the presence of a learning disability. Others can have academic problems because of missed learning opportunities caused by their disruptions in class; missing classes because of detentions or suspensions; truancy; or being arrested and detained in the juvenile justice system. These latter problems could be particularly problematic for youth with the LPE specifier, who tend to show more severe conduct problems and are more likely to engage in criminal behavior and have contact with the justice system, which has been linked to lower levels of school achievement. For example, in a study we conducted following 1,216 adolescents who had been arrested for the first time for a criminal offense of moderate severity, we found that those who were formally processed for their crime were less likely to be enrolled in school during the 5 years following their first arrest compared with youth who had been diverted from the justice system after their arrest (Cauffman et al., 2021). Also, youth with the LPE specifier do not appear to be motivated to do well in school. In fact, a lack of motivation to do well in school, work, or important activities is one of the defining features of the LPE specifier. These youth often do not care if they get good or bad grades, they are not motivated to put effort into studying and completing assignments or homework, and they do not care about being recognized or rewarded for good performance. They also tend to have more conflicted and less close relationships with their teachers. Because of these different reasons, assessments for youth with serious conduct problems should involve a comprehensive assessment of the youth's academic potential (e.g., intelligence), as well as their academic performance (i.e., academic achievement).

One final problem that is often found in children and adolescents with serious conduct problems is in their relationships with peers. They are often disliked and rejected by same-aged peers. For those without the LPE specifier, this rejection can be due to their difficulty regulating their behavior (e.g., getting angry; being intrusive) or a lack of social skills, which leads them to be ostracized by their peers. For those with the LPE specifier, they are often viewed by their peers as being mean, aggressive, and untrustworthy. Youth with the LPE specifier may have the skills needed to make friends, but their friendships tend to be shorter, more conflicted, less warm, and less satisfying compared to youth without the LPE specifier. As a result, assessments of youth with serious conduct problems should not only involve an assessment of their friendships but also the nature, quality, and length of their current and former peer relationships.

When assessing children with the LPE specifier, an important diagnostic decision that often arises is how to distinguish between the empathy deficits associated with the LPE specifier and the difficulties in perspective taking associated with autism spectrum disorder (ASD). First, children with ASD often show several deficits in social communication and interaction (e.g., reduced sharing of interests, minimal back-and-forth communication), highly restricted interests (e.g., preoccupation with unusual objects or topics), or repetitive patterns of behavior (i.e., insistence on sameness, stereotyped behaviors such as lining up toys) that are not typically shown by youth with the LPE specifier. Second, a child with ASD typically has trouble understanding and interpreting social cues. Because of this, they often have difficulty manipulating others, and, when they hurt someone, they struggle to understand why the person was hurt. In contrast, a child with the LPE specifier can typically read social cues and can use them to manipulate or trick others into doing things. Also, when they hurt someone, they often know why the other person is hurt but they do not care about the other person's feelings. Carefully assessing the types of aggressive acts that a child engages in can help make this distinction between whether the child has difficulty in perspective taking or whether the child does not care about the consequences of their acts on others. Third, children with ASD tend to have problems with cognitive empathy and theory of mind (e.g., understanding the thoughts and feelings of others), whereas children with the LPE specifier often show deficits in their emotional empathy (e.g., experiencing emotional reactions to distress in others). This difference is exemplified by a study by Schwenck and colleagues (2012), who showed boys with ASD and boys with the LPE specifier film clips involving emotional situations and asked them to explain why the protagonist in the film felt as he did (i.e., cognitive empathy). They also asked the child how emotionally affected they felt by the film (i.e., affective empathy). Children with ASD were less accurate in labeling the protagonist's emotion (i.e., cognitive empathy), whereas children with the LPE specifier reported feeling less strong emotions during the film (e.g., affective empathy).

Assessing Multiple Risk Factors

As noted in Chapter 3, children with serious conduct problems often show multiple risk factors. Further, as also noted in Chapter 3 and summarized in Table 4.1, there are some common pathways through which these multiple risk factors can influence the developing child to make them more likely to act in ways that harm others or break major rules and norms. Knowing these common developmental pathways can help clinicians focus their assessment on certain key risk factors that can then lead to more tailored and individualized treatments.

Specifically, the adolescent-onset pathway typically involves youth whose behavior problems started around adolescence because of an exaggeration of the normal rebelliousness that an adolescent goes through as part of their identity development. This exaggeration can be encouraged by antisocial peers, a lack of monitoring and supervision by caregivers, and a generally rebellious personality. Thus, in addition to assessing the timing of onset to the child's conduct problems, assessments should consider the adolescent's peer group, their caregivers' level of knowledge of the child's whereabouts and companions, and their personality. This can be especially important where the caregiver is unaware of the child's engagement in serious conduct problems and the youth is not forthcoming with such information, and because official contacts with police and the justice system often lag years behind a child's engagement in criminal activities.

Another common pathway to serious conduct problems involves children who show a childhood-onset to their problem behavior but who do not show the LPE specifier. These children seem to have problems regulating their behavior because of emotional hyperreactivity (i.e., a tendency to quickly react angrily and with hostility toward others) or poor planning abilities and difficulties anticipating the consequences of their actions (i.e., poor executive control of behavior). These emotional and cognitive difficulties are often exacerbated by caregivers who use hostile and inconsistent discipline, or by exposure to violence in the child's home or community. Thus, in addition to assessing the onset of a child's behavior problems, it is important to assess a child's emotional control, indicators of executive functioning, and the quality of parenting the child is experiencing.

The third pathway to serious conduct problems involves youth with the LPE specifier, whose conduct problems also start early in childhood. However, rather than being highly sensitive to others distress and to signs of danger (i.e., fearlessness), they are underreactive and less responsive to these emotional situations. Also, their behavior is often more strongly motivated by potential gain rather than potential punishment. Their relationships with caregivers are often characterized by a lack of warmth or closeness, which further limits their development of empathetic concern for others and guilt for their misdeeds that harm others. Thus, in addition to assessing the timing of onset of their behavior problems and the presence of CU traits, it is also important to assess their level of fearlessness, their response to punishments, and the degree of warmth they experience at home and at school.

Assessing Key Indicators for Common Causal Pathways

As noted in Chapter 3, we outlined three common causal pathways to CD that are differentiated by the timing of onset of the child's conduct problems and the presence or absence of elevated levels of CU traits. Specifically, there is an adolescent-onset pathway to CD and then two types of childhood-onset pathways, differentiated by the presence or absence of CU traits (i.e., with or without the LPE specifier). Assessing these traits will be the focus of the rest of this chapter and the next two chapters. However, in the case of evaluating older children and adolescents, it is also important to highlight the need to provide an accurate assessment of when a child's conduct problems started. The *DSM-5-TR* defines childhood-onset CD for individuals showing at least one symptom prior to the age of 10 and adolescent-onset CD for individuals showing no symptoms prior to age 10. There has been some debate about whether this age is too conservative, with many youths not starting adolescence until later, and whether the distinction should be made based on physical signs of puberty rather than by age. Furthermore, determining the age of onset often requires caregivers and youth to use retrospective recall of past behaviors and research has suggested that the accuracy of such recall is often poor (Moffitt et al., 2008).

Given the importance of assessing age of onset despite this limited accuracy, we recommend assessing it in a number of different ways, using as many different informants and sources of information as possible. For example, one of the most common ways of determining age of onset is, when assessing each symptom of CD, to follow up with a question: "When did they/you first do this?" The earliest age provided by either the caregiver or child is considered one indicator of age of onset. Also, there can be objective indicators of impairment that help to pinpoint the timing of onset. For example, a caregiver may indicate that a child was "asked to leave a preschool due to hitting other children," suggesting that the child had been showing aggression at least prior to entering school. As another example, a caregiver or child can report on the number of detentions and suspensions that a child has experienced and can then indicate the grade the first incident occurred. Similarly, an adolescent who has gotten into legal trouble can report on the age at which they had their first contact with the police. Finally, a caregiver or child could provide the age at which they first sought treatment for behavior problems, again providing an objective anchor for determining when the behavior problems began. Each of these different sources and methods can be used to determine whether or not serious behavior problems were present prior to age 10 years.

Assessing for Callous-Unemotional Traits

The final important part of the assessment of children and adolescents with serious conduct problems is whether or not they show elevated levels of CU traits. The most common way this has been done in research is through behavior rating scales, whereby the child rates themselves on questions related to CU traits or the child's caregivers and teachers rate the child on these questions. Early research often used items from existing rating scales that seemed to assess CU traits for this assessment (see, e.g., Pardini et al., 2006). However, as research began to accumulate supporting the importance of CU traits for designating important subgroups of children with serious conduct problems, rating scales were developed to specifically assess them. Some examples of these scales include the Antisocial Process Screening Device (APSD; Frick & Hare, 2001), the Child Problematic Traits Inventory (CPTI; Colins et al., 2014), the Proposed Specifiers for Conduct Disorder (PSCD;

Salekin & Hare, 2016), and the Triarchic Psychopathy Measure (TriPM; Drislane et al., 2014).

All of these measures have evidence supporting their ability to assess CU traits. However, it is important to note that these scales were developed to assess not only CU traits but also other dimensions associated with the construct of psychopathy in adults. As a result, these scales typically include only a small number of items directly assessing CU traits. For example, the APSD and PSCD include only six and five items, respectively, on their CU subscale. The small number of items, combined with the low base rate of many items in community samples, often led to psychometric problems for the scales, such as low internal consistency among the items (i.e., items not working well together to measure the same construct; see Sharp & Kine, 2008, for a review).

In addition to their limited focus on assessing CU traits, these scales also assess other dimensions related to psychopathy, many of which overlap significantly with constructs already included in definitions of childhood disruptive behavior disorders (see Frick, 2022, for a discussion of this issue). For example, while the PSCD includes a scale for conduct problems, it does not capture the full range of conduct problems defined in the *DSM-5-TR* criteria for ODD and CD. Similarly, all of the scales include items assessing impulsivity, a core part of the ADHD criteria, but these subscales often fail to address the full diagnostic criteria for ADHD. Although screening for additional dimensions relevant to children with serious conduct problems can be useful for research, the inclusion of these additional subscales increases the length of the assessment process. This added length is particularly burdensome in clinical settings, where elevated scores would require further assessment with more specialized measures.

Another limitation of most of these measures is that the subscales assessing CU traits often do not correspond directly to the LPE specifier criteria. For example, two of the six items on the APSD's CU subscale (i.e., "Is good at keeping promises" and "Keeps the same friends," both inversely scored to assess CU traits) do not align with any LPE specifier symptoms. Similarly, the meanness subscale of the TriPM includes items related to sensation seeking (e.g., "I would enjoy being in a high-speed chase," "Things are more fun if a little danger is involved"), which are not part of the LPE diagnostic criteria. Finally, with the exception of the APSD's CU subscale, none of the scales include items addressing one of the four LPE specifier symptoms: "Does not care about performance in important activities."

Another limitation of these measures for clinical assessments is the lack of clear guidelines on when CU ratings should be considered "elevated." While this is not a significant issue for most research purposes, where continuous scores are typically preferred for data analyses, it poses challenges in clinical settings. One exception is the APSD manual, which provides T-scores for the CU subscale that can help identify scores outside the normative range. However, these T-scores are only available for the caregiver and teacher versions of the APSD, not the self-report version. Additionally, they are based on a limited normative sample of 1,120 school children between 9 and 13 years old from two school districts in the southern United States.

Given these limitations of existing behavior rating scales, we developed the Inventory of Callous–Unemotional Traits (ICU; Kimonis et al., 2008). The next chapter outlines its development and provides guidance for its use in clinical assessments. However, it is important to note that no rating scale, including the ICU, should be used alone to make clinical diagnoses such as the LPE specifier. Rating scales rely on self-reports or informant reports (e.g., caregivers and teachers), and it is crucial to ensure that the informants understood the questions, provided thoughtful responses, and accurately considered the traits being assessed. Further, while behavior rating scales often anchor responses (e.g., assessing the frequency or typicality of the trait being assessed), the LPE specifier requires that CU traits are persistent (i.e., present for at least 12 months) and occur across multiple relationships and settings. This level of detail is often difficult to ascertain from rating scales alone, as they may reflect occasional behaviors rather than an individual's typical pattern of interpersonal or emotional functioning. Furthermore, assessments for the LPE specifier should incorporate information from multiple informants. However, research consistently shows discrepancies among informants (e.g., a child rating themselves as empathetic, while a caregiver rates them as callous and uncaring, or one caregiver reporting significant problems while the other reports few symptoms; De Los Reyes, 2024). Such inconsistencies can make it challenging for clinicians to determine how to integrate such discrepant information and arrive at a reliable diagnosis when relying solely on behavior rating scales.

To accurately diagnose the LPE specifier, it is essential to gather detailed clinical information. One tool that can be used for this purpose is the Psychopathy Checklist: Youth Version (PCL-YV; Forth et al., 2003), a clinician rating system that assesses constructs similar to those in the LPE specifier. Trained clinicians obtain detailed information from multiple sources to rate items as being (0) "Definitely not present," (1) "Somewhat present," or (2) "Definitely present." Scores on the PCL-YV have demonstrated strong reliability and validity in samples of adolescents (Forth et al., 2015). However, like the rating scales summarized in Table 4.1, the PCL-YV assesses CU traits as part of the broader construct of psychopathy. Consequently, only four of its 21 items are directly relevant to the LPE specifier. Moreover, these items were not specifically designed to align with the LPE specifier symptoms. For example, the LPE symptom "Failure to put forth effort in important activities" is most closely related to the PCL-YV item "Unable to take responsibility for actions," which is not an exact match. Additionally, the PCL-YV was developed for adolescents aged 12 to 18 years and has been primarily tested and validated in forensic settings (Forth et al., 2015). Its applicability for younger children and its validity in mental health settings remains unclear. In Chapter 6, we introduce the Clinical Assessment of Prosocial Emotions (CAPE; Goetz et al., 2024), a clinician rating system specifically designed to assess the criteria for the LPE specifier, and we provide guidance on its use.

WHAT IS IN A NAME? MINIMIZING STIGMA

Before we provide detailed guidance on how to use the ICU and the CAPE in clinical assessments of youth with serious conduct problems, it is important to be aware of the potential stigmatizing effects of assigning a diagnosis of LPE. Unfortunately, in many societies, mental health diagnoses are often stigmatized and perceived as a sign of personal failing—either in the individual or their caregivers. This stigma can discourage people from seeking treatment because of a fear of negative judgement, limit opportunities for future education and employment because of misconceptions by others regarding the causes and consequences of mental health problems, and lead to self-stigmatization, where people internalize these diagnoses as evidence of personal flaws and weaknesses (see Frick, 2021). Diagnostic labels related to serious conduct problems, such as ODD and CD, and associated constructs like antisocial behavior, aggression, and psychopathy, can be especially stigmatizing. These behaviors are often viewed as morally undesirable rather than as symptoms of mental health conditions. In fact, they are frequently interpreted as indicative of "bad people" rather than "sick people." Even many mental health professionals may hesitate to diagnose a child with ODD or CD, fearing it will be seen as blaming the child for problems within their family. Implicit in this hesitation is the concern that assigning such a diagnosis implies fault rather than identifying a mental health issue requiring treatment.

Research supports concerns about the stigma associated with labels related to antisocial behavior. Much of this work has focused on the attributions attached to terms like "psychopathy" or "psychopathic." Studies have shown that these terms often lead to increased perceptions of dangerousness and reduced perceptions of treatment amenability, for both adult (Berryessa & Wohlstetter, 2019) and adolescent defendants (Jones & Cauffman, 2008; Murrie et al., 2007). However, these attributions seem to be driven more by the behaviors associated with the term "psychopathic" than by the diagnostic label itself. For instance, in a study of 891 adult jury pool members, researchers disentangled the effects of describing symptoms (i.e., antisocial behavior and personality traits related to psychopathy) from the effects of using diagnostic labels (i.e., CD or psychopathic disorder; Boccaccini et al., 2008). Using vignettes of an adolescent offender, they found that descriptions of symptoms led to greater perceptions of the youth's risk for future crime and increased beliefs that the youth deserved harsher punishment. Critically, the addition of a diagnosis (i.e., labeling the youth as having CD or with a psychopathic disorder) did not amplify these negative perceptions. Instead, it slightly increased perceptions that the youth might benefit from treatment. Notably, the one label that did lead to heightened perceptions of risk—beyond the description of symptoms—was labeling the youth as a "psychopath."

This research highlights that using strongly pejorative terms, such as calling someone a "psychopath," can have harmful consequences with little benefit. In contrast, assigning a label that includes the term "disorder" can increase perceptions of the need for treatment. This underscores the importance of using mental health labels carefully to convey the seriousness of a condition and the significant impairment and suffering it can cause to the individual and those around them. Appropriate labeling also emphasizes that these problems require intervention by trained mental health professionals, rather than being addressed solely through support from friends and family or punitive measures from schools or the justice system. Therefore, diagnostic labels should be used thoughtfully to convey the need for treatment, while minimizing potential stigmatizing effects. Not only is this crucial for reducing the potential harm caused by labeling, but overly stigmatizing labels may also be avoided by mental health professionals altogether. This can result in some youth being denied access to treatment for a serious and impairing disorder.

These considerations influenced the decision-making process in selecting the name for the LPE specifier. Several terms were rejected because they were unclear, insufficiently descriptive, or could cause confusion about the nature of the construct (e.g., "undersocialized"). Other terms were rejected because of their potential for significant stigmatizing effects, which could outweigh any diagnostic benefits or lead to reluctance among professionals to use them for fear of the potential consequences to the person being diagnosed (e.g., "psychopathic"). This concern also applied to the term "CU traits," the term most commonly used in research to describe the criteria for the LPE specifier. Additionally, other terms were rejected because they appeared to describe normative behaviors, failing to effectively convey the serious impairment associated with atypical levels of CU traits. Such terms ran the risk of leading clinicians to overdiagnose children who did not require treatment (e.g., "with uncaring features"). After careful deliberation, the final label chosen for this specifier, as included in the *DSM-5* (American Psychiatric Association, 2013) and the *ICD-11* (World Health Organization, 2018), was "with limited prosocial emotions."

Some research has tested whether the choice effectively balances the need to document that the individual requires treatment of this label against the potential negative effects of labeling. In a study by Edens and colleagues (2017), 326 potential jury members were randomly assigned to one of four vignette conditions depicting court testimony by a forensic evaluator about the background and mental health status of a fictional defendant. The conditions manipulated the mental health symptoms and diagnosis to assess whether the LPE label led to worse perceptions of the fictional defendant. The results indicated that participants perceived adolescents with an LPE label as more dangerous, evil, and psychopathic compared with those with only a CD label. However, critically, this study did not separate the effects of the symptoms from the effects of the diagnostic label. Specifically, the vignettes depicting defendants labeled with CD + LPE included both descriptions of LPE symptoms and the diagnostic label itself. Therefore, it was not clear if the negative connotations were based on the use of the "limited prosocial emotions" specifier or the behaviors that were described leading to this diagnosis.

Therefore, we conducted a study to disentangle these possible explanations. We studied 294 adult mock jurors who were randomly assigned to one of six conditions that similarly depicted court testimony by a forensic evaluator about a juvenile defendant (Prasad & Kimonis, 2018). The first independent variable included conditions where (a) no symptoms or diagnosis were described, (b) the defendant was described as showing both CD and LPE symptoms without a formal diagnosis, (c) the CD symptoms were combined with a CD label, or (d) the CD + LPE symptoms were paired with a CD + LPE label (the fifth and sixth conditions tested involved the latter two groups being further divided into whether or not etiological information was included alongside the diagnostic label). Consistent with previous research on psychopathy, defendants described as having CD + LPE symptoms were perceived as less amenable to treatment, more dangerous, and deserving of a more restrictive sentence. However, the addition of an LPE diagnostic label did not further amplify these negative perceptions. Rather, the diagnostic label led to increased recommendations for psychiatric treatment compared with other restrictive sentencing options. These findings again highlight some potential benefits of diagnostic labeling, as including diagnoses can encourage access to mental health treatment, while not necessarily exacerbating negative perceptions.

In summary, diagnosing youth with serious conduct problems must be undertaken with great care. The terms used to identify disorders should be carefully chosen to convey the need for treatment while minimizing harmful attributions. Throughout this book, we have emphasized that children and adolescents with serious conduct problems require mental health treatment. In fact, the primary purpose of this book is to guide clinicians in providing individualized treatment for a specific group of youth with serious conduct problems: those with the LPE specifier. However, because this type of mental health problem is particularly vulnerable to harmful interpretations, it is critical that clinicians carefully consider when a diagnosis of the LPE specifier is warranted, which is the focus of the next two chapters. Additionally, clinicians must go beyond simply assigning a diagnosis; they should provide a clear explanation of what the diagnostic terms mean. It is particularly important that the use of diagnostic labels facilitates access to enhanced treatment rather than exclusion from it (e.g., expulsion from mainstream education or incarceration).

To illustrate the potential dangers of misusing this label, a number of years ago, we were asked to present to a very large school system about how to use our measure of CU traits to determine whether a child had an "emotional disability" qualifying them for special education services or was "behaviorally disturbed," warranting suspension, expulsion, or transfer to an alternative school. Instead of endorsing such an arbitrary and unclear distinction between these two terms, we educated the school system on how CU traits align well with the school system's definition of emotional disturbance, characterized by emotional responses that adversely affect performance in an educational environment. We reviewed research showing how underreactivity to others' emotions and difficulty accurately interpreting others' emotions (i.e., inappropriate emotional responses) contribute to the behavior problems and learning difficulties faced by youth with CU traits. Additionally, we discussed ways schools could provide tailored interventions to these youth in a manner that ensures the safety of all students. In essence, we advocated for the appropriate use of the scale assessing CU traits to enhance the services provided to these youth, rather than for an inappropriate use to deny them access to critical services.

CHAPTER SUMMARY

In the next two chapters, we provide clear guidance on how to assess the criteria of the LPE specifier. However, it is only assigned when a person also exhibits significant and impairing conduct problems that meet diagnostic criteria. Therefore, the assessment of CU traits needs to be conducted within the context of a broader assessment of a person's conduct problems. Conduct problems can vary widely in severity, often co-occurring with adjustment issues, and they can arise from diverse risk factors that differ between individuals. As a result, this broader assessment process is typically extensive. To ensure efficiency, the assessment of CU traits needs to be focused and streamlined to fit within this broader assessment context. While behavior rating scales can provide a time-efficient method for assessing CU traits, most existing scales include dimensions that are not specific to the LPE specifier and overlap with areas that are more thoroughly evaluated in other parts of the assessment process. In the next chapter, we discuss the use of a behavior rating scale, the ICU, which was specifically developed to assess the full criteria for the LPE specifier and focuses exclusively on the criteria for this specifier.

5

Using the Inventory of Callous–Unemotional Traits in Clinical Assessments of the Limited Prosocial Emotions Specifier

As noted in the previous chapter, research on callous–unemotional (CU) traits has relied heavily on behavior ratings scales to assess the limited prosocial emotions (LPE) specifier and its associated symptoms. Unfortunately, existing scales have significant limitations in their usefulness for clinical assessments. Most notably, CU traits are often assessed alongside other emotional and behavioral dimensions related to conduct problems, resulting in relatively few items on the scale that directly assess the LPE specifier criteria and a large number of items not directly related to assessing CU traits. Further, most rating scales were not developed to assess the specifier and, thus, include numerous items that are not relevant to the assessment of the diagnostic criteria and omit certain symptoms, such as a lack of concern about performance.

To address these limitations, we developed the Inventory of Callous–Unemotional Traits (ICU; Kimonis et al., 2008). The ICU provides a comprehensive assessment of CU traits and only includes items assessing this construct. Importantly, the 24 items of the ICU were chosen to directly assess the four symptoms of the LPE specifier, which themselves were chosen as the most consistent indicators of CU traits across samples (Kimonis et al., 2015). As shown in Table 5.1, the ICU includes six items for each of the four symptoms of the LPE specifier: three positively worded (i.e., higher ratings are indicative of greater levels of CU traits) and three negatively worded (i.e., lower ratings are indicative of greater levels of CU traits) items. Items on the ICU are rated on a four-point Likert-type scale ranging from 0 (*not at all true*) to 3 (*definitely true*).

https://doi.org/10.1037/0000500-006
A Clinical Guide to Working With Youth With Conduct Disorders and Limited Prosocial Emotions, by P. J. Frick and E. R. Kimonis

TABLE 5.1. Items on the Inventory of Callous-Unemotional Traits and Their Correspondence to the Symptoms of the Limited Prosocial Emotions Specifier

Items worded in the CU direction	Items worded in the prosocial direction	Items worded in the CU direction	Items worded in the prosocial direction
Lack of guilt or remorse		**Callous–lack of empathy**	
2. What I think is "right" and "wrong" is different from what other people think.	5. I feel bad or guilty when I do something wrong.	4. I do not care who I hurt to get what I want.	8. I am concerned about the feelings of others.
9. I do not care if I get in trouble.	13. I easily admit to being wrong.	12. I seem very cold and uncaring to others.	17. I try not to hurt others' feelings.
18. I do not feel remorseful when I do something wrong.	16. I apologize to persons I hurt.	21. The feelings of others are unimportant to me.	24. I do things to make others feel good.
Unconcerned about performance		**Shallow or deficient affect**	
7. I do not care about being on time.	3. I care about how well I do at school or work.	6. I do not show my emotions to others.	1. I express my feelings openly.
11. I do not care about doing things well.	15. I always try my best.	10. I do not care who I hurt to get what I want.	14. It is easy for others to tell how I am feeling.
20. I do not like to put the time into doing things well.	23. I work hard on everything I do.	22. I hide my feelings from others.	19. I am very expressive and emotional.

Note. For items worded in the callous-unemotional (CU) direction, higher ratings indicate greater levels of CU traits. For items worded in the prosocial direction, lower ratings indicate greater levels of CU traits. The items in this table use the wording from the self-report version of the Inventory of Callous-Unemotional Traits (Frick, 2004).

This response format does not allow for a neutral midpoint, requiring the informant to rate the item as leaning either toward higher CU traits or greater prosociality. The rating anchors were specifically chosen to assess how descriptive or "typical" the item is for the person being rated, rather than focusing on the frequency of the behavior. This type of anchor is different from many behavior rating scales, which assess how often a behavior occurs. The ICU's approach was chosen because an important way to distinguish maladaptive from normative levels of prosocial emotions is that the maladaptive pattern tends to be present across multiple relationships and settings.

The ICU was designed to have multiple versions. First, it was intended for use with children and adolescents aged 5 to 21 years. Consequently, it includes a self-report version, where the individual being assessed rates their own behavior, as well as informant-report versions, which allow caregivers, teachers, or other individuals familiar with the person to provide ratings. Second, a preschool version of the ICU was developed to assess children who are too young for school, typically aged 2 to 4 years. This version is nearly identical to the main ICU scale, with one modification to reflect age-appropriate activities. Specifically, the item "Is concerned about schoolwork" was changed to "Seems motivated to do his/her best in structured activities." The preschool version of the ICU is only available in informant-report (i.e., for caregivers and teachers) versions, as self-reporting is not appropriate for this age group. Third, the ICU has been translated into over 30 languages. All language versions, along with the original English versions, are freely accessible. All versions of the ICU and all supporting information to guide its use is available from the official ICU website (Frick, 2004; see Appendix for a QR code and a full URL to the webpage).

PSYCHOMETRIC PROPERTIES

Since we published the first paper using the ICU in 2008 (Kimonis et al., 2008), the ICU has been used extensively in research. As a result, there are substantial data supporting many aspects of its psychometric properties. In this section, we review several characteristics of the ICU that have emerged from research studies that should be considered when using it in clinical assessments.

Item Wording

As explained previously, the ICU was developed with half of its items worded positively, where higher ratings indicate greater CU traits (e.g., "I do not feel remorseful when I do something wrong"). For these items, being rated "3" (i.e., *definitely true*) reflects higher levels of CU traits. The other half of the items are worded negatively, where lower ratings indicate greater CU traits (e.g., "I feel bad or guilty when I do something wrong"). For these items, being rated "0" (i.e., *not at all true*) reflects higher levels of CU traits. This approach was intended to reduce response biases by encouraging raters to carefully consider how true each item is rather than consistently rating items as either high or low across the scale. However, the differences in item wording have important implications for both the psychometric properties of the ICU and for the clinical interpretation of its scores.

Specifically, we conducted a study of 1,190 adolescents who completed the self-report version of the ICU shortly after their first arrest (Ray et al., 2016b). The results revealed distinct response patterns for the positively (i.e., in the CU direction) and negatively worded items (i.e., in the prosocial direction). Specifically, youth were more likely to rate prosocial items low, indicating higher CU traits (e.g., to rate "I feel bad or guilty when I do something wrong" as *not at all true*), than to endorse items indicative of callousness as being very high (e.g., to rate "I do not feel remorseful when I do something wrong" as *definitely true*). Using item response theory (IRT) analyses in this same sample, we found that these response patterns led to very different levels of difficulty between items. That is, the prosocial items were most useful for discriminating among youth with low levels of CU traits, whereas the callously worded items were most useful for discriminating among youth with high levels of CU traits. Since the ICU is designed for use in diverse contexts (e.g., community, clinical, forensic), it is important for the scale to include items that perform well across the full range of CU traits. This balance ensures that the ICU can provide meaningful scores in samples with varying prevalence rates of CU traits. However, the differences in item difficulty mean that the usefulness of specific items may vary depending on the population. For instance, items assessing prosocial traits may be more informative in community samples (e.g., school children), whereas items assessing callousness may be more relevant in forensic samples (e.g., adolescents arrested for criminal offenses). These differences in item functioning also have implications for interpreting the results of factor analyses of the ICU.

Factor Analyses

The ICU was developed to assess a general dimension of CU traits, structured around four symptom clusters corresponding to the LPE specifier. Theoretically, factor analytic support for this scale structure would be to have a general CU factor that consists of four subfactors, corresponding to the four clusters of items for each LPE symptom. However, in a review of 13 factor analyses of the ICU, we did not typically find support for this hierarchical four-factor structure (Ray & Frick, 2020). While most factor analyses identified a general CU factor, they typically found three distinct subfactors: one with items mostly worded in the CU direction (often called a "callousness factor"), another with items mostly worded in the prosocial dimension (often called an "uncaring factor"), and a third related to restricted affect (often called an "unemotional factor"). Although this factor structure provided the best fit in many samples, it still often had poor fit without deleting items and demonstrated inconsistent factor correlates across samples. Consequently, the factor structure of the ICU did not align with its theoretical foundation, nor did it produce reliable findings that advanced our understanding of CU traits.

We were concerned, however, that this lack of support for the factorial validity of the ICU might stem from differences in response patterns to positively and negatively worded items. That is, we were concerned that the greater variability in responses to prosocially worded items could be influencing the factor analytic results. To address this, we asked researchers from around the world who had collected data using the ICU in large representative community samples to share their data, so that we could conduct a factor analysis testing the structure of the ICU while accounting for the "method variance" due to item wording. In a multinational sample of 4,683 adolescents from five different countries, we found that controlling for item wording effects resulted in a factor structure consistent with the way the ICU was developed

(Kemp, Ray, Frick, Robertson, et al., 2024). Specifically, we reported that, after controlling for differences in response patterns due to item wording, the best-fitting factor model included a general CU factor and four subfactors of items corresponding to the four symptoms of the LPE specifier, as outlined in Table 5.1. Further, we demonstrated that this four-factor structure was invariant for younger and older adolescents and for boys and girls, suggesting that the ICU was measuring CU traits in the same way for these different subgroups of the sample. We then replicated these findings in a sample of 1,216 adolescent boys who had been arrested in three different regions of the United States (Kemp, Ray, Frick, Speck, et al., 2024). In this second study, we demonstrated that this four-factor structure was invariant across racial and ethnic groups. Taken together, these results confirm that, when method variance is accounted for, the ICU aligns with the structure of the diagnostic criteria for the LPE specifier (i.e., four symptom clusters loading on an overarching CU dimension). This correspondence to diagnostic criteria distinguishes the ICU from other rating scales, reinforcing its utility as a measure of the LPE specifier in clinical and research settings.

Reliability

As noted in Chapter 4, a key limitation of many existing scales used to assess CU traits was that they were fairly short. This brevity, combined with the fact that CU traits are relatively uncommon in community samples of children and adolescents, often resulted in low internal consistency for many of the existing rating scales. To address this, one goal in developing the ICU was to include more items to increase this form of reliability. Several reviews of research using the ICU support that this goal has been met. In a review of studies including 115 samples with a combined sample size of 27,947 participants, Cardinale and Marsh (2020) reported a mean internal consistency of 0.83 for the self-report version of the ICU, which indicates a level of reliability that is quite good for a rating scale. In another review of studies including 146 samples from around the world, Deng et al. (2019) found similar support for the internal consistency of the self-report version of the ICU, with a mean internal consistency of 0.79 across the studies reviewed. These authors also found support for the internal consistency of the parent-report version (0.83) and the teacher report version (0.88), although these estimates were based on fewer samples (23 and 7, respectively). Further, Deng et al. reported that this level of reliability was found across different age groups, with mean internal consistency of 0.80 for samples of children, 0.80 for adolescents, and 0.78 for adults.

While internal consistency is the most commonly reported form of reliability, test–retest reliability also provides important evidence of score stability. Moore et al. (2017) examined test–retest reliability of the parent-report version of the ICU in a sample of 339 twins (ages 9–14) and found a reliability coefficient of 0.84 over the 3 weeks. Similarly, Hawes et al. (2014) reported a test–retest reliability coefficient of 0.85 for the parent-report version of the ICU over 30 days, although they only used a subset of the 24 ICU items. Finally, our study tested the temporal stability of the ICU self-report version across several 6-month intervals in a sample of adolescents, yielding an average stability coefficient of 0.67 (Ray et al., 2019). These findings provide support for the ICU's reliability and stability across repeated administrations.

Validity

Since the first publication on the ICU (Kimonis et al., 2008), over 600 studies published in peer-reviewed journals have used the ICU. A list of these studies is available at Frick (2004; see Appendix for a QR code and a full URL to the webpage). The sheer volume of research demonstrates the ICU's widespread use by researchers worldwide and suggests that they have found the ICU useful. However, this vast body of work makes it challenging to summarize the findings in a way that is useful to clinicians. A meta-analytic review by Cardinale and Marsh (2020) provides a helpful synthesis of this research. They reported an average effect size of 0.46 for the correlation between the ICU and other measures of the affective component of psychopathy, based on 16 samples with 5,041 participants. The ICU has also been validated through its associations with behavior problems, aggression, and criminal behavior. They reported an average effect size of 0.34 based on 44 samples with 13,899 participants for the correlation between the ICU and other measures of the conduct problems, an average effect size of 0.41 based on 14 samples with 3,627 participants for its correlation with proactive aggression, and an average effect size of 0.34 based on 18 samples with 3,952 participants for its correlation with criminal behavior. Additionally, CU traits are theorized to assess deficits in prosocial emotions, such as empathy. Cardinale and Marsh (2020) reported an average effect size of –0.42 for its correlation with other measures of empathy, based on 8 samples with 2,575 participants. Importantly, all of these effect sizes were based on the self-report version of the ICU. There is much less data on the parent-report and teacher-report versions, and the strength of the evidence for their validity may depend on the age of the child. We discuss these considerations in our recommendations for use of different informants for the ICU across age groups.

Cutoff Scores

Another limitation of most behavioral rating scales used to assess CU traits is the lack of validated diagnostic cutoffs. Most research treats CU traits scores from rating scales as continuous variables, such as by correlating the measure of CU traits with other measures (e.g., warm parenting, aggression). While this approach is appropriate and typically recommended for research, clinical assessment requires a determination of when the CU traits scores are "elevated" or "clinically significant," which is crucial for diagnosing the LPE specifier and guiding treatment decisions.

The primary indicator of clinical significance is whether CU traits contribute to serious functional impairment, such as

- serious aggression toward others,
- peer relationship difficulties,
- discipline problems at school, or
- engagement in illegal behaviors.

Thus, a critically important marker for the clinical significance of CU traits is based on a careful assessment of the level and severity of the child's antisocial behavior, which we discussed in the previous chapter. As we also noted earlier, elevated CU traits can still cause significant impairment, even in the absence of conduct problems. Moreover, treatment recommendations should be tailored, as not all children and adolescents with serious conduct problems require the same interventions. Therefore, clinicians need clear guidelines for determining when ICU scores are elevated and indicate a need for modified treatment approaches.

One early attempt to establish clinical cutoffs involved conducting item response theory analyses to guide selection of the four best performing ICU items that corresponded to LPE specifier symptoms. A score of 2 (*very true*) or 3 (*definitely true*) on at least two of the four items was used to indicate elevation (Kimonis et al., 2015). However, this method did not replicate well across multiple samples (Colins et al., 2020), likely due to psychometric limitations. That is, this method uses a very limited item pool (only four items) and a restricted range of scores (0 to 3) on each item to determine elevations. More stable estimates are likely to be obtained when using multiple items to assess the presence of each LPE symptom, consistent with how the ICU was developed to have six items assessing each of the four symptoms.

Given these limitations, we tested alternative methods for determining ICU cutoffs across multiple samples. We tested the validity of different cut scores (i.e., scores that indicate clinical significance) that we determined in several ways (Kemp et al., 2023). First, we used empirical methods by determining what ICU scores optimally predicted a number of important areas of clinical impairment, such as aggression, criminal behavior, school behavior problems, and peer relationship problems. Second, we tested cutoffs based on norm-referenced scores, showing when the scores were above the 90th percentile from a large sample of older children and adolescents. These analyses enabled us to establish scores on the ICU at which a clinician should begin to be concerned (i.e., at risk) and scores at which the clinician should definitely have concerns (i.e., clinical). These score ranges are provided in Table 5.2. Because these scores were based on older children and adolescents, we developed cut scores for younger children using data collected by Ezpeleta and colleagues (2013) on the parent-report version of the ICU with 622 children ages 3 and 4 in Spain. We used scores that were one standard deviation above the mean to indicate when scores should be of concern and two standard deviations above the mean to indicate when scores are in the clinical range. Scores for the parent-report preschool version of the ICU are also provided in Table 5.2.

TABLE 5.2. Guide for Using Cut Scores for the Different Informant Versions of the Inventory of Callous-Unemotional Traits

Version	Gender	At risk	Clinical
Self-report	Boys	24	34
	Girls	24	29
Parent report	Boys	21	34
	Girls	21	30
Teacher report	Boys	35	46
	Girls	NA	35
Parent report preschool	Boys	24	35
	Girls	20	29

Note. NA = not available. Cut scores for the first three child and adolescent versions are based on findings from Kemp et al. (2023) using all 24 items and validating different methods for determining cut scores in samples ages 8 to 17. Cutoffs for the preschool version were based on scores falling 1 standard deviation (*SD*; at risk) or 2 *SD* (clinical) from the 24-item mean ICU (Inventory of Callous-Unemotional Traits) score in a community sample of preschool children in Spain (Ezpeleta et al., 2013).

It is important to recognize that validating cut scores is an ongoing process. Further research is needed to refine these thresholds and evaluate their predictive validity across different populations. These recommendations may need to be adjusted depending on the outcomes of further testing. Also, no diagnosis, including the LPE specifier, should ever be made based on a single score from one measure. ICU scores should always be integrated with other assessment information within a broad assessment of serious conduct problems (see Chapter 4). ICU scores should also be integrated with other methods for assessing CU traits, such as the Clinical Assessment of Prosocial Emotions (CAPE), which we discuss in the next chapter. Scores from the ICU can be used with the CAPE to help determine when a diagnosis of LPE is warranted. Since the CAPE requires highly trained clinicians and is time consuming, a tiered assessment approach may be useful:

Step 1: Use the ICU as a screening tool to identify children at risk.
Step 2: Assess for an impairing level of conduct problems.
Step 3: Administer the CAPE only to those who score above ICU cutoffs, using the cutoffs provided in Table 5.2, and who show severe and impairing conduct problems to determine if an LPE diagnosis is warranted.

Use of Different Informants

A critical aspect of assessing children and adolescents with emotional and behavioral problems is the need to gather information from multiple sources (Frick et al., 2020). However, research has long shown that ratings from different informants often correlate only modestly. For example, in a study we conducted using the ICU with 236 school children in grades 3, 6, and 8, self-reported ICU scores correlated $r = 0.22$ ($p < 0.01$) with caregiver-reported ICU scores and $r = 0.29$ ($p < 0.001$) with teacher-reported ICU scores (Matlasz et al., 2023). Caregiver and teacher ratings were also correlated modestly at

$r = 0.18$ ($p < 0.01$). Although statistically significant, these correlations are modest but are consistent with findings for ratings using other emotional and behavioral problem measures in children and adolescents (De Los Reyes et al., 2015).

Several factors contribute to these discrepancies across informants (Frick et al., 2020). First, a child's behavior and emotions may vary across different settings and relationships. Some problems may be more likely to occur at home, where parents are the primary caregivers, while others may emerge in school settings, where teachers observe peer interactions. Also, one caregiver, who is primarily responsible for caregiving, may have more opportunities to experience problem behaviors than the other caregiver, who is not the primary caregiver. Also, a caregiver may have limited opportunities to witness their child being mean or bullying others, just as a teacher may not observe stealing or the types of rule-breaking behavior that occurs at home or in the community. Additionally, some characteristics, such as how a child experiences emotions or processes social interactions, may be difficult for any external observer to assess because they are internal events that may only be apparent to the child themselves. In these cases, self-reporting may provide the most valid assessment, provided the child is at an appropriate developmental level to accurately describe their own emotions and behaviors. The child's ability to report on these internal events changes over development, with young children having more difficulty reporting on their emotions and behaviors than older children.

The ability of different informants to report on a child's emotions and behaviors also changes over development. Teachers in early grades, who often spend the entire day with a single group of students, may develop a well-rounded understanding of a child's behaviors and social interactions. However, as children advance to higher grades and rotate through multiple teachers throughout the day, any one teacher's observations become more limited. A similar shift occurs with caregivers, who tend to have close and frequent contact with younger children but may have less direct knowledge of their adolescent's behavior as they spend more time with friends and in extracurricular activities (e.g., sports, band, working). Furthermore, informants may have their own biases or motivations that influence their ratings. A caregiver's perception of their own parenting ability may make them reluctant to acknowledge their child's lack of prosocial emotions, leading to underreporting. Conversely, some caregivers may exaggerate symptoms to gain access to services or financial support.

Given these many different factors that can influence the report of any single informant, it is unsurprising that ICU scores often vary across informants. Rather than viewing these discrepancies as measurement errors, clinicians should interpret them as a source of valuable information about a child's behavior across different contexts (De Los Reyes, 2024). The low correspondence across informants also reinforces the importance of integrating multiple sources of information rather than relying on a single informant or measure. No diagnosis, including the LPE specifier, should be based on one score alone. Instead, discrepancies should be evaluated in the broader context of other assessment information to determine whether they reflect meaningful differences in behavior across settings or potential biases in reporting. However, an important rule of thumb that we observed in our assessments is that the presence of elevations on a behavior rating scale tends to be more clinically important than the absence of elevations. In other words, there is a multitude of reasons for a person to underreport on their level of CU traits, given that these traits are often considered undesirable. However, the reasons to overreport high levels of CU traits during a psychological evaluation when they are not there are much fewer. Thus, an elevation on a measure of CU traits should always be taken seriously. It may not always result in a diagnosis of the LPE specifier (i.e., a caregiver may have misunderstood the questions), but it should not be ignored.

In addition to this general rule, we provide some additional guidelines to help clinicians determine which informants may provide the most valid ICU ratings for children at different ages, based on research findings that suggest that their ratings should be given more weight in trying to resolve discrepancies. In a study we conducted with a sample of 236 school children (grades 3, 6, and 8), we compared the validity of ICU ratings across caregiver, teacher, and self-reports (Matlasz et al., 2023). We found that teacher reports were the most valid in third grade but decreased in validity over time, becoming the least valid by eighth grade. These trends likely reflect the decreasing amount of time that teachers spend with individual students in later grades. In contrast, self-reports showed strong validity at all ages. Specifically, they were the most valid way of assessing CU traits in grades 6 and 8 and were second in validity to teachers in grade 3. These findings suggest that CU traits, which involve emotions and internal motivations, are often best reported by the child, once they reach an age where they can reliably complete a rating scale. Based on this research, children as young as 9 years old appear to be capable of validly reporting on their CU traits using the self-report ICU. Caregiver ratings were somewhat valid across all ages but were never the most reliable source at any of the grade levels examined (grades 3, 6, 8).

These findings inform our recommendations regarding which informants are most appropriate when using the ICU in clinical assessments of children at different ages. These recommendations, summarized in Table 5.3, suggest that

TABLE 5.3. Guide for Selecting the Best Informants to Complete the Inventory of Callous–Unemotional Traits by Child Age

Age	Best primary informant	Best secondary informant
Prior to age 5	Parent	Teacher
Ages 5 to 9	Teacher	Parent
Ages 10 to 12	Self-report	Teacher
Ages 13 to 21	Self-report	Parent

Note. Recommendations are based on findings from Matlasz et al., 2023.

teachers serve as the primary informants for younger school-aged children, while youth serve as primary informants in later years. However, these recommendations are based primarily on school-aged children. For younger children (ages 5 and under), additional research has guided our approach. For example, we found that teachers can provide valid ICU ratings for children as young as 3 years old (Kimonis, Fanti, et al., 2016), suggesting that once a child enters school, teacher reports should be prioritized. However, preschool settings vary widely in structure, class size, and in the stability of teachers, which may influence the validity of teacher ratings. Additionally, some young children do not attend preschool or daycare, limiting the availability of teacher reports. In these cases, parent-report ICU scores provide the best alternative. In support of this recommendation, Ezpeleta and colleagues (2013) used the parent-report version of the ICU in a sample of 622 children ages 3 and 4 in Spain. Their results supported the validity of the parent-report ICU for this age group. Based on this research, we recommend that for children under age 5, the parent-report ICU should be the primary version used, with the teacher-report ICU serving as a secondary source of information when available.

Understanding which informants, or combinations of informants, are likely to provide the most valid ICU scores at different ages is essential for accurate assessment and diagnosis of the LPE specifier. In short, to make well-informed decisions when interpreting ICU scores, clinicians should consider

- variations in a child's behaviors and emotions across settings and relationships,
- developmental changes in the accuracy of self-report versus other informant ratings, and
- potential biases in information ratings.

Using multiple sources of information increases the reliability and validity of assessments and ensures that clinical decisions are based on the most comprehensive and informed understanding of a child's level of CU traits.

Treatment Monitoring

Thus far, this chapter has focused on using the ICU for diagnostic purposes, particularly how it can be integrated into broader assessments of serious conduct problems to inform the diagnosis of the LPE specifier. However, another important clinical application of the ICU is its use for monitoring treatment progress. Once a child with the LPE specifier is referred for treatment, it is essential to assess whether or not they are responding to treatment. A growing body of research supports the ICU as a valid tool for tracking treatment effects over time. For example, we conducted an open trial of an intervention for children with the LPE specifier and we found that parent-reported ICU scores showed a substantial decline from pretreatment to posttreatment, and these improvements maintained at a 3-month follow-up (Kimonis et al., 2019). Similarly, in a randomized controlled trial of the same intervention, we found that parent-reported ICU ratings significantly decreased from pretreatment through follow-up (Fleming et al., 2022; Fleming et al., 2023). Similarly, in a study where we tested a universal teacher intervention for student disruptive behavior, we found that teacher ratings on the ICU showed greater declines over treatment for the intervention group compared to a no-treatment control group (Boulton et al., in press). Further, in an older sample of adolescents, self-reported ICU scores declined in response to treatment (Muratori et al., 2019). Taken together, these findings indicate that continuous scores on the parent-, teacher-, and self-report ICU versions can provide valuable treatment monitoring data, helping clinicians track whether an intervention is effectively reducing CU traits in youth with the LPE specifier.

CHAPTER SUMMARY

In this chapter, we described the development and use of a behavioral rating scale specifically designed to assess the LPE specifier. The ICU provides a relatively brief (24-item) assessment of the four symptoms of the LPE specifier described in the fifth edition of the *Diagnostic and Statistical Manual of Mental Disorders* (*DSM-5*) and is available in multiple freely accessible versions (see Appendix), allowing clinicians to obtain ratings from the person being assessed (i.e., self-report), as well as from knowledgeable informants (e.g., caregivers and teacher). Additionally, the ICU has been translated into numerous languages, expanding its applicability across diverse populations. Research supports the reliability and validity of ICU scores across a wide age range, from early childhood (age 3) to young adulthood. Also, research provides guidance on selecting informants based on a child's age (see Table 5.3) and provides cut score recommendations to assist clinicians in identifying elevated or clinically significant CU traits for diagnostic purposes (see Table 5.2).

Despite its strengths, the ICU should never be used in isolation to diagnose the LPE specifier. First, it should be integrated into a broader assessment of conduct problems, as discussed in Chapter 4. Second, while the ICU offers a time-efficient method for assessing CU traits from the perspective of multiple informants, additional information is necessary before making a clinical diagnosis. It is crucial to evaluate whether informants understood the questions, provided thoughtful responses, and attempted to rate the individual accurately. It is also important to consider the contexts within which their ratings are informed. These factors are essential for interpreting discrepancies between informants, which must be carefully considered in diagnostic decision making. In the next chapter, we introduce a structured clinical assessment for the LPE specifier, which can be used alongside the ICU to support a comprehensive and accurate diagnosis of the LPE specifier.

6

Using the Clinical Assessment of Prosocial Emotions (CAPE) in Clinical Assessments of the Limited Prosocial Emotions Specifier

As we discussed in Chapter 5, the Inventory of Callous–Unemotional Traits (ICU) rating scale provides a time-efficient way to assess the full criteria for the LPE specifier from the perspective of multiple informants. By asking people to rate 24 standardized questions about themselves or others, the ICU can be completed quickly and does not require extensive training for administration or scoring. Its ease of use makes it useful for research and, as a result, there is a substantial body of evidence supporting its psychometric properties that can help guide its clinical application. In Chapter 5, we provided examples of this research, such as studies that determined when scores should be considered elevated and how to interpret discrepancies between different informants.

Despite these very useful qualities, behavior rating scales also have some important limitations in clinical assessments. First, they do not clarify the reasoning behind ratings, making it difficult to verify whether informants understood the questions correctly or provided thoughtful, accurate responses. Second, while behavior rating scales all have some method of anchoring the ratings of the items (e.g., frequency of the trait being assessed, how typical it is), the limited prosocial emotions (LPE) specifier requires callous–unemotional (CU) traits to be persistent (i.e., present for at least 12 months) and pervasive (occurring across multiple relationships and settings). When relying on behavior rating scales, it is often difficult to obtain such detailed information about whether the traits being assessed reflect the individual's typical pattern of interpersonal or emotional functioning and not just occasional occurrences in

https://doi.org/10.1037/0000500-007
A Clinical Guide to Working With Youth With Conduct Disorders and Limited Prosocial Emotions, by P. J. Frick and E. R. Kimonis

some situations. Finally, it is important when assessing for the LPE specifier to get information from multiple informants. Moreover, since different informants may provide conflicting reports (e.g., a child rating themselves as empathetic, while the caregiver rates them as callous and uncaring), clinicians face challenges in integrating such discrepancies to make a diagnosis.

Thus, clinical assessments cannot rely solely on the information provided by behavior rating scales to diagnose the LPE specifier. Clinicians need additional information to assess the symptoms of the specifier comprehensively. While some structured tools exist to guide this process, as noted in Chapter 4, they were not specifically designed to assess the LPE criteria and, as a result, have significant limitations for this purpose. To address these gaps, we developed the Clinical Assessment of Prosocial Emotions (CAPE; Goetz et al., 2024). The CAPE was developed specifically to assess the four symptoms of the LPE specifier, focusing entirely on gathering all of the necessary information to make this diagnosis. It provides a structured method for evaluating symptom persistence and pervasiveness, while allowing flexibility to accommodate developmental, educational, and cultural differences across persons being assessed. Consequently, it can be used for a fairly wide age range of children and adolescents, spanning ages 3 to 21 years old. The CAPE's flexible administration also enables clinicians to explore why informants responded in certain ways, aiding in the interpretation of conflicting responses in order to make a final diagnosis. Additionally, while archival information (e.g., institutional or medical records) can be used to score the CAPE, they are not required, making it suitable for use in a wide range of mental health settings.

Despite these important advantages, the CAPE has some drawbacks. It is time intensive, often requiring 45 minutes to an hour for administration and scoring. Further, the CAPE should only be used by trained clinicians who meet the following requirements outlined in its manual (Frick, 2013; see Appendix for a QR code and a full URL to the webpage):

- possess an advanced degree in the social, medical, or behavioral sciences;
- have at least 3 years of experience assessing the emotional and behavioral adjustment of children and adolescents;
- have training and expertise in psychopathology, child development, and clinical interviewing;
- be familiar with the research literature on CU traits in children and adolescents;
- hold the necessary credentials to be legally authorized to conduct clinical assessments;
- be knowledgeable of the relevant ethical standards guiding clinical assessment; and
- be trained in the CAPE's administration and scoring procedures.

This book provides foundational training by summarizing research on CU traits (Chapters 1 to 3) and outlining CAPE administration and scoring procedures in this chapter. However, we do not provide the broader training in child and adolescent clinical assessment. Proper training also requires initial supervision by a clinician experienced in the administration of the CAPE to ensure appropriate administration and scoring. This involves having at least two cases observed by a trained clinician, either in person or by video, with feedback provided on the administration of interviews and scoring of CAPE items. In certain research settings where CAPE scores are not used for clinical decision making, the same level of training may not be required, provided users are supervised by a qualified clinician who meets these requirements.

INITIAL TESTS OF RELIABILITY AND VALIDITY

An important consideration in using the CAPE is that its psychometric properties have not been as extensively tested as the ICU. However, we have been involved in several published studies testing the reliability and validity of the CAPE, yielding encouraging findings that support its cautious clinical use. Nonetheless, further research is needed to refine the CAPE and enhance its utility for use in clinical assessments across diverse populations.

Given the CAPE's flexibility in how clinician raters obtain information to assign scores, a critical test of its psychometric properties is whether raters can do this reliably. We found an acceptable level of interrater reliability in a Spanish sample of incarcerated adolescents (ages 14–18 years; Molinuevo et al., 2020) and excellent reliability in a sample of clinic-referred children and adolescents (ages 6–18 years; Goetz et al., 2024). Further, in both samples, as well as in a sample of young children (ages 2–8 years) referred to a mental health clinic for conduct problems (Neo et al., 2023), the reliability of individual LPE specifier symptoms was within an acceptable range. These findings suggest that trained clinicians can reliably score the CAPE.

Across these samples, as well as in a fourth sample of clinic-referred children (ages 3–15 years) in Australia (Hawes et al., 2020), CAPE scores showed convergent validity by significantly correlating with measures of empathy (Hawes et al., 2020; Molinuevo et al., 2020; Neo et al., 2023) and measures of conduct problems and aggression (Goetz et al., 2024; Hawes et al., 2020; Molinuevo et al., 2020; Neo et al., 2023). Furthermore, CAPE scores explained unique variance in measures of empathy (Hawes et al., 2020; Neo et al., 2023), measures of conduct problems (Goetz et al., 2024; Hawes et al., 2020; Neo et al., 2023), and measures of aggression (Goetz et al., 2024; Neo et al., 2023), after controlling for ICU scores. These findings suggest that CAPE scores provide clinically valuable information beyond that obtained from rating scales assessing CU traits, supporting the incremental clinical utility of this more time-intensive measure. Also, clinicians that we have trained and supervised also anecdotally report that the CAPE provides valuable insights beyond several other rating scales assessing CU traits, particularly regarding the reasons behind informant ratings and discrepancies between raters.

Perhaps the most crucial test of the CAPE's validity is its ability to identify a subgroup of children with a conduct problem diagnosis who differ meaningfully from others with the same diagnosis. This ability to distinguish subgroups of youth with serious conduct problems is why the LPE specifier is included in diagnostic classification. In both the Hawes et al. (2020) and Neo et al. (2023) studies, support for this aspect of the CAPE's validity was modest. Hawes et al. (2020) reported that children diagnosed with oppositional defiant disorder (ODD) or conduct disorder (CD) who met LPE specifier criteria on the CAPE did not differ from other children with ODD or CD on any of the measures of conduct problem severity or aggression but did exhibit lower empathy levels. Neo et al. (2023) reported that young children diagnosed with ODD or CD who met LPE specifier criteria on the CAPE differed from those who did not meet these criteria only on measures of proactive aggression and poor treatment outcome. In contrast, Goetz et al. (2024) found stronger support for the CAPE in a clinic-referred sample of children and adolescents. In this study, we found that children with an ODD or CD diagnosis who met LPE specifier criteria on the CAPE showed more severe conduct problems and aggression on five of the seven measures included in the study compared to other children with either an ODD or CD diagnosis. Importantly, Goetz et al. (2024) used both caregiver and child reports to score the CAPE, whereas Hawes et al. (2020) and Neo et al. (2023) relied solely on caregiver reports on the CAPE. These findings could suggest that including self-report, when the child is old enough to provide such information, may be important for defining clinically important subgroups of youth with serious conduct problems.

HOW TO ADMINISTER THE CAPE

The most important thing to remember when administering the CAPE is that it utilizes the *structured professional judgement method* for assessment. What this means is that the CAPE provides very clear and detailed descriptions of the constructs being assessed—the four symptoms of the LPE specifier. Further, there are very clear scoring guidelines for each of these constructs. The CAPE provides extended prototypical descriptions for each of the LPE symptoms. The clinician must obtain whatever information is needed to rate how descriptive the prototype is for the person being assessed. The ratings are made on a three-point scale:

0. Not descriptive or mildly descriptive
1. Moderately descriptive
2. Highly descriptive

The clinician then determines if the person being assessed has at least two of the four symptoms rated as being "highly descriptive" (i.e., at a "2") and thus meets the LPE criteria according to the CAPE.

While the protypes and scoring are very standard and structured, the clinician is given great flexibility in how to obtain the information needed to score the CAPE. The one very clear rule is that the ratings should never be based solely on a single answer from a single source of information. The CAPE includes semi-structured interviews to aid in gathering this information, one designed with questions for the person being assessed (i.e., self-report interview) and one designed to be answered by an informant (i.e., informant interview) that could be a caregiver (or multiple caretakers), teacher, or someone else who knows the person being assessed quite well. For most assessments, the clinician should have conducted the self-report interview and at least one informant interview prior to making the CAPE LPE symptom ratings. In young children (before the age of 9), a second informant interview can take the place of the self-report interview and it is highly recommended that the two informants be a caregiver and a teacher.

While the semi-structured interviews are required, clinicians can use other sources to obtain information to score the CAPE as well. The availability of such information may vary across settings. It can include ratings on the ICU or other measures of CU traits; a review of records of the person being assessed (e.g., medical, mental health, educational, legal), observations of the person being assessed, and any other information that has been collected as part of a clinical evaluation of the person being assessed. All of this information is then weighed by the clinician to make a rating as to how well the person being assessed matches the prototypical description of each LPE symptom.

The CAPE Semi-Structured Interviews

While the CAPE administration includes semi-structured interviews, it is important to remember that these interviews are not the CAPE. They are simply aids to help the clinician gather the needed information to score the prototypical descriptions of the LPE symptoms. The interviews allow for extensive follow-up questions to obtain the information needed to score the CAPE. Thus, interviewers cannot just be familiar with the interview questions. It is just as critical that the interviewer be very familiar with the prototype description of symptoms that need to be scored, so that they will know what follow-up questions are needed to make the ratings. The interviews also allow the assessor to gain detailed information about why a person may have answered a question in a certain way. This information can be critical when scoring the CAPE items because the clinician will need to weigh information across multiple sources to determine the most accurate rating. Finally, the interviews allow the assessor to tailor questions based on the age of the child, as well as to tailor the questions to the educational and cultural backgrounds of the persons being assessed.

The interviews all revolve around two to three *stem questions* for each of the four LPE symptoms. These questions are provided in Tables 6.1 through 6.4. These are critical parts of the interview because they were carefully selected to ask questions most highly related to the core features of each LPE symptom. For example, the first stem question assessing the symptom "lack of remorse and guilt" is: "Do you feel bad or guilty if you do something wrong or if you hurt someone?" It is critical that the interviewer gets a "yes" or "no" answer to all stem questions before doing any follow-up questions or providing clarification to the person being interviewed. So, if a person answered this question with "Well it depends on if the person deserved it or not," the interviewer would follow up by asking, "How would you describe how you typically feel? Would you say it's more 'yes' or more 'no'?"

Once the person being interviewed provides a "yes" or "no" answer to a stem question, the interviewer is then allowed to clarify why the person answered in this way. It is good to vary these follow-ups and tailor them to stem questions. It can be "Can you give me examples of this?" or "Can you tell me about a time when you/they felt this way?" or "Can you tell me why you said 'yes' [or said 'no']?" These follow-up questions are where the flexibility in the interviewing is most apparent. An answer to a stem question may be so clear that the clinician feels that no follow-up is needed. For example, if a caregiver's response to the question "Does your child seem to care and be concerned about the feelings of others?" is "Oh, absolutely; in fact, he often worries too much about other people and how they are feeling," the interviewer may feel that no additional information is required. However, if a caregiver says "no" to this question, the interview should follow up with "Tell me why you say that." The interviewer should then continue asking questions until they feel comfortable that they will be able to determine how well the child fits the prototypical description of "the person consistently disregards and is unconcerned about the feelings of others."

Depending on the response to the stem question, the interviewer is routed to additional standard follow-up questions to further aid in making CAPE ratings. Some are specific to the LPE symptom being assessed. For example, as noted in Table 6.1, if a person responds "yes" to the question "Do you feel bad or guilty if you do something wrong or if you hurt someone?" the interviewer is directed to the follow-up question "Do you only feel bad or guilty if you are caught doing something wrong and are going to be in trouble?" There are also several questions that are important for scoring the CAPE that are asked following any stem question that is answered as being potentially indicative of the presence of the specifier. The first set of questions helps the clinician determine how persistent and pervasive the trait being assessed is for the person—in other words, how the person "typically" is with most people and in most situations. This is done using the following standard questions included in the informant interview:

- Is this how they are most of the time and with most people?
- Have they been like this for a long time, that is, for at least a year?

The second type of standard follow-up question is to ask for counter-examples. We have found that these questions are a very helpful way to determine how descriptive or typical a trait is for a person. For example, if an informant answers "no" to the stem question about feeling bad or guilty, a standard follow-up question is "Can you think of any time recently, say, over the past month, when they have felt bad or guilty about something?" The various ways that this question can be answered are quite informative for scoring the CAPE. For example, if an informant cannot think of an example, it reinforces the possibility that the lack of remorse is how the person is most of the time. If the informant gives an example and describes "being shocked by it because that is not how he usually acts," this again supports that a lack of guilt or remorse is more typical for the person. If the informant answers this question with an example of showing remorse or guilt with "his one good friend," the interviewer can then follow up with questions assessing whether the lack of remorse or guilt is present in most relationships or only in a few. For example, the interviewer can ask "Can you think of anyone else he shows remorse and guilt with?" If the informant provides a number of examples, this may help determine that the lack of remorse and guilt is not "with most people" but maybe only with their caregivers and immediate family members.

Given the "stem with follow-up question" format of these interviews, the length of time they take can vary greatly depending on how many stem questions require follow-up questions, how succinct the informant is, and how adept the interviewer is at asking follow-up questions that provide information that is most needed for scoring the CAPE.[1] Each interview can take between 15 minutes to an hour to complete. Also, at the end of each interview, the interviewer provides ratings of accuracy.

For the self-report interview, the rating is based on the following question:

How accurate and honest did the informant seem to be?

Not at All	Somewhat	Moderately	Very
0	1	2	3

For the informant interview, the rating is based on two questions:

How well did the informant seem to know the client?

Not at All	Somewhat	Moderately	Very
0	1	2	3

How accurate and honest did the informant seem to be?

Not at All	Somewhat	Moderately	Very
0	1	2	3

HOW TO SCORE THE CAPE

Once these semi-structured interviews are completed, the information gathered from these interviews, as well as any other information that is available on the person being assessed, must be used to score the four CAPE items. In this

[1]Adapted from *Clinical Assessment of Prosocial Emotions: Version 1.1* (*CAPE Version 1.1*), by P. J. Frick, 2013, LSU, Developmental Psychopathology Lab (https://faculty.lsu.edu/pfricklab/cape.php). Copyright 2013 by Paul J. Frick.

section, we provide information to guide clinicians in this process. We start with general considerations that apply to all items and then we follow this by providing guidelines to aid in scoring individual items.

Guidelines for Integrating Information

The most challenging aspect of scoring the CAPE is determining how to weigh different sources of information when making the final symptom ratings. This can be particularly difficult when the sources of information provide inconsistent answers. As noted in the previous chapter on the ICU, this is a broader issue in assessing children and adolescents using almost any assessment method. Research has shown that information from different sources provides varying perspectives on a child's emotions, behaviors, and social adjustment. For example, caregivers may interpret their child's emotions and behaviors differently, teachers may provide distinct observations based on school interactions, and children themselves may offer accounts that differ markedly from their caregivers. Additionally, a child may report one thing while other evidence suggests otherwise. Unlike a simple behavior rating scale, the CAPE incorporates responses to follow-up questions and supporting information to help determine which information is most accurate. Interviewers can use follow-up questions to help resolve discrepancies. For example, if a caregiver says "yes" to the question about the child making fun of or teasing other people, but the child says "no" during their interview, the interviewer might ask the child, "Your mom mentioned that you got detention for calling someone fat. Do you remember that incident? Can you tell me what happened?" If the caregiver provides school documentation supporting this detention, the child's denial can be disregarded when making a final symptom score.

General Considerations for Scoring the CAPE Items

We have been training and supervising clinicians administering the CAPE for several years. In doing so, we have learned some helpful suggestions for scoring the CAPE items. Before providing some helpful strategies for scoring individual LPE symptoms, we provide several general guidelines that are important for scoring all of the CAPE items.

1. **Weighing positive responses more heavily:** Positive endorsements (i.e., answers indicating CU traits) typically carry more weight than denials of symptoms. Indicators of CU traits are generally not socially desirable and there are many reasons why informants or the person being assessed might minimize or deny them but fewer reasons for endorsing high levels of CU traits when they are not actually displayed by the person being assessed. While rare, assessors should consider possible exceptions to this rule, such as a caregiver exaggerating symptoms to secure a certain placement for their child in a residential treatment center, a teacher seeking removal of a disruptive student from their classroom, or a child's misunderstanding of the interview questions. However, in most cases, a single source reporting the

presence of a symptom should be given more weight than a denial unless there is a compelling reason to disregard it.

2. **Considering informant validity at different ages:** Research summarized in Chapter 5 (see Table 5.2) suggests that different informants on the ICU provide the most valid reports at different ages of the child or adolescent. This finding could be useful in determining how to integrate information across informants for the CAPE as well.
   - **Prior to age 6**, self-reporting by the child is generally unreliable. CAPE interviews should primarily involve caregivers and, where feasible, teachers. The weight given to caregiver or teacher informants should depend on the amount of time the child spends with them. More weight should be given to the teacher's report if the teacher sees the child interact with other children on a daily basis.
   - **Ages 6 to 9** represent a transitional period where the validity of self-report depends on the child's ability to understand and verbally articulate answers to the CAPE interview questions. It is very important for the interviewer to let young children talk and provide examples for questions in their own words, to determine how well the child understands what is being asked.
   - **After age 9**, self-reports become increasingly reliable and should be a primary source of information. While this recommendation was based on research using the ICU, our validation research on the CAPE indicates that including self-reports in assessments of the LPE specifier improves differentiation between important subgroups of children with conduct problems.
3. **Distinguishing between presence and severity of LPE symptoms:** In our experiences supervising a large number of CAPE interviews, we have found that deciding between a score of "0" (*not descriptive* or *mildly descriptive*) and "1" or "2" (*moderately descriptive* or *highly descriptive*) is usually fairly straightforward. Informants are often clear on whether certain descriptors do not apply at all to the person being assessed. We have found that the more difficult decision arises when a trait is present but its descriptiveness (i.e., moderately or highly) needs to be determined. As noted earlier, the CAPE interviews provide a number of follow-up questions to help to make this decision. The key decision is: How "typical" is this descriptor across different relationships and settings? If the behavior is pervasive across multiple contexts, it warrants a score of "2." If it is limited to certain situations, a score of "1" may be more appropriate. Sometimes, very direct questions are needed for scoring. For example, a caregiver describes their child as showing a lack of empathy in some situations but not others. The clinician, knowing that they will need to decide whether to rate the symptom of callous–lack of empathy as *moderately descriptive* (1) or *highly descriptive* (2) of the child, can ask, "So, would you say that lacking empathy and not caring about others is how Noah is to just some people or is that how he is to most people?"

4. **Focusing on expressed traits and not perceived capability:** When interpreting information gathered for scoring the CAPE, assign scores based on observed behaviors indicating the person actually displays the trait of interest, and not on a person's perceived potential. For example, if a caregiver describes a child as having emotions but "they are buried deep inside and he is scared to let them come out," a key follow-up question for scoring the CAPE is about whether the child actually expresses these emotions to others. Similarly, if a child describes "feeling bad when hurting someone," follow-up questions should be, "How do you show it?" and "Can other people tell that you feel bad?"

5. **Separating cause from presence:** CAPE scores should not be influenced by what the child, the caregiver, or even the assessor thinks may have caused the child or adolescent to show the traits. For example, two children might show a lack of emotion—one caused by a long-standing trait and the other following a very traumatic experience—but both should be scored in the same way, should all of the criteria for persistence and duration be met. Although these differences are crucial for treatment planning, they should not affect the scoring of CAPE items.

Scoring of the Individual CAPE Items

In this section, we focus on providing guidance for scoring the individual CAPE items. Tables 6.1 to 6.4 provide each of the four LPE symptom descriptions and the corresponding interview questions from the self-report interview version. To reiterate, it is critical that assessors are thoroughly familiar with these symptom descriptions, so that they know how and when to ask additional relevant follow-up questions during the interview in order to obtain all of the needed information to accurately score the item. The questions in the interview were designed to help the assessor gather the information needed to score the CAPE. However, the interview questions only serve as a starting point and additional probing is almost always necessary to score each item. In the following sections, we provide recommendations to guide these follow-up questions based on our training and supervising of clinicians administering the CAPE.

Lack of Remorse or Guilt

As shown in Table 6.1, the first item to be scored on the CAPE relates to a lack of guilt or remorse. This item is rated based on whether the person rarely, if ever, feels bad or guilty when they do something wrong and shows a general lack of concern about the negative consequences of their action. This item is often one that assessors have the most difficulty scoring on the CAPE (see Goetz et al., 2024; Molinuevo et al., 2020). That is, many informants have difficulty deciding whether the person "really" feels guilt or remorse (i.e., whether the remorse is genuine or not). As a result, it is important that the assessor not spend a lot of time determining if the person genuinely feels bad

TABLE 6.1. Scoring the Symptom "Lack of Remorse or Guilt"

Ratings (Circle)	Description
0 1 2	The person rarely, if ever, feels bad or guilty when he or she does something wrong (except if he or she shows remorse when caught and/or facing punishment). The individual shows a general lack of concern about the negative consequences of his or her actions. For example, the individual is not remorseful after hurting someone or does not care about the consequences of breaking rules, unless the consequences inconvenience the person. This lack of guilt occurs in a range of situations both serious and nonserious and it occurs with most people (i.e., it is not confined to only certain people or relationships).
Stem questions	**Follow-up questions**
Do you feel bad or guilty if you do something wrong or if you hurt someone?	**If no:** Is this how you are most of the time and with most people? Have you been like this for a long time; that is, for at least a year? Can you think of any time recently, say over the past month, when you did something wrong or hurt someone and you felt bad or guilty about something? **If yes:** Do you only feel bad or guilty if you get caught doing something wrong and are going to be in trouble?
Do you find it easy to admit to being wrong; that is, do you take responsibility for your actions and apologize to people you have hurt?	**If no:** Is this how you are most of the time and with most people? Have you been like this for a long time; that is, for at least a year? Can you think of a time recently, say over the past month, when you admitted to being wrong or apologized to someone you hurt?

Note. Adapted from *Clinical Assessment of Prosocial Emotions: Version 1.1* (*CAPE Version 1.1*), by P. J. Frick, 2013, LSU, Developmental Psychopathology Lab (https://faculty.lsu.edu/pfricklab/cape.php). Copyright 2013 by Paul J. Frick.

or guilty but focuses instead on how the person shows this. As a result, after the stem question (i.e., "Does your child feel bad or guilty if he/she does something wrong or if he/she hurts someone?"), we often find that it is most helpful to focus questions on how this feeling is displayed by the person being assessed. For example, if the informant answers "yes" to this question, a good follow-up question is "How does Jane show this?" If the informant answers "no" to this question, a good follow-up question is "What makes you say that?" Similarly, if the person being assessed answers "yes," a similar follow-up question that is often helpful is "How do you show this?" with additional follow-up questions being "Can other people see that you feel bad or guilty?" and "How can they tell?" In short, the follow-up questions should focus on how the guilt and remorse is displayed and not whether the person actually feels this way.

The second stem question also helps to focus in on how the guilt is displayed, as opposed to whether the person truly feels this way. In the informant interview, it asks, "Does he/she find it easy to admit to being wrong; that is, does he/she take responsibility for his/her actions and apologize to people he/she hurts?" Follow-up questions can focus on getting examples of times when the person apologized for doing something wrong or for hurting someone and whether it is a typical or a rare response for the person being assessed. Again, this question focuses on how the person being assessed shows remorse, not whether they actually feel remorse. A critical follow-up to this question is also to determine if the person being assessed apologizes for things without being told to do so.

Another helpful guide for questions that can aid in scoring this item is to focus on the range of situations in which a person shows feelings of guilt and remorse. It is important to ask questions to determine whether the lack of guilt occurs across a range of situations, both serious and nonserious. For example, if a person says they feel bad or guilty and they give examples of apologizing when they seriously injured their sibling, it is important to follow up with "Can you give me other examples?" The interviewer should continue to probe for multiple situations in which the person may have shown signs of guilt, such as "What if you have gotten in trouble at school and your teacher is upset?" or "What if your parents are angry with you for something you have done?" and then follow up with "Do you apologize?" If the displays of remorse and guilt are only shown in serious situations, it suggests that the guilt and remorse may only be shown to avoid negative consequences. However, if the person being assessed or the informant provides clear examples of the person showing guilt and/or apologizing in a range of situations both serious and minor, this can help in establishing that guilt and remorse are a typical characteristic of the person being assessed.

Finally, a unique follow-up question to the stem question related to guilt and remorse is asked if the stem question is answered positively ("yes" to feeling bad or guilty). In this case, the informant or person being assessed is asked if this occurs "only if he/she gets caught doing something wrong and is going to be in trouble?" It is often helpful to follow up with the question "Can you think of a time when he/she admitted to doing something wrong that you didn't even know he/she had done and he/she would have gotten away with it if he/she hadn't told you?" (informant interview) or "Can you think of time when you admitted to doing something wrong to your parents or teacher, even if they didn't know that you had done it?" (self-report interview). In an interview we did with a child who ended up meeting criteria for the LPE specifier, the child responded to this question with, "Well no, that would be stupid." Such a response clearly implies that they only show guilt or remorse to avoid getting in trouble.

Callous–Lack of Empathy

The next item to score on the CAPE relates to a lack of empathy. This item and the questions that are provided to help gather information to score it are provided in Table 6.2. The first stem question asks directly does the person "care about other people's feelings?" and, as with all items on the CAPE, follow-up questions should focus on how the person shows this, not try to determine whether they "truly" or "genuinely" care about other people's feelings. While this first question is most directly related to the item being scored, we have found that the next two stem questions are actually more helpful for scoring this item. The next stem question asks if the person actually does things to hurt other's feelings (i.e., "Does he/she make fun of or tease others, even if hurts their feelings?"). It is important to focus on hurting others' feelings, not whether they hurt others physically. Some children may physically hurt others because they are impulsive and anger easily, not because they are callous and do not care about others' feelings. For example, in one of our assessments, the caregiver answered this question by describing their child being suspended after being in a fight at school, where the child bloodied another student's nose. They then described how the other child would not leave their son alone and their son "just lost it." By the time the child got home from school that day, he expressed feeling bad that he hurt the other child but said that "he just wanted the other child to stop being an ass." This statement would suggest that their son did feel bad about hurting the other child after he had cooled down and was no longer angry. The third stem question asks if "they do nice things for other people, even if there is nothing in it for them, like trying to cheer someone up?" The follow-up questions should focus not only on how the person does this but also whether it is done for a range of people. Some children with the LPE specifier may do nice things for a very select group of people. For example, one person we assessed was described as having a very close relationship with his grandmother and he would do nice things for her, but his caregivers stated that they "sure wished he acted that way with us and with others." Also, in the interview with the child, he was asked why he did nice things for his grandmother and he said, "Because she gives me money when I help her out."

There are two unique follow-up questions added to the interview to aid in scoring this item based on clinical work and research. First, a follow-up probe to the first stem question about caring about other people's feelings is "Do people find him/her/you cold and uncaring?" The response to this question is particularly helpful in the informant interview. When we were developing our first measure of CU traits, we would have the assessors ask caregivers of children who seemed to show the LPE specifier, "In your own words, how would you describe your child?" One of the most frequent responses was "He/she just seems so cold and callous." This common descriptor made by caregivers led to the term "CU traits" to describe the symptoms of the LPE specifier.

TABLE 6.2. Scoring the Symptom "Callous-Lack of Empathy"

Ratings (Circle)	Description
0 1 2	The person consistently disregards and is unconcerned about the feelings of others. The individual is described as cold, callous, and uncaring by others. The person appears more concerned about the effects of his or her actions on himself or herself, rather than their effects on others, even when they result in substantial harm to others. The person frequently mocks and teases other people or says things that may hurt others' feelings. The person rarely does things to try to make others feel good, like trying to cheer someone up or doing something to help someone without any possible gain from it. This callousness and lack of empathy is evident in a range of situations and it occurs with most people (i.e., it is not confined to only certain people or relationships).
Stem questions	**Follow-up questions**
Do you care about other people's feelings?	**If no:** Is this how you are most of the time and with most people? Have you been like this for a long time; that is, for at least a year? Do people find you cold and uncaring? Can you think of any time recently, say over the past month, when you showed concern about someone else's feelings?
Do you make fun of or tease others, even if it hurts their feelings?	**If yes:** Is this how you are most of the time and with most people? Have you been like this for a long time; that is, for at least a year? Do people say you are mean or cruel?
Do you do nice things for other people, even if there is nothing in it for you, like trying to cheer someone up?	**If no:** Is this how you are most of the time and with most people? Have you been like this for a long time; that is, for at least a year? Can you think of any time recently, say over the past month, when you did something nice for someone?

Note. Adapted from *Clinical Assessment of Prosocial Emotions: Version 1.1* (*CAPE Version 1.1*), by P. J. Frick, 2013, LSU, Developmental Psychopathology Lab (https://faculty.lsu.edu/pfricklab/cape.php).

Also, in our research, we found that one of most common descriptors that classmates of children with CU traits use to describe them is that they do "mean things" to others (Matlasz et al., 2022). Furthermore, in research differentiating children and adolescents with behavior problems who did and did not show the LPE specifier, we found that the aggression of those with the specifier was more likely to be described as "cruel" (Kahn et al., 2012). Thus, these descriptors (i.e., being mean or cruel) seem to be unique and specific to youth with the LPE specifier and were added to the interview to aid in scoring this item. As result, a follow-up probe to the stem question "Do you make fun of or tease others, even if it hurts their feelings?" Is the question "Do people say that you are mean or cruel?" Again, as is evident from how this question is worded, the important issue is to determine if people describe the child being assessed as mean or cruel, not necessarily whether the person being assessed accepts these labels as accurate. In one interview, the adolescent being assessed said, "Yeah, my teacher keeps telling me to quit being mean, but it's not true." When the interviewer followed up with the question, "Why don't you think it's not true?" the adolescent stated that "I just do those things to make people scared of me, so they don't mess with me." While the child denied considering himself "mean," his response reinforced his callous attitude toward hurting others.

Unconcerned About Performance

The third item to score on the CAPE relates to a lack of concern about performance in important activities. The symptom description and standard questions on the interviews to gather information needed for scoring are provided in Table 6.3. There are several important considerations that can help in scoring this item. First, it is important to determine whether the person does not care about both poor and good performance. That is, this item is designed to tap a lack of caring and concern about the expectations of others. Many children who are having difficulties at school begin to become accustomed to negative feedback and seem to become habituated to negative feedback. However, they still become very excited when they do well and are praised by others. What is often unique about children with the LPE specifier is that they generally do not care about doing well or receiving praise. So, some helpful follow-up questions to the stem question "Do you care a lot about how well you do in school, at work, or in other important activities?" can be "Have you gotten very upset if you haven't done well at school, like gotten a bad grade?" or "Have you ever been really excited and proud about something you have done well? If so, tell me about this." Many children with behavior problems would say "no" to the first question (feel bad about getting a bad grade) but "yes" to the second (excited about an accomplishment). Those with the LPE specifier are more likely to say "no" to both. Also, it is important to consider activities beyond school as well. If the responses on the interview focus largely on school, it is important to follow up with questions to see if any lack of concern extends to other areas, such as asking an informant, "Does he/she care about how well he/she does in anything else besides school?" or "Can you think of anything that he/she was really proud to have done well?"

TABLE 6.3. Scoring the Symptom "Unconcerned About Performance"

Ratings (Circle)	Description
0 1 2	The person typically shows little concern about the quality of his or her performance in most, if not all, important activities. He or she rarely, if ever, puts forth the effort necessary to perform well, even when expectations are clear. The person does not seem concerned by poor performance indicators (e.g., poor grades, poor work evaluations) or negative feedback from others about his or her performance. He or she often blames others or circumstances for his or her poor performance or minimizes the importance of performing well.
Stem questions	**Follow-up questions**
Do you care a lot about how well you do in school, at work, or in other important activities?	**If no:** Is this how you are most of the time and with most people? Have you been like this for a long time; that is, for at least a year? Can you think of any time recently, say over the past month, when you felt really bad because you didn't do something well?
Do you try your best and work hard in most things?	**If no:** Is this how you are most of the time and with most people? Have you been like this for a long time; that is, for at least a year? Do you often blame others if you don't do well in something?

Note. Adapted from *Clinical Assessment of Prosocial Emotions: Version 1.1* (*CAPE Version 1.1*), by P. J. Frick, 2013, LSU, Developmental Psychopathology Lab (https://faculty.lsu.edu/pfricklab/cape.php). Copyright 2013 by Paul J. Frick.

Another important focus to questions following the stem one related to performance in important activities is to determine how the person being assessed reacts to negative performance evaluations. As noted earlier, the important issue for scoring this symptom on the CAPE is whether the person cared about their performance. So, if the person being assessed says they received a failing grade, you can follow up with "How did you react to this?" or "How did this make you feel?" People with the LPE specifier often describe not caring about this failure or it "not being a big deal." In one interview we observed, the interviewer asked the child, "Were your parents upset that you got an F on the test?" and the child responded, "Yeah, they care about stupid things like that." Another common response to consider when scoring this item is whether the person blames others for their poor performance. That is, people with LPE are more likely to attribute their poor performance to other people (e.g., a mean teacher, an incompetent coach or teammates) and not their own fault.

A final consideration in scoring this item is the importance of focusing on the effort put forth by the child, not the outcome. That is why the second stem question for the interview is very important for scoring this item: "Does he/she try his/her best and work hard in most things?" We observed an interview in which a caregiver answered the question about whether their child cared how well he did in school by saying, "Yes, he gets straight As." The interviewer then followed up with "Does he seem proud of this and does he brag to others about how well he does in school?" to try to determine if he cared about doing well. The interviewer also asked, "Does he study hard for his grades?" The caregiver responded, "Absolutely not; he doesn't study at all. He is just really smart, and it makes his sister so mad that he doesn't have to work at it." In another interview, the child was described by his caregivers as not caring about how well he did in school and the interviewer asked, "How about things outside of school?" The caregiver responded that "he was really good at soccer," to which the interviewer asked, "Does he work hard and practice at it?" The caregiver then responded, "Not at all; he's just really good. In fact, his last coach threatened to kick him off the team because he kept missing practice but never followed through because he is the best player on the team." When the child was asked about this, he described himself as being really good at soccer and that "he liked being good," but also admitted that he did not really work at it. He also described usually being on good teams, except for one year when he was "on a team with a bunch of losers who couldn't walk and chew gum at the same time." All of this led the interviewer to conclude that, while the child was really good at soccer, there was no evidence that he put great effort into it and he often blamed others for poor performance.

Shallow or Deficient Affect

The final symptom to be scored on the CAPE relates to shallow or deficient affect, with the symptom description and standard interview questions provided in Table 6.4. The most important consideration in scoring this item is to focus on whether the person shows emotions openly to others and not whether the person actually experiences emotions. A very common way that caregivers describe children with the LPE specifier is that "I just never can tell exactly how he is feeling." It is very important for the interviewer to be sure that the child is actually showing emotions and that the caregiver is not making an assumption about their child's emotions. For example, in an interview we observed, the caregiver answered the question, "Does Johnny show his feelings and emotions to others?" as a "yes." The interviewer followed up with the question, "Can you give me some examples of this?" The caregiver then stated that "Johnny seems unemotional on the outside but I can tell they are in there" and "I am the only one who can see this in Johnny because he doesn't show emotions the way other people do." These follow-up questions made clear that Johnny was not showing emotions openly but his caregiver was attributing emotions to him. In general, a helpful follow-up question when asking about a child's emotions is to ask "Is it easy for you *and* others to know how he/she is feeling?" Focusing on how easy it is to know what the child is feeling is helpful because this focuses on their expression of the emotion and not on whether the child actually feels the emotion.

TABLE 6.4. Scoring the Symptom "Shallow or Deficient Affect"

Ratings (Circle)	Description
0 **1** **2**	The person rarely, if ever, expresses strong feelings or intense emotions to others, except in ways that seem shallow, insincere, or superficial (e.g., actions contradict the emotion displayed; can turn emotions "on" or "off" quickly). When the person describes a distressing event (e.g., an animal or person getting hurt or dying; someone losing a job), it is without showing emotions appropriate to the situation. When the individual shows intense emotional expressions they are typically used for gain such as to manipulate (e.g., get out of a punishment) or intimidate (e.g., scare someone into doing what he or she wants) others.

Stem questions	Follow-up questions
Do you show your feelings and emotions openly to others?	**If no:** Is this how you are most of the time and with most people? Have you been like this for a long time; that is, for at least a year? Can you think of any time recently, say over the past month, when you have shown a lot of emotion? **If yes:** Do you only show emotions when you get in trouble or when you don't get your way? Do others think your feelings and emotions are fake and insincere?
When something bad happens to someone, do you get upset?	**If no:** Is this how you are most of the time and with most people? Have you been like this for a long time; that is, for at least a year? Can you think of any time recently, say over the past month, when something bad happened to someone and you got upset?

Note. Adapted from *Clinical Assessment of Prosocial Emotions: Version 1.1* (*CAPE Version 1.1*), by P. J. Frick, 2013, LSU, Developmental Psychopathology Lab (https://faculty.lsu.edu/pfricklab/cape.php). Copyright 2013 by Paul J. Frick.

The other important consideration in scoring this item is that persons with the LPE specifier can show emotions, even strong emotions, in certain situations. For example, a standard follow-up question on the informant interview is "Does he/she only show emotions when he/she gets in trouble or doesn't get his/her way?" However, the scoring of the item should focus on whether the person typically shows emotions, even if they have emotional outbursts in certain situations, usually when things have not gone the way they want. For example, we observed an interview where a caregiver had previously described a very serious angry outburst in which the child being assessed hurt another child at school. Yet, the caregiver answered the question about showing feelings and emotions with "no." The interviewer asked for clarification about these two answers: "Earlier, you described Noah as losing it on another child. I am trying to put this answer together with your description of him as not showing emotions." They responded, "Oh, I thought you meant about his emotions most of the time. Most of the time you can't tell how he is feeling, but if he thinks something is unfair to him or he feels that someone has disrespected him, he will lose it."

Another important consideration in scoring this item is whether or not the person shows emotions that seem fake and insincere to others. In fact, a standard follow-up question in CAPE interviews asks about this specifically (see Table 6.4). A helpful way to follow up on these questions about emotions is to ask if the person can "turn on or off their emotions quickly" or if the person has "ever shown emotions that seem inappropriate to the situation." We observed an interview where the caregiver was describing the death of a family dog, where most of the members of the family were very upset, but the person being assessed seemed excited and asked, "When can we get a new dog?" Another helpful consideration in determining if any emotions are solely self-serving are responses to the second stem question on the CAPE interview that asks "When something bad happens to someone, does he/she get upset?" What is critical here is to determine whether the event had no impact at all on the person being assessed, but they still seemed to feel bad about it. For example, in an interview we observed, a caregiver described their child as being upset about a neighbor dying. However, when discussing this, the caregiver said, "I think this was just because the neighbor used let her drive his tractor around their property." The interviewer followed up with the question, "Can you think of a time when the child was upset like that but there wasn't anything in it for her?" and the caregiver was unable to provide such an example.

INTEGRATING CAPE RESULTS INTO BROADER ASSESSMENT OF CONDUCT PROBLEMS

By providing a comprehensive clinical assessment of the symptoms of the LPE, the CAPE overcomes many of the limitations of other methods used to assess the LPE specifier. However, as with the results of any single assessment instrument, it should only be used as part of a broader clinical assessment. Specifically, diagnosis of the LPE specifier can only be made when a person also shows serious conduct problems and meets diagnostic criteria for either ODD or CD. Further, it can only add to understanding the person's conduct problems when it is integrated with the broader assessment of conduct problems outlined in Chapter 4. For example, while elevated CU traits are associated with more aggression toward others, children with the LPE specifier can still vary greatly on the severity of their behavior problems and this can determine how intensive of an intervention they may require. Similarly, the presence of attention-deficit/hyperactivity disorder (ADHD) as a comorbidity may warrant treatment recommendations to determine if a trial of stimulant medication is indicated, given research evidence that it improves outcomes for children with ADHD, even when significant levels of CU traits are present (Blader et al., 2013). Similarly, the treatment we outline in the remaining chapters of this book often requires substantial parental involvement; as a result, the assessment of potential familial risk factors that may be related to the person's conduct problems is also important for tailoring intervention. As we noted in previous chapters, CU traits often lead to reductions in warmth in the caregiver–child relationship, which can, in turn, increase conduct problems and CU traits in the child. Information about parenting style and caregiver–child relationship quality would therefore be important for identifying important treatment targets.

As noted previously, the CAPE should not be scored based on the potential causes of the person's behavior problems or the causes of the LPE specifier. However, potential causes can be helpful in informing treatment recommendations. As noted in Chapter 3, some children with the LPE specifier have histories of significant trauma, including child abuse, neglect, or exposure to violence. These children often show the most severe levels of conduct problems and aggression. Such people may need treatment tailored to this presentation by including components that focus on helping them cope with their trauma histories.

CHAPTER SUMMARY

In short, assessment of the LPE specifier is important to clinical decision-making to help tailor treatment for children with serious conduct problems. The CAPE provides one of the most comprehensive tools for assessing the symptoms of the LPE specifier. The CAPE is unique in having content that was designed specifically to assess the criteria for the LPE specifier and the emerging research on its reliability and validity support its cautious use in clinical assessments.

There are a few critical considerations to ensure that the CAPE is used appropriately:

1. **Qualified administration:** The CAPE should only be used for clinical purposes by experienced clinicians who meet the required qualifications. This includes being appropriately trained in its administration.
2. **Continued research monitoring:** As the CAPE is in its early stages of development, users should stay informed of emerging research on it. This is essential to determining if changes in administration are warranted, based on research findings.
3. **Avoiding harmful labels:** CAPE users should recognize the potential harmful effects of labels that we discussed in Chapter 4. The CAPE should never be used to assign highly pejorative labels like "psychopath" or "predator."

4. **Enhancing access to treatment:** CAPE ratings should facilitate people's access to appropriate treatment for their behavior problems and should never be used to restrict access to services.

A final consideration in using the CAPE is that it is expensive and time consuming to administer. It requires a high level of training to administer and score the CAPE. Also, it is very time intensive to administer, often taking 45 minutes to an hour to administer and score. These characteristics of the CAPE could limit its usefulness in some clinical settings. As a result, it will be important to test other potentially less time-intensive methods for assessing the LPE specifier (see, e.g., Walker et al., 2021) and compare their validity relative to diagnoses made by the CAPE. Also, the administrative burden suggests that, in most clinical settings, the CAPE could only be administered to a limited number of clients. One possibility suggested by Goetz et al. (2024) is to use rating scales, like the ICU, as an initial screening. The CAPE would then only be administered when a possible LPE diagnosis is likely based on scores from the rating scales. This would substantially limit the number of youths who require the CAPE and, as a result, the number of clinicians needed to administer it. Such a multiple-gating diagnostic procedure has not been tested but doing so should be an important focus of clinical research to determine how to use the CAPE most cost-effectively.

III

TREATING CHILDREN AND ADOLESCENTS WITH LIMITED PROSOCIAL EMOTIONS

7

An Overview of Treatments That Work for Children and Adolescents With Limited Prosocial Emotions

The next four chapters focus on treating children and adolescents who show serious conduct problems with the limited prosocial emotions (LPE) specifier. In this chapter, we provide an overview of the available treatments that have been tested for children with elevated callous–unemotional (CU) traits, focusing on what has proven to be most effective in these interventions. This literature converges in finding that many existing evidence-based treatments do effectively reduce the conduct problems and improve the prosocial emotions of youth with elevated CU traits. However, it also indicates that children and adolescents with the LPE specifier (a) often start treatment with more serious conduct problems than youth low on CU traits; and (b) despite improving with treatment, still show conduct problems that are severe, at clinically significant levels, and exceed diagnostic thresholds after treatment ends (Perlstein et al., 2023).

This state of treatment research provides an important context for our approach to the clinical management of children and adolescents with the LPE specifier. Specifically, it makes clear that children with elevated CU traits are not "untreatable"; they do respond to many treatments. Also, given that many treatments have been somewhat successful in reducing conduct problems and CU traits in youth with the LPE specifier, these treatments should not be entirely abandoned. However, the fact that children with the LPE specifier do end treatment with clinically significant behavior problems also suggests that these treatments need to be improved. Our approach has been to refine treatments based on research—both our own and that of others—examining

https://doi.org/10.1037/0000500-008
A Clinical Guide to Working With Youth With Conduct Disorders and Limited Prosocial Emotions, by P. J. Frick and E. R. Kimonis

the unique emotional, cognitive, and social characteristics of youth with elevated CU traits. We focus on modifying treatments to directly address these characteristics. In short, our treatment approach combines research on children and adolescents with the LPE specifier, as discussed in earlier chapters, with research on existing effective treatments for serious conduct problems. This integration allows us to develop a treatment approach that is more tailored to the specific needs of those with the LPE specifier. In addition to discussing effective treatments, this chapter also briefly touches on treatments with no or limited efficacy for treating youth with the LPE specifier.

Several reviews of controlled treatment outcome studies identify that the following treatments have proven effective for treating children with serious conduct problems (see Kaminski & Claussen, 2017; McCart & Sheidow, 2016, for further discussions):

- parent management training (PMT),
- cognitive behavioral interventions, and
- multimodal treatments that use various modalities to target multiple risk factors.

Of these treatments for child conduct problems, PMT, sometimes also called "behavioral parent training" or "parent training," is arguably the most extensively studied. Findings from systematic reviews and meta-analyses support the efficacy of PMT for preschool- and elementary school–aged children for improving child conduct problems and for improving other parent or family outcomes (Beelmann et al., 2023; Comer et al., 2013; van Aar et al., 2017). Consequently, PMT has been recommended as the first-line treatment for children aged 11 years and younger with conduct problems (National Institute for Health and Care Excellence, 2017; Sheidow et al., 2022).

PARENT MANAGEMENT TRAINING

PMT works by teaching caregivers strategies to alter their child's behavior in the home. These strategies address antecedents to problem behaviors (e.g., preventing attention-seeking behaviors by providing regular, high-quality caregiver–child interaction, often known as "special play"; using descriptive praise to positively reinforce desirable child behavior; providing clear and explicit rules, expectations, and instructions), teach replacement behaviors (e.g., modeling and reinforcing use of appropriate or prosocial behaviors in place of antisocial behaviors to get needs met), and change parental responses or consequences to these behaviors by implementing structured contingency management programs (Kazdin, 2005). Caregivers learn how to implement predictable limit-setting strategies, including providing immediate, consistent, calm, and nonforceful consequences (e.g., time out for noncompliance, aggression, and destruction) to extinguish learned problematic child behaviors to prevent their recurrence. Changing both positive and negative parenting behavior is expected to produce positive change in child behavior, a process that is supported by numerous studies (Fagan & Benedini, 2016; Forehand et al., 2014; Mestre et al., 2022).

PMT techniques and principles are grounded in social learning theory and operant learning theory, which are integrated in Patterson's (1982, 2016) coercion model for explaining how conduct problems develop and are maintained. Patterson suggests that childhood conduct problems are primarily maintained by coercive interactional cycles between the parent and child. Figure 7.1 illustrates how a caregiver places a demand on the child ("Turn off the iPad. It's time for dinner"), to which the child responds with problematic behavior (e.g., whining, pleading for more time) and to get out of the directive. The caregiver persists with their request, becoming increasingly louder and issuing threats in response to the child's continued noncompliance ("Turn off the iPad *now* or you won't get to use it anymore!"). The child responds by

FIGURE 7.1. Illustrating the Parent-Child Coercive Cycle

Note. Figure created by Hana Kinoshita Thomson. Used with permission.

escalating their own negative behavior (e.g., screaming, throwing items around them, hitting the parent). These behaviors may function to get the child out of the directive and/or to get the desired goal of more iPad time. The parent withdraws their request, and the child continues using the iPad, resulting in positive reinforcement of their problematic behaviors (i.e., verbal and physical aggression, destruction) that increases the child's likelihood of behaving similarly in the future when the caregiver issues demands. The caregiver's response is also negatively reinforcing to the child because the unpleasant and aversive parental demand is withdrawn. Simultaneously, the caregiver's withdrawal behavior is negatively reinforced because the child's unpleasant, coercive behaviors end, leading the parent to be more likely to withdraw demands of the child that produce similar aversive behaviors in the future. These sorts of negative reinforcement traps occur repeatedly during the caregiver–child interactions of children with conduct problems and often carry over to future relationships, such as between children and their teachers at school. A key goal of PMT is to break these coercive caregiver–child cycles.

A range of parent training programs have been manualized and disseminated, most of which are grounded in operant and social learning principles. Some interventions emerged directly from Patterson's coercion model and the broader Social Interaction Learning framework developed at the Oregon Social Learning Center (e.g., Parent Management Training—Oregon Model [PMTO]; Forgatch & DeGarmo, 1999). In parallel, Constance Hanf's two-stage intervention, developed at Oregon Health Sciences University (Hanf, 1969), later informed programs such as Parent–Child Interaction Therapy (PCIT; Eyberg & Funderburk, 2011; https://www.pcit.org/); The Incredible Years: Early Childhood BASIC Parent Training Program (Webster-Stratton, 2011; https://www.incredibleyears.com/); Helping the Noncompliant Child (HNC; McMahon & Forehand, 2019); and Barkley's Defiant Children program (Barkley, 2013). Other widely implemented PMT models sharing similar behavioral roots include Kazdin's Parent Management Training program (Kazdin, 2005; https://alankazdin.com/) and the Triple P–Positive Parenting Program (Sanders, 1999; https://www.triplep.net/).

Programs vary in their length (less than 10 to more than 20 sessions); whether they are delivered in a self-administered, group, or individual format; and whether they include caregivers only or the caregiver–child dyad in treatment. Most PMT programs begin by strengthening the caregiver–child relationship before introducing behavior management strategies. However, the scope and depth of this initial phase vary widely across programs. This two-step approach is based on the premise that a strong relationship between caregiver and child serves as a foundation for and enhances the effectiveness of behavior management techniques. Research supports this integrated model, showing that treatments that incorporate relationship building alongside behavior management, and also those that actively involve the child in treatment, produce larger effect sizes than those that do not (Baumel et al., 2021; Florean et al., 2020; Kaminski et al., 2008; Leijten et al., 2018).

PMT programs also differ in whether they employ in vivo coaching, where parents receive real-time guidance on implementing skills taught in the intervention. Some programs provide direct live coaching to enhance skill acquisition and application, while others rely solely on didactic instruction or role-playing. For example, PCIT involves therapists observing a parent–child dyad from behind a one-way mirror (or via a webcam when delivered through the internet) and providing the parent with immediate feedback in real-time via a parent-worn wireless bug-in-ear device to facilitate their learning and proper use of intervention strategies. Similarly, another Hanf-based PMT program, Helping the Noncompliant Child, involves the therapist providing the parent with in-session feedback on their use of skills with the child (McMahon & Forehand, 2019). Critically, this appears to be an important moderator of treatment effectiveness, with interventions involving in vivo coaching producing the greatest improvements in child and parent behavior (Kaminski et al., 2008). As we note later, in vivo coaching may be particularly important when using PMT approaches to treat children with the LPE specifier.

Although PMT is identified as the most efficacious and effective treatment for child conduct problems, it does not work for a lot of children. Estimates suggest that one third to one half of treated cases do not complete treatment, fail to benefit from it, or do not sustain improvements over time and across settings (Beauchaine et al., 2005; Chacko et al., 2016; Sheldrick et al., 2001). These findings have prompted interest in identifying whether certain children and families are systematically less likely than others to benefit from PMT. Identification of treatment moderators clarifies for whom and under what conditions treatment works (Kraemer et al., 2002). Across research findings, there is a great deal of inconsistency, but factors more consistently linked with better PMT outcomes include younger child age, more severe pretreatment conduct problems, and a positive pretreatment parent–child relationship, whereas a combination of high parental stress and parental psychopathology consistently predict poorer treatment outcomes (Baumel et al., 2021; Dedousis-Wallace et al., 2021; Lavigne et al., 2008).

As noted previously, although children with elevated CU traits do respond to treatment with improved behavior, they often end treatments with more severe conduct problems than other children (Perlstein et al., 2023). This pattern has also been found specifically in studies of PMT outcomes. Overall, these studies find that children with conduct problems and elevated CU traits start and end PMT with more severe conduct problems than children low on CU traits (Perlstein et al., 2023). Some studies also find higher dropout rates among families of children high on CU traits receiving PMT (Dadds, Cauchi et al., 2012; Kimonis et al., 2014). An early study investigating the impact of children's CU traits on treatment outcomes examined whether CU traits moderated changes in conduct problems. The study included 49 parents of boys aged 4 to 8 years (*M* age = 6.29 years) diagnosed with oppositional defiant disorder (ODD) or conduct disorder (CD) who participated in a 9-week PMT program at two Australian university–based psychology clinics (Hawes & Dadds, 2005). This study found that boys with higher CU traits at pretreatment were most likely to be rediagnosed with ODD at a 6-month posttreatment follow-up, independent of treatment dose, parents' implementation of treatment components, socioeconomic status, child age, and pretreatment ODD severity. Several studies conducted since Hawes and Dadds (2005) have similarly found that PMT is less likely to normalize the conduct problems of children with elevated CU traits (see Perlstein et al., 2023, for a review). The negative impact of CU traits on clinical outcomes of PMT also extends beyond conduct problems. That is, CU traits also predict poorer posttreatment child outcomes, including more attention problems, fewer social skills, higher rates of depression and loneliness, and poorer therapist-rated therapeutic success in children treated for conduct problems (Bjørnebekk & Kjøbli, 2017; Högström et al., 2013).

This link between CU traits and inferior treatment outcomes is evident across "brands" of PMT programs, including but not limited to the PMTO (Bjørnebekk & Kjøbli, 2017; Ogden et al., 2005), PCIT (Kimonis et al., 2014; Neo et al., 2023), Integrated Family Intervention (Dadds & Hawes, 2006), Project Support (Jouriles et al., 2001), Hitkashrut (Hebrew word for "attachment"; Somech & Elizur, 2012), and internet-based COmmunication METhod (iCOMET; Högström et al., 2013). As one example of this moderation effect, we conducted a study in which we tested whether CU traits modified treatment effects for PCIT using secondary data from two existing data sets (Bagner & Eyberg, 2007; Bagner et al., 2010) comprising 63 families of young children with conduct problems (*M* age = 46.48 months, 73% boys), with or at risk for developmental delay (IQ < 75 or premature birth < 37 weeks gestation, respectively; Kimonis et al., 2014). Our results showed that children with higher pretreatment CU traits had higher post-PCIT conduct problems, and across samples they were significantly more likely to drop out of treatment. Importantly, the inferior treatment outcomes for youth with elevated CU traits occurs cross-nationally (i.e., for children in the United States, Australia, Norway, Sweden, Israel); is not explained by the greater severity of conduct problems for children with CU traits; and is not explained by comorbid attention-deficit/hyperactivity disorder (ADHD), anxiety, or autism spectrum disorder (ASD) symptoms (Hawes & Dadds, 2005; Hawes et al., 2013).

Beyond conduct problem outcomes, several studies have investigated whether PMT improves the child's CU traits themselves. In a meta-analytic review of treatment studies of children and adolescents with elevated CU traits, treatments overall did not have an appreciable effect on levels of CU traits. However, of the broad range of treatments investigated, PMT was one of the few to show at least some effectiveness in reducing levels of CU traits, albeit with relatively small effect sizes (Perlstein et al., 2023). Other research suggests that only a subset of treated children with elevated CU traits show a reduction in their levels of CU traits. For example, Hawes and Dadds (2007) found that, out of the 49 boys with ODD who received PMT, 10 boys showed unstable CU traits and 13 boys showed stable high CU traits across treatment. That is, less than half of the boys with high pretreatment CU traits showed marked reductions in these traits with treatment. Boys in the stable high CU group had the most severe conduct problems at follow-up, irrespective of pretreatment conduct problem severity, but this was not because of their parents more poorly or less frequently implementing behavior management strategies.

While modest, the effectiveness of PMT for reducing CU traits may be because of its targeting of dysfunctional harsh or coercive and inconsistent parent–child interactions that research finds maintain and increase children's CU traits over time (McDonald et al., 2011). In a randomized controlled trial of 66 mothers of 4- to 9-year-old children recruited from domestic violence shelters, McDonald et al. (2011) found that children randomized to receive PMT showed greater and more rapid reductions in their CU traits from baseline to an 8-month follow-up, relative to a services-as-usual comparison group, and beyond the effects of the intervention on conduct problem severity. In contrast, the services-as-usual group showed no significant change across the active intervention period, and over the follow-up period, their CU traits worsened (see also Somech & Elizur, 2012). Follow-up mediation analyses indicated that the reductions in CU traits were partially due to reductions in mothers' use of harsh or coercive and inconsistent parenting (see also Elizur et al., 2017). Increasing parental consistency and reducing parental physical and verbal aggression (e.g., shouting, threatening, grabbing, hitting) toward the child appear to be important treatment targets for reducing CU traits (Perlstein et al., 2023).

One feature of PMT that has emerged as being especially important for improving outcomes for children with elevated CU traits is higher treatment dose or intensity. Notably, the "Project Support" parenting intervention provided in McDonald et al. (2011), which produced large within-group effect sizes in reducing CU traits (baseline to posttreatment: Cohen's $d = 0.95$; baseline to 8-month follow-up $d = 0.89$) relative to medium effect sizes reported in other treatment studies, was intensive ($M = 20$ sessions, $SD = 9$) sessions. It also provided mothers exposed to physical intimate partner violence with an adjunctive supportive intervention (i.e., emotional support, providing referrals to address current needs, delivering donated goods; Hawes & Dadds, 2005; Kolko et al., 2009). Higher treatment intensity may be especially important for shifting coercive exchanges between parent–child dyads when child CU traits are high. When intervening with children with CU traits, these findings indicate that those with clinically significant conduct problems require more intensive PMT programs.

In summary, research conducted with samples of children with conduct problems and varying levels of CU traits demonstrates that children with higher CU traits benefit from PMT, especially if it is administered with a high degree of intensity, but they fall short of typical gains achieved by other children with severe behavior problems. A key explanation for why PMT is not as effective at reducing conduct problems to within normal limits for children with higher CU traits is that these treatments were founded on theoretical principles that explain the conduct problems of children low on CU traits. That is, PMT programs often do not explicitly address those risk factors and processes that are uniquely involved in the development and maintenance of conduct problems for those with the LPE specifier. While PMT works by altering harsh and coercive parent-child cycles through structured parent-implemented behavioral strategies, targeting these processes may be insufficient for children with

CU traits who develop their conduct problems for different reasons, as we discussed in Chapter 3.

Making Parent Management Training More Effective for Children and Adolescents With the Limited Prosocial Emotions Specifier

Although PMT does not typically normalize the conduct problems of children with the LPE specifier, researchers have identified some ways in which it can be tailored to be more effective. We review some of those adaptations next, which include individualized coaching of parents to consistently implement time-out with the child, modifying the time-out procedure to have more meaningful consequences for children with CU traits, increasing the use of rewards to incentivize positive behaviors, and encouraging parents to be warmer and more responsive during interactions with their child to strengthen their bond.

Improving the Use of Time-Out

Some of the core strategies used in PMT to shift dysfunctional parent–child interactions may also be undermined by characteristics of children with elevated CU traits. That is, "time-out" is a core limit-setting behavior management strategy used in most PMT models as a consequence to modify problematic child behavior. Time-out involves withdrawing attention from the child for misbehavior, such as noncompliance with directives, aggression, or destruction, by briefly placing them in a time-out chair and removing all verbal and nonverbal attention during the time-out period. From an operant learning framework, this removal of attention is a form of negative punishment that serves to extinguish the problematic child behavior. However, as detailed in Chapter 3, individuals with CU traits often do not respond in typical ways to many forms of punishment. Anecdotally, many of the parents who come to our clinics for treatment tell us that their child with CU traits does not seem to change their behavior with any form of discipline. This insensitivity to punishment can interfere with the child developing conditioned associations between wrongdoing and its consequences, such as time-out. To illustrate this, research has shown that children with conduct problems and elevated CU traits display less emotional reactivity while in time-out, suggesting that they do not experience this form of punishment as aversive. For example, in Hawes and Dadds's (2005) treatment trial of 4- to 8-year-old boys with conduct problems receiving PMT ($N = 49$), those with higher CU traits were less responsive to time-out. At posttreatment and follow-up, these boys reacted with less negative emotion (i.e., sadness, anger, fear) and more neutral emotions during time-out, after controlling for their conduct problem severity and observed differences between parents in their implementation of time-out. In this same sample, parents also rated time-out as significantly less effective when their child was higher on CU traits (Hawes & Dadds, 2007). Similarly, a small pilot study observed the emotional responses to time-out of 7- to 11-year-olds ($N = 11$, 1 female) with conduct problems, elevated CU traits, and comorbid ADHD receiving behavioral therapy in a summer treatment program (STP; Pelham & Hoza, 1996). Counselors were more likely to rate children with elevated CU traits as "calm" or "unemotional" when they were first placed in time-out and also during the time-out procedure (Bansal et al., 2020).

Some studies also find that children with CU traits escalate their problematic behavior while in time-out, which may undermine parent's ability or willingness to consistently implement this discipline strategy. For example, in another study of 190 young children with conduct problems (*M* age = 4.92 years, 76% boys, 66% with comorbid ADHD) receiving the 8-week STPs, counselors observed that children higher on CU traits received more time-outs because of problematic behavior and spent longer in time-out in the later stages of treatment, controlling for initial levels of conduct problems and ADHD symptom severity (Garcia et al., 2018). Time-out is longer when the child misbehaves during the procedure, since many programs require the child to be calm and quiet before they can get out of the time-out chair. In yet another study of the STP using a mixed-sex sample of 7- to 12-year-old children ($N = 51$) with conduct problems and ADHD, counselors observed children with higher CU traits to engage in more aggressive and destructive behaviors while in time-out, after controlling for conduct problem severity (Haas et al., 2011). Other studies involving parents in PMT administering time-out have failed to find this increased escalation of behavior for children with CU traits (Kimonis et al., 2024). However, it is possible that, in the summer camp context, time-out had a less punishing impact for children with CU traits as they may have been simultaneously rewarded for their manipulative, destructive, and aggressive behavior in time-out by gaining social influence with their onlooking peers. Taken together, this research suggests that children with CU traits experience time-out as less aversive, and, in some cases, escalate their antisocial behavior (Dadds & Salmon, 2003). When this occurs, it may lead parents to prematurely abandon attempts at using time-out, reduce their likelihood of using it as a discipline strategy again in the future, and lead to perceptions that time out is ineffective.

As a result of these characteristics of children with CU traits, teaching time-out in the context of PMT programs that use in vivo coaching of parents to implement behavior management techniques with the child in treatment may be especially important for children with CU traits. We conducted a study using PCIT, which involves using in vivo coaching (i.e., therapist line feeding a standardized time-out script) of caregivers to administer a time-out procedure via a parent-worn bug-in-ear device. The study involved 87 families of mixed-sex 2- to 7-year-old children with conduct problems (*M* age = 4.88 years, *SD* = 1.32, 78% boys). Consistent with other research, we observed that children with CU traits initially responded to time-out for noncompliance with more calm and neutral emotion and less negative emotion than children without CU traits (Kimonis et al., 2024). However, for the remainder of the child's time-out period, we did not observe this attenuated emotional response in children with CU traits, suggesting that they may experience time-out as increasingly aversive the longer they are removed from parental reinforcement and not in control of when they can return to play. During extended time-out periods, the lack of external stimulation may become aversive for children with CU traits who are high in boredom susceptibility (Fanti et al., 2013). In our study, PCIT therapists were also trained to ensure that the child sat in time-out for the full 3 minutes and 5-seconds quiet, calm period required before they can return to play, as outlined in the PCIT protocol (Eyberg & Funderburk, 2011). Importantly, by the fourth PCIT session in which caregivers received in vivo coaching to implement time-out, only a minority of children (n =17) continued to go to time-out for noncompliance, although a greater proportion of them had high CU traits. These findings suggest that when implemented in this PCIT context using intensive in vivo coaching of parents with the child in treatment, time-out was an effective disciplinary strategy, even for most children with CU traits.

The importance of enhanced methods of observing and coaching for children with CU traits is also supported by a study by Parent and colleagues (2023). The authors compared the effects of a standard PMT program (HNC) with a technology-enhanced version of HNC in a sample of 101 low-income families with children aged 3 to 8 years with clinically significant conduct problems. The enhancement used a mobile app that video recorded caregivers' skill use during homework practice for therapists to review and provide feedback; provided caregivers with automated feedback on their skill use; enabled a video call midweek to reinforce caregivers' practice of skills and problem solve issues in implementation; and reminded them about weekly sessions, midweek calls, and skills practice. Results showed that children with CU traits had poorer treatment outcomes (i.e., higher child noncompliance and lower positive parenting), but only in the standard treatment condition. In the technology-enhanced condition, children with CU traits did just as well as other children. These results further support the need for more individualized coaching for families of children with CU traits. They also provide promising evidence that this need could be achieved using technology enhanced intervention. This hybrid intervention format has the potential to extend the reach of effective PMT implementation to economically distressed families, such as those participating in the Parent et al. (2023) study, as we discuss further in Chapter 10.

One hypothesis offered for the differences in punishment learning seen in individuals with CU traits across PMT approaches is that they have a wider "learning window" than other children (Moul et al., 2021). A key aim of most PMT programs is to increase parental consistency and predictability in delivering consequences for noncompliant child behavior. Thus, extensive therapist-supported in-clinic coaching sessions with the child, as well as regular structured between-session home practice to facilitate parent's consistent delivery of the scripted time-out procedure, may be necessary in PMT to provide ample opportunities for children with CU traits to learn the necessary contingencies. Other research suggests that deficits in learning punishment associations seen in punishment insensitive individuals can be overcome by supplying them with information about how their behavior relates to punishment, but this relies on consistent delivery of punishing consequences for problematic behavior (Jean-Richard-dit-Bressel et al., 2023). This means that, for children with CU traits, an important part of a PMT approach is to use a time-out script with a standardized explanation provided to the child that they must sit in time-out because they did not do what they were told (acted aggressively/destructively), providing an informational frame for them to appropriately interpret the consequences they are experiencing (i.e., that their behavior was the cause). For example, in PCIT, parents are coached to tell the child "You didn't do what I told you to do, so you have to sit in the time-out chair" when the child does not comply with the parent's command.

In summary, the characteristics of children with CU traits undermine core behavior management strategies used in PMT (i.e., time-out). This may be overcome by using in vivo individualized coaching of parents to consistently implement these strategies and by using a time-out script designed to support these children's learning that their behavior was the cause of the punishing consequence. Another approach for increasing the effectiveness of PMT for children with CU traits is to use reward-based behavior management strategies.

Increasing the Use of Reward-Based Behavior Management

Research finds that children with the LPE specifier respond well to reward-based behavior management strategies. For example, while parents of children with conduct problems receiving PMT rated the punishing time-out procedure as less effective when their child had elevated CU traits, they rated reward as equally effective for children with and without CU traits (Hawes & Dadds, 2005). This finding aligns with research we reviewed in Chapter 3 showing that children with CU traits tend to overly focus on the potential for reward, such as having difficulty inhibiting a response that was previously rewarded when that same response is subsequently punished. Additional support for the potential benefits of reward-oriented behavior management strategies for treating children with CU traits comes from a series of studies conducted by Waschbusch and colleagues as part of the STP program described earlier. The STP delivered several behavioral management strategies by trained counselors that included reinforcement using social reinforcers and a comprehensive point system, daily report cards, time-out, and social skills training over an 8-week period. Overall, results from this intervention for children with CU traits were similar to other interventions. That is, the 7- to 12-year-old children with conduct problems and elevated CU traits showed the largest pre- to posttreatment change (Bansal et al., 2019) but still ended treatment with the most severe conduct problems (Haas et al., 2011; Waschbusch, Carrey, et al., 2007).

Miller et al. (2014) compared behavioral management strategies administered during the STP that de-emphasized punishment, emphasized reward techniques, or combined treatment that minimized punishment and maximized rewards against a standard behavior therapy condition. Using a within-person design and single-case research methods with a sample of 11 children with conduct problems and CU traits, they found that the low-punishment condition produced the best treatment responses in terms of the reduction in conduct problems, whereas the combined condition produced the worst. However, children varied substantially in their treatment responses to the various conditions. The authors concluded that the optimal approach to behavior modification for children with CU traits may involve a combination of shaping positive behavior using reward-based strategies tailored to the child's self-interests and minimizing punishment by responding to problematic behavior with planned ignoring where possible or applying punishing consequences only for behaviors that cannot be ignored. This research group later conducted an extended study of 46 children (*M* age = 9.3 years, *SD* = 1.4) attending the STP with conduct problems who were oversampled to be high on CU traits. They found immediately and consistently delivering consequences for misbehavior appeared to be as important or more important than the relative effectiveness of rewards and punishment for children with CU traits (Waschbusch et al., 2020).

Most PMT programs work with parents of children with conduct problems to use both reward-oriented and punishment-oriented behavioral management strategies consistently. For example, Kazdin's (2005) PMT program teaches parents how to increase positive child behaviors using selective attention to (e.g., parent signals of approval such as a smile, thumbs up) and verbal praise of these behaviors, in addition to rewarding them using a point incentive chart collaboratively developed by the therapist and parent. The child can trade in the tokens they earn from this points system for more valuable tangible items (e.g., toys, preferred foods) and for privileges or preferred activities (e.g., tablet time, going to the movies, choosing what to eat for dinner). The target child behaviors that parents reward with tokens, their value in points, and the menu of reinforcers are determined by therapist and parents, and, in some cases, with older children. They also consider the child's current interests or preferences and the level of difficulty for the child to achieve behavior targets. Kazdin's PMT program also teaches parents how to reduce minor misbehavior using praise of positive opposite behaviors (e.g., complimenting the child politely asking after they aggressively demand something from the parent) paired with consistent planned ignoring. For more serious problem behaviors, punishing behavior modification strategies are used (i.e., time-out, privilege removal, assigning low-rate chores—those that occur infrequently, require effort, and are not yet part of the child's routine, such as folding laundry, setting the table, taking out the garbage).

In sum, the research outlined in this section highlights that children with the LPE specifier respond equally well to reward-based strategies as other children with conduct problems, and that effective behavior change rests on parents immediately and consistently responding to positive child behavior with reinforcement and negative child behavior with punishment.

Increasing Parental Warmth to Improve the Parent–Child Relationship

When using disciplinary strategies such as time-out or planned ignoring as a punishing consequence for child misbehavior, another important consideration for children high on CU traits is "time-in." Time-in refers to the typical interactive environment from which the child is removed during a time-out. Time-in environments with high levels of engaging activities and positive reinforcement provide a more pronounced contrast against time-out. This means that the child experiences greater costs for choosing to engage in antisocial over more prosocial alternative behaviors. As noted in Chapter 3, children and adolescents with CU traits often have parent–child relationships characterized by lower levels of warmth. This lower level of warmth seems to be (a) quite important for maintaining the child's elevated levels of CU traits and (b) highly related to the conduct problems of children with CU traits. As we explain in this chapter, one of the striking differences between children with and without the LPE specifier is the relative importance of hostile and coercive parenting versus warm and responsive parenting, with the former being most important for children without the LPE specifier and the latter being most important for children with the LPE specifier. We also tied these findings to research in developmental psychology showing that a warm and responsive parent–child relationship can lead a child to be more willing to accept, cooperate with, embrace, and internalize parent's values, standards of conduct, and socialization attempts (Kochanska et al., 2010; Kochanska, Boldt, et al., 2015). This importance of a warm and responsive parent–child relationship is particularly relevant for children who are insensitive to punishment, like those with elevated CU traits, since they may behave in ways that are more sensitive to the rewarding aspects of the parent–child relationship and will be less motivated to act in ways that avoid punishment.

Unfortunately, children with the LPE specifier often do not experience the type of parenting that would be most effective for reducing their behavior problems. That is, research finds that children with CU traits often evoke less warm responses from their caregivers and, in fact, can evoke greater levels of hostile parenting that increases the chances of coercive cycles developing between the parent and child. Further, the limited positive reinforcement and warmth in the parent–child relationship for children with CU traits can make the time-out procedure that is critical to many PMT programs less effective by reducing the quality of the time-in experiences of the child. As a result, it is important that PMT interventions for children with the LPE specifier focus even more attention on the first phase of these programs designed to improve the quality of the parent–child relationship.

As noted earlier, several PMT interventions start by seeking to improve the parent–child relationship. Specifically, in the case of PCIT, as an example, this involves teaching parents a set of behaviors to do and identifying behaviors to avoid while they engage in child-led play in session and during 5 minutes of daily home practice. Although we elaborate on these relationship enhancement strategies in Chapter 8, in brief, they involve the parent complimenting the child on their appropriate behaviors, activities, or creations; repeating back or paraphrasing appropriate things the child says; narrating and copying the appropriate behaviors the child is doing; and expressing warmth via verbal and nonverbal signs of happiness, enthusiasm, and affection, while simultaneously avoiding asking questions, issuing commands, or making disapproving or sarcastic comments about the child. A treatment outcome study by Kjøbli and colleagues (2018) supports the particular importance of this relationship enhancement part of PMT interventions for children with elevated CU traits. Pooling data across three randomized controlled trials of a PMT approach implemented with 551 families of children ages 3 to 12 with conduct problems, they reported that reductions in the child's CU traits after treatment were accounted for by changes in parents' levels of warm and responsive parenting. Pasalich et al. (2016) also reported similar findings in their study investigating outcomes of a comprehensive intervention including PMT that was provided to kindergarteners with conduct problems. They found that increases in parental warmth following the intervention predicted decreases in the level of CU traits in treated children 6 to 7 years following the intervention.

Summary of Parent Management Training Approaches to Treating Children With the Limited Prosocial Emotions Specifier

From this discussion of research, it is clear that PMT approaches to treatment are critical to the clinical management of children with the LPE specifier for a number of reasons:

- PMT treatments have shown the most consistent evidence for their effectiveness in treating children with serious conduct problems.
- PMT treatments have also proven to be effective in reducing the level of conduct problems and the level of CU traits in children with the LPE specifier.
- There are several ways that PMT treatments can be enhanced based on research on the characteristics of children with the LPE specifier that can potentially provide even greater clinical utility for these children.

In the next chapter, we outline a treatment model that we developed that uses this knowledge to enhance a well-tested PMT intervention in order to increase its effectiveness for children with the LPE specifier. We feel that this type of intervention should be a core part of any treatment delivered to children with serious conduct problems who show the LPE specifier. However, it is also clear from the existing research that PMT interventions have their limitations and do not work for all families of children with serious conduct problems. Therefore, it is also important to consider other approaches to intervention that can be used to enhance PMT approaches in the clinical management of children with the LPE specifier.

STIMULANT MEDICATION

Another intervention that has a significant amount of research supporting its effectiveness in reducing conduct problems in children is the use of stimulant medication. Stimulant medication has long been considered an effective treatment for children diagnosed with ADHD (Pelham & Fabiano, 2008), provided either alone or in combination with behavioral interventions like PMT (Conners et al., 2001; Jensen et al., 2001). Most important for this book, the effectiveness of stimulants for reducing conduct problems in children with ADHD has been demonstrated in several controlled medication trials (see Pringsheim et al., 2015, for a review). Further, ADHD is often present in children who show serious conduct problems that start before adolescence (i.e., the childhood-onset type) and, in fact, the vast majority of children referred for mental health treatment for either ODD or CD prior to adolescence have a co-occurring diagnosis of ADHD (Moffitt, 2018; Waschbusch, 2002). Finally, this link between ADHD and serious conduct problems may be even more prevalent among children with the LPE specifier compared with children with conduct problems alone (Frick et al., 2000; Haas & Waschbusch, 2012). Thus, a significant number of children referred to treatment for serious conduct problems with the LPE specifier have co-occurring ADHD.

As a result of this high rate of ADHD in children with the LPE specifier and given the effectiveness of stimulant medication in the treatment of ADHD, several studies have directly tested whether the presence of elevated CU traits influences the effectiveness of stimulant pharmacotherapy in the treatment of children with ADHD and severe conduct problems. The available research suggests that the presence of elevated CU traits does not change the effectiveness of stimulant medications for reducing conduct problems in children with ADHD (Masi et al., 2020). For example, Blader and colleagues (2013) studied 160 6- to 13-year-old children receiving a family-focused behavioral intervention for serious conduct problems, all of whom also had a diagnosis of ADHD, and who began a trial of stimulant medication. The medication reduced the level of aggression shown by the treated children and this was not moderated by the level of the child's CU traits. Importantly, the reduction in aggression associated with the medication trial was related to a reduction in CU traits. Similarly, in a sample of 37 7- to 12-year old children with serious conduct problems and comorbid ADHD (*M* age = 9.67, *SD* = 1.63, 78% boys, 90% white) and being treated with the intensive STP behavior therapy, results showed that administering methylphenidate (generic drug name Ritalin) led to superior improvement in the conduct problems of children with co-occurring CU traits relative to behavior therapy alone (plus placebo medication; Waschbusch, Carrey, et al., 2007). In other words, children with conduct problems without CU traits responded to both behavioral interventions alone and behavioral interventions with medication. However, for children with CU traits, combining behavioral treatments with the stimulant medication regimen was necessary to see a substantial improvement in their behavior problems.

OMEGA-3 SUPPLEMENTS

Another pharmacological treatment tested with children with the LPE specifier involves omega-3 nutritional supplementation. This focus on omega-3 is based on findings that children with conduct problems show poor nutritional status that is thought to increase risk for antisocial behavior via changes to brain structure and function (Liu et al., 2004), and meta-analytic findings from

30 intervention studies that omega-3 supplementation produces small effects in improving antisocial behavior (Gajos & Beaver, 2016). Raine and colleagues (2020) conducted a randomized double-blind trial with 145 young offenders. Those randomized to receive daily omega-3 supplements (840 milligrams in a 200 milliliter Smartfish Recharge drink) over 3 months showed improved self-reported posttreatment antisocial and reactive aggression outcomes relative to those receiving standard institutional services. The omega-3 group showed better outcomes than both placebo and treatment-as-usual groups at 12-month follow-up. However, this study did not test moderation by CU traits and there was no significant condition by time effect for predicting CU trait outcomes. No adverse events were reported. In a larger study of 324 school children (*M* age = 11.9 years), Raine et al. (2021) tested moderation by CU traits. They found that when CU traits were high, children randomized to the omega-3 intervention showed improved self-reported antisocial outcomes relative to placebo or no-treatment control groups, with a small effect size ($d = 0.19$), but not when CU traits were low (Raine et al., 2021). However, another trial in a high-risk community sample of 290 11- to 12-year-old children found that neither nutritional supplementation of omega-3 alone nor as an adjunct to psychosocial treatment (CBT) were superior to a no-treatment control group for improving CU traits (Raine et al., 2016).

It is important to note that more research is needed investigating the effectiveness of medication in treating children with the LPE specifier. However, the evidence that is available suggests that stimulant medication could be very helpful in reducing the conduct problems and impulsive aggression of children with the LPE specifier in the presence of comorbid ADHD, especially when combined with behavioral interventions like PMT. While we have not conducted medication trials ourselves, in our experience in treating children with the LPE specifier and very severe behavior problems and aggression, they often show seriously dysregulated and impulsive behaviors that can undermine treatment. These behaviors make it very difficult for parents to implement behavioral management strategies consistently and effectively and the child is often so emotionally and behaviorally dysregulated that they do not respond to many of the interventions. Thus, while we recognize that further research is needed to determine for whom pharmacological treatment is indicated, our experiences do match the findings of Waschbusch, Carrey, et al. (2007) in that stimulant medication for those children with the LPE specifier who also have a diagnosis of ADHD could enhance the effectiveness of the behavioral interventions. In short, the presence of the LPE specifier does not seem to change the recommended standard of care for children with ADHD that includes stimulant medication as an important component of treatment.

COGNITIVE BEHAVIOR THERAPY

One limitation of PMT is that it focuses heavily on modifying adult caregiver behaviors to improve children's outcomes. Again, the success of such programs suggests that caregiver involvement in treatment is important when possible.

However, there are several interventions that place greater emphasis on teaching children and adolescents new skills to modify their own behavior. These are cognitive behavior therapies (CBTs) that teach how to overcome deficits in social cognition, social problem solving, self-control, anger management, and social skills experienced by many children and adolescents with disruptive disorders, including those shown by youth with the LPE specifier. For example, some children with aggressive conduct problems are more likely to attribute hostile intent to peers during ambiguous interactions, which leads them to act aggressively toward peers. Other children with conduct problems engage in aggressive behavior because they overestimate the likelihood that it will produce positive outcomes, such as enhanced peer status or getting a desired object. This cognitive bias increases the likelihood that a child will select an aggressive alternative when solving peer conflict (Lochman et al., 2022). As noted in Chapter 3, this latter cognitive style seems to be especially frequent in children with the LPE specifier. Whereas most of the research on PMT has been conducted with younger children with conduct problems, evidence supports the effectiveness of CBT approaches with older children and adolescents with conduct problems (McCart et al., 2006). This is not surprising given that adolescents are less reliant on and influenced by parents and have greater capacity to reason, understand, and utilize cognitive strategies.

Like PMT, there are a number of different brands of CBT for treating children and adolescents with serious behaviors. These include, but are not limited to, Kazdin et al.'s (1989) problem-solving skills training (PSST), Stop-Now-And-Plan (SNAP, Augimeri et al., 2007), Promoting Alternative Thinking Strategies (PATHS, Kusche & Greenberg, 1994), and Coping Power (Lochman et al., 2009). Coping Power is one of the most widely studied and translated of these CBT programs and is an expansion of a program originally called Anger Coping (Larson & Lochman, 2010). Coping Power was developed as an indicated prevention program for at-risk youth and is one of the few evidence-based interventions to target older children (i.e., late preadolescent years) with conduct problems, using both child- and parent-focused small group sessions (four to six children) that target multiple empirical risk factors (e.g., social problem-solving deficits, angry arousal, negative peer influences, poor parent–child relationship quality, dysfunctional parenting practices) involved in the development of antisocial and aggressive behavior (Lochman & Wells, 2002a, 2002b). Research finds that this treatment program reduces teacher-rated externalizing problems and aggression with moderate effect sizes (Lochman & Wells, 2003, 2004; Lochman et al., 2009) and that gains are maintained at 1- and 3-year follow-ups (Lochman & Wells, 2003, 2004; Lochman et al., 2013).

Another important characteristic of the Coping Power intervention is that it is one of the few interventions for which there is research directly testing its potential benefit to children with the LPE specifier. Specifically, in a sample of 98 at-risk 9- to 12-year-old Italian children (87% male) with serious conduct problems, those who received the Coping Power Program ($n = 33$) showed a greater reduction in CU traits relative to children receiving a nonmanualized, generic multicomponent individual treatment ($n = 37$) or treatment-as-usual "child therapy" ($n = 28$) (Muratori et al., 2017). This significantly greater reduction in CU traits remained significant at 12-month and 6-year follow-ups (Muratori et al., 2019). In another controlled study of 241 racially diverse (68% Black) preadolescents (*M* age = 10.7 years, *SD* = 0.56) with conduct problems, those receiving a brief version of Coping Power showed greater teacher-rated reductions in CU traits three years later relative to a control group (Lochman et al., 2014).

Thus, there are some promising findings for using CBT treatments to treat children with the LPE specifier and indications that they can lead to reductions in CU traits in older children and adolescents. However, we want to be clear that there have only been a few studies testing these effects. Thus, the evidence in support of their effectiveness is not as clear as it is for PMT. Further, it is important to note that, in a meta-analysis of treatment for children and adolescents with CU traits, Perlstein and colleagues (2023) did not find that child-focused interventions overall led to significant reductions in CU traits. Thus, it is not clear if these findings are specific to CBT skills-building approaches to intervention or even more specific to the Coping Power approach to intervention. However, the promising findings for Coping Power involving child-focused CBT plus PMT clearly warrant additional research, especially given its effectiveness for older children and adolescents.

MULTIMODAL INTERVENTIONS

Another approach to treatment that has proven to be effective for adolescents with severe conduct problems are multimodal interventions, most notably functional family therapy (FFT; Alexander et al., 2013; Robbins et al., 2016) and multisystemic therapy (MST: Henggeler, 2011). There are two commonalities between these approaches that likely account for their effectiveness for adolescents with serious conduct problems. Both treatments are comprehensive, targeting multiple risk factors that could be contributing to the adolescent's behavior problems, and both treatments have systems in place to individualize the treatments to the specific needs of the case. As a result, these treatment approaches recognize that conduct problems often develop through a host of different risk factors and that the causal factors leading to conduct problems may differ across individuals. Thus, they can be tailored to address the unique risk factors that may be leading to the conduct problems of adolescents.

While there is evidence for both the short- and long-term effectiveness of MST for reducing the level of serious conduct problems in adolescents (Curtis et al., 2004; Satodiya et al., 2024; van der Stouwe et al., 2014), the evidence for its effectiveness for adolescents with the LPE specifier is limited at present. In one of the few studies testing the effectiveness of MST for adolescents with elevated CU traits, Manders et al. (2013) found that in a sample of 256 ethnically diverse adolescents (*M* age = 16 years, *SD* = 1.31, 73% male), MST only produced superior reductions in self- and parent-reported conduct problems at posttreatment relative to treatment as usual (i.e., variety of alternative community programs) when CU traits were not high.

In contrast, there is some promising evidence that FFT may show effectiveness in treating adolescents with the LPE specifier. FFT was developed by Alexander and colleagues (2013) by combining elements from behavioral, CBT, and family systems orientations to treatment to address the factors maintaining the youth's problematic behavior within a short-term (3–6 months) family-focused treatment (McCart & Sheidow, 2016). FFT may employ many of the interventions we discussed previously, such as PMT, CBT, and even medication. However, what specific interventions are used for a given adolescent are tailored to the needs of the case. That is why the length of treatment can vary greatly.

In addition to being comprehensive and individualized, FFT has several other features that could account for its effectiveness for youth with elevated CU traits. First, FFT has a very heavy emphasis on "engagement," with much of the initial part of the intervention focused on enhancing families' expectations for success in treatment and addressing barriers to attendance. This emphasis in FFT is important, given findings from past treatment research that families of children and adolescents with the LPE specifier often show lower participation rates in interventions (Frick et al., 2014b). Second, a key focus of FFT is on developing an appropriate "motivational context for change" (Robbins et al., 2016, p. 544). That is, FFT was given its name because a critical part of treatment is to determine the "function" that an adolescent's problem behavior is serving for the child and family and then finding ways for the adolescent and their family to meet this need in more adaptive ways. In short, it focuses on determining what is motivating an adolescent's problematic behavior, which for an adolescent with the LPE specifier may be related to self-interest (e.g., showing dominance, gaining something), and then working with the adolescent to reach that goal in ways that do not harm others or violate major rules.

Given these promising features of FFT, we conducted an open trial (i.e., no control group) of the intervention with 134 adolescents (ages 11 to 17; *M* age = 15.34; *SD* = 1.34 years) referred to a community health center due to involvement with the legal system (White et al., 2013). Our findings showed that CU traits were unrelated to treatment participation (i.e., number of sessions attended, dropping out of treatment), suggesting that FFT's focus on engagement was effective in promoting family participation, even for adolescents with CU traits. More important, CU traits predicted the greatest reduction in conduct problems from pre- to posttreatment, demonstrating FFT's effectiveness in treating adolescents with elevated CU traits. However, as with other treatments for childhood conduct problems, CU traits were associated with more severe conduct problems at pretreatment. While adolescents with CU traits showed the most improvement over the course of treatment, they still exhibited more severe conduct problems at treatment completion compared to their low-CU counterparts. At 6-month and 1-year follow-ups, CU traits were no longer associated with risk for reoffending. However, during treatment, adolescents with CU traits were more likely to commit a violent offense. Additionally, the variability in outcomes for adolescents with CU traits was notable: They were more likely to show reliable improvement in conduct problems compared with those without CU traits (49% vs. 28%, respectively). Yet, they were also more likely to experience reliable worsening of conduct problems over treatment (i.e., 23% vs. 15%, respectively).

Another study of FFT supports these somewhat mixed findings. Using a randomized controlled trial design, Thøgersen et al. (2022) assigned 159 clinic-referred adolescents with conduct problems (*M* age = 14.7, *SD* = 1.47) to either FFT or an active control condition (e.g., MST, PMT). Consistent with our open trial results, CU traits predicted greater reductions in aggression and rule-breaking outcomes, as well as greater improvements in social skills across conditions. However, there was little evidence that the intervention effectively reduced CU traits. These findings suggest that multimodal, individualized treatments like FFT can lead to meaningful improvements for adolescents with the LPE specifier. However, as with other treatments we have reviewed, adolescents with elevated CU traits often complete treatment with more severe conduct problems despite showing improvement. They may also experience little improvement in CU trait outcomes. Additionally, our study of FFT highlighted that adolescents with CU traits may be at greater risk for aggression and violence during treatment, emphasizing the need for careful consideration about how to safely provide outpatient clinical intervention to this population.

As a result, there are some comprehensive treatment programs that have been tested for youth with elevated CU traits within secure mental health or forensic settings. One example of this type of intervention is provided at the Mendota Juvenile Treatment Center (MJTC; Caldwell et al., 2006), which is a secure facility that admits violent justice-involved youth who are unresponsive to standard correctional interventions. In contrast to standard correctional facilities that rely largely on sanctions to manage institutional misbehaviors, MJTC uses a contingency management strategy that emphasizes rewards or privileges to reinforce on-task prosocial behavior and focuses on weakening antagonistic social bonds and replacing them with conventional social bonds. Trained staff complete a daily behavior rating scale that measures the quality of the youths' interactions with peers and staff, their compliance, and performance in treatment groups and school. Ratings are translated into points that can be exchanged for privileges. Expectations for behavior are initially set low (e.g., brief periods of compliant behavior) and increased progressively to enable the youth to gradually develop meaningful relationships with staff and have sufficient behavioral control to engage meaningfully in the full MJTC treatment program (Caldwell & Van Rybroek, 2001). The full program adopts an intensive multimodal approach that includes individual or family counseling; group treatment for anger, social, and problem-solving skills training; substance abuse treatment; pharmacological treatment; and school services.

In an outcome study of this program, youth high on CU traits who received the MJTC program had lower 2-year violent recidivism rates, and were less likely to be charged with serious violent offenses, than youth matched on several factors (demographic, delinquency history, intellectual and academic functioning, substance use problems, CD, general reoffending risk, psychopathy) who received treatment as usual (Caldwell et al., 2006).

TREATMENTS DEVELOPED SPECIFICALLY FOR CHILDREN AND ADOLESCENTS WITH THE LIMITED PROSOCIAL EMOTIONS SPECIFIER

Our selective review of interventions thus far in this chapter has focused on treatments that have research support for successfully reducing conduct problems in children and adolescents, including those with the LPE specifier. These programs were all developed largely to treat children and adolescents with serious conduct problems in general. This may account for why youth with elevated CU traits often still end treatment with more severe conduct problems than other children and adolescents across all of these interventions. Through this chapter, we have discussed ways that these interventions may be enhanced to be more effective for youth with the LPE specifier. However, it is important to note that there have been some attempts to develop interventions specifically to address some of the emotional, cognitive, and social deficits associated with the LPE specifier.

These interventions utilize an experimental therapeutics framework that has been promoted by the National Institute of Mental Health toward identifying new treatments for mental health problems (Insel, 2015). In brief, experimental therapeutics involves developing an intervention to target, a priori, a key risk factor or disease mechanism that is hypothesized to contribute to symptoms or functional impairment, contrasted against a clinical efficacy approach focused on symptom reduction. As noted in Chapter 3, a common emotional deficit that is associated with elevated CU traits is difficulty recognizing and correctly labeling emotions in others. Utilizing this experimental therapeutics approach, Dadds, Cauchi, and colleagues (2012) attempted to directly target this deficit by providing children with a computerized emotion recognition training, which was originally developed to help children with autism to improve their accurate perception and interpretation of others' emotions (Mindreading program, Autism Centre of Excellence at Cambridge, n.d.; Baron-Cohen et al., 2004). Families were randomized to receive four 90-minute parent-only PMT sessions either with ($n = 90$) or without ($n = 105$) Mindreading administered to the child by the therapist during active treatment or by the parent after treatment ended and before the 6-month follow-up assessment. When CU traits were high, this enhanced PMT was superior to PMT alone in reducing conduct problems and increasing affective empathy at 6-month follow-up in 6- to 16-year-old children ($N = 195$, M age = 10.52 years, 76% boys) referred for treatment due to ODD, CD, ADHD, ASD, or anxiety or depressive disorder symptoms (Dadds, Cauchi, et al., 2012). Unexpectedly, improvements in children's conduct problems associated with emotion recognition training were not explained by improved emotion recognition or affective empathy (i.e., mediating therapeutic mechanisms). The authors hypothesized that improvements may instead have operated through the embedding of Mindreading within an intervention targeting an increase in warm parent–child interactions. However, this study was important for demonstrating the potential of emotional recognition training as an adjunctive intervention to PMT for children with CU traits.

Dadds, English, and colleagues (2019) extended this work by investigating whether emotional responding in children with CU traits can be improved by increasing children's eye contact with their primary caregivers. Foundational to this perspective is research and theory proposing that the source of the facial emotion recognition deficits seen in individuals high on CU traits is in a failure to attend to the critical eye region of the face (Dadds et al., 2006; Dadds et al., 2014; Fox & Damjanovic, 2006). Eyes serve as "super stimuli" that capture and direct attention via activation of the amygdala (Adolphs et al., 2005). When the amygdala registers these socially relevant stimuli, it activates several complex autonomic and behavioral processes that are critical for human survival in signaling another person's emotional state (i.e., via prototypical facial microexpressions such as wide-open eyes for fear; Ekman & Friesen, 1975) and in assessing potential threats, promoting healthy parent–child attachment, and eliciting socially competent and prosocial behavior (e.g., Blair, 2003; Carlson & Reinke, 2014; Marsh & Ambady, 2007; Skuse, 2003). Conversely, individuals with damage to the amygdala show "fear blindness" in their neglect of the eye region of fearful faces, resulting in fear recognition deficits (Adolphs et al., 2005; Davis & Whalen, 2001). This atypical eye gaze pattern may influence fear recognition most adversely because fear is the one emotion for which recognition is highly dependent on the eyes (Adolphs et al., 2005).

Several studies support "fear blindness" in individuals with CU traits, leading theorists to posit that reduced spontaneous attention to the eye region when processing facial expressions may be a critical mechanism in the development of CU traits (Billeci et al., 2019; Dadds & Rhodes, 2008; Dadds et al., 2007). For example, using a static eye-tracking task with 100 private school boys (*M* age = 12.4 years, *SD* = 2.2), Dadds and colleagues found that CU traits were associated with fewer and shorter fixations to the eye region during a facial expression recognition task, with the strongest effects for fear faces (Dadds et al., 2007; see also Dadds et al., 2006; Dadds et al., 2011). Others have found that the eye gaze deficits of individuals with elevated CU traits may be more broadly seen across facial emotional expressions (Demetriou & Fanti, 2022) or faces in general (neutral faces; Kyranides et al., 2020), expressed as increased fixations instead to the mouth region of faces across emotional expressions (Demetriou & Fanti, 2022), and a similar pattern is observed in interactions with caregivers during infancy (Bedford et al., 2015).

Given this research supporting the importance of gaze to the eyes for correctly interpreting other distress, studies have attempted to experimentally manipulate attention to the eyes of emotionally expressive faces, and these studies have been able to temporarily correct emotion recognition deficits in individuals with CU traits (Dadds et al., 2006, 2007). To illustrate this approach, providing children with conduct problems and CU traits with a simple verbal instruction to fixate on the eye region of emotional faces led to improved facial recognition accuracy (Dadds et al., 2006). However, other studies using "silent" cognitive retraining approaches, such as a visual probe (i.e., asterisk on a computer screen) directing individuals to look at the eye, nose, or mouth regions of emotional face stimuli, as we used in our eye-tracking intervention study, could not modify eye gaze patterns in individuals with CU traits (Kyranides et al., 2020). To translate these experimental methods for manipulating eye gaze into a clinical intervention for young children, Dadds, English, and colleagues (2019) developed a novel 6-session emotional engagement (EE) adjunctive intervention module to increase shared eye gaze between children with CU traits and their caregivers using a variety of daily in-session and homework activities completed by parent and child (e.g., reviewing and receiving therapist feedback on video-recorded positive parent–child interactions; Kennedy et al., 2017). For example, dyads completed the "read my mind" game involving parent and child acting out and identifying each other's facial emotional expression. Results showed that young clinic-referred children ($N = 49$; 3–8 years old) with conduct problems selected for stable high CU traits who were randomized to receive 10-week PMT + EE showed an immediate increase in reciprocated parent–child eye contact. Unfortunately, this change was not sustained to follow-up nor did it differ significantly from children randomized to receive a relationship building module adjunctively to PMT. The authors concluded that a more intensive intervention may be needed to achieve a longer-term shift in eye gaze patterns, which are likely established early in life.

A final example of this experimental therapeutics approach applied to children with CU traits is an intervention called facial affect sensitivity training (FAST; White et al., 2022). FAST is an 11-session computerized intervention designed to automate attentional orientation to the eye region during facial emotion recognition and to use incentives to increase children's accurate interpretation of distressed facial emotions. The task cues children's eye gaze by frequently instructing them to "look at the eyes" when presented with black-and-white standardized photos of men and women models from the Ekman's (1993) pictures of facial affect. In each trial, children must indicate whether the eyes of emotional faces are directed to the left, right, or straight ahead and select the correct emotion displayed from a list, while electroencephalography measures neural markers of sensitivity, encoding, and face processing (N170 and P200 components). Children are provided real-time automated feedback on their accuracy using an auditory tone combined with tangible reinforcement for accurate facial emotion recognition responses (i.e., points earned toward a prize). While the results testing this intervention have not yet been published, preliminary pilot data indicated promising findings, with FAST improving emotion recognition of fear faces and eye gaze fixations in a small sample of school-aged children with CU traits (B. White, personal communication, December 12, 2024).

In summary, there have been some promising attempts to address the specific mechanisms that may lead to the development of conduct problems with elevated CU traits in children and adolescents. Such attempts at experimental therapeutics are a critically important focus for future research. However, currently, the available research in support of their effectiveness is limited, and they are not available to the vast majority of children and adolescents with the LPE specifier. Furthermore, given the substantial number of risk factors that can lead to serious conduct problems and the many areas of impairment associated with them, it is likely that these focused mechanistic interventions would need to be integrated with broader models of intervention to be effective.

CHAPTER SUMMARY

The goal of this chapter was to provide a summary of the current state of research for treating children and adolescents with the LPE specifier. First, the most important overall conclusion that can made is that there are several treatments that work for this clinically important group. Second, youth with the LPE specifier also present with unique clinical challenges that must be considered when treating them. From our review of this work, we can make several specific recommendations for treatment.

Treatment Recommendation 1: The treatment for children and adolescents with the LPE specifier requires intervention with a PMT component. This first recommendation is informed by meta-analytic research finding that only interventions with a PMT component significantly reduced levels of CU traits, whereas solely child-focused interventions did not (Perlstein et al., 2023). This approach also aligns with overall best practice guidelines for treating children with conduct problems (National Institute for Health and Care Excellence, 2017). Furthermore, basic and applied research highlights several important features of PMT treatments that may optimize their outcomes for children and adolescents with the LPE specifier. These include:

- a relationship enhancement component that places heavy emphasis on increasing caregiver warmth and responsiveness, which is administered before teaching behavior modification strategies;
- use of tangible rewards (i.e., token economy system) in addition to social rewards (i.e., labeled praise) by the child's caregivers to immediately and consistently reinforce desirable and prosocial behaviors (these rewards are tailored to the child's motivations and self-interests); and

- in vivo coaching of caregiver(s) with the child in treatment to ensure that consequences are given immediately and consistently for positive behaviors (i.e., social and tangible rewards), minor misbehaviors (i.e., consistent planned ignoring wherever possible), and for significant escalation in response to planned ignoring and other major misbehaviors including chronic noncompliance, aggression, destruction, and other major rule violations (i.e., for children ages 7 and under or for older children where the parent is able to safely maneuver them to the time-out chair: time-out using a script with a standardized explanation to the child that their behavior was the cause of the punishing consequence; for older children and adolescents: privilege removal or assigning low-rate chores, as defined in the Reward-Based Behavior Management section).

Treatment Recommendation 2: Children and adolescents with the LPE specifier who also show comorbid ADHD should be evaluated to determine if a trial of stimulant medication is medically indicated. Again, this recommendation is consistent with best practice guidelines for treating children and adolescents with ADHD. The Clinical Practice Guideline for the treatment of ADHD published by the American Academy of Pediatrics recommends both PMT and stimulant medication as first line treatments for ADHD (Wolraich et al., 2019). Available research does not suggest that the presence of the LPE specifier changes this recommendation.

Treatment Recommendation 3: Treatment of older children and adolescents can be enhanced with adjunctive CBT interventions. As we reviewed in this chapter, there are some CBT interventions that specifically target the dysfunctional cognitive styles (e.g., emphasizing the positive outcomes of acting aggressively in situations involving peer conflict) and emotional processing deficits (e.g., impaired emotion recognition) that are associated with the LPE specifier.

Treatment Recommendation 4: Treatment of older children and adolescents can be enhanced with individualized multimodal interventions. We think much of the success of multimodal treatments, like FFT, in the treatment of adolescents with the LPE specifier is the involvement of the family in treatment, its focus on tailoring the intervention to the individual adolescent, and its integration of PMT and CBT components into the intervention. So, in some respects, FFT provides a model for how to tailor a comprehensive approach to treatment to the individual needs of the adolescent with serious conduct problems, considering the unique needs of those with the LPE specifier. However, we also feel that FFT's focus on engaging the child and family in treatment and systematically assessing and addressing the adolescent's motivation for acting in ways that hurt others or violate rules and norms can be especially helpful in treating youth with the LPE specifier.

These are broad recommendations for clinical practice based on our integration of the currently available research. We have spent the last 2 decades developing and testing a comprehensive intervention approach based on these recommendations. In the next chapter, we describe the systematic and iterative approach we took to developing and testing an evidence-based PMT intervention enhanced with CBT for children with CU traits, called Parent–Child Interaction Therapy: Callous–Unemotional version (PCIT-CU; Fleming & Kimonis, 2018; Fleming et al., 2022; Kimonis et al., 2019). Importantly, we describe this process in a way that illustrates how the treatment recommendations we make here can be translated into concrete and usable approaches to enhance the treatment of children and adolescents with the LPE specifier. In short, we modified an empirically supported PMT approach (i.e., PCIT) to target three key risk factors for the development of the LPE specifier: low parental warmth (directly and via reducing high parenting stress), punishment insensitivity, and lack of responsiveness to others' emotions. Results of our initial trials testing this intervention have been promising enough for us to recommend it as a state-of-the-art treatment approach for young children with the LPE specifier.

8

Parent–Child Interaction Therapy Adapted for Callous–Unemotional Traits

This chapter demonstrates how we applied the recommendations we made in the previous chapter, based on available research on children and adolescents with the limited prosocial emotions (LPE) specifier, to modify a highly effective treatment for young children with conduct problems, making it more suitable for those with elevated callous–unemotional (CU) traits. Specifically, we systematically enhanced Parent–Child Interaction Therapy (PCIT), a treatment for 2- to 7-year-old children with conduct problems, to address the unique causal mechanisms that can lead to CU traits. This section begins by describing the original format of the PCIT intervention, which we adapted for children with CU traits (called Parent–Child Interaction Therapy: Callous–Unemotional version [PCIT-CU]). It is then followed by a detailed explanation of the specific changes that we made to each phase of this standard PCIT treatment protocol to create the PCIT-CU protocol based on the theoretical and empirical foundations reviewed in the previous chapters. We then describe the clinical research we conducted to test and refine this enhanced intervention, which we conducted exclusively with children with elevated CU traits, and which provides evidence for its efficacy. We provide links in the Appendix for clinicians to access the treatment manuals needed to deliver PCIT-CU along with other resources, including all of the handouts described throughout the chapter. We conclude this chapter with practical guidance on implementing PCIT-CU with families of children with the LPE specifier, including a discussion of common challenges clinicians may encounter during treatment.

https://doi.org/10.1037/0000500-009
A Clinical Guide to Working With Youth With Conduct Disorders and Limited Prosocial Emotions, by P. J. Frick and E. R. Kimonis

OVERVIEW OF PARENT–CHILD INTERACTION THERAPY

PCIT (Eyberg & Funderburk, 2011) is a brand of parent management training (PMT) program for treating 2- to 7-year-old children with conduct problems. Meta-analytic studies have found that PCIT in its standard form produces large effect sizes for reducing children's conduct problems (Thomas et al., 2017; Ward et al., 2016). PCIT's effectiveness did not differ depending on session length, setting (university clinic vs. community clinic), the child's gender, or any co-occurring emotional or behavioral problems the child had in addition to conduct problems (Thomas et al., 2017; Ward et al., 2016). PCIT produced larger effects than PMT approaches that only included the caregiver in the intervention (Thomas & Zimmer-Gembeck, 2007) and larger effects than treatment as usual for child conduct problems (i.e., individual child therapy, caregiver counseling, play therapy, family therapy; Bjørseth & Wichstrøm, 2016). A hallmark of PCIT among other parenting programs is its use of in vivo coaching of caregivers as they practice skills with their child in session, to improve the positive quality of caregiver–child interactions, engage in emotional communication, and use time-out correctly and consistently, which resulted in larger improvements in child and caregiver behavior than programs not including live coaching of these skills (Kaminski et al., 2008; Leijten et al., 2018; Leijten et al., 2019). This method is shown in Figure 8.1, with caregiver and child actors. Beyond conduct problems, PCIT also improves parenting skills; reduces caregiver internalizing symptoms, parenting-related stress, child

FIGURE 8.1. Demonstration of Live Coaching

Note. A caregiver (actor) is wearing a wireless bug-in-ear device while in therapeutic play with the child (actor) and is receiving live coaching from a therapist, Dr. Eva Kimonis, who is behind a one-way mirror. Photo by Georgette Fleming. Used with permission.

internalizing symptoms, trauma symptoms, and stress (Phillips & Mychailyszyn, 2021, 2023; Thomas et al., 2017; Ward et al., 2016; Warren et al., 2022); and reduces the incidence of child physical abuse recidivism among physically abusive families (Kennedy et al., 2016).

Given its broad effects, PCIT has been adapted for various populations and settings with positive results, including for children with attention-deficit/hyperactivity disorder (ADHD; Chronis-Tuscano et al., 2016), anxiety and separation anxiety (Comer et al., 2018; Pincus et al., 2008), selective mutism (Cotter et al., 2018), autism spectrum disorder (ASD; McNeil et al., 2019), intellectual disability and developmental delays (Bagner & Eyberg, 2007; Lesack et al., 2014), and obesity (Niec et al., 2022), as well as to reduce risk for child maltreatment (Zhang et al., 2024). Consequently, PCIT is described by clinical researchers as a transdiagnostic intervention (Niec, 2018). It has also proven effective for families from various culturally and linguistically diverse populations (e.g., Matos et al., 2006), and when adapted for delivery over the internet (Comer et al., 2017), as a group-based treatment (Niec et al., 2016), in primary care settings (Berkovits et al., 2010), and in school settings as a universal prevention delivered to teachers (Budd, 2018). This robust evidence base has positioned PCIT as a strong foundational PMT intervention to enhance for children with CU traits.

Like several PMT programs, PCIT is delivered in two phases, the first of which is called child-directed interaction (CDI) and the second parent-directed interaction (PDI). Standard CDI aims to strengthen the caregiver–child relationship by increasing use of positive parenting strategies. Each treatment phase begins with a caregiver-only teach session in which the therapist explains the core CDI and PDI skills to the caregivers and the rationale for their use, and provides an opportunity for caregivers to role-play these skills without the child present. The following sessions involve the therapist coaching the caregivers, one at a time (where applicable), on how to use these skills during play-based interactions with the child that involve CDI-specific toys (i.e., toys that can be used in unstructured play, such as building blocks or tiles, marble run, drawing, Lego). The CDI phase is heavily focused on caregiver–child relationship enhancement by teaching caregivers five "do" skills and three "don't" skills that help to develop a more positive and responsive interaction with the child that fosters a high-quality, securely attached relationship. Specifically, caregivers are taught to use descriptive **p**raise, speech **r**eflections, behavior **i**mitation and **d**escription, and to **e**xpress enjoyment. Caregivers are coached to use these skills, known as the PRIDE or CDI do skills, to increase their sensitivity and responsiveness during interactions with their child.

PCIT is highly data driven in that data collected throughout treatment are used for clinical decision-making purposes. For example, at the beginning of each coaching session the therapist closely observes the caregiver–child dyad, one at a time (where applicable), in unstructured play for 5 minutes and codes parental verbalizations using a manualized system called the dyadic parent–child interaction coding system (DPICS; Eyberg et al., 2013). The codes serve multiple purposes, including to determine which caregiver skills to target in session with coaching and to determine when the caregiver has met "mastery" of CDI skills and is ready to move on to the second PDI treatment phase. CDI mastery is met when, in one 5-minute observation period, the caregiver uses each of the three key CDI skills 10 times and uses less than three don't skills. The three key skills are labeled **p**raise (i.e., complimenting the child on their appropriate behaviors or products of these behaviors, e.g., "Thanks for sharing," "Your drawing is beautiful!"), **r**eflections (i.e., repeating back or paraphrasing the child's appropriate speech with the same meaning, e.g., child: "I draw-ded a circle"; caregiver: "You did draw a circle"), and behavior **d**escriptions (i.e., describing the child's appropriate behaviors like a sports commentator, e.g., "You're driving your car up the ramp"), which, together with **i**mitation of the child's appropriate actions (e.g., copying the child pretending to use blocks like a camera) and **e**nthusiasm (i.e., positive affect, enjoyment, and enthusiasm for what the child is doing), form the core PRIDE do skills of CDI. The don't skills that the caregiver is instructed to avoid during this therapeutic play period are questions (e.g., "What is that you're making?"), commands (e.g., "Put that bigger piece there and it will work better"), and criticism (e.g., "That's not how you do it"). The PCIT protocol (Eyberg & Funderburk, 2011) provides the rationale for these skills, which are not only explained to the caregiver in the first teach session but also throughout coaching as live feedback to the caregiver (e.g., "I can see how your regular practice of the PRIDE skills is really strengthening your relationship with [child's name]"). Caregivers are also taught how to effectively use planned ignoring for minor misbehaviors (e.g., whining, interrupting) by pairing it with labeled praise of the positive opposite behavior (i.e., asking nicely, waiting patiently, respectively). In standard PCIT, once it has been determined, through DPICS coding, that the caregiver has mastered the CDI skills, they move on to the second PDI phase of treatment.

The goal of the second PDI phase of PCIT is to teach caregivers how to give commands effectively and how to consistently respond to the child behavior that follows. Caregivers are taught to implement a structured behavior modification sequence involving either enthusiastic labeled praise for quick listening behavior or a calmly delivered, predictable, and structured consequence of time-out from reinforcement for noncompliant child behavior. A version of this sequence is also taught in a later session to use when the child violates house rules by engaging in aggressive, destructive, and otherwise seriously inappropriate behaviors that cannot be ignored (e.g., spitting, lying, stealing). Where required, later PDI sessions focus on using PCIT skills in public settings and within group dynamics involving siblings. As in the CDI phase, the first session of PDI is delivered to caregivers alone and it begins by teaching them the eight rules for giving effective commands, which are intended to prevent misbehavior by enhancing the likelihood that the child will comply. Specifically, this content teaches caregivers that commands are most effective when they are

- direct in clearly telling the child they must do something (e.g., "Put the toys in the basket");
- stated positively instead of telling the child not to do something (e.g., "Please put your feet on the ground" instead of "Stop jumping on the couch");
- given one at a time in that only one task is requested at a time;
- specific in telling the child exactly what they are expected to do ("Please ask politely");
- developmentally appropriate in telling the child to do something they are capable of doing or understanding;
- given in a neutral, calm, but assertive tone of voice that may be preceded with the word "please" to teach polite behavior via modeling;
- given with a reason that is thoughtfully timed either before the request is given (e.g., "It's time to go to school. Please hand me the tablet") or after the child complies ("Thank you for quick listening. Now we'll get to school on time"); and
- given only when necessary to maximize the likelihood of caregiver's follow-through and consistency.

After teaching the eight qualities of an effective command, the next section of the PDI teach session instructs caregivers on how to consistently and predictably respond to the child's behavior following an effective command. This begins by defining noncompliance for the caregiver by explaining the "5-second rule" that the child must obey the effective command within 5 seconds of the caregiver issuing it. If the child does not comply within 5 seconds because they are not moving toward complying, are ignoring the caregiver, or are negotiating (i.e., "dawdling" in PCIT terminology), this is defined as noncompliance and the structured time-out sequence begins. If the child complies within the 5 seconds, the caregiver is encouraged to issue labeled praise for quick listening as a reinforcing response. The therapist explains that the time-out sequence used in PCIT is very different from typical uses of time-out because of its initial use to target child noncompliance and also its use of a backup procedure to ensure the child stays sitting in the chair. Following child noncompliance with an effective command (e.g., "Please hand me the red block"), caregivers are instructed to first provide the noncompliant child with a consistent warning that restates the original command (e.g., "If you don't hand me the red block, you'll have to sit on the time-out chair"). If the child complies with the warning within 5 seconds, the caregiver is instructed to immediately provide a labeled praise for listening (e.g., "Thanks for quick listening. Now we have more time to play together.").

If the child is noncompliant with the time-out warning, the caregiver begins the structured time-out procedure. This begins by quickly, calmly, and safely moving the child to a safely placed, sturdy time-out chair that is facing, but not within reach of, the corner of a room with no distractions nearby and telling the child, "You didn't do what I told you to do, so you have to sit on the time-out chair. Stay on the chair until I say you can get off." The child must sit on the chair for 3 minutes, receiving no verbal or nonverbal caregiver attention. After an additional 5 quiet seconds of sitting on the chair, the caregiver returns and asks if the child is ready to complete the original command (e.g., "You're sitting quietly in the chair. Are you ready to hand me the red block?"). If the child complies with the original command within 5 seconds the caregiver acknowledges the compliance (e.g., "Okay" or "Fine"), before immediately giving a second follow-up effective command (e.g., "Please put the red block on the top of the tower"). If the child complies within 5 seconds, the caregiver immediately and enthusiastically issues a labeled praise for the quick listening behavior they are working to increase (e.g., "Thank you for listening the first time. Now we get to keep playing"). If the child is noncompliant after sitting in the chair, the caregiver tells them to "Stay on the chair until I say you can get off" and the child must sit in the chair for another 3 minutes and 5 quiet seconds before the caregiver repeats the steps above. The sequence must always end with praise for complying with the second follow-up command.

A unique feature of time-out in PCIT, which is not used in many other PMT programs, is its use of a standardized backup procedure to teach the child to stay sitting in the chair. This step is important because caregivers' attempts at using time-out at home are often undermined by the child getting off the chair when they want and caregivers being unsure of how to handle this scenario or providing the child significant and reinforcing attention by escalating their physical or verbal attempts to return the child to the chair. The third component of the PDI teach session instructs caregivers on what to do when the child prematurely gets off the time-out chair, before completing the required sitting period of 3 minutes and 5 quiet seconds. When the child gets off, or more than 50% of their body is off, the chair for the first time in a PDI coaching session, the caregiver is coached to give the child a once ever warning: "You got off the chair before I said you could. If you get off the chair again, you will go to the time-out room," while quickly, calmly, and safely placing the child back on the chair for another 3 minutes and 5 quiet seconds. For safety reasons, this warning is repeated if the child moves, rocks, or stands on the chair for the first time during the time-out procedure. The next time the child gets off, moves, stands on, or rocks the chair, the caregiver is instructed to move the child quickly, calmly, and safely to the time-out room while explaining, "You got off the chair before I said you could, so you have to go to the time-out room."

The time-out room is a safe, lit, and well-ventilated room with nothing inside, where the child must stay with the door closed and the caregiver standing just outside the door for 1 minute and 5 quiet seconds. After this time elapses, the caregiver opens the door and silently, quickly, calmly, and safely guides the child back to the time-out chair before stating, "Sit on the chair until I say you can get off." The procedure above repeats, such that the child returns to the time-out room for all future instances of getting off, moving, rocking, or standing on the chair, before the 3 minutes and 5 quiet seconds of chair time. The discipline procedure ends and the dyad resumes special play when the child complies with the caregiver's follow-up command. This ensures that the child receives enthusiastic labeled praise for the quick listening behavior that the program is focused on increasing. In between PDI sequences, the caregiver returns to using CDI skills in special play with the child. At the end of the PDI teach session, the therapist engages the caregiver in role-play practice of the PDI sequence. Caregivers are encouraged to practice daily CDI special play, and to review handouts about effective command rules and the time-out diagram over the following week, but to wait until the next PDI coaching session to practice the PDI sequence with the child.

In the first PDI coach session, the therapist teaches the PDI procedure to the child in a developmentally appropriate way using a "Mr. Bear" teddy bear role-playing the steps or via an explanation for older children within the 2- to 7-year-old PCIT age range. The majority of each PDI coach session is spent coaching caregiver(s) via the wireless bug-in-ear device to use the PDI procedure with the child, alternating between using CDI skills and issuing effective commands. The coaching style in PDI sessions differs markedly from coaching in CDI in that the therapist is highly directive by telling the caregiver(s) what to say and do and immediately correcting any mistakes. For example:

Therapist: We're going to start PDI now. Say, "I like the blue car. Please hand me the blue car."

Caregiver: Could you hand me the blue car?

Therapist: Say, "Please hand me the blue car."

Caregiver: Please hand me the blue car.

Therapist: Great direct command.

Over the course of the PDI phase, the therapist's directiveness tapers to allow caregiver(s) increasing independence to deliver the steps of the PDI procedure, with the goal being the caregiver's accurate and consistent independent implementation of the time-out procedure with the child. (Conversely, in the CDI phase the therapist begins by following the caregiver's lead by responding to their behaviors and verbalizations with coaching statements, becoming increasingly directive in later sessions to aid the caregiver in mastering CDI skills.) PDI mastery criteria include: 75% use of effective commands, 75% correct follow-through (i.e., labeled praise for compliance or time-out warning for noncompliance), and, if needed, correct implementation of time-out ending with labeled praise for child's compliance with the follow-up command, during a 5-minute observational coding period.

If public behavior is a problem, a public outing is planned for one PDI session once the child is reliably staying in the time-out chair and generally compliant with the PDI procedure. If sibling rivalry is a problem, a sibling session is conducted with one sibling in the PCIT age range to allow the caregiver to practice CDI and PDI skills simultaneously with both children. The family is ready to graduate from PCIT once caregiver(s) have mastered CDI and PDI, the child is showing conduct problems within normal limits on standard behavior rating scales, and the caregiver feels confident in managing the child's behavior alone. As we noted in the previous chapter, we conducted two tests of PCIT with children who showed elevated CU traits. Both studies showed results similar to those found with other treatments for conduct problems (Perlstein et al., 2023); that is, PCIT was effective in reducing conduct problems even for children with elevated CU traits. However, those with CU traits started treatment with more severe conduct problems and, despite improving with treatment, ended treatment with more severe behavior problems (particularly aggression) than children without CU traits (Kimonis et al., 2014; Neo et al., 2023). Also, one of these studies found that children with elevated CU traits were more likely to drop out of PCIT treatment (Kimonis et al., 2014). Thus, both studies found that standard PCIT significantly improved conduct problems, even in children with the LPE specifier. However, they also highlighted the need to adapt PCIT to better address the unique needs of children with CU traits.

PARENT-CHILD INTERACTION THERAPY: CALLOUS-UNEMOTIONAL VERSION: ADAPTATIONS TO PARENT-CHILD INTERACTION THERAPY

As we noted in the previous chapter, most PMT programs like PCIT were developed without consideration of the unique characteristics of children with elevated CU traits that may make treatment less effective for these children with conduct problems. As a result, we adapted PCIT to target the distinct mechanisms thought to underpin the behavior problems in children with the LPE specifier. We called this adaptation of PCIT for children with CU traits "PCIT-CU," and it differs from standard PCIT in three key ways. First, PCIT-CU explicitly trains caregivers to engage in warm, emotionally expressive, and sensitive parenting behaviors, which, as we have noted, seem to be particularly important for families of children with elevated CU traits. Whereas standard PCIT already emphasizes increasing caregiver responsiveness by using CDI skills for appropriate child behaviors and aims to increase caregiver positivity specifically with its "enjoy" skill of positive affect, verbalizations, and touch with the child, PCIT-CU turns the dial up on caregivers' use of warmth. Given findings that parental warmth and other forms of positive parenting are undermined by high levels of parental stress, and that parental stress is highest among caregivers of children with CU traits, the CDI phase of PCIT-CU also explicitly aims to reduce parental stress levels (Kaouar, 2025). Whereas, in standard PCIT, the therapist briefly (< 5 minutes) checks in with caregivers about their stressors unrelated to the child's behavior since the last session, PCIT-CU involves a brief assessment of caregiver's current life stressors, provides caregivers with a menu of evidence-based stress management strategies, encourages them to schedule stress reduction strategies into their weeks, and monitors their use of these strategies over treatment.

Another adaptation of PCIT for children with CU traits is in the PDI procedure. PCIT-CU integrates tangible child incentives (i.e., token economy system) into the time-out sequence, aiming to emphasize reward-based behavior modification strategies over punishment-based strategies, to respectively address the reward-dominant and punishment-insensitive learning styles seen in children with CU traits that we discussed previously. Consistent with this research, caregivers who are referred to our clinic for treatment of a child with the LPE specifier frequently explain in their pretreatment assessments that punishment does not work with their child, leading them to try out a wide variety of strategies (e.g., ignoring, scolding, spanking, privilege removal), which they experience as either inconsistently effective or mostly ineffective.

Finally, we modified PCIT by supplementing it with a novel third treatment phase to systematically target the deficient affective experience dimension that is associated with CU traits; namely, the reduced emotional attention, recognition, and physiological and behavioral responses to others' distressed emotions. This final treatment phase is delivered using the adjunctive Coaching and Rewarding Emotional Skills (CARES) module. The CARES protocol outlines a variety of activities incrementally aimed at fostering improved emotion recognition, perspective taking, emotional regulation, and prosocial behavior in the child, which are completed by the caregiver, child, and therapist together in the treatment room. This phase deviates most markedly from the caregiver training modality of standard PCIT in its cognitive behavioral, problem-solving, and skills-building approach to targeting child deficits associated with CU traits; however, it also emphasizes teaching caregivers new skills to model and reinforce the child's use of CARES skills from a social learning framework.

Research trials of PCIT-CU (inclusive of CARES) have tested it delivered using a fixed-session format. This format involves one caregiver-only teach session followed by six coaching sessions within each of the three treatment phases, which also deviates from the prototypical variable treatment length format of standard PCIT (Eyberg & Funderburk, 2011). For example, in standard PCIT families progress from the CDI to the PDI phase when the caregiver has mastered the PRIDE skills by demonstrating 10 labeled praises, 10 reflections, 10 behavior descriptions and no more than three don't skills during a 5-minute observational period that is coded by the therapist using the DPICS at the beginning of the session. The rationale for using a fixed-session format for PCIT-CU came from research findings that treatment retention and outcomes were better for high-risk, complex families with a history of child maltreatment when using a fixed-length versus variable-length format, possibly countering therapy fatigue that is known to contribute to drop out (Thomas & Zimmer-Gembeck, 2012). An interesting and little-known fact is that PCIT was originally delivered in this fixed format, prior to the development of evidence-based CDI mastery criteria (Kurtz et al., 2024).

In the following sections, we describe these three changes to the standard PCIT protocol in more depth, with their supporting research. We also explain in greater depth how PCIT-CU is administered to families (see Table 8.1 for session-by-session goals).

Increasing Parental Warmth in Child-Directed Interaction

The driving goals of most PMT programs are to reduce dysfunctional parenting (i.e., harsh and coercive practices) and to increase positive parenting. For some PMT brands, including PCIT, another central goal is to strengthen the caregiver–child relationship that is often strained for children with conduct problems (Leijten et al., 2018). Although PCIT in its standard form does not explicitly coach or measure changes in parental warmth, its CDI phase was found to increase observed parental warmth or positive affect and sensitivity (i.e., prompt, appropriate responses to child's bids) measured immediately and 3- and 6-months posttreatment among a sample of young racially or ethnically minoritized children (*M* age = 13.52 months; Blizzard et al., 2018). These findings support standard CDI as a suitable platform for adapting intervention to more explicitly target warm, emotionally expressive, and responsive parenting behaviors for children with the LPE specifier.

Increasing the focus of PCIT more explicitly on improving warm, sensitive, and responsive parenting is especially important for the development of CU traits and for the development of conduct problems in children with the LPE specifier, as we noted in Chapter 3. For example, low levels of observed and expressed parental warmth in high-risk 2-year-olds (*N* = 731) predicted CU traits at age 3, over and above conduct problem severity (Waller et al., 2014). Also, relative to mothers of 2- to 7-year-old children with conduct problems alone, mothers of children with co-occurring CU traits expressed fewer warm cognitions and reported a more negative relationship with their child (Kaouar et al., 2024).

Finally, as we discussed in Chapter 3, low parental warmth seems to be more strongly related to the conduct problems of children with elevated CU traits, whereas harsh and coercive parenting seems to be more strongly related to the development of conduct problems among children without the LPE specifier (Oxford et al., 2003; Pasalich et al., 2012). This difference, and the fact that most children who show conduct problems do not show the LPE specifier, is likely why most PMT programs focus more on reducing harsh and coercive parenting and less on increasing warmth and responsivity. However, there is substantial research suggesting that improving the affective quality of the caregiver–child relationship, by increasing parental warmth, sensitivity, and emotional communication, may lower conduct problems in children and even reduce the level of CU traits themselves. For example, in a community sample of 100 typically developing children, greater mother–child closeness, warmth, and mutual cooperation and father–child shared positive affect between ages 3 and 4.5 predicted fewer mother-reported behavior problems

TABLE 8.1. PCIT-CU Session-by-Session Goals and Materials

Phase	Session	Session title	Session goals	Materials provided to caregivers
PCIT-CU CDI	1	CDI-CU teach session (caregiver only)	• Establish rapport with the family • Educate caregivers on the procedures and course of therapy • Teach caregivers the CDI-CU skills • Educate caregivers on the importance of expressing warmth/affection and labeling emotions with their child • Provide rationale for each skill tailored to the individual family, helping caregivers understand why each skill and CDI-CU as a whole is important for their child	• PCIT-CU PRIDE skills handout and poster/flyer • Warmth and Affection handout • CDI-CU homework sheets (for each caregiver) • Policy for cancellations and no-shows (optional) **From the standard PCIT manual:** • CDI "Don't Skills" handout • Suggested toys for CDI handout • "How to Create Great Labeled Praises" handout (optional) • "Practicing Labeled Praise for Positive Opposites" handout (optional)
	2	CDI-CU Coach Session 1	• Strengthen rapport with the family • Establish the importance of regular homework completion • Build caregiver confidence in their ability to use the CDI-CU skills	• CDI-CU homework sheets
	3	CDI-CU Coach Session 2	• Continue to stress importance of homework • Continue to shape caregivers' use of CDI-CU skills, guided by the DPICS coding data • Instill positive expectations for mastery • Explain social story activity	• CDI-CU homework sheets • "Showing You Care" social story • Laptop or tablet with social story video example (optional)

(continues)

TABLE 8.1. PCIT-CU Session-by-Session Goals and Materials (*Continued*)

Phase	Session	Session title	Session goals	Materials provided to caregivers
	4	CDI-CU Coach Session 3	• Fine-tune caregivers' CDI-CU skills, with an emphasis on skills not yet at criteria • Instill positive expectations for mastery • Educate caregivers on the importance of taking time for themselves to relieve stress and suggested activities proven to be effective • **Activity:** Have caregivers generate a list of stress-reduction strategies they will try and schedule them by day into the homework sheet	• "How Stressed Am I?" questionnaire • Parenting Stress Index • Guide to Stress Relief handout • CDI-CU Homework Sheet 2
	5–9	CDI-CU Coach Session 4 and beyond (to mastery)	• Review caregivers' use of stress relief activities • To achieve mastery of CDI-CU skills • To increase caregiver motivation if not meeting CDI mastery criteria	• CDI-CU Homework Sheet 2
PCIT-CU PDI	10	PDI-CU teach session (caregiver only)	• Educate caregivers on the eight qualities of an effective command • Educate caregivers on the token economy system and discuss the importance of reward versus punishment to achieve compliance in children with LPE • Teach all steps of the PDI-CU discipline procedure, incorporating tokens to reinforce compliance • Help caregivers set up their own token economy system at home • Stress importance of consistency	• "Benefits of Using a Token Economy" handout (2–3 years and 4+ years versions) • Reward list handout • Sample sticker chart (age 2–3) • PCIT-CU time-out diagram • CDI-CU homework sheets **From the PCIT manual:** • PCIT "Effective Commands" handout • "Using a Time-Out Room in Your Home" handout

11	PDI-CU Coach Session 1	• Describe the PDI-CU procedure to the child • Coach caregivers to deliver PDI-CU • Discuss PDI-CU homework: daily 5–10-minute PDI practice in play following CDI	• Mr. Bear PCIT-CU script and Mr. Bear stuffed animal • Mr. Bear video link (optional) • Reward list handout • Token economy homework sheet (2–3 years and 4+ years versions) • First PDI-CU homework assignment handout • Sample script handout • CDI-CU homework sheets • PDI-CU homework sheet (play situation)
12	PDI-CU Coach Session 2	• Continue to coach PDI and work toward mastery • Begin to move from play commands to real-life commands and clean up	• CDI-CU homework sheets • PDI-CU homework sheet ("Using PDI-CU in Clean-Up and Other Selected Situations")
13	PDI-CU Coach Session 3	• Review the effect treatment has had on the child's behavior • Continue to strengthen the caregivers' skills in both CDI-CU and PDI-CU • Focus on generalization of PDI-CU skills beyond the formal coaching situation	• CDI-CU homework sheets • PDI-CU homework sheet ("Using PDI-CU Throughout the Day When Needed") • "Target Behavior List" handout

(*continues*)

TABLE 8.1. PCIT-CU Session-by-Session Goals and Materials (*Continued*)

Phase	Session	Session title	Session goals	Materials provided to caregivers
	14	PDI-CU Coach Session 4	• Provide intensive coaching of skills needed to reach CDI-CU and PDI-CU skills mastery criteria • Identify remaining issues that need addressing using house rules	• PCIT-CU house rules time-out diagram handout (for aggression and property destruction) • "Getting Started Tips" handout (2–3 years, 4+ years version) • Sample script for explaining behavior chart to child • CDI-CU homework sheets • PDI-CU homework sheet (with running commands and house rules) **From the PCIT manual:** • "Setting Up House Rules"
	15	PDI-CU Coach Session 5	• Continue to coach PDI-CU skills, working toward mastery • Add another house rule if indicated • Introduce public behavior, if needed • Begin preparing families for graduation	• "Dealing With Your Child in Public Places" handout • CDI-CU homework sheets • PDI-CU homework sheet (with running commands and house rules)
	16	PDI-CU Coach Session 6	• For families not close to mastery criteria, focus on CDI-CU and PDI-CU skills that remain problematic • Add another house rule, if indicated • Practice public behavior, if indicated • Continue preparing families for graduation	• CDI-CU homework sheets • PDI-CU homework sheet (with running commands and house rules)

17	PDI-CU Coach Session 7 and beyond	• Address remaining barriers to reach graduation criteria • Discuss using the token system and behavior chart to monitor school behaviors • Discuss using the token system to monitor school behaviors	• Phasing out the token system handout • CDI-CU homework sheets • PDI-CU homework sheet (with running commands and house rules)
17(a)	Sibling session (optional)	• Explain how the sibling session will be conducted to caregivers and children (5 minutes of coaching with target child followed by coaching with both children together) • Practice CDI-CU and PDI-CU skills with both the target child and their sibling in the PCIT age range • Discuss which specific CDI-CU or PDI-CU skills were most helpful in facilitating cooperation and avoiding conflict	• CDI-CU homework sheets • PDI-CU homework sheet (with running commands and house rules)
18	Graduation session	• Review treatment progress and success • Plan for future maintenance of treatment gains and token system • Discuss phasing out the token system	• Therapy Attitude Inventory • Phasing out the token system handout • Ribbon/certificate of completion (optional)

Note. PCIT-CU = Parent–Child Interaction Therapy: Callous–Unemotional version; CDI = child-directed interaction; CDI-CU = Child-Directed Interaction: Callous–Unemotional version; PRIDE = praise, reflect, imitate, describe, and enjoy; PDI = Parent-Directed Interaction. Adapted from *Parent–Child Interaction Therapy: Callous–Unemotional Version Treatment Manual* (PCIT-CU, Version 2.2, pp. 1–5), by E. R. Kimonis, 2024, Lulu Press (https://www.lulu.com/shop/eva-kimonis/parent-child-interaction-therapy-callous-unemotional-version-treatment-manual-pcit-cu-version-22/paperback/product-2mjrj9n.html?q=Parent-Child+Interaction+Therapy+Callous-Unemotional+Version+Treatment+Manual). Copyright 2024 by Eva R. Kimonis.

between ages 6.5 to 8.5 for children with elevated CU traits but not for children with conduct problems alone (Kochanska et al., 2013). Thus, enhancing parental warmth and sensitive responding to child emotion are deemed critical components of treatment for children with the LPE specifier.

Specific Adaptations to Child-Directed Interaction

In the CDI phase of PCIT-CU, the goal of increasing parental warmth is made more explicit by replacing the enjoy skill of PRIDE with the "emotional expression and identification" skill. Emotional expression emphasizes increasing parental displays of warmth using both nonverbal and verbal expressions of affection, including use of emotional language ("feelings talk") and statements validating the child's emotional states (i.e., acknowledging, showing understanding, and acceptance of the child's feelings, such as "You're feeling frustrated because the pieces are so hard to join together"). During the CDI-CU teach session with caregivers alone, therapists provide psychoeducation accompanied by handouts on why warm and affectionate parenting is especially important for children with the LPE specifier, even when the child seems unresponsive or appears to find it aversive. The "Warmth and Affection" caregiver handout (Exhibit 8.1) offers examples of warm behaviors for caregivers to use, including verbalizations that communicate about emotional experiences and that express affection in their content (e.g., "I love you," using terms of endearment) and their tone (i.e., interested, enthusiastic, joyful, excited) and also nonverbal physically affectionate behaviors (e.g., hugging, kissing, patting, stroking the child's hair, and other child-engaging actions), facial expressions (e.g., animated, smiling, laughing), and body language (e.g., relaxed, facing and sitting close to the child during interactions, using good eye contact). This last "E" skill related to eye contact is particularly important given research showing that children high on CU traits make less eye contact with their mothers in both free play and directed situations (Dadds, Allen, et al., 2012).

After reviewing this "E" skill from the PCIT-CU–adapted PRIDE skills, the therapist models to the caregivers the difference between delivering the skills with and without warmth. For example, the therapist may demonstrate delivering a labeled praise "Great job using your inside voice" with a flat tone of voice, and no eye contact or physical proximity, contrasted against the same labeled praise accompanied by facial and vocal animation (e.g., smiling, excited or genuinely interested tone of voice), eye contact, open body posture (i.e., in close physical proximity to and facing the child), and/or physical affection (e.g., gentle pat on back), to demonstrate the importance of the emotional expression skill.

The emotionally expressive "E" warmth behavior targets of CDI in PCIT-CU were refined over time based on clinical experiences with many families and based on research described in this chapter focused on operationalizing the construct of warmth in caregivers of young children, specifically for those clinic-referred children with the LPE specifier. First, as we have explained,

EXHIBIT 8.1

Warmth and Affection Handout From the PCIT-CU Manual

Expressing warmth and affection to children is important for many reasons. It provides models of caring and kind behavior, increases closeness, is comforting, and shows children that caregivers love, approve of, and enjoy being with them. Labeling and linking emotions to their causes is one form of warmth that helps children develop empathy and healthy relationships.

Ways of Showing Warmth: 5 Key Types of Affection to Practice

1. Physical touch
2. Tone/pitch of voice
3. Body language
4. Vocally expressed affection
5. Actions

Type	Reasons	Examples
Physical touch	Interacting through positive physical contact teaches appropriate behavior and communicates to children that they are safe, secure, liked and loved	• Hugs, kisses • Gentle pat on the head/shoulder/back • Putting arm around child • Playing with child's hair (e.g., braid), lovingly adjusting child's clothing
Tone/pitch of voice	Voice can be a powerful tool for conveying meaning, including interest, enthusiasm, excitement and enjoyment to a child	• Talking enthusiastically • Exaggerated, playful speech • Laughing/cheering/sounding happy • Higher pitch voice (e.g., "woohoo, I'm proud of you for sharing so nicely")
Body language	Our faces and bodies communicate to children how we are feeling, and can cue children to respond to us in certain ways	• Frequent eye contact • Facing, leaning in, relaxed, and sitting close together while talking/playing • Smiling • Playful, exaggerated, animated facial expressions (e.g., excited face) • Encouraging gestures (e.g., nodding)
Vocally expressed affection	Like labeled praise, telling a child what we like or enjoy about them increases closeness and connection	• Using special nicknames (e.g., "sweetie") • Explicitly expressing affection (e.g., "I love your smile," "I missed you," "you are cute/lovely/nice/thoughtful," "I love you") • Talking about happy memories together • Talking about feelings
Actions	Children learn by watching our actions and responses. Positive actions are a great way to communicate affection	• Play actions (e.g., doing silly things to make child laugh) • Helping child when they're struggling • Letting child take the lead in play

Note. Adapted from *Parent-Child Interaction Therapy: Callous-Unemotional Version Treatment Manual* (PCIT-CU, Version 2.2, p. 30), by E. R. Kimonis, 2024, Lulu Press (https://www.lulu.com/shop/eva-kimonis/parent-child-interaction-therapy-callous-unemotional-version-treatment-manual-pcit-cu-version-22/paperback/product-2mjrj9n.html?q=Parent-Child+Interaction+Therapy+Callous-Unemotional+Version+Treatment+Manual).

PCIT is notable in that all sessions are observed and the caregiver–child interactions are coded, using several codes designed to operationalize signs of positive and negative interactions. However, we did not find that the standard observational coding system used in PCIT (i.e., DPICS) was able to capture the full complexity of warmth behaviors that were important in treating families of children with the LPE specifier. To address this limitation, we developed the novel observational Warmth/Affection Coding System (WACS-II; Prasad et al., 2023). The WACS-II emerged through a detailed review of video recorded caregiver–child interactions during clinic-based pretreatment assessment sessions with families of children with the LPE specifier to identify warm behaviors. These behaviors were then refined based on expert review and confirmatory literature review, and organized into eight comprehensive coding categories, allowing researchers to evaluate parental warmth with greater precision (Koh et al., 2024). These theoretically and empirically derived coding categories signaling affection and engagement include

- tone/pitch of voice,
- verbal affection,
- positive facial expression,
- positive physical touch,
- eye contact,
- body posture,
- child-oriented action, and
- appropriate responsiveness.

The WACS-II integrates both macro (global impressions) and micro (specific behaviors) coding methods, ensuring a nuanced understanding of how warmth is expressed during caregiver–child interactions (Prasad et al., 2023).

Warmth behaviors listed in the "Warmth and Affection" caregiver handout (Exhibit 8.1), which caregivers are instructed and coached to increase over the course of the first CDI-CU phase of PCIT-CU, were informed by the WACS-II, as well as by the Parental Affection/Warmth Scale (PAWS). The PAWS builds on the observational insights of the WACS-II, by adapting its behavioral indicators into measurable self-report items intended to comprehensively capture essential elements of parental warmth that are particularly relevant to early childhood, and, more specifically, the 2- to 7-year-old age range for which PCIT is robustly empirically supported. While observational coding systems, such as the DPICS and the WACS-II, are considered the "gold standard" for assessing evaluative behaviors like parenting and parental warmth, self-report questionnaires like the PAWS offer a practical supplement for monitoring parental warmth levels within clinical and research contexts when the ability to use observations is limited. Self-report tools are quick to administer and easy to interpret and, therefore, are a cost-efficient method for obtaining valuable clinical data.

To develop the PAWS into a usable clinical tool, we surveyed 899 caregivers of 2- to 8-year-old children on a first set of PAWS items that were generated based on the WACS-II, and then used exploratory and confirmatory factor analyses to refine this item set into the 29-item PAWS scale (Koh et al., 2024). Interestingly, results showed that warmth as measured by these 29 items was a unitary construct (i.e., formed a single factor) consisting of various nonverbal and verbal behaviors detailed in the Warmth and Affection handout (Exhibit 8.1). We also found that PAWS scores were internally consistent and correlated in the expected directions with other validated measures of positive and negative parenting, child empathy, conduct problems, and CU traits in this community sample of children. In a different sample including children clinic-referred for conduct problems, we also found that PAWS scores were internally consistent, and at low levels were associated with decreased child empathy and increased CU traits (Henery et al., 2025). The PAWS scale is freely accessible online (https://research.conductproblems.com/measures/wacs-self-report-warmth-measure).

When combined, these novel tools offer the means to robustly and comprehensively measure parental warmth, providing valuable data to help with treatment planning. For example, information obtained from the WACS-II and PAWS in the initial assessment prior to the start of treatment can provide valuable insights into caregivers' use and levels of a variety of warmth behaviors that the therapist can integrate into their delivery of PCIT-CU. For example, for caregivers showing low levels of eye contact and physical affection toward their child during interactions at pretreatment, PCIT-CU therapists can look out for parental displays of these behaviors and can reinforce their continued use by providing immediate praise (e.g., "That's beautiful eye contact"; "Nice job pairing your praise with a loving pat on the back"). An important future research direction for the WACS-II and PAWS is to test their clinical utility for monitoring progress in interventions targeting warmth behaviors like PCIT-CU.

The CDI-CU teach session is followed by coaching sessions, which follow a similar structure to one another and to standard PCIT. This involves

- the caregiver completing a standardized rating of the child's conduct problems (i.e., the Eyberg Child Behavior Inventory [ECBI]; Eyberg & Pincus, 1999),
- a brief (< 5 minute) check-in with the caregiver about any stressors unrelated to the child over the past week,
- review of homework sheets to identify and problem solve barriers to caregiver's home practice of CDI-CU skills (5–10 minutes),
- coding of each caregiver's CDI-CU skills for 5 minutes using the in-session DPICS coding sheet,
- provision of brief feedback on specific skills and coaching goals,
- live coaching through the caregiver-worn earpiece for about 30 minutes (or about 15 minutes each when there are two caregivers present),
- reviewing in-session coding and ECBI data with the caregiver, and
- assigning caregivers 5 minutes of daily CDI play as homework to be recorded on a homework sheet.

During coaching sessions, therapists explicitly coach caregivers to increase their frequency in using a variety of verbal and nonverbal warmth behaviors toward their child. For example, caregivers are coached to increase their own eye contact with their child during these interactions, but to also reinforce their child's eye contact using labeled praise (e.g., "I love it when you look me in the eyes"; "Fantastic looking!"). Throughout CDI-CU, parental thoughts and feelings about the child and the caregiver–child relationship can be targeted using higher-order coaching statements that reiterate the importance of expressed warmth in the development of children's socio-emotional skills. For example, during the coaching session, a therapist might tell a caregiver through their earpiece that "I can tell from his big smile that he's genuinely enjoying your affection and feels close to you" or "Your regular eye contact will help him develop meaningful connections with others." Importantly, caregivers are instructed in the teach session and also coached in each session to only use these positive expressive behaviors in response to positive or otherwise appropriate child behavior. That is, neither attachment-rich positive nor negative emotional expressions (e.g., negative talk, shouting, aggressive physical contact) should be used in response to problematic child behavior, to avoid reinforcing it. As in standard PCIT, caregivers are taught and coached to instead use either planned ignoring to extinguish attention-seeking behaviors or to terminate CDI play in response to destructive or aggressive child behavior.

As with other PRIDE skills, the "E" skill is assessed and monitoring via therapist coding at the beginning of each coaching session. In PCIT-CU this involves using a simpler and less time-consuming clinician's version of the WACS-II coding system that is integrated into in-session DPICS behavioral coding sheets. During the 5-minute DPICS observation at the beginning of each CDI coaching session, therapists tally how many WACS-II warmth behaviors they observe alongside the other PRIDE skills, which they use to prioritize session coaching goals for the family. Monitoring of caregivers' warmth behaviors during special play at home involves having caregivers complete a modified version of the CDI homework sheet in which they rate the level of warmth of special play each day of practice across the week, from "1" (*not at all*) to "4" (*extremely*). Together, these data provide information that therapists can use to determine the caregiver's week-by-week need for prioritizing warmth over other coaching goals for a given session.

Each CDI-CU coach session follows a similar structure, with some session-specific nuances. The CDI-CU Coach Session 2 diverges from other sessions by providing caregivers with a personalized social story designed to teach the child about various ways of expressing warmth and affection toward others. Its purpose is to increase the child's warmth behaviors in close relationships. Social stories use a storyline personalized to the child to describe a skill, concept, or situation, by highlighting common responses, perspectives, and social cues (Gray, 2000). The therapist instructs caregivers to read this "Showing You Care" social story to their child daily as part of their home practice activities (see Table 8.2).

In the CDI-CU Coach Session 3, the therapist follows up on caregiver's use of the social story and problem solves any issues in its use. For example,

TABLE 8.2. Sample Text From the PCIT-CU "Showing You Care" Social Story

Page	"Showing You Care" social story
1	Sometimes I want to show someone I care about them. There are a lot of people that I care about, like: • My family • My friends • My teachers
2	There are a lot of ways to show you care about someone. I can give someone a HUG. A hug sometimes means, "This is my friend." A person might give a hug to make someone feel better if they are sad, hurt, uncomfortable, or frightened. A hug can mean, "I'm proud of you." Sometimes a teacher or parent might give a child a hug to let them know they've done a good job.
3	There are a lot of ways to show you care about someone. I can SMILE when I'm around them. A person might smile when they're around someone they care about because it shows they like being together. A smile can mean "I'm happy to see you" or "I'm having fun with you." Sometimes my mom, dad, or teacher might smile at me to say they're happy I did a good job. It's nice when people smile at each other.
4	There are a lot of ways to show you care about someone. I can give someone a KISS. Giving mommy or daddy a kiss is a good way to tell them "I Love You." It tells them that you care about them and you want to let them know.
5	There are a lot of ways to show you care about someone. I can give someone a PAT ON THE BACK. Sometimes, a coach or teacher will do this to show support. It might mean "Way to go" or "I'm proud of you." It might also make someone feel better by reminding them that you're a good friend.
6	There are a lot of ways to show you care about someone. I can PLAY and SPEND TIME with them. This is a really good way to show affection to another person. It shows that you want to spend time doing stuff with them. You can play, or watch TV, or read stories—it's just fun to be together!
7	How many other ways can you think of to show someone you care about them?

Note. Adapted from *Parent–Child Interaction Therapy: Callous–Unemotional Version Treatment Manual* (PCIT-CU, Version 2.2, pp. 216–222), by E. R. Kimonis, 2024, Lulu Press (https://www.lulu.com/shop/eva-kimonis/parent-child-interaction-therapy-callous-unemotional-version-treatment-manual-pcit-cu-version-22/paperback/product-2mjrj9n.html?q=Parent-Child+Interaction+Therapy+Callous-Unemotional+Version+Treatment+Manual). Copyright 2024 by Eva R. Kimonis.

caregivers may report that their child was disinterested, difficult to engage, and/or resistant to reading the social story. Therapists can discuss ways to make the story more fun for the child, such as by acting it out with toys, pets, or other family members. If the social story was not originally personalized to the child, the therapist and/or caregiver may collaboratively revise it to better tailor the story to the family using the name, images, preferences of the child client, and preferred warmth behaviors. Caregivers are encouraged to persist in trying to engage the child in the social story activity.

In this session, the therapist also engages the caregivers in a discussion about their stress levels and provides psychoeducation about how stress is known to impact the ability to engage in calm, consistent, positive, warm, and responsive parenting behaviors. To facilitate this discussion, caregivers are asked to complete a stressful life events questionnaire to identify which common sources of stress they are currently experiencing (e.g., new job, financial difficulties, increased arguments at home). Using the "Guide to Stress Relief" handout, the therapist encourages caregivers to identify and implement personalized, feasible daily stress management strategies (e.g., brief meditation, connecting with others, gratitude journal, exercise) as part of their homework activities. In the CDI-CU sessions that follow, using the CDI-CU homework sheet, the therapist follows up on caregivers' use of their selected stress management strategies, helping to problem solve barriers to regular practice. Where possible, it can be helpful to link caregivers' regular practice of stress relief strategies with improvements in the regularity of their CDI-CU home practice, their CDI-CU skills, caregivers' perceptions about their ability to effectively engage in targeted positive parenting behaviors, and to reductions in their child's disruptive behavior on the ECBI.

Following each coaching session, caregivers are instructed to fill in adapted CDI-CU homework sheets to record their daily practice of special play and

- its level of warmth,
- caregiver's use of feelings talk, and
- caregiver's practice of stress relief strategies.

As in standard PCIT, therapists review completed homework sheets at the beginning of the following session and problem solve with the caregiver any issues identified in implementing the weekly strategies. For example, where a caregiver indicates low levels of warmth during special play in each week, the therapist would engage them in a discussion about possible reasons (e.g., a particularly stressful work week, illness, more severe child behavior, breaks in routine). This process can also be helpful for caregivers to make the link between their daily use of stress relief activities and levels of warmth, which can be beneficial for encouraging particularly resistant caregivers to engage with stress management interventions.

All CDI-CU coaching sessions also involve reviewing the progression of the child's ECBI scores (i.e., intensity of conduct problems), as reported by each caregiver. A flattened chart of weekly ECBI scores can indicate the need to have an "ECBI talk" with caregivers to explore and discuss possible reasons for continued or increasing child misbehavior. Some common reasons for unchanging or worsening child misbehavior may include

- caregiver(s) providing attention for attention-seeking behaviors;
- irregular or minimal home practice;
- incorrect implementation of CDI play or skills; and
- increased stressors such as injury or illness, changes in routine, or relationship, financial, or work problems.

It can be helpful to engage caregivers in detailed questioning to better understand barriers to home practice, walk through how caregivers are implementing skills at home, and discuss how stressors are impacting the home environment or caregivers' use or practice of PCIT-CU skills. Where proper implementation is in question, it can be useful to have caregiver(s) video record home practice sessions and provide this recording for therapist review and feedback. Questioning around caregiver's thoughts about using PCIT-CU skills can be useful for uncovering and addressing cognitions that undermine a caregiver's correct or consistent implementation. For example, if a caregiver explains that they did not practice CDI play on a given day because the child was badly behaved and they felt the child did not deserve it, this can prompt the need to return to psychoeducation on the natural tendency for caregivers of children with LPE to withdraw their warmth, which results in a vicious cycle involving worsening child problems. A commonly used analogy in standard PCIT is to liken CDI play to administering a daily dose of medicine. Just as a prescribed medicine works best when taken consistently, regardless of immediate symptoms, the benefits of special play accumulate over time to produce lasting change and improvement in child behavior.

Addressing Child Punishment Insensitivity and Reward Dominance in Parent-Directed Interaction

As we noted in previous chapters, abnormalities in learning from punishment and reward cues are other unique risk factors related to CU traits. In the previous chapter, we noted that punishment insensitivity has been found specifically within a treatment context, with several studies finding that children with the LPE specifier do not show a typical response to time-out. That is, these children often show more calm or neutral emotion and less negative emotion when first placed in time-out and, as a result, time-out in typical PMT programs does not appear to be as effective for children with the LPE specifier (Hawes & Dadds, 2005, 2007; Kimonis et al., 2024). Thus, PCIT-CU emphasizes reward-focused behavior management strategies (e.g., descriptive praise, use of token economies). In other words, PDI in the standard PCIT intervention teaches caregiver(s) to implement a consistent, predictable time-out sequence in response to child noncompliance and/or disobedience. This discipline procedure is adapted in PCIT-CU by integrating an intensive and individualized token economy system directly into the time-out sequence.

In the PDI-CU teach session, after reviewing the eight rules for giving effective commands detailed earlier, caregiver(s) are educated on how to use a token economy system to motivate target child behaviors. Using the "Benefits of Using a Token Economy" handout, the therapist explains to caregiver(s) that token economies are

- effective across time and situations;
- convenient and subtle (i.e., can be taken anywhere and delivered without interrupting the activity or behavior); and
- sustainable, since tokens can be delivered immediately following desirable behavior and later exchanged by the child for a variety of rewards or privileges.

The therapist explains that tokens are never removed for misbehavior, since this may affect the child's motivation to engage with the system. The therapist then assists caregiver(s) to set up the token economy system, including selecting a token type (e.g., older children: poker chips, plastic coins; younger children: stickers), and assigns homework of generating a list of eight to 10 reward possibilities that are highly motivating to their child (e.g., 30 minutes of tablet time, visit to the playground). A reward menu is provided to aid caregiver(s) who are struggling to identify possible developmentally appropriate rewards (e.g., playdate, trip to the park, preferred food; Table 8.3). It can be useful for therapists to identify and use existing child privileges as rewards, explaining to caregiver(s) that the child will now need to earn them by trading in tokens. For homework, caregivers are asked to generate a list of everyday rewards (e.g., 15 minutes of tablet time, preferred activity) and exceptional rewards (e.g., eating at a favorite restaurant). The latter cost more tokens than the former, taking the child longer to earn them. They are encouraged to collaborate with older children to identify motivating rewards. In the following session, the therapist will make sure that caregivers can feasibly give these rewards when earned, considering the family's financial and time constraints. The therapist will also monitor on an ongoing basis how motivating the identified rewards are to the child, refreshing the list as required. For example, if a caregiver relies on daily TV time to allow them to cook dinner and, thus, it could not be taken away, this would likely be deemed an unsuitable reward for the family.

The therapist then explains to caregivers how to incorporate the token system into the PDI procedure (see Figure 8.2). Specifically, child compliance with effective commands (i.e., "listening the first time") is the first target behavior that earns the child tokens. The therapist explains that tokens must be paired with labeled praise and given immediately following compliance (i.e., "Great listening! You get a token because you listened the first time!"). Similar to standard PCIT, caregivers are coached to give the child a time-out warning after 5 seconds of dawdling time when the child is noncompliant with an effective command. In contrast to standard PCIT, the time-out warning in

TABLE 8.3. Home Reward Possibilities From the PCIT-CU Manual

Going to the park	Having a playdate with friends	Reading a bedtime story
Calling a friend	Spending the night with friends or grandparents	Going to a sports game
Playing a game with mom or dad	Planting a garden	Feeding a pet
Eating out	Going someplace alone with dad or mom	Baking something in the kitchen
Planning a day's activities	Riding on a bicycle	Going on a fishing trip with dad or mom
Choosing a TV program	Taking time off from chores	Holding hands while walking
Using the phone	Dressing up in parent's clothes	Computer/tablet time
Camping in the backyard	Going to the library	Chewing gum
Buying a new toy	Having a special snack	Helping to make Jell-O, popcorn, or something similar
Helping to take a gift to a friend	Feeding the baby	Staying up late
Going to the movies	Making a special craft with mom or dad	Ordering pizza
Coloring	Riding in the window seat of the car	Riding in the front seat
Sleeping in a different place in the house	Choosing the menu for a meal	Calling grandma to tell of their successes
Going skating, swimming, or bowling	Going for a picnic	Having a special treat in their school lunch

Note. Adapted from *Parent–Child Interaction Therapy: Callous-Unemotional Version Treatment Manual* (PCIT-CU, Version 2.2, p. 78), by E. R. Kimonis, 2024, Lulu Press (https://www.lulu.com/shop/eva-kimonis/parent-child-interaction-therapy-callous-unemotional-version-treatment-manual-pcit-cu-version-22/paperback/product-2mjrj9n.html?q=Parent-Child+Interaction+Therapy+Callous-Unemotional+Version+Treatment+Manual). Copyright 2024 by Eva R. Kimonis.

PCIT-CU states that the child risks forgoing a token if they continue to be noncompliant (i.e., "If you don't [original command], you won't get a token for listening and you'll have to sit on the time-out chair"). When the child complies after the warning, they still receive labeled praise for listening plus a token from the caregiver. Following the warning, if the child continues to be noncompliant the caregiver begins the time-out procedure following the standard PCIT protocol, detailed earlier. After a time-out, the child does not receive a token for complying with the original command. However, the time-out procedure requires the caregiver to give a follow-up command, and if the child complies with it, which typically occurs, they give the child a token with labeled praise to reinforce quick listening (i.e., rather than for listening after time-out).

After a brief check-in and review of homework sheets, the first PDI coach session starts with the therapist reviewing the caregiver-completed rewards list and collaboratively deciding how much each reward "costs." For example,

FIGURE 8.2. Graphic of the PDI-CU Time-Out Procedure From the PCIT-CU Manual

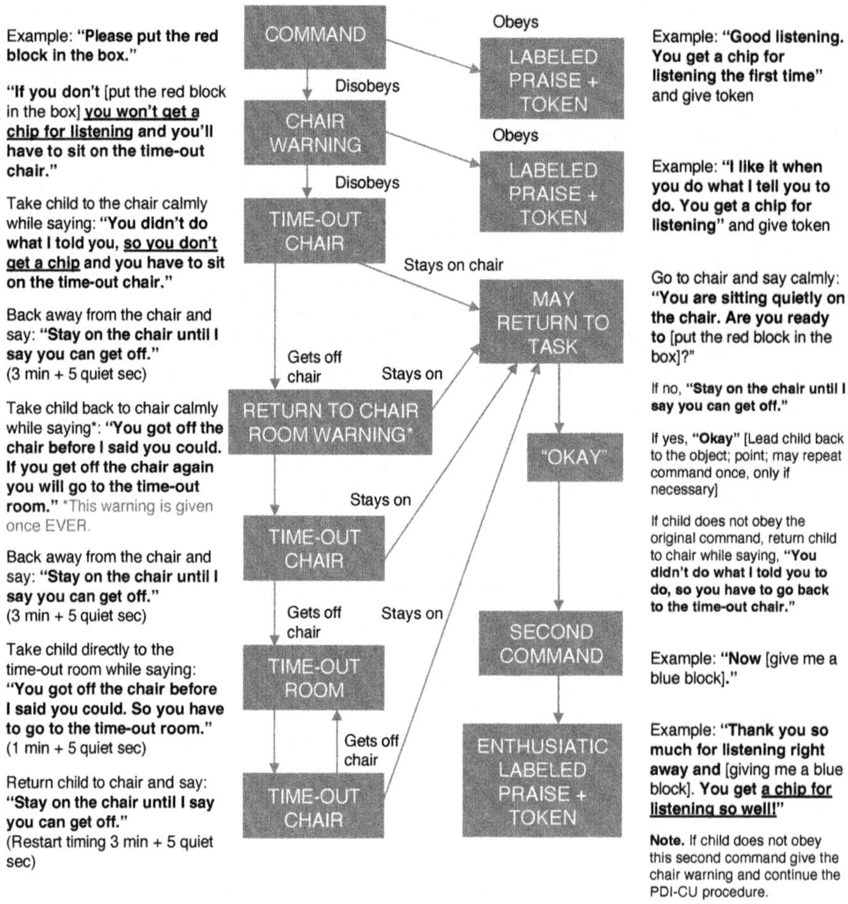

Note. PDI-CU = Parent-Directed Interaction: Callous–Unemotional version. Adapted from *Parent–Child Interaction Therapy: Callous–Unemotional Version Treatment Manual* (PCIT-CU, Version 2.2, p. 72), by E. R. Kimonis, 2024, Lulu Press (https://www.lulu.com/shop/eva-kimonis/parent-child-interaction-therapy-callous-unemotional-version-treatment-manual-pcit-cu-version-22/paperback/product-2mjrj9n.html?q=Parent-Child+Interaction+Therapy+Callous-Unemotional+Version+Treatment+Manual). Copyright 2024 by Eva R. Kimonis.

rewards that can be earned daily may be assigned three tokens, whereas rewards earned weekly may be assigned 10 to 15 tokens. Next, the therapist explains and/or models the token economy system to the child and caregiver using a stuffed animal bear within the Mr. Bear role-play that teaches the PDI-CU procedure in a developmentally appropriate way (see Kimonis, n.d.-e., for an animated demonstration). It is not uncommon for children to not fully engage with or attend to the role-play but accept that they are nonetheless absorbing some of its content. Regardless, the role-play also serves to remind caregivers about the steps of the PDI-CU procedure before commencing PDI coaching within the remaining PDI phase sessions.

At this first coaching session, caregivers are reminded that they will be coached to deliver the PDI-CU steps, even if they have memorized the procedure. This involves the therapist line feeding the PDI-CU script to ensure it is correctly delivered the first time it is used with the child. In this first coaching session, the therapist aims to coach caregivers to give enough effective commands to enable the child to earn three to five tokens per caregiver, to facilitate the child's buy-in with the token procedure by receiving a reward for good listening. If caregivers have not brought tokens with them to the session, the therapist provides these to the caregiver prior to coaching. PDI coaching sessions intentionally begin by providing caregivers with simple play-based commands to give their child ("Please hand me the blue car") to maximize the child's likelihood of compliance and the caregiver's success in implementing the PDI procedure, before gradually increasing the demands on the child. For some caregivers, it can be helpful to frame this approach as being most fair for the child by helping them learn to comply with easy requests before expecting them to listen to harder, real-life commands. It is not uncommon for children with the LPE specifier to be highly compliant in this first PDI coaching session given their reward-dominant response styles. At the end of the first coaching session, the therapist explains to caregiver(s) the importance of the child being able to trade in tokens earned daily if they choose to do so, including tokens earned during the clinic coaching sessions.

At the end of the first PDI-CU coaching session, the therapist reviews the token economy homework sheet with the caregivers. This sheet instructs them to

- purchase tokens,
- engage the child in a fun activity to make a "bank" to store tokens earned,
- create a poster visually detailing how many tokens the child needs to trade in for each reward, and
- explain the reward system to the child with instructions and a sample script.

Throughout the PDI phase, caregivers are instructed to do and record on homework sheets their daily home practice of the PDI-CU procedure. Over the course of the PDI phase, homework begins with lower demand play-based commands following 5 minutes of CDI-CU play for the first home practice, and gradually increases in demand to clean-up commands, then two to four real-life commands throughout the day (e.g., "Turn off the TV"), and, finally, real-life commands as needed. For the first home practice, it is recommended that caregivers be encouraged to call the clinic if they encounter difficulties implementing PDI-CU at home rather than waiting to discuss these problems in the following session.

Subsequent PDI-CU sessions follow a similar format beginning with a brief check-in (less than 5 minutes), followed by review of CDI-CU and PDI-CU homework sheets, including caregivers' use of the token system, and review of child ECBI scores. Using completed CDI-CU homework sheets, therapists continue to monitor caregivers daily use of stress relief strategies, encouraging continued daily practice and problem-solving barriers. It may be necessary to return to psychoeducation on how high levels of parental stress are known to undermine caregiver(s) ability to engage in warm, responsive parenting and increase problematic harsh, critical, and reactive parenting behaviors. With one caregiver at a time, the therapist codes CDI-CU for 5 minutes and provides brief feedback on CDI-CU skills, before spending most of the session coaching caregivers on the use of PDI-CU with the child. In PDI-CU Coach Session 3 and from Coach Session 5 onward, the therapist codes PDI-CU for 5 minutes to inform their prioritization of session goals (e.g., making commands direct, independently generating effective commands, improving timing of time-out warning, immediately responding to child compliance with labeled praise for listening plus a token) and to provide caregivers with feedback. PDI sessions end with a review of the child's rewards list to ensure that rewards remain motivating to the child and their point value remains appropriate. At the end of PDI sessions, caregivers are also assigned homework practice with the goal of increased generalization of PDI-CU skills (e.g., use of the skills throughout the day).

Additional target behaviors are added in later PDI-CU sessions to increase children's prosocial behaviors. During the PDI-CU Coach Session 3, caregivers are provided the "Target Behavior List" handout and asked to write down on it any remaining problem behaviors that have not been adequately addressed with the time-out procedure. In PDI-CU Coach Session 4, the therapist reviews this completed "Target Behavior List" with caregiver(s) to collaboratively identify, where possible, incompatible, positive opposite behaviors (e.g., using "gentle hands" or "kind words" in place of hurting others physically or verbally, respectively) and identify one to two target behaviors to prioritize for the week. These additional target behaviors are collaboratively generated with caregivers to be tailored to the family's goals and the child's specific LPE symptoms. For example, these could include the following:

- sharing,
- taking turns,
- caring behaviors,
- being kind,
- doing things to make others feel good,
- showing concern for others' well-being,
- taking responsibility for wrongdoing,
- apologizing,
- doing the "right thing,"
- trying their best, or
- working hard on schoolwork or other important activities.

Caregivers are encouraged to look out for these target behaviors and to generously and immediately reinforce them with tokens plus enthusiastic labeled praise (e.g., "It's so great how you used gentle hands with your brother. You get a token!").

In this fourth coaching session, house rules are also introduced for serious problem behaviors, including aggression, destruction, and sneaky behaviors such as lying. These behaviors may overlap with identified target behaviors. The therapist helps caregivers to prioritize the most problematic of these behaviors when implementing a house rule over the following weeks. They are taught a variant of the time-out procedure in which they immediately implement it for children breaking this house rule, explaining, "You broke the no hurting house rule, so you have to sit on the time-out chair." This procedure does not involve a warning statement or return to completing an original command. Instead, when the child has successfully sat on the time-out chair for 3 minutes and 5 quiet, calm seconds, they are told, "You're sitting quietly on the chair. You can get off now. Remember, no hurting." Caregivers are advised to be vigilant to and immediately reinforce with labeled praise plus token any subsequent positive opposite target behaviors (e.g., gentle play).

In PDI-CU Coach Session 5, an additional house rule is added if there has been sufficient progress in the first house rule behavior. For caregivers with concerns about the child's behavior in public places, the therapist explains the public behavior time-out procedure and collaboratively plans a public behavior coaching practice for the following session. To proceed to this procedure, the child must be consistently staying seated in the time-out chair. Otherwise, the previous coaching session outline is repeated until the family is ready to progress. Using the "Dealing With Your Child in Public Places" handout, the therapist explains how to plan the public outing, explain to the child what will happen and expectations for their behavior, implement preventions such as a busy bag of activities, and use regular labeled praise and issuing of tokens for target and other prosocial behaviors. A small blanket or placemat is used in place of a time-out chair, and the therapist helps caregiver(s) identify a suitable, safe public time-out room option.

The PDI-CU Coach Session 6 can be used to practice this planned public behavior coaching outing. PDI-CU Coach Session 7 and subsequent sessions focus on addressing any remaining barriers to treatment completion and how to use a home–school notes system to target problem behaviors occurring at school. This can begin with a meeting with the child's teacher(s) to identify and prioritize one or two of the most problematic behaviors and to develop a system for their daily monitoring and communication back to caregivers about whether they occur during discrete portions of the school day. This monitoring system enables caregivers to provide contingencies using PCIT-CU skills (e.g., time-out for child engaging in the problem behavior at school, tokens for not doing the problem behavior or engaging in other positive or prosocial behaviors). For caregivers identifying problems in the sibling relationship where the sibling falls within the recommended age range for PCIT, an optional sibling session can be provided. This session focuses on practicing CDI-CU and PDI-CU skills with the target child and their sibling together but typically begins with 5 minutes of special play with the target child alone.

In all PDI-CU sessions, caregivers complete adapted PDI-CU homework sheets that include a column for tallying tokens given. Where caregivers identify problems implementing the token system or time-out, the therapist problem solves how to address these. They are ready to move on to the final CARES treatment phase when they have mastered PDI-CU skills, the child's ECBI intensity score is within normal limits, and they feel confident in managing the child's behavior on their own. PDI-CU mastery criteria is defined as

- 75% effective commands,
- 75% correct follow-through after delivering an effective command (token plus labeled praise for child compliance, time-out warning for noncompliance), and
- correct follow-through with time-out for noncompliance with the warning (ending with token plus labeled praise for compliance with the second follow-up command).

In the final "graduation session," using a handout, the therapist explains to caregivers when and how to phase out the token economy. Tips include keeping the system active for at least 2 months before letting it naturally and gradually phase out once the child is reliably engaging in target behaviors and, thereafter, maintaining target behaviors with labeled praise for desirable child behaviors and reinstating the token system if problem behaviors return. Therapists also encourage families to continue regular CDI-CU play after treatment ends, particularly where problems resurface, or new problems emerge. Families can also be offered booster sessions where they return to the clinic for extra sessions in the future, as required.

Modifying Parent–Child Interaction Therapy to Improve Child Emotional Recognition, Regulation, and Empathic Skills

As noted in Chapter 3, a core deficit observed in children with CU traits is abnormalities in their processing of emotional stimuli. These deficits include reduced attentional orienting to others' distress cues (Kimonis, Fanti et al., 2016), poorer recognition of others' distress cues such as fearful facial expressions or body postures (Dawel et al., 2012; Marsh & Blair, 2008), less distress over the negative effects of their behavior on others and more impairment in their moral reasoning and empathic concern toward others (Pardini et al., 2003), reduced facial mimicry of others' emotions (Kimonis et al., 2023), and physiological reactivity to aversive stimuli (Fanti, 2018) and when responding to peer provocation (Kimonis et al., 2008), relative to youth with conduct problems alone. Given that deficient emotional processing is central in developmental theory for CU traits and associated conduct problems, a few interventions have been tried to directly improve emotional functioning in children with LPE specifier. As we noted in the previous chapter, only a few interventions of this kind have been tested, and they often require a level of expertise that is beyond the capabilities of many clinicians. Further, we noted the limited effectiveness of delivering these interventions alone, explaining that they need to be integrated into more comprehensive interventions, like PMT. Consequently, we developed the seven-session CARES treatment protocol to be part of PCIT-CU. The aim of this final treatment component is to improve emotional attention, recognition, mimicry, regulation, perspective taking, and appropriate and prosocial responses to others' emotions, with an emphasis on emotions that communicate distress (i.e., fear, sadness).

The Coaching and Rewarding Emotional Skills Adjunctive Module

CARES was created by drawing upon existing evidence-based interventions for improving emotional literacy in clinical populations and typically developing individuals and tailoring these to target the specific emotional deficits associated with CU traits. The CARES module is timed to be delivered after the PDI phase when the child is most compliant. This is critical since CARES involves engaging in various emotional learning activities with which the child may struggle. However, CARES places less emphasis on compliance, and more emphasis on making activities fun and engaging for the child. Consequently, caregivers are discouraged from applying the PDI-CU time-out procedure for child noncompliance with CARES activities, placing greater emphasis on rewarding cooperation with tokens.

The CARES phase also begins with a caregiver-only teach session. This teach session involves educating caregivers about why emotional literacy is especially important for children with CU traits. Therapists also discuss the caregiver's critical role in teaching children with the LPE specifier to recognize emotions through modeling, using emotional language, and emotion coaching. In the six CARES sessions that follow, the therapist engages the caregiver–child dyad or triad in several activities to teach various emotional literacy skills. Where appropriate, siblings are invited to participate in CARES sessions to provide opportunities for real-time coaching of CARES skills. Table 8.4 outlines the session-by-session goals of the CARES module.

The key treatment objectives of the CARES module are explained to caregivers in the first CARES teach session using the "CARES Staircase to Success" handout (Figure 8.3). This graphic outlines the following progression of CARES skills taught in this third and final treatment phase, which aim to

- enhance attention to critical facial cues (i.e., microexpressions) signaling a variety of emotions and particularly distressed emotions in the self and others;
- apply this microexpression approach to improve emotion recognition and emotional labeling and generally increase caregiver–child emotion communication ("feelings talk");
- improve perspective taking skills by linking emotional expressions to contexts, by identifying common situations that trigger emotions in self and others, with an emphasis on experiences of negative emotions of anger, frustration, sadness and fear;
- increase awareness of internal experiences linked with negative emotional states and link these experiences to emotional labels;

TABLE 8.4. CARES Session-by-Session Goals and Materials

Session	Session title	Session goals	Materials provided to caregivers
1	CARES Session 1: Teach session (caregiver only)	• Explain the importance of children's emotional development • Provide an overview of the CARES program using the "CARES Staircase to Success" handout • Explain why CARES emphasizes distressed emotions • Educate caregivers on how to improve their child's ability to recognize their own and others' emotions • Educate caregivers on the importance of labeling emotions and "feelings talk" • Explain the importance of developing prosocial behaviors in the child • Discuss using a token economy system to reward child compliance with CARES activities	• Measure of Empathy in Early Childhood (MEEC; Chan et al., 2023) • "Emotional Literacy" handout • "CARES Staircase to Success" handout • CARES teach session homework sheet • Feelings flash cards
2	CARES Session 2: Learning to recognize others' emotions	• Explain token economy system to the child • Teach caregiver and child to identify and understand basic feelings – **Activity:** Microexpression training – **Activity:** Feelings flash card game • Demonstrate to caregivers how to reinforce child's compliance with learning activities using tokens and praise	• Token system handout • "Emotion Skills Training" homework sheet
3	CARES Session 3: Learning to recognize caregiver–child emotions	• Continue teaching emotion recognition skills, focusing on the caregiver and child labeling their own and each other's emotions – **Activity:** Child microexpression activity review – **Activity:** Blank face activity – **Activity:** "Musical feelings" flash card game with caregiver(s), child, and therapist(s) using a mirror	• "Labeling Emotions" homework sheet • Feelings book (optional)

4	CARES Session 4: Linking emotions with context	• Continue teaching emotion recognition skills, focusing on understanding the link with context (i.e., situation-based emotions) • Teach the child to predict how someone will feel in different situations – **Activity:** "Feelings" application – **Activity:** Situation-based emotions activity – **Activity:** Freeze face charades game with mirror • Explain social stories activity	• "I Want to Play" and "I Like to Help" Just for Me or social stories • "Labeling Emotions" homework sheet
5	CARES Session 5: Coping with negative emotions	• Review emotion recognition skills – **Activity:** "Emotions" application – **Activity:** Feelings face charades game with mirror • Teach the stop–breathe–think sequence to cope with negative emotions (e.g., anger, frustration) – **Activity:** Stop–breathe–think "Just for Me" social story – **Activity:** Stop–breathe–think role-play – **Activity:** Stop–breathe–think scenarios • Explain how to incorporate stop–breathe–think into the token system	• Stop–breathe–think poster • Stop–breathe–think social story • "Labeling Emotions" homework sheet
6	CARES Session 6: Recognizing and responding to signs of distress	• Teach how to recognize early signs of distress – **Activity:** Volcano analogy – **Activity:** Body map: Sam example and blank version • Teach strategies for emotion regulation – **Activity: "**My Cool Down Toolbox" – **Activity:** Role-play of frustrating situation – **Activity:** "My Cool Down Toolbox" social story	• "CARES Feelings Volcano Explained" handout • **"**My Cool Down Toolbox" poster • **"**My Cool Down Toolbox"social story • "Labeling Emotions" homework sheet

(continues)

TABLE 8.4. CARES Session-by-Session Goals and Materials (*Continued*)

Session	Session title	Session goals	Materials provided to caregivers
7	CARES Session 7: Review and graduation	• Discuss and review new skills the child has learned throughout treatment: – How to identify emotions through facial features – Understanding how situations can lead to different emotions – Recognizing our own internal cues of emotion, particularly anger and frustration – Coping with negative emotions to make better decisions • Review treatment progress/successes and plans for future maintenance of treatment gains • Schedule a follow-up session (optional)	• Therapy Attitude Inventory (TAI; Eyberg & Johnson, 1974) • Stop–breathe–think poster • "My Cool Down Toolbox" poster • Graduation certificate/ribbon (optional)
F/U	CARES follow-up session	• Same outline as CARES Session 7	• Same as above

Note. From *Coaching and Rewarding Emotional Skills (CARES) Treatment Manual* (CARES Module; Version 5.1, pp. 1–4), by E. R. Kimonis, Lulu Press (https://www.lulu.com/shop/eva-kimonis/coaching-and-rewarding-emotional-skills-cares-treatment-manual-cares-module-version-51/paperback/product-7kqjpym.html?q=Parent-Child+Interaction+Therapy+Callous-Unemotional+Version+Treatment+Manual). Copyright 2024 by Eva R. Kimonis.

FIGURE 8.3. CARES Staircase to Success From the CARES Manual

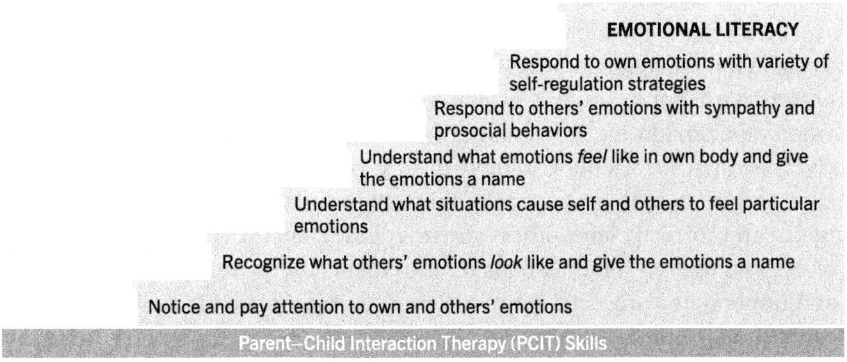

Note. From *Coaching and Rewarding Emotional Skills (CARES) Treatment Manual* (CARES Module; Version 5.1, p. 17), by E. R. Kimonis, Lulu Press (https://www.lulu.com/shop/eva-kimonis/coaching-and-rewarding-emotional-skills-cares-treatment-manual-cares-module-version-51/paperback/product-7kqjpym.html?q=Parent-Child+Interaction+Therapy+Callous-Unemotional+Version+Treatment+Manual). Copyright 2024 by Eva R. Kimonis.

- teach, model, and reinforce empathic, sympathetic, and prosocial responses to others displaying negative emotions using caregiver and therapist modeling, role-plays, and social stories;
- use a variety of cognitive behavioral strategies to manage negative emotions (e.g., anger, frustration); and
- reinforce daily practice and use of these learned strategies using social and tangible positive reinforcement by the therapist and caregiver(s) (i.e., labeled praise plus tokens using the token economy system initially established in the PDI-CU phase).

The therapist explains how each skill builds on previous CARES skills to address the emotional deficits seen in children with the LPE specifier, aiming to tailor this discussion to the child's individual difficulties. For example, where caregivers identified that the child fails to show empathy after hurting their sibling, the therapist can link the progressive CARES steps to providing the essential emotional foundation to supporting the desired empathic and prosocial child behavior.

Using a session handout, the therapist defines emotional literacy, links it to the difficulties seen in children with CU traits, and explains that CARES skills are the building blocks of emotional literacy. The therapist emphasizes how caregivers play a critical role in teaching children emotional literacy, using a social learning framework. The therapist explains how labeling everyday emotions models and increases emotion communication in the child, which is foundational to their emotional literacy. Caregivers are advised to look out for natural emotional displays occurring around them, such as on television, in books, and in everyday events, to draw the child's attention to these cues and begin to label them with the child. To individualize delivery of CARES material, the therapist aims to gain a deeper understanding of the family's current emotion communication practices and the caregiver's personal experiences and perspectives on increasing "feelings talk."

The therapist explains the connection between emotional literacy and prosocial behavior, again aiming to tailor this discussion to the individual child's presentation. For example, for a child who caregivers describe as uninterested when other children express sadness, the therapist may explain how the caregiver can increase attention to these distress cues by pointing out relevant facial cues and labeling these cues as sadness and reinforcing the child when they notice and correctly label others' distress cues. Then the therapist may explain how this attention is foundational to the child's ability to share in that emotion and respond in a prosocial way such as by asking if the child is okay or getting something to comfort them. The therapist engages caregivers in a discussion about the types of prosocial behaviors they would like to see more of in their child to identify the target behaviors to reinforce. The therapist explains how the token economy system set up in the second PDI-CU phase of PCIT-CU will be applied during CARES in session and at home to reinforce their child's use of these prosocial behaviors, CARES emotional literacy skills, and cooperation with CARES activities as target behaviors.

At the end of the CARES teach session, caregivers are given a homework sheet with four activities to complete with the child. These homework activities are

- labeling their own and child's emotions throughout the week;
- playing a feelings flash card game involving identifying various emotions displayed in images of children and praising the child's efforts and correct responses;
- reading or listening to emotional literacy books, for which caregivers can be provided a YouTube playlist of read-aloud books; and
- creating a surprise box with inexpensive tangible rewards to reinforce the child's cooperation with CARES homework activities using the established token economy system.

Caregivers are also encouraged to continue daily CDI-CU special play with the child and are provided the standard CDI-CU homework sheet weekly. Caregivers are instructed to bring the child to the following CARES coaching sessions.

In the second CARES session with caregiver(s) and child, the therapist first reviews homework sheets and resolves any identified issues, and then briefly recaps key points from the first teach session before explaining the token system to the child. The therapist explains to the child that they will be doing activities together focused on "feelings and emotions" and that the child can earn tokens from the therapist and caregiver to earn a prize from the clinic's prize box for target behaviors of sitting still and staying calm, keeping their hands to themselves, using good listening, and trying their hardest. For all CARES activities, caregiver(s) are active participants alongside the child and therapist and regular "wiggle breaks" are offered as needed when the child appears restless or loses concentration. The primary activity in this session is the

"Learning to Recognize Feelings" microexpression computer-based training. This activity was developed by adapting strategies from Ekman's microexpression training for adults (Paul Ekman Group, n.d.) for use with young children. The goal of this activity is to improve emotion recognition by directing attention to critical microexpressions, namely the salient eye and mouth regions, when processing facial emotional expressions. This focus is informed by research we reviewed in the previous chapter that children with CU traits show atypical eye gaze and poor recognition when processing fear stimuli, which can be at least temporarily ameliorated by directing their gaze to the eye region (Dadds et al., 2006). Using the analogy of a "feelings detective," the therapist guides the child and caregiver through a series of emotional faces on a computer, looking out for clues in the form of critical microexpressions that are signaled in the slides using embedded arrows. For example, for fear faces, these feelings clues include a wide, long stretched-out mouth, big and wide eyes, and raised eyebrows. These microexpression "clues" are also reviewed for happy, angry, sad, and surprised emotional faces. The therapist and caregivers engage as active participants in the microexpression activity, aiming to make it fun and engaging for the child by using animated speech, facial expressions, and gestures. The therapist and caregivers continually reinforce the child's engagement with the task using labeled praise and tokens.

The next optional activity is an "emotions photoshoot" involving the therapist or caregiver taking photos of the child expressing the emotions from the microexpression activity. These photos will be used to tailor future CARES content to the child. At the end of each CARES session activity, the child trades in tokens for a prize out of the in-clinic prize box if enough tokens were earned. If the child did not earn enough tokens, the therapist can record the number of tokens earned to apply to the following session. At the end of the session, caregivers are given a homework sheet to complete two activities with the child:

- an emotions collage involving cutting out and pasting printed emotional faces onto a poster board and
- a feelings flash card game involving caregiver and child taking turns picking up flash cards faced down, pointing out microexpressions ("feelings cues"), and labeling emotions.

The third CARES session begins with a review of the homework sheets and a brief discussion with caregivers about any observations around the child's increased emotional communication. This discussion is intended to prompt the caregiver to be vigilant to and reinforce any improvements in the child's emotional literacy skills, and is repeated in the CARES sessions that follow. Emphasis is increasingly placed on the distress emotions of sadness, fear, and pain. After providing an overview of the session and reminding the child about the opportunity to earn tokens for target behaviors, in the third CARES session, the therapist delivers a brief refresher version of the microexpression training. The next blank face activity involves using cutouts of eyes, eyebrows, and mouths depicting various emotional expressions to create emotional faces, building on the microexpression training. The last in-session activity is a musical feelings flash card game involving drawing flash cards with emotional faces from a container when the music stops, using a handheld mirror to mimic the emotion on the card, and having others guess the feeling. Throughout subsequent CARES activities, the therapist returns to concepts taught in previous sessions such as identifying microexpressions. The session concludes with trading in tokens earned for rewards, where indicated, and assigning homework involving

- emotion labeling and
- a variant of the feelings flash card game.

The fourth and fifth CARES sessions begin with a review of emotion recognition and microexpression skills using a gamified emotion-focused mobile application delivered on a tablet. Apps in the Apple store offer various options for software that presents faces expressing various emotions, requires the player to identify the correct emotion, and provides feedback (e.g., Emotions and FACES applications compatible with current iPhone operating systems available at the time of writing). The therapist actively participates in this activity with the child to help them identify microexpression "clues" for deciphering the displayed emotion. In the fifth session, this activity is followed with the situation-based emotions activity that involves teaching children perspective taking skills by linking emotional experiences to contexts that may trigger them. This activity was informed by strategies from the mind reading program (Baron-Cohen et al., 2004) designed for children with ASD, and from the Center on the Social and Emotional Foundations for Early Learning's (n.d.) Preschool Training Module 2 designed to teach children the link between context and emotions. Following this activity, in the fourth and fifth CARES sessions, the child is engaged in variants of the feelings flash card game involving mimicking the displayed facial expression, having others guess it, and generating real-life examples of situations or contexts that triggered their own experience of that emotion. In the fourth, fifth, and sixth CARES sessions, caregivers are encouraged to continue practicing labeling emotions and linking them to contexts or situations at home, aiming to encourage the child to generate multiple possible reasons for a given emotion. The therapist assigns the caregiver social stories to read to the child at home, which demonstrate the application of microexpression training, situation-based emotions, and prosocial, helping behaviors. To facilitate the child's engagement, the CARES social story templates (Table 8.5) can be personalized to the child and family by using the names of the child, family members, and friends; real-life conflicts as examples; and photographs of the child acting out elements of each story taken in the previous session(s). (Referred to as "Just For Me" stories in Table 8.4.) Social stories were incorporated to teach prosocial behaviors and in later sessions frustration tolerance strategies, given their demonstrated promise as an intervention for teaching social skills and improving distress sensitivity in children with ASD (Ospina et al., 2008).

TABLE 8.5. Sample Text From the CARES "I Want to Play" Social Story

Page	"I Want to Play" social story
1	School is fun! I get to learn new things and see my teacher.
2	I am always **happy** during recess because I get to see my friends and play. I show everyone how happy I am by laughing and smiling really big.
3	I want to play with toy cars today. Most days, nobody is playing with toy cars.
4	But today, Max is building a house with the toy cars.
	"Hey, I was going to play with cars today!" I say to Max.
5	Max says "Well, you can't play right now because I had them first!"
6	I feel very **angry** inside because I really want toy cars today. My heart starts to beat very fast, and I feels like I am about to explode. "You need to give me those cars RIGHT NOW!" I yell at Max.
7	When I'm angry, my eyebrows go down in the middle and sometimes my mouth opens to yell.
8	Max becomes **scared** of me because I look so angry. Max's eyebrows go up and his mouth is open to the sides. His palms are sweaty and he starts shaking with fear.
9	I am so angry that I push Max on top of the toy cars, and they make a huge mess.
10	Max feels **sad** because the toy cars hurt him when he fell down. He frowns (mouth goes down) and his eyebrows go up in the middle. He starts to cry because I am being so mean.
11	I want to walk away, but I see how sad Max is because he is frowning and crying. I feel very **sad** about what I did to Max.
12	I take a long, deep breath. I can feel that I am starting to calm down.
	I tell Max, "I'm sorry for pushing you down on the Legos. I should not have gotten angry at you. Maybe we can play together?"
13	Max and I are friends again and we are **happy**. We can have fun and laugh together when we share. I am the best when I care!

Note. From *Coaching and Rewarding Emotional Skills (CARES) Treatment Manual* (CARES Module; Version 5.1, pp. 170–182), by E. R. Kimonis, Lulu Press (https://www.lulu.com/shop/eva-kimonis/coaching-and-rewarding-emotional-skills-cares-treatment-manual-cares-module-version-51/paperback/product-7kqjpym.html?q=Parent-Child+Interaction+Therapy+Callous-Unemotional+Version+Treatment+Manual). Copyright 2024 by Eva R. Kimonis.

The fifth CARES session introduces the stop–breathe–think emotion regulation strategy using a poster and social story. The therapist can encourage the child to generate their own special term to prompt their use of stop–breathe–think (e.g., "traffic light"—image used in the poster). The therapist engages the caregivers in a role-play activity to model each step as a calm down strategy to use when feeling angry or frustrated, encouraging the child to imitate their actions. Cognitive behavioral strategies to teach children how to manage frustration-based anger toward preventing reactive aggression were adapted from the preschool version of the Promoting Alternative Thinking Strategies (PATHS) curriculum (Domitrovich et al., 2005). This training is followed by the stop–breathe–think scenarios activity, in which children decide whether it would be appropriate to use the strategy in different scenarios. These scenarios are also used to help children generate okay and not okay choices, facilitate discussion around situation-based emotions, and encourage perspective-taking skills in identifying the impact of the child's choices on others. The therapist provides psychoeducation to caregivers that mastering the stop–breathe–think strategy requires practice, reinforcement using labeled praise and/or tokens, and that they can best facilitate the child's learning by appropriately timing their prompting of its use in the early stages of conflict and other situations triggering emotion dysregulation. The following session involves problem solving any issues arising in using stop–breathe–think at home.

The sixth CARES session teaches children to link their emotions to internal cues and introduces the "Cool Down Toolbox" of emotion regulation cognitive behavior therapy (CBT) strategies. This begins by using a volcano analogy to teach about early physiological cues associated with anger that can precede acting out behaviors. Using a body map exercise, the therapist acts out and draws "body clues" as early warning signs of anger. They engage the child in recalling a time they felt angry and identifying what physiological signs they experienced in different parts of their body, such as heart racing, red and hot face, and hands scrunched into fists. For older children, this may involve eliciting thoughts linked with anger. Next, the "Cool Down Toolbox" is introduced using a poster activity involving identifying various emotion regulation strategies ("tools") that can be used to help the child calm down (see Table 8.6). After collaboratively identifying, with the child and caregiver, the tools they could use in their own cool down toolboxes, the therapist role-plays situations that commonly lead to anger or frustration to practice how to identify body signs, use stop–breathe–think, and then select emotion regulation tools from the toolbox to calm down. Using a handout, caregivers are provided guidance on when and how to respond to the child's different stages of anger from validating and redirecting and planned ignoring in the early stages to prompting the child's use of stop–breathe–think, followed by the Cool Down Toolbox or a calm down corner as angry arousal increases. Importantly, caregivers are encouraged

TABLE 8.6. Cool Down Toolbox Strategies

Color	Sing a song
Count forward or backward	Tense then relax your muscles
Cuddle a stuffed animal	Hug a parent
Talk to a trusted adult about how you're feeling	Do a jigsaw puzzle
Build Legos	Have some quiet or alone time
Take a rest or a nap	Take some deep breaths
Do jumping jacks	Imagine a favorite happy place
Read a book	Draw
Play soccer/football	Do yoga
Stretch	Listen to calming music
Use a calm down corner	Look at a favorite book
Think about a happy memory	Blow bubbles
Use a fidget toy or stress ball	Jump or run in place
Swing or rock in place	Squeeze a pillow

Note. From *Coaching and Rewarding Emotional Skills (CARES)* Treatment Manual (CARES Module; Version 5.1, pp. 121–125), by E. R. Kimonis, 2024, Lulu Press (https://www.lulu.com/shop/eva-kimonis/coaching-and-rewarding-emotional-skills-cares-treatment-manual-cares-module-version-51/paperback/product-7kqjpym.html?q=Parent-Child+Interaction+Therapy+Callous-Unemotional+Version+Treatment+Manual). Copyright 2024 by Eva R. Kimonis.

to consistently implement time-out for broken house rules such as aggression and destruction resulting from emotion dysregulation. For homework, caregivers are instructed to read the "My Cool Down Toolbox" social story to model to the child how to apply these strategies in emotionally charged scenarios.

The seventh and final CARES session reviews each of the emotional literacy skills taught in previous sessions. These include

- using microexpressions like a "feelings detective" to recognize what others are feeling;
- linking emotions to situations that can trigger them;
- recognizing our own internal cues of emotion, particularly anger and frustration; and
- using emotion regulation tools such as stop–breathe–think and the Cool Down Toolbox to calm down and make good decisions.

Emphasis is placed on having caregivers lead this refresher to support their continued use of the strategies with their child after treatment ends. At the end of this session, as in standard PCIT, caregivers can be asked to complete the Therapy Attitude Inventory (TAI; Eyberg & Johnson, 1974) to assess their satisfaction with the process and outcomes of treatment. Caregivers are encouraged to continue using CARES strategies, CDI-CU special play, and PCIT-CU behavior management strategies after treatment ends, and, if problem behaviors return, to reimplement the strategies daily. It can be helpful to organize a follow-up booster session to facilitate the caregivers' continued implementation of PCIT-CU or CARES skills.

RESEARCH SUPPORTING PARENT–CHILD INTERACTION THERAPY: CALLOUS–UNEMOTIONAL VERSION

From this description of the modifications made to develop PCIT-CU, it hopefully is evident that we attempted to make each modification based on the most current research base. In addition, through this development process, we have systematically tested the feasibility, acceptability, and efficacy of PCIT-CU among families of children with the LPE specifier.

Our early tests of the intervention were through a serious of case studies. In Kimonis and Armstrong (2012), we reported that an intensive token economy system improved the defiance, aggression, and angry moods of a 5-year-old boy with the LPE specifier, above and beyond the limited effects of 12 standard PDI sessions of PCIT. However, findings suggested that this adaptation was insufficient to improve the child's CU traits. Accordingly, in Datyner et al. (2016), we described the development of the CARES module to target the multilevel emotional deficits that characterize CU traits, which was implemented with the same family treated in Kimonis and Armstrong (2012). Following CARES, the child's facial emotional expression accuracy on a computerized emotion recognition task, and affective empathy as reported by the mother, improved. In another case study of PCIT-CU with a 4½-year-old boy and his caregivers, we found preliminary support for sustained improvement in observed parenting skills following PCIT-CU (Agazzi et al., 2020).

Following the initial case studies, we moved on to testing the intervention in treatment trials. In Kimonis et al. (2019), we reported on an initial open trial of PCIT-CU implemented with 3- to 6-year-old children with the LPE specifier ($N = 23$) and their families. Caregivers in this trial reported statistically significant and clinically meaningful improvements in child conduct problems, CU traits, and empathy, while significant improvement in child compliance was also observed, measured using the DPICS coding system. Caregivers perceived PCIT-CU as acceptable, reporting a high level of satisfaction with the process and outcome of therapy. However, without a no-treatment comparison control group, this open trial could not rule out whether these improvements were due to parental expectancy effects, child maturation, regression to the mean, or adjustment to the clinic setting over time.

Thus, we moved on to a more rigorous test of PCIT-CU. In Fleming et al. (2022), we reported on a randomized controlled trial comparing PCIT-CU against standard PCIT in a sample of 3- to 7-year-old children with the LPE specifier ($N = 43$) and their families. Children in both treatment groups demonstrated statistically significant and clinically meaningful improvement in conduct problems during the active treatment period. Both groups also had high treatment retention rates and parental satisfaction, and they did not differ on their number of missed or canceled appointments or homework completion rates. Further, no adverse events were reported for either treatment group. However, 3 months after treatment ended, families randomized to the standard PCIT group reported an increase in the number of conduct problems and frequency of aggressive behavior. In contrast, families randomized to receive PCIT-CU maintained their treatment gains during the follow-up period, with medium to large effect sizes for group differences ($d = -0.44$ to -0.73). Although there was a similar pattern of group differences in improvement in CU traits, this effect did not reach statistical significance ($p = 0.09$, $d = -0.34$).

Together, our research provides some initial support for the feasibility, acceptability, safety, and efficacy of PCIT-CU for children with the LPE specifier, and its superiority to the standard version of PCIT for maintaining improvements for this group of children after treatment ends. Notably, this approach to treatment is also consistent with the approach recommended by experienced clinicians who provide treatment to children and adolescents with serious behavior problems. Specifically, a study of expert practitioners across nine countries reported strong consensus among them that practitioners working with complex presentations of conduct problems should be skilled in delivering content such as that found in PCIT-CU, which includes caregiver–child relationship enhancement, emphasizing positive reinforcement strategies using both social and tangible rewards, and promoting child emotion recognition (Barker & Hawes, 2024).

COMMON CHALLENGES AND STRATEGIES IN IMPLEMENTING PCIT-CU

In providing this support for the efficacy of PCIT-CU and its promise for providing a treatment model for young children with the LPE specifier, we want to acknowledge that these children present quite a treatment challenge. Thus, we would like to highlight some of the specific challenges we have faced when implementing PCIT-CU with families of children with the LPE specifier. Although these challenges are divided by PCIT-CU treatment phase, some pervade treatment phases. This is not intended to be an exhaustive list of challenges and, where a specific challenge is not addressed, clinical judgement that applies an understanding of foundational theoretical principles, understanding of the function of the child's behavior, and a comprehensive understanding of the individual child and family is essential.

Child-Directed Interaction: Callous-Unemotional Version

Monitoring child conduct problems at each session using the standardized ECBI parenting rating of their child's conduct problems is a useful tool for determining when there may be issues in implementation. When ECBI scores are not declining, it is important to determine early on in treatment why this is happening and to address the problem. A common reason for a flatlined ECBI graph may be that caregivers are not practicing the PRIDE skills or are practicing them improperly at home. In cases of suspected improper implementation, it can be useful to question the caregiver and child, where appropriate, about what time-out looks like at home to ensure that the setting, toys, and process are correctly administered to facilitate the caregiver's practice of CDI-CU skills. Where caregivers are not practicing, it is critical to identify and address the barriers early in treatment.

Where caregivers' cognitions are interfering with home practice (e.g., believing the child does not deserve special play time, thinking the CDI-CU play skills are silly or unhelpful, thinking that the child does not want to play with them), it may be necessary to pause dyadic sessions to have a caregiver-only session to address these issues. Although less common, some children refuse to engage in CDI-CU, and some problem solving is needed to determine and address reasons for this. For example, for children with highly restricted interests who do not want to play with the available toys, it may be necessary to modify the selection of toys to this interest for several sessions before gradually introducing a broader selection of PCIT-appropriate toys. For others who are prone to quickly becoming bored with toys, it can be helpful to engage the child in selecting special PCIT-appropriate toys that are only taken out and used during CDI-CU play or using toys that can be built over several sessions, such as more advanced Lego kits for some older children. In some cases, stable high ECBI scores may stem from caregiver attention maintaining the problem behavior because the caregiver struggles to apply planned ignoring. Some caregivers may actively avoid using planned ignoring because of prior experiences with child escalation to aggression or destruction when ignored. In these cases, it is critical to find opportunities to practice planned ignoring in clinic sessions. In extreme cases of child aggression when caregivers practice planned ignoring, it may be necessary to coach the caregiver to temporarily remove themself from the playroom for safety reasons. Every 1 minute and 5 quiet seconds, the caregiver can be coached to check back in with the child to see if the child is ready to play gently, and they can return to the playroom when it is safe to do so. This approach is consistent with an early small research trial testing the order of PCIT treatment phases, in which Eyberg and colleagues recommended that

> In clinical practice, it may be advisable to present the discipline stage before the play therapy stage for certain types of children and presenting problems. For example, for children whose behavior is seriously out of control and potentially dangerous (e.g., extreme aggression toward younger siblings), the more rapid decrease in conduct-problem behaviors produced by starting with PDI may be decisive. (Eisenstadt et al., 1993, p. 49)

Parent-Directed Interaction: Callous-Unemotional Version

Some children may comply with caregiver commands but do so in an inappropriate way, which, in some cases, may stem from the child's attempts to maintain control. For example, when told to pick up an item they threw, they may aggressively or destructively slam the item on the table instead of placing it gently. In these cases, clinical judgment is needed to determine the best strategy. One strategy might be to have caregivers reward the compliance behavior and increase the specificity of their future commands by telling the child exactly how to complete it, such as by saying "Please put the container on the table gently." Another strategy might be to coach the caregiver not to give a token and to instead immediately restate their original command, qualifying that the item must be placed down gently. In other cases, children will comply with a command to receive the labeled praise and token and then immediately return to the problematic behavior or undo what they were told to do, often to elicit another opportunity to earn a token. For example, a child drawing on the wall may comply with a command to draw on paper, for which the caregiver gives them a token, and then immediately return to drawing on the wall. It is important to understand the function of the child's behavior, such as earning another token or regaining control over the situation. In these cases, the therapist might coach the caregiver to again increase the specificity of the command such as by stating, "Draw only on the paper," and to only give the token after a brief period of compliance. Although this would be defined as "ineffective" in PCIT terms because the child cannot technically comply within the required 5-second compliance period, this adjustment to the structure of commands can prevent children with the LPE specifier from manipulating the system by repeatedly being rewarded with a token for complying with the same command multiple times in a row. Another strategy might be to give a warning after the child returns to the problem behavior: "If you don't draw only on the paper, you will go to the time-out chair for not listening."

Children with the LPE specifier who tend to show higher levels of aggression generally can also be highly aggressive and destructive during time-out. This can mean that caregivers face injury when transporting the child to the time-out room or chair and/or clinic or household property can be damaged. Important preventive measures can be put in place to minimize the risk of injury and damage, such as

- placing the time-out chair away from reach of walls and household items and as close as possible to the time-out room,
- having caregivers tie up long hair and avoid wearing dangling earrings/jewelry or loose-fitting clothing,
- ensuring the bug-in-ear system is tucked into caregivers clothing and any loose cords are out of the child's reach,
- removing hard toys or unnecessary furniture from the room,
- instructing caregivers not to bring to session hard items such as metal water bottles that can be used as weapons, and
- having the child remove their shoes before the session to avoid these items being used as weapons.

Some children intentionally urinate or defecate in the time-out room, weaponize their bodily fluids during the time-out procedure, or claim the need to use the bathroom to get out of time-out, and so it is highly recommended to have children use the toilet prior to PDI-CU coaching sessions.

Ideally, therapists should strive to implement the standard time-out procedure involving the caregiver transporting the child quickly, calmly, and safely to the time-out chair and room, for which it can be helpful to coach the caregiver to back away quickly when placing the child on the chair to avoid getting hit or kicked; however, in some cases where the child is extremely aggressive or the caregiver indicates they are not comfortable with the level of physicality shown by the child, it may be necessary to modify the time-out sequence to more closely resemble the PCIT "swoop-and-go" procedure. This involves the caregiver leaving the playroom where the time-out chair is located if it becomes too difficult or dangerous to get the child to sit on the time-out chair. In this case, the playroom becomes the time-out room. In the traditional PCIT "swoop-and-go" procedure, caregivers are advised to remove as many toys as possible from the room as they leave, for which a container or laundry basket can be placed in the room. However, in our experience, children are not too interested in toys left in the room once the caregiver leaves, although clinical judgement about each individual case is important. In the PCIT-CU modification of swoop and go, the caregiver is coached to say, "Please sit yourself on the chair" and to begin backing away from the child toward the exit door. If they do not comply within 5 seconds, the caregiver is coached to leave the room, stating, "You didn't sit yourself on the time-out chair so now you're in the time-out room." After 1 minute and 5 quiet seconds, the therapist coaches the caregiver to peek into the playroom and ask the child, "Are you ready to sit yourself on the time-out chair?" If the child does not comply, the caregiver closes the playroom door and waits for another 1 minute and 5 quiet seconds, repeating these steps until the child independently sits in the time-out chair. Once the child sits on the time-out chair, the caregiver returns to the room and says, "Stay on the chair until I say you can get up." They ignore the child in the chair for the standard 3 minutes and 5 quiet seconds before saying, "You're sitting quietly on the chair, are you ready to [original command]?" resuming the standard PDI-CU procedure. Once the swoop-and-go modification has been put in place for a highly aggressive child, it can be used for all future PDI-CU coaching sessions and by the caregivers at home after problem solving how to set up the time-out room and chair at home. For example, for home practice with very aggressive children, it is important to place the time-out chair inside the time-out room when feasible. Once a child is reliably independently sitting in the time-out chair, it may be possible to reinstate a separate time-out room consistent with the standard PDI-CU procedure.

For slow-moving caregivers, it is important to coach them to move quickly while implementing this procedure to avoid the child escaping the room or turning it into a game of cat and mouse, where they are in control and obtaining high levels of attention from the chasing caregiver. It may also be necessary to have a caregiver-only session to address unhelpful cognitions that may be getting in the way of their adherence to PCIT-CU procedures (e.g., believing that asking the child to complete a play-based command is unfair, thinking that the child is not listening because they do not understand, thinking that they should not have to reward the child with a token for behaviors they should be doing anyway). For therapists to engage in the quick decision making needed to effectively address the various creative child behaviors that arise during the fast-moving PDI-CU coaching sessions, it is important to get adequate sleep and practice self-care.

Where children are not motivated by the token economy system, this can be an important indicator that it is likely being incorrectly implemented. The clinician can question the caregiver and child, where appropriate, about what the token system looks like in the home to understand and address any issues. It will be important to ensure that children are only receiving rewards identified on their reward list by regularly trading in tokens. It may be necessary to provide caregivers with psychoeducation from an operant conditioning framework about why this is important for child buy-in. It is important to regularly check in throughout PDI-CU sessions to ensure that the rewards on the list remain motivating to the child and to refresh them often where indicated. It will also be important to monitor the balance of tokens to rewards to ensure that it is not too easy or too hard for children to receive rewards and that caregivers can still feasibly give the rewards. It is expected that the number of tokens required to receive rewards may gradually increase as the child becomes more compliant and engages in increasing prosocial behaviors. Also, it is critical for children with the LPE specifier to have caregivers do the following:

- immediately reinforce target behaviors with labeled praise and a token;
- implement the token economy system consistently, which requires always having tokens on them when with the child;
- provide the opportunity for the child to regularly trade in tokens for rewards; and

- not remove tokens for problematic behavior, given the punishment insensitivity of children with CU traits.

In clinic sessions, therapists may need to prompt the caregiver to give a token where the child has engaged in an unreinforced target behavior (e.g., compliance, positive opposite behaviors to problematic behaviors, prosocial behaviors). A helpful strategy is to reinforce the caregiver's behavior while providing the rationale for using this strategy (e.g., "Great job rewarding his sharing. He'll share more now because you're consistently rewarding it.").

Coaching and Rewarding Emotional Skills

One of the biggest challenges when delivering the CARES module is child engagement. The CARES module was temporally ordered to be delivered after the family completes PDI-CU, so the child is both at their most compliant and familiar with the active token economy system that is adapted in CARES to reinforce child compliance with activities. Several strategies can be used to overcome a child's lack of engagement in this treatment phase. First, the therapist's and the caregiver's use of PRIDE skills, particularly verbal and nonverbal emotion expression and animation, is important for engaging the child in CARES tasks and reinforcing their use of CARES skills. Second, for children with the LPE specifier who are prone to boredom and may have higher activity levels, it is important to make the activities as fun as possible for the child while ensuring that session goals are achieved. Therapists will need to be flexible and creative in how they teach various skills. Examples include

- outlining the child's head or body while they lie down on butcher's paper and using this outline to draw facial expressions or identify internal emotional experiences;
- using the one-way mirror to have child or caregiver first practice their emotional expression before showing it to others during this variant of the feelings flash card game;
- affixing facial feature expressions around the room and having child and caregiver search for the correct ones to generate a facial emotional expression in the blank face activity, instead of requiring them to stay seated; and
- using materials relevant to the child's interests or using personalized examples from the child's recent life events to help increase engagement.

It may be necessary to revisit the rewards to ensure they remain motivating to the child. Critically, CARES sessions should be delivered flexibly and tailored to the child and their caregivers, while ensuring that the goals of each session are achieved.

Another common challenge during this treatment phase is caregiver engagement with and resistance to practicing CARES strategies at home. Again, it is important to formulate possible reasons for this resistance and engage in a conversation with caregivers, taking a curious stance when asking about how CARES activities are implemented at home, to rule out alternative hypotheses. One reason for parental resistance may be their discomfort or unfamiliarity with the skills and strategies (e.g., increasing "feelings talk") that may stem from the caregiver's own experiences in their family of origin. While the CARES teach session builds in some discussion around this, it may be necessary to spend more time understanding the caregiver's relevant childhood experiences and uncovering cognitions that may be contributing to their resistance. Where and when appropriate, it can be helpful to link CARES strategies to the caregiver's treatment goals to increase buy-in and engagement. It is also important to explain that CARES skills can take longer for the child to learn and so it is important that caregivers are equipped with the skills so they can continue to support the child's learning after treatment ends. Another reason for resistance may be caregiver's lack of understanding about when to implement CARES versus PCIT-CU strategies. When this comes up, it can be helpful to explain how the CARES phase provides additional strategies on top of those learned in PCIT-CU for addressing challenging child behaviors. The sixth CARES session provides guidance to caregivers on what factors to consider when deciding whether to apply CDI-CU, PDI-CU, and/or CARES management strategies.

CHAPTER SUMMARY

In this chapter, we detail the systematic adaptation of standard PCIT into the PCIT-CU protocol, which was developed to address the unique needs of children with CU traits. The chapter begins by reviewing the standard PCIT program and its robust evidence base for reducing conduct problems in young children. It highlights the challenges standard PCIT faces in treating children with the LPE specifier, such as their insensitivity to punishment and their emotional deficits. PCIT-CU incorporates three key primary enhancements: (a) increasing parental warmth and emotional expression and reducing parental stress during the CDI phase; (b) integrating a token economy system in the PDI phase to emphasize reward-based learning strategies; and (c) introducing a novel CARES module to directly target children's deficient emotional recognition, regulation, and empathy.

In this chapter, we outlined the theoretical and empirical foundations for these adaptations and then systematically described how they are used in the PCIT-CU intervention. We also described case studies and clinical trials demonstrating PCIT-CU's feasibility, acceptability, and efficacy, including its superiority over standard PCIT for sustaining improvements posttreatment for young clinic-referred children with the LPE specifier.

We concluded this chapter by providing practical guidance to clinicians on implementing the PCIT-CU and CARES protocols, addressing challenges such as child aggression during time-out and parental consistency with the token economy system. In this guidance, we emphasized the importance of tailoring

PCIT-CU to individual families, highlighting its potential to transform caregiver–child interactions and effectively address the emotional and behavioral deficits associated with CU traits. To further provide practical guidance to clinicians, in the next chapter, we provide a detailed case example of PCIT-CU implemented with a child with the LPE specifier. There, we will discuss how we have attempted to expand PCIT-CU to overcome barriers to treatment access, with innovative implementations in diverse formats and settings, such as via online face-to-face and school-based delivery, to increase its reach and impact for families in need.

9

Illustrative Clinical Case Study Involving Parent–Child Interaction Therapy Adapted for Callous–Unemotional Traits

As we noted in the last chapter, treating families of a child with the limited prosocial emotions (LPE) specifier is quite challenging. We want to make clear it is also quite rewarding. Many of these children have been labeled as "bad," "untreatable," "psychopathic," "demons," and other pejorative terms. It is hard to express how rewarding it is when a treatment makes changes in these children and their families that they and others did not think was possible. In this chapter we provide a case description of a child that was treated using Parent–Child Interaction Therapy: Callous–Unemotional version (PCIT-CU). This detailed, step-by-step case study intends to highlight important clinical issues and challenges that can arise when implementing the PCIT-CU and Coaching and Rewarding Emotional Skills (CARES) protocols with families of children with severe conduct problems and the LPE specifier, such as addressing in-session aggressive child behavior and how to prevent caregiver frustration and burnout. It also intends to highlight the victories that can be achieved by providing an effective treatment. This case was one that was seen in our clinic and the mother provided consent for this description. We have modified a number of descriptive characteristics of the case to protect the family's anonymity but have tried to faithfully describe the treatment process as it unfolded for this family.

https://doi.org/10.1037/0000500-010
A Clinical Guide to Working With Youth With Conduct Disorders and Limited Prosocial Emotions, by P. J. Frick and E. R. Kimonis

CASE INTRODUCTION

Leo (not his real name) is a 5½-year-old boy who was referred to us for treatment by his mother due to behavioral concerns. At age 4, he was diagnosed with global developmental delay by a school counselor. His mother denied any other prior mental health diagnoses or a history of trauma for Leo (although note prenatal substance exposure detailed later). However, she reported that when he was 2 years old, a child neighbor in their complex was violently murdered during a home invasion, which was followed for 2 weeks by a heavy police presence. She explained that Leo heard about but did not directly witness these events, which she felt he was too young to understand. Later into treatment, she disclosed that her intellectually disabled daughter had been verbally and physically abusive toward Leo since he was 2 years old. At this time, a risk assessment was conducted to ensure no imminent risk of harm to Leo, and safety planning was undertaken to limit the amount of time the siblings spent alone together. This involved developing strategies aimed at preventing sibling conflict when it is most likely to occur (e.g., implementing a consistent routine involving the siblings taking turns either choosing what music to play in the car or listening to music on headphones). Leo's mother denied any history of domestic violence, involvement with child protective services, or other legal involvement. She described the home environment as "always chaotic." She also reported that Leo had not previously received any psychological or pharmacological treatment. However, she was on a waiting list for speech therapy and occupational therapy after requesting services for Leo's speech and toileting difficulties, respectively. At intake, Leo wore diapers on most days because he was not yet being toilet trained.

Leo lives in public housing with his 40-year-old biological mother. In addition to his 14-year-old half-sister, he also has two adult half-brothers who do not live in the home. His mother denied any contact with Leo's biological father. However, she and Leo visit his teenage sister daily at the apartment she lives in with her biological father, who is not involved in parenting Leo but helps to support his practical living needs. Leo's mother identified herself as his primary caregiver. She self-identified as Aboriginal Australian with English as the family's primary language. She reported her highest level of education as year 10 and that she is unemployed and receiving governmental income support. Leo attends preschool 2 to 3 days each week, after it was recommended that she delay him starting kindergarten because he was not ready. She denied any school suspensions or expulsions. Since starting preschool, she reported improvements in Leo's willingness to play with others and in his toileting.

ASSESSMENT

Leo's mother participated in the initial comprehensive assessment at a school-based outreach clinic of the University of New South Wales (UNSW) Parent–Child Research Clinic. According to his mother, Leo's presenting problems include hitting, pushing, noncompliance, arguing and "talking back" at home and school, temper tantrums, screaming and yelling, whining, blaming others for his wrongdoing, and running away at drop-off to preschool or his aunt's house. She described Leo as "territorial" because he will not let others touch his things, refuses to use spaces or equipment if other children are using them, and behaves poorly unless he is one-on-one with her. His teacher reported that Leo is noncompliant, defiant, and aggressive toward teachers and teacher's aides and aggressive with peers, typically expressed as overly "rough play" and pretending to hurt or threaten others using toy knives. The teacher described the content of his conversations as "dark," as he talked about hurting people with swords and knives. His mother reported that, from a very young age, Leo preferred to play alone rather than with peers. These problem behaviors reportedly presented from age 2 years old and worsened during the COVID-19 pandemic isolation period. She reported using a variety of discipline strategies, none of which appeared to change Leo's behavior. Strategies she reported using included trying to reason with Leo, giving in, walking away, offering incentives, providing reminders about rules, yelling, and "giving up." She rated her confidence in managing Leo's behavior as 6 out of 10. When asked about his strengths, his mother described Leo as usually being happy and loving to play dress up and catch. Her goals for treatment were to learn strategies to help Leo better regulate his emotions and increase his social skills (e.g., sharing).

Regarding Leo's developmental history, his mother reported having gestational diabetes, low amniotic fluid, and first trimester bleeding during her pregnancy. Leo had an enlarged kidney. She denied smoking or drinking alcohol during her pregnancy but reported taking methadone. Leo was born full-term at 40 weeks and delivery was uncomplicated. However, he did not cry for 30 minutes after birth and was transported to special care, transferred to a second hospital, and diagnosed with a congenital condition affecting the vocal cords. In the neonatal intensive care unit (NICU), he was treated for an infection with antibiotics and started on morphine for methadone withdrawal. He was sent home after 2 weeks in the NICU with a morphine reduction schedule. His mother denied any feeding problems during infancy but reported he had poor sleep patterns, colic, and was very restless in his first year. Leo reportedly did not like hugs or other forms of affection as an infant. Leo's sleep is irregular, varying drastically between preschool and nonpreschool days in terms of sleep and waking times. He reportedly goes to bed as late as midnight on some days and sleeps on average 10 to 11 hours each night. Leo's mother described him as an extremely fussy eater who prefers "bland" foods such as pasta and breaded chicken and refuses fruits and vegetables. His mother denied any other child hospitalizations, surgeries, or serious accidents.

Regarding family history of mental illness, Leo's mother reported that she was diagnosed with depression and took antidepressants but stopped taking them because they "didn't work." She denied experiencing postnatal depression. She reported that her feelings of social isolation and withdrawal worsened following COVID-19. She also reported Leo's sister was diagnosed with autism spectrum disorder (ASD) and intellectual disability, his adult brother was diagnosed with schizophrenia, and her own father was diagnosed with posttraumatic stress disorder, depression, and antisocial personality disorder. Leo's grandfather and two older brothers were previously incarcerated. She reported experiencing several stressful life events, including health problems and her father's death.

Leo's mother completed several standardized rating scales. On the Child Behavior Checklist (CBCL; Achenbach & Rescorla, 2001), Leo scored in the clinical range for oppositional defiant problems and on the internalizing problems composite, in the borderline clinical range on the externalizing problems composite, but in the normal range for other *Diagnostic and Statistical Manual of Mental Disorders* (*DSM*)-oriented scales. Leo's teacher scored him in the clinical range on most *DSM*-oriented scales—depression, anxiety, ASD, and oppositional defiant disorder (ODD)—and on the internalizing and externalizing problems composites, and in the borderline clinical range on the attention-deficit/hyperactivity disorder (ADHD) scale. Mother and teacher also endorsed high rates of callous–unemotional (CU) traits on the Inventory of Callous–Unemotional Traits (ICU). On the Eyberg Child Behavior Inventory (ECBI; Eyberg & Pincus, 1999) completed by his mother and the Sutter-Eyberg Student Behavior Inventory-Revised (SESBI-R; Eyberg & Pincus, 1999) completed by his teacher, scores were in the clinically significant range with T-scores of 79 and 62 for intensity of conduct problems, and 75 and 52 for problematic nature of child's conduct problems, respectively. On the Diagnostic Interview Schedule for Children, Adolescents, and Parents (DISCAP; Tissue et al., 2022), his mother endorsed ODD symptoms of arguing, defiance at home and school, blame externalization, and being touchy or easily annoyed by others occurring for greater than 6 months and interfering with daily life in social and academic domains. His mother only endorsed the aggressive behavior symptom of conduct disorder (CD) on the DISCAP. Based on this information, Leo met diagnostic criteria for ODD, moderate severity.

On the Clinical Assessment of Prosocial Emotions (CAPE; Frick, 2013), his mother endorsed lack of remorse or guilt, callous–lack of empathy, and lack of concern about performance symptoms presenting most of the time, across settings, and for at least 1 year, supporting a diagnosis of the LPE specifier. She provided examples of Leo telling other children they deserved it or "too bad" if he hurt them, not caring or laughing if others are hurt, and not caring if he is in trouble. The assessor scored the family as 45 (obvious problems) on the Children's Global Assessment Scale (CGAS; Shaffer et al., 1983), which ranges from 1 to 100.

His mother was observed with Leo during three structured play situations, child-led play, parent-led play, and cleanup, and coded using the Dyadic Parent–Child Interaction Coding System (DPICS; Eyberg et al., 2013). The DPICS is a behavioral observation measure designed to be part of the standard Parent–Child Interaction Therapy (PCIT) intervention and it assesses the quality of caregiver–child interactions by coding the verbalizations, vocalizations, and behaviors of the caregiver and child. Across the DPICS observation period, the demands on the caregiver to exert control over the child are progressively increased to (a) allow the child to direct the play (child-led play), (b) direct the play with the child adhering to the caregiver's rules (parent-led play), and (c) instruct the child to clean up the toys independently (cleanup). Leo's mother's DPICS skills during child-led play were low: zero reflections, behavior descriptions, labeled praise, or unlabeled praise; 15 questions; 4 commands; 4 negative talks (e.g., "Don't do that," "No, you're being silly"); and 26 neutral talks. She mainly stood or sat watching Leo play rather than engaging in play together with him, her eye contact was limited, and her affect was flat. However, Leo readily engaged in play with his mother. She reported that Leo was "better behaved" during the child-led play session and it was not typical of his play at home, which tended to be more aggressive and destructive using toys such as monster trucks. During parent-led play, Leo's mother used numerous indirect and several direct commands, none of which Leo complied with. He often dawdled, ignored commands, or refused to follow his mother's requests to change tasks or follow her lead. She reported he was more noncompliant during this play session than at home. In the cleanup observation, Leo complied with 11% of his mother's effective commands. She gave "machine-gun commands," one after the other, of which many were indirect (e.g., "Clean up, okay?" "You can pick up the block and put it in the container," "Come on quick before [therapist] comes back," "Let's pack away these blocks"). She described Leo's noncompliance during this observation as typical of his behavior at home and she explained that she has "given up" on asking him to clean up at home.

TREATMENT USING PARENT–CHILD INTERACTION THERAPY: CALLOUS–UNEMOTIONAL VERSION

The family received treatment using the PCIT-CU protocol we described in the previous chapter. Consistent with the fixed session approach of the clinical trial in which they were enrolled, the family received seven child-directed interaction (CDI-CU adaptation) sessions, seven parent-directed interaction (PDI-CU version) sessions, and seven CARES sessions over an 8-month treatment period. This course of treatment is described in detail in this section.

Before providing a detailed description of the course of treatment for Leo, we would like to note some important considerations we made based on Leo's cultural background. Although Leo's presentation was consistent with criteria for the LPE specifier, diagnostic labels such as "CU traits" and "LPE" were intentionally avoided in early sessions to reduce the risk of harmful attributions. Instead, the therapist employed a stepped, family-centered approach to communicating the child's emotional and behavioral profile. In the CDI-CU teach session, the therapist introduced the idea that children differ in their emotional capacities, which can help explain behaviors of concern identified by the mother, including Leo's limited sharing and reduced empathy. Later, in the PDI-CU teach session, this discussion was extended to include how reduced emotional sensitivity makes certain children less responsive to typical forms of discipline, thereby reinforcing the need for structured strategies like the token economy system. Finally, during the CARES teach session, these ideas were integrated into a broader discussion of the treatment rationale for children like Leo with lower than typical development of emotional literacy skills. This gradual, relational approach supported the mother's understanding of Leo's mental health needs, while minimizing the risk that diagnostic labels would inadvertently contribute to feelings of blame, exclusion, or hopelessness. Critically, the therapist framed Leo's limited emotional capacities relative to his peers as malleable and capable of growth with tailored, supported learning opportunities, promoting optimism about treatment.

Given the mother's self-identified Indigenous Australian background, cultural responsiveness was embedded throughout treatment planning and delivery. A key framework guiding this approach was the social and emotional well-being (SEWB) model articulated by Dudgeon et al. (2017), which emphasizes seven interconnected domains as central to Indigenous health and healing: body, mind and emotions, family and kinship, community, culture, Country (i.e., referring to the lands, waterways, and skies with which First Nations peoples maintain deep ancestral, cultural, and family connections), and spirituality. This holistic understanding shaped the therapeutic alliance and informed how the therapist framed child behavior, caregiver strengths, and treatment goals. For example, in addition to carefully and respectfully introducing diagnostic terminology, the therapist placed strong emphasis on supporting the mother's self-determination in therapeutic engagement by recognizing and praising her advocacy for her child through her voluntary participation in the program. Collaborative decision making was also prioritized. Later in treatment, when exploring the possibility of a neuropsychological assessment of the child for ADHD or ASD, the therapist encouraged the mother to pursue this through her existing and trusted health care provider, the Aboriginal Health Service, with which she was already engaged. This respected her agency and aligned with the SEWB domain of culturally safe connection to services. Finally, the therapist actively supported the mother's connections to family and community, key domains in the SEWB model. From the third CDI-CU coach session onward, when discussions around caregiver stress levels begin, the therapist regularly checked in on the mother's self-care and the well-being of important people in her life, including her daughter's father (who had epilepsy) and her own mother (diagnosed with cancer during treatment). These discussions acknowledged the relational nature of Indigenous identity and the impact of family and community stressors on parenting and well-being. In this way, PCIT-CU was flexibly adapted to affirm cultural values, foster relational and emotional strength, reduce stigma through thoughtful communication about diagnosis, and support Indigenous-defined pathways to healing.

The Child-Directed Interaction: Callous-Unemotional Version Phase

The first phase of treatment is the CDI-CU phase and it consists of seven sessions, which focus primarily on improving the quality of the parent–child relationship. The first session is a parent-only teach session. The remaining sessions primarily focus on in vivo coaching of the caregiver, to implement the skills they learned about in the teach session with the child during child-directed interactions.

CDI-CU Teach Session

In the CDI teach session, session goals include:

- establishing rapport with the family,
- educating caregivers about PCIT-CU procedures and the course of therapy, and
- teaching the caregiver CDI-CU skills, such as to increase warmth and to use differential attention in response to minor child misbehavior (e.g., rough play) paired with labeled praise for positive behavior (e.g., gentle play).

The session begins with an orientation to the treatment by discussing expectations for therapy, briefly reviewing assessment results, revisiting caregiver-identified concerns from the pretreatment assessment, and affirming the relevance and evidence base of the PCIT-CU model in addressing these concerns.

Next, therapists provide an overview of PCIT-CU that includes discussion of its three treatment phases and an overview of CDI-CU, with rationale for why it is taught before the PDI-CU discipline phase (i.e., because children are better able to accept limits and discipline once the caregiver–child relationship is strengthened). This is followed by an explanation of the PRIDE do and don't skills. When explaining the PRIDE (praise, reflect, imitate, describe, enjoy) do skills to the caregiver, therapists standardly provide a rationale for why using each individual skill is important and this rationale is tailored to each individual child and family. For example, given Leo's speech difficulties, the therapist emphasized that using reflections improves children's speech and increases verbal communication. When reviewing the reflection skill, his mother also raised concerns about Leo's speech either being minimal or highly negative in content. The therapist emphasized that she should only use reflections for Leo's appropriate speech. As another example of tailoring, when explaining the differential attention skill, the therapist instructed the mother to use planned ignoring when Leo makes nonverbal threats toward her (e.g., using his finger to draw a line across his mother's neck after losing or gesturing to threaten to punch her by raising up his arm) and to keep an eye out for gentle behaviors to descriptively praise. When reviewing the labeled praise skill, the mother raised concerns that Leo often tells her to "shut up" when she praises him. The therapist explained that this is not uncommon for children like Leo with the LPE specifier and encouraged the mother to use planned ignoring when this happens and to persist with praising his positive behaviors.

Leo's mother was engaged throughout the CDI-CU teach session and was able to recall the PRIDE skills discussed without prompting. When role-playing

PRIDE skills with the therapist, the mother used many questions. When the therapist prompted her to use a do skill instead, she explained that she often asks Leo questions to encourage him to talk more because of his speech problems, but she acknowledged that too many questions often frustrate him. She also reported that Leo becomes frustrated when she asks him to repeat himself because she cannot understand what he is saying. The therapist encouraged her to try and reflect back only one or two words if she cannot understand all of what Leo is saying. During the discussion around implementing CDI-CU special play for 5 minutes daily at home, Leo's mother raised concerns around how to do it alone with Leo given his sister's high needs. The therapist engaged in a collaborative discussion with Leo's mother to problem solve ideas, and she settled on occupying her daughter with some limited screen time while doing the 5 minutes of special play with Leo. During this session, the mother reported a recent escalation in Leo's problem behaviors at school, including hitting teachers and swearing.

CDI-CU Coach Session 1

One week later, the mother attended her first CDI-CU coaching session with Leo. In this first CDI coaching session, session goals include:

- continuing to strengthen rapport with families,
- establishing the importance of regular home practice of CDI-CU skills during 5 minutes of daily special play, and
- building the caregiver's confidence in their ability to use PRIDE skills through in vivo coaching.

Typically, in PCIT this coaching is done with one caregiver at a time playing with the child in the therapy room and the therapist behind the one-way mirror providing the caregiver with real-time live feedback via a wireless, caregiver-worn bug-in-ear device. Where there are two caregivers involved in treatment, they take turns being coached by the therapist, and it can be useful for the other caregiver to learn by observing the one who is being coached to implement CDI skills.

In this session, as in every CDI session, the CDI-CU homework sheet was reviewed with Leo's mother to see how often she practiced special play during the week, the level of warmth and affection during the play according to her (i.e., 1, *not at all,* to 4, *extremely*), and any problems she encountered during special play, in order to problem solve and collaboratively generate solutions. She reported practicing special play 4 out of the 7 days since the last session and she denied any problems with Leo during special play. Her homework sheet warmth ratings ranged from 2 (*somewhat*) to 4 (*extremely*). During this session, the mother reported continued difficulties with Leo's noncompliance or defiance, aggression, and disruptive behavior, most notably interrupting her during conversations. Leo was also observed to engage in significant disruptive behavior during the check-in and debrief sections before and after coaching, respectively. Leo frequently pulled his mother's clothing and the therapist's lanyard, used a plastic toy knife from the toy kitchen set to threaten to cut the therapist, and climbed on the furniture. She initially responded to Leo's attempts to interrupt her conversation with the therapist, who then coached her to used planned ignoring of these attention-seeking behaviors paired with specific praise for positive opposite behaviors (e.g., waiting patiently). She was observed in child-led play with Leo for 5 minutes and coded by the therapist using the DPICS. The mother showed improved use of labeled praise and reflections (Figure 9.1) along with decreased use of questions and negative talk (Figure 9.2). Figures 9.1 and 9.2 show the fluctuation of do and don't skills throughout all phases of treatment, respectively, as well as posttreatment and at a 3-month follow-up assessment. The therapist provided Leo's mother with feedback after the observation and told her that behavior descriptions would be prioritized during coaching, since she used none during the coding period. She was receptive to coaching and increased her use of descriptions, reflections, and labeled praise during the coaching period. Leo's mother gave several unlabeled praises (e.g., "good job"), which she successfully converted to labeled praises (e.g., "good counting") when prompted by the therapist. She also showed increased reciprocal play, appropriate eye contact, and low to moderate warmth during coaching. She infrequently smiled or laughed with Leo during play. Leo was mostly engaged in play with his mother, displaying occasional eye contact and attempts to engage her in his play. He showed some instances of misbehavior including touching his mother's bug-in-ear device and pretending to use the toy knife to cut the wire leading to the receiver or

FIGURE 9.1. Leo's Mother's CDI-CU "Do" Skills Across PCIT-CU Treatment and at 3-Month Follow-Up Assessment

Note. CDI-CU = Child-Directed Interaction: Callous-Unemotional version; PDI = parent-directed interaction; PCIT-CU = Parent-Child Interaction Therapy: Callous-Unemotional version.

FIGURE 9.2. Leo's Mother's CDI-CU "Don't" Skills Across PCIT-CU Treatment and at 3-Month Follow-Up Assessment

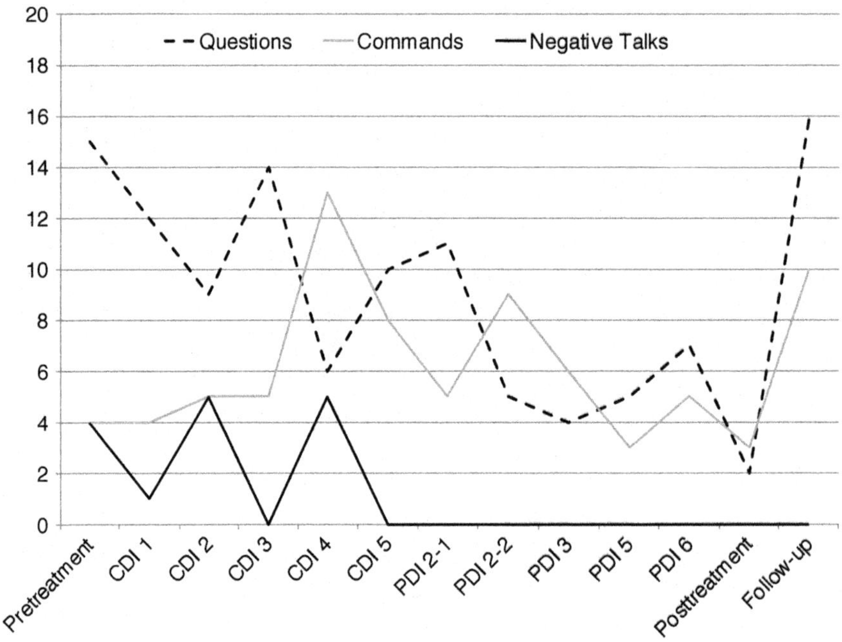

Note. CDI-CU = Child-Directed Interaction: Callous-Unemotional version; PDI = parent-directed interaction; PCIT-CU = Parent–Child Interaction Therapy: Callous-Unemotional version.

to hurt his mother. The mother was coached to use planned ignoring paired with specific praise for positive opposite behavior in response. In the debrief, the therapist expanded on the rationale for using planned ignoring. She was reminded to end special play at home if Leo's behavior became aggressive or destructive, by saying, "Special play is over for today because you hurt me. I bet tomorrow you'll be able to play gently during special time." The mother reported she found the coaching helpful for knowing what to say with Leo, as she was not used to playing with him. She was instructed to focus on increasing her behavior descriptions and reducing her questions during special play practice at home.

CDI-CU Coach Session 2

The following week, Leo's mother attended the second CDI-CU coaching session. Sessions goals include the following:

- continuing to stress the importance of regular homework (i.e., practice of CDI-CU skills during 5 minutes of daily special play);
- continuing to shape caregivers' use of CDI-CU skills, guided by in-session DPICS data; and
- instilling caregiver's positive expectations for mastery of CDI-CU skills (see the previous chapter for definition of mastery).

Leo's mother reported practicing special play at home 5 out of the 7 days since the last treatment session, for which the therapist provided labeled praise. She reported using appropriate special time activities and denied any problems. She rated each day of home special play as somewhat warm (2 out of 4). She observed a reduction in her own use of questions. She reported continued difficulties over the week with Leo's noncompliance or defiance and aggressive and destructive behavior, which he again displayed during the check-in and debrief. Leo interrupted his mother's conversation with the therapist, pulled on her clothes and lanyard, threw and banged toys, and climbed on furniture. The mother was coached in using planned ignoring. During coding, she was observed to increase her use of all three PRIDE do skills and decrease her use of questions, but she also increased her commands and negative talk. She used negative talk in response to Leo's disruptive behavior during coding (e.g., "No, don't break things" when he suggested breaking a toy). During coaching, the mother was guided to decrease questions and commands and to use planned ignoring for disruptive behavior. She was receptive to coaching, decreasing her use of questions and negative talk, as well as converting her questions to reflections. She also engaged in appropriate eye contact and reciprocal play, as well as low to moderate warmth (i.e., infrequent smiling and laughter). Leo appeared to enjoy special play with his mother, in the form of eye contact and attempts to engage her in play. He continued showing disruptive behavior including wearing and touching the bug-in-ear device. His mother used planned ignoring with specific praise for positive opposite behaviors. Initially, Leo escalated his behavior in response to his mother's ignoring, by increasing the intensity of his swearing (e.g., "fucking pig"), trying to escape the treatment room, and climbing on furniture to turn off the lights. His mother was coached to position herself against the exit door so Leo could not escape the room.

During the debrief, the therapist explained the rationale for not ending special play at home when it is apparent that the function of Leo's aggressive behavior is to escape the play, in order to avoid reinforcing this behavior. Given the mother's low use of descriptions during coaching, she was instructed to focus on this skill for her daily CDI-CU homework practice. In this CDI-CU Coach Session 2, Leo's mother was provided a "Showing You Care" social story and was instructed to read it every day with Leo. This social story describes different ways people can show they care about others, including physical affection, smiling and laughing, playing, and spending time together. The mother was instructed to talk with Leo to generate ideas about others' caring behaviors. At the end of the debrief, Leo swore at the therapist, told her he wanted to hurt her, and pulled her finger when she tried to block him from opening the clinic door to escape the room. For their safety, therapists at the Parent–Child Research Clinic are trained to keep long hair tied up; avoid wearing dangling earrings, other accessories, or loose clothing; remove all hard objects from the room that could be used as a weapon; position themselves between a client with a history of violence and the exit door; avoid turning their back to this client; and remove themselves and caregiver(s) from the room when the child escalates to violence.

CDI-CU Coach Session 3

Goals for this treatment session include

- fine-tuning the caregiver's CDI-CU skills using coaching of skills not yet at mastery level (where multiple skills are deficient, in-session DPICS coding is used to prioritize which skill(s) to focus on in coaching), and
- providing psychoeducation on the importance of reducing caregiver's stress levels using personalized strategies.

This conversation was initiated by having Leo's mother complete the "How Stressed Am I?" questionnaire, which originates from the Helping Our Toddlers, Developing Our Children's Skills universal group parenting intervention (Agazzi et al., 2017; Armstrong et al., 2006). Leo's mother's score on this tool that assesses stressful life events was 170, indicating a "boiling stage" or overstressed level. Stressors endorsed by the mother included death of a close family member, change in health of a family member, less than 8 hours of sleep per night, trouble with children, and family get-togethers. She also completed the Parenting Stress Index–Short Form (PSI-SF; Abidin, 1995), which assesses three domains of parenting-related stress: parental distress (i.e., distress relating to the parenting role itself), difficult child (i.e., specific child behavior and temperament factors), and caregiver–child dysfunctional interaction (i.e., caregiver's perceptions of their child and the caregiver–child relationship as not meeting their expectations). The mother's raw scores on the PSI-SF were highest for difficult child at 44, followed by 42 for parental distress, and 40 for caregiver–child dysfunctional interaction subscales (> 95th percentile for all scores), producing a total PSI score of 126 (> 99th percentile).

Leo's mother reported completing special play with Leo on 6 of the 7 days since her last treatment session. Warmth ratings ranged from "1" (*not at all*) to "2" (*somewhat*). She reported that on one day, he refused to engage in special play, so she played alone for the 5 minutes. She denied any other problems during special play and explained that he typically enjoys it. She explained that CDI-CU skills still feel unnatural for her and that she is noticing that she used more don't skills. She denied completing the social story with Leo, explaining that he refused to sit down and engage, saying, "Reading is dumb." She was advised to look out for times when he is calm over the following week to read the social story, not requiring that he sit down while she reads it. The mother reported an improvement in Leo's behavior at school, indicating no instances of hitting peers or teachers over the past week. She attributed this change to her giving him a treat when he behaves at school, explaining that he is highly motivated by rewards. She denied any changes in Leo's disruptive behavior at home. During check-in, Leo engaged in disruptive behaviors, including pretending to cut himself with the toy knife, throwing toys, using rude language, and attempting to escape the therapy room. Often, PCIT therapists will remove objects like toy knives from the therapy room; however, the therapist intentionally kept it in the therapy room to provide an opportunity to coach Leo's mother in planned ignoring, since she initially attended to these behaviors by using negative talk. After the check-in, Leo's disruptive behaviors increased in intensity to include swearing, hitting his mother, pointing his middle finger at the in-room mounted cameras, throwing toys at the cameras, and attempting to escape the therapy room. Consequently, the therapist decided to immediately coach the mother to apply planned ignoring, labeled praise for positive opposite behaviors, and to redirect Leo by describing her own play in an enthusiastic and fun way. These strategies were effective at reengaging Leo in the play, at which point the therapist began coding using the DPICS.

During coding, Leo's mother increased reflections and decreased negative talk. She also decreased labeled praise, increased questions, continued using commands, and rarely used descriptions. She struggled to ignore Leo's minor misbehaviors, including throwing toys and bossy behavior, by responding to them with CDI-CU do and don't skills. Coaching focused on increasing labeled praises and decreasing questions. She was receptive to coaching and improved in these skills. She often required prompting to convert unlabeled praises to labeled praises (e.g., "Good job for . . .") and continued using commands and negative talk. She showed appropriate eye contact and reciprocal play, but warmth was low to moderate (e.g., infrequent smiling). Leo appeared to enjoy the play, showing eye contact and sustained play with his mother after redirection. He continued displaying instances of disruptive behavior including swearing, throwing, and putting toys in his mouth, for which his mother was coached to use planned ignoring. During the debrief, psychoeducation was provided on the importance of using planned ignoring instead of negative talk to respond to Leo's attention-seeking misbehavior. Given Leo's escalation in disruptive behavior when he observed the therapist coaching the mother to use planned ignoring during the check-in and debrief, the therapist explained to the mother she would instead use a discrete nonverbal hand signal cue for future sessions. Using the "PCIT-CU Guide to Stress Relief" handout, the therapist engaged her in a discussion about what stress relief strategies she finds most effective, and to practice those ones identified daily. For Leo's mother, this included chatting with friends online. She was also instructed to focus on increasing descriptions and reducing questions during daily special play at home.

CDI-CU Coach Session 4

The goals for this treatment session are

- achieving mastery of CDI-CU skills using in vivo coaching, and
- increasing caregiver motivation if mastery criteria are not yet met.

Leo's mother reported completing special play in all of the 7 days since her last treatment session and denied any major problems. She reported that sometimes Leo initially did not want to engage in special play but that he will do so later in the day. After discussion, it was determined that this was due to introducing special time when Leo was engaged in a highly desirable activity like TV or video games. The therapist recommended that the mother introduce a "first–then" strategy of first doing special play, then letting Leo use these media. Leo's mother denied reading the social story, explaining that Leo refused to engage because he viewed her reading as a form of homework. She also denied engaging in any stress relief strategies over the week due to a lack of capacity. She reported improved school behavior based on teacher feedback, which she continued to attribute to her use of rewards for good school behavior. She denied any significant changes in behavior problems at home.

Leo continued engaging in disruptive behavior during check-in by throwing toys, using rude language, and attempting to escape the therapy room to enter the observation room. His mother responded to these behaviors with a mix of negative talk and planned ignoring, which she was coached to continue using with paired labeled praise for positive opposite behaviors (e.g., using polite words, returning to the play room). Leo's behavior escalated to swearing, climbing on furniture, and trying to escape the therapy room. Consequently, Leo's mother was coached in planned ignoring and redirection by enthusiastically describing her own play, before beginning coding using the DPICS when Leo eventually engaged in play with her.

During coding, the mother increased her use of labeled praise and decreased her use of questions. However, she reduced her use of the other do skills and increased her use of don't skills. She applied a mix of planned ignoring, commands to redirect Leo to play, and negative talk in response to his disruptive behavior. Much of the coaching session was spent on applying planned ignoring and redirection in response to Leo's escalating attempts to escape the therapy room. For example, the therapist coached the mother to position herself in front of the exit door with toys and enthusiastically describe her own play. On a couple of occasions, the therapist entered the playroom to coach the mother and model redirection because Leo escaped the playroom and the mother's infrared bug-in-ear device stopped working when she went after him. She was somewhat receptive to coaching, often inconsistently applying planned ignoring by responding to Leo's disruptive behavior with negative talk and commands. Disruptive behaviors included swearing, using a bossy and demanding tone of voice, putting toys in his mouth or throwing them, climbing on furniture, miming cutting the clinician in a threatening way, and escaping the playroom. The mother successfully used labeled praise for positive opposite behaviors (e.g., playing on the floor) and returned to following his lead using CDI-CU skills whenever Leo briefly engaged in appropriate play. At the end of the session, the mother explained that Leo told her he escalates his disruptive behavior during therapy sessions because he does not like being ignored. She attributed his severe behavior in this session to him drinking a sugary Slurpee drink immediately before it began. Due to Leo's escalation in disruptive behavior during the debrief, it was ended and resumed in a phone call to the mother later in the day. In this call, she was instructed to focus on increasing descriptions and reflections during special play homework, to continue to attempt reading the social story to Leo at a calm time, and to aim to use daily stress relief strategies.

Following this session, the therapist also sought supervision from her clinical supervisor on how to manage the escalation in negative behaviors. This discussion prompted scheduling a caregiver-only teleconference session to gather further information about Leo's home behavior and whether and how planned ignoring is being used. This information could be useful for providing more tailored psychoeducation on this skill and the importance of consistency for supporting learning for children like Leo who show the LPE specifier. It was also determined that more detailed information about the mother's use of special play at home was needed to better understand her slow progress in CDI-CU skill development and Leo's persistently high-intensity conduct problems reported by her on the weekly ECBIs. In this teleconference, it was determined that a reason for Leo's in-session escape behaviors was likely his high need for control. The therapist discussed using several strategies to avoid Leo's escape behavior and behavioral escalation, including providing him with the choice to either see the observation room before or after special play with his mother and choosing between toys to use for special play. Other strategies included the mother restricting the child's access to sugary foods before the session, instructing Leo's mother to explain expected session behaviors to Leo prior to the next treatment session (e.g., keeping his hands and feet to himself, keeping his feet on the ground, staying in the playroom), and the therapist removing furniture from the playroom that he could climb on. The therapist provided additional psychoeducation on consistent use of planned ignoring for disruptive behaviors at home, which the mother described as challenging because Leo makes threats to destroy things when she ignores him. The therapist also suggested using a nonverbal hand signal with verbal cue of "brick wall" to prompt planned ignoring during session check-ins and debriefs so as not to alert Leo to the therapist's instruction. She was also asked to video record herself doing special play at home for the therapist to see how it was being done and to provide feedback.

CDI-CU Coach Session 5

The goals of this treatment session are

- achieving mastery of CDI-CU skills using in vivo coaching, and
- increasing caregiver motivation if mastery criteria are not yet met.

The mother reported practicing special play on 5 of the 7 days since her last treatment session. She denied any problems except for Leo not wanting to engage in special play once or twice, but she successfully reengaged him later in the day. Warmth ratings were mostly "3" (*very*), except for 1 day that was rated a "2" (*somewhat*). She reported forgetting to video record herself in special play with Leo at home but remembering to explain expected session behaviors to him before this treatment session. She denied completing the social story or stress relief strategies because of Leo's refusal and her particularly stressful week, respectively. She explained she had added strain this week because she had to take her daughter to multiple medical appointments because her father was too unwell to take her. Leo reportedly began newly engaging in spitting behavior at home. The therapist and mother discussed stress relief strategies she found effective to do the following week, including taking a warm shower, clothes shopping, and talking to friends. They problem solved together barriers to using these daily stress relief strategies.

When provided the two choices at the beginning of the session, Leo chose to see the observation room first before engaging in special play with his mother, and he chose what toy he wanted to play with. However, he continued to display disruptive behavior during the check-in, including using rude language, climbing on the table, attempting to leave the playroom, and kicking the therapist while she left the playroom during the check-in and debrief. Leo's mother responded to these behaviors with a mix of negative talk, reminders about expected behaviors during the session, and planned ignoring, which she was coached to continue using paired with labeled praise for positive opposite behaviors. Leo's behaviors escalated after the check-in to swearing, throwing toys, and attempting to escape the playroom. When he was reengaged in play after coaching the mother in using planned ignoring and redirection, coding with the DPICS commenced. During coding, the mother increased her use of all three do skills and questions and decreased her use of commands and negative talk. She struggled to independently use planned ignoring for Leo's aggressive and bossy behaviors by continuing to engage in play with him and occasionally using negative talk and commands. Coaching focused on reducing questions and commands. The mother was receptive to coaching and decreased her use of these don't skills while simultaneously increasing her descriptions and labeled praise and maintaining use of reflections. She showed appropriate eye contact, reciprocal play, and low to moderate warmth (e.g., occasional smiling, laughing). Leo was engaged in play with his mother but occasionally swore, spit, put toys in his mouth, threw and kicked toys, pulled on the bug-in-ear device, climbed on the table, banged the playroom door, and took his mother's phone. The mother was coached to use planned ignoring of these behaviors with labeled praise for positive opposite behaviors and to use PRIDE skills in response to his appropriate behaviors. Leo kicked his mother on a few occasions, to which the therapist instructed her to provide a PCIT "swoop-and-go" warning that if he kicked her again she would leave the playroom. At the end of coaching, the mother reported her impression that his behaviors were more manageable in this session, which she attributed to having discussed expected behaviors with him before the session and having more boundaries in play during the session as preventions. She attributed her difficulties in holding back commands and negative talk and applying planned ignoring in response to Leo's problem behaviors as being due to her high level of frustration. The therapist returned to the importance of the mother using daily brief stress relief strategies to reduce her high stress levels.

During the debrief, Leo's mother provided him with her phone to listen to music, and he was observed to listen to rap music with explicit lyrics. His mother reported her belief that Leo models his sister's aggressive and swearing behavior from hearing her explicit rap music. The therapist provided psychoeducation on social learning and modeling and the need to limit Leo's access to inappropriate media content as a prevention strategy, such as having his sister use headphones when listening to explicit and loud music at home. The mother was instructed to focus on decreasing questions and commands during special play at home, continue attempting to read the social story to Leo, and use the identified daily stress relief strategies. Following the session, the therapist emailed a reminder to the mother to record herself doing special play at home with Leo.

CDI-CU Coach Session 6

The goals of this treatment session are

- achieving mastery of CDI-CU skills using in vivo coaching, and
- increasing caregiver motivation if mastery criteria are not yet met.

Leo's mother reported practicing special play every day in the week since her last session and denied any major problems, except for Leo on occasion not wanting to engage or being less engaged than usual. She successfully reengaged him in special play later in the day. Warmth ratings were mostly "2" (*somewhat*). She provided the therapist with a video recording of her special play at home to review. She also reported that Leo newly began engaging in aggression toward others in public, including hitting a person she was talking to. He displayed many disruptive behaviors during the check-in, including using rude language and swearing, drawing on playroom walls, climbing on toy boxes, throwing toys, moving and climbing on furniture, and multiple attempts to run and jump onto the time-out room door. He kicked and threw toys at the therapist a couple of times. Leo's mother responded with a mixture of negative talk and planned ignoring, and she was coached to consistently use planned ignoring with labeled praise of positive opposite behavior. Additional instruction was given on the importance of consistent responding to misbehavior to support Leo's learning style.

No coding could be conducted and, instead, coaching proceeded because of his escalating disruptive behavior following the check-in, including threatening motions toward his mother, throwing toys at her, and attempting to kick her. During this session, his mother was provided extended coaching on how to consistently apply planned ignoring and redirection by describing her own play. With prompting, she was able to provide labeled praise for positive opposite behaviors (e.g., "putting feet on the floor"). She very occasionally continued to use negative talk and commands. Leo was observed to initially significantly escalate his disruptive behavior in response to her planned ignoring, including hitting and kicking. The mother was instructed to use a "swoop-and-go" warning to prevent further aggression. She briefly left the room on one occasion when he hit her again. When Leo engaged in appropriate play, she was able to return to using CDI-CU skills with some prompting. She often struggled to withhold using commands and negative talk when Leo engaged in behaviors such as putting toy food in his mouth. She repeatedly let Leo know how much time was left in the session before he could reenter the observation room as a reward for engaging in special play with her.

During the debrief session, Leo's mother was instructed to focus on reducing negative talk and increasing labeled praise, especially for positive opposite behaviors occurring during special play homework. The therapist provided her with a typed sheet of labeled praise ideas for positive opposite behaviors personalized to Leo, which included "Thank you for . . . / Good job for . . . / I like when you are . . . sitting on the floor, keeping feet on the floor, staying close to me, returning to play with me, using your inside voice, playing quietly, using your manners, asking nicely, playing gently with toys, keeping toys in your hands, keeping hands and feet to yourself, playing gently with me, taking turns, sharing." In this final session of the CDI phase, the therapist stressed the importance of practicing special play at home every day. Consistently engaging in special play strengthens the caregiver–child bond, fostering a positive, emotionally close, and mutually cooperative relationship. This, in turn, increases the likelihood of successfully implementing discipline within a supportive and nurturing context.

The Parent-Directed Interaction: Callous-Unemotional Version Phase

The second phase of PCIT-CU is the PDI-CU phase. While the CDI-CU phase focused greatly on helping improve the caregiver–child relationship, the PDI phase focuses more on helping the caregiver develop skills to appropriately manage their child's behavior. This phase, like the CDI-CU phase, lasts seven sessions in its fixed session format. The first session is a caregiver-only teaching session and the remaining sessions primarily focus on coaching the caregiver through interactions with their child to implement PDI-CU discipline skills.

PDI-CU Teach Session

As in standard PCIT, the mother attended a teach session without the child to start this phase of treatment. Goals for this session include the following:

- providing the caregiver with psychoeducation on the eight qualities of an effective command;
- helping the caregiver to learn the importance of using a personalized token economy system with children with LPE to achieve compliance; and

- helping the caregiver learn how to implement the structured PDI-CU time-out procedure for noncompliance, paired with tokens to reinforce compliance.

When explaining the PDI-CU procedure, therapists explain that it is necessary to gradually progress from first using it in play with very simple in-clinic play–based commands (e.g., "Please hand me the red Lego") to eventually using it outside of the clinic and in public settings and throughout the day as needed for real-life commands, over the course of several weeks. As we noted in the previous chapter, research suggests that difficulties in learning punishment associations that children with the LPE specifier often experience may be overcome by consistently delivering punishment and by using a scripted procedure that explains to the child that their behavior was the cause of the punishment (Jean-Richard-dit-Bressel et al., 2023). The PCIT-CU time-out script provides children with a standardized explanation that they must sit in time-out because they did not do what they were told (i.e., an information-laden consequence), providing an informational frame to the child with LPE that helps them to appropriately interpret the consequences they are experiencing.

In Leo's case, his mother reported practicing special play 5 days in the past week and explained she was unable to practice on 2 days because her daughter broke her arm. She reported a stressful week because she needed to drive her daughter to multiple medical appointments. She also reported that Leo's school provided positive feedback about his behavior improving over the past week. She attributed this to the teachers spending more one-on-one time with him and giving him more labeled praise. She also reported an increase in learning by Leo, evidenced by him asking her questions about counting. However, she also reported continued difficulties with his noncompliant and defiant behavior at home. She expressed positive feelings about the CDI phase, saying she felt more confident in managing his behavior because of the new skills she learned, in particular planned ignoring.

The mother was engaged throughout the teach session, offering appropriate comments and questions about the material. For example, when explaining that one feature of an effective command is that it should be direct, she reflected that she often uses indirect commands with Leo in the form of a question ("Can you please . . .?"). She also explained that she often over-explains commands to get Leo to comply instead of providing the explanation before issuing the command or after he has complied with it, another quality of an effective command. She also reflected that Leo typically responded to her indirect commands with outright refusal (e.g., "No" or "I don't want to because . . ."). Leo's mother explained that she often responds by withdrawing her demand or escalating into a coercive cycle with Leo and eventually giving in when his behavior escalates. She predicted that PDI coaching would be difficult because Leo is likely to be very defiant since he has previously never learned to comply. However, she was open to implementing the discipline sequence in session with therapist support. She appropriately identified an adult-sized spare chair in her dining room that she could face toward the wall as her time-out chair, and she appropriately identified the laundry room as her time-out room, to which the therapist recommended temporarily removing the laundry powder and any other chemicals for safety reasons. When discussing the token economy system to reward Leo's quick listening, the mother reported that she will use poker chips as tokens and rewards of ice cream or Leo choosing a small toy from the store.

The mother engaged well in the PDI-CU role-play with the therapist and was receptive to coaching on how to sequence caregiver statements. She reported some concerns about her ability to remember the exact PDI-CU sequence lines, and the therapist reassured her that she would line-feed them in the next PDI-CU Coach Session 1. The therapist also provided psychoeducation about the usefulness of consistent use of CDI skills and planned ignoring in response to child behaviors maintained by attention (e.g., tantrums, yelling, backtalk) versus calm use of PDI skills specifically for compliance. Homework assigned for the week included daily special play and reading the "Showing You Care" social story with Leo, and engaging in a daily personal stress relief activity. The mother was given handouts titled "Eight Rules of Effective Commands" and "Using a Time-Out Room in Your Home" from the standard PCIT protocol, as well as "Benefits of Using a Token Economy" and the "PCIT-CU Time Out" diagram from the PCIT-CU protocol.

PDI-CU Coach Session 1

The goals for this session are to

- teach the PDI-CU discipline sequence to the child using a Mr. Bear teddy bear model, who is listening and rewarded with tokens he exchanges for honey, or not listening and being placed in time-out;
- intensively coach the caregiver, through the bug-in-ear system, to deliver the sequence with the child; and
- discuss PDI-CU homework: daily 5–10-minute PDI practice in play following CDI.

Leo's mother reported practicing special play 6 days out of the past week and denied any difficulties. Her warmth ratings ranged from 2 (*somewhat*) to 3 (*very*). She reported continued positive feedback from the school about maintaining his improved behavior, including no instances of hitting other children over the past week. However, she reported continued problems with Leo's noncompliant and defiant behavior at home and instances of him using his middle finger with others at school pickup. She brought poker chips to the session, as requested. During the check-in, Leo engaged in appropriate play and behavior, except for one instance of turning off the playroom lights. His mother responded by ignoring this behavior, and she was coached to provide labeled praise for him turning the lights back on. Leo's disruptive behavior was notably reduced relative to CDI sessions, including fewer instances of interrupting and throwing toys and no aggression or climbing on furniture.

During the therapist's Mr. Bear role-play, Leo engaged in several disruptive behaviors including snatching, kicking, and punching the teddy bear, to which the therapist used planned ignoring paired with labeled praise for playing gently with and then letting her have a turn with Mr. Bear, once he had let go of it. As is standard, coaching began with CDI play, during which the mother was coached to use planned ignoring of initial disruptive behaviors (i.e., putting a toy in his mouth, throwing toys, moving the time-out chair) and to redirect his attention by describing her own play with the toys using animated, enthusiastic speech. Once Leo was engaged in appropriate play with his mother and they were playing comfortably together, she was coached to deliver a play-based effective command ("Please hand me the carrot"). Leo initially did not respond and then threw the toy. She was then coached to deliver the warning ("If you don't hand me the carrot, you won't get a token for listening, and you'll have to sit on the time-out chair"), to which Leo did not comply and was taken to the time-out chair. He sat on the chair for 30 seconds before getting off, at which point his mother was coached to give him the once ever warning that "You got off the chair before I said you could. If you get off the chair again, you'll have to go to the time-out room." Leo continued to not comply and his mother was coached to take him to the time-out room, saying, "You got off the chair before I said you could. Now you have to go to the time-out room." Leo displayed several disruptive behaviors in the time-out room, including yelling, crying, spitting, taking off his shoes and throwing them, and climbing the walls. After 1 minute and 5 quiet seconds, his mother was coached to move him from the time-out room to the time-out chair, saying "Stay on the chair until I say you can get off." Additionally, he was given the once ever warning for standing on, rocking, and moving the time-out chair before he was placed in the time-out room for these behaviors (e.g., "You rocked the chair. If you rock the chair again, you'll have to go to the time-out room"). In total, during this session Leo sat in the time-out chair seven times and was placed in the time-out room six times for getting off the chair. On the seventh instance of sitting on the time-out chair after not complying with original command, Leo sat for the full 3 minutes and 5 quiet calm seconds. His mother was coached to say to him, "You're sitting quietly on the chair, are you ready to hand me the carrot?" (i.e., the original command), and Leo picked up the carrot and handed it to her. She was coached to immediately give a follow-up play-based effective command, "Okay, please give me the apple," and Leo immediately complied by handing her the apple. The mother was coached to give enthusiastic labeled praise for quick listening and a token: "Great quick listening. You get a token for listening right away." She was then coached to return to CDI for several minutes before being line fed a new effective command. Leo immediately complied with this command and his mother was coached to give labeled praise and a token for his quick listening.

Leo's mother was coached to end with several minutes of CDI play. She was receptive to CDI and PDI coaching, effectively repeating lines fed by the therapist and using a calm tone of voice when delivering PDI-CU statements.

She effectively ignored Leo's disruptive behavior while he was in time-out. Her use of planned ignoring during CDI coaching was mostly effective, except for a couple of occasions of involving Leo when attempting to redirect his play. She used a moderate level of labeled praise, including for positive opposite behaviors (e.g., keeping feet on floor, playing gently with toys) when prompted. Her eye contact and reciprocal play were appropriate but warmth was low (e.g., flat tone of voice).

In the debrief at the end of the session, the therapist emphasized the importance of accurately, consistently, and calmly implementing PDI-CU, including ignoring while Leo is in time-out and remaining silent after issuing an effective command or warning statement to allow him the opportunity to comply within the PCIT-stipulated 5-second response period. The mother reflected that this diverges from her typical approach of attempting to talk to and reason with Leo during these emotionally heightened periods, which typically results in him escalating his disruptive behavior. She and the therapist reviewed how to properly set up the time-out chair and room once the mother confirmed she felt comfortable practicing PDI following daily special play at home. Using the "Reward List" and "Home Reward Possibilities" handouts, Leo's mother was asked to generate a list of additional rewards, in addition to the ice cream reward for three tokens discussed in this session, for which Leo could trade in his earned tokens daily. The therapist emphasized the importance of Leo only receiving the reward if he had earned the correct number of tokens, and that his mother should decide when he receives the reward on the day he chooses to cash in his tokens. The mother was instructed to practice daily CDI for 5 minutes, followed by PDI in play for 5 to 10 minutes, aiming to use enough commands to allow the child to earn five daily tokens over the following week. She was encouraged to call the clinic if she encountered any issues in implementing PDI-CU at home. She was given the token economy homework sheet to complete with Leo over the week, including making a token bank together (e.g., decorated canister), posting a reward list in the home, and explaining the reward system to Leo using the sample script.

PDI-CU Coach Session 2

The goals for this session are to

- continue coaching PDI-CU skills toward mastery criteria (see Chapter 8 for a definition), and
- begin shifting from play-based commands to real-life and clean-up commands.

Leo's mother reported completing home practice 6 of the 14 days since her last session. She canceled a session because she found out her mother was diagnosed with cancer. She reported being unable to practice at all in the second week since her last appointment since she stayed at her mother's house to help care for her. She denied any problems with CDI or PDI home practice, explaining that Leo complied with all of her commands during the play. Her warmth ratings ranged from 2 (*somewhat*) to 3 (*very*). On her PDI-CU homework sheet, she recorded giving Leo between three and five tokens each day for compliance. She reported that Leo did not exchange any of his tokens for rewards but that he was frequently getting ice cream without trading in his tokens. She was provided psychoeducation on why it is important that he does not receive a reward without trading in his tokens. The mother reported improved home behavior, which was reflected in her ratings on the ECBI. She described improved social skills over the past week, including using his manners to ask for permission before engaging in a behavior and waving at others. She also reported that the school provided positive feedback about his behavior over the past week. She denied any specific behavior problems at home as well. She reported recently engaging with a service to provide occupational therapy support around Leo's toilet training and motor skills, to improve school readiness as he begins kindergarten in the coming months.

During the check in, Leo engaged in both independent play and appropriate play with the therapist while his mother completed the ECBI. He did not engage in any disruptive behaviors. He easily transitioned to CDI play with mother and she was coded for 5 minutes using the DPICS before some brief CDI coaching. During coding, she showed moderate use of labeled praise and decreased commands but also decreased descriptions and reflections and increased questions. CDI coaching focused on reducing questions and commands. Leo's mother was coached in PDI to deliver effective play and real-life commands (e.g., "Sit beside me"). She was not coached to have Leo clean up because the toy containers were removed from the playroom prior to the session for safety reasons because of Leo's high level of aggression and destruction in the first PDI-CU coach session. Leo complied with all 10 of the effective commands his mother issued during PDI-CU coaching and required only one time-out warning for the first play command, after initially dawdling and then throwing the car instead of handing it to his mother as she requested. He tended to comply toward the end of the 5-second waiting period, however. Consequently, he did not have to sit on the time-out chair or go to the time-out room during the entire coaching session. The mother was receptive to both CDI and PDI coaching, increasing her CDI do skills and reducing questions. She showed appropriate eye contact and reciprocal play, but warmth was low, as evidenced by her flat tone of voice and limited physical affection. She converted her indirect commands to effective direct commands when prompted but often used multistep commands (e.g., "Please come over here and help me to . . ."). She was observed to experience some difficulty staying silent after issuing a command, sometimes repeating parts to prompt Leo's compliance or verbally clarifying her request. She was effectively coached to make commands simpler and more specific, and to use pointing to prompt and clarify compliance while staying silent after her command, to which Leo responded well. She struggled to issue labeled praise for compliance, either giving the token without praise or praising the specific behavior instead of the targeted behavior (e.g., "Thank you for handing me the car" instead of "Thank you for quick listening"). Leo was engaged and receptive in play and did not engage in any disruptive behaviors. He appeared enthusiastic and interested in earning tokens and trading them in for rewards.

During the debrief, there was a notable reduction in Leo's disruptive behaviors as he engaged in very few instances of throwing toys, moving furniture, interrupting his mother, yelling, or aggressive behavior. The mother initially responded to this behavior with negative talk, but then effectively used planned ignoring when prompted. The therapist problem solved barriers to completing homework with Leo while staying at his grandmother's house. She was encouraged to continue using labeled praise for targeted positive behaviors displayed by Leo (e.g., keeping feet on floor, playing gently, calmly). The therapist discussed increasing the value of rewards but continuing to make them attainable, such that Leo continues frequently earning tokens. Leo's mother explained that Leo engages in more disruptive behaviors when around his sister's father, noticing that he tends to respond to Leo's aggressive and disruptive behavior with negative talk that leads to an escalation. The therapist encouraged the mother to invite him to attend and observe a future PCIT session and to share her knowledge of CDI skills with him to support consistent behavior management strategies across adults in the home. She reflected that her relationship with Leo had improved because of their special play time. She was assigned daily CDI followed by PDI for cleanup. She was assigned issuing two to four effective commands each day for important behaviors (e.g., getting his drink bottle, standing beside her when getting ready to leave the house), carefully planning them by ensuring she has enough time to follow through with time-out if he does not comply. She was encouraged to call the clinic if she encountered any problems implementing time-out at home.

Leo's mother requested to reschedule her following treatment sessions for various reasons including family sickness, summer holidays, and her mother starting radiation treatment. Since 70 days had passed since her last treatment session and the mother denied completing PDI home practice or using the token economy system, and she had only completed 3 days of CDI practice (all rated "2": *somewhat warm/affectionate*), the therapist and a senior clinician determined it would be in the family's best interest to repeat the content of the PDI-CU Coach Session 2. The goals of this session were to provide Leo's mother with a refresher on the PRIDE do and don't skills and the PDI-CU procedure, transition from using it with play-based commands to real-life commands, and address barriers to regular home practice of CDI-CU and PDI-CU skills. Leo's mother reported some improvements in Leo's behavior at home, describing him as being calmer and yelling, swearing, and hitting her less than usual. However, Leo's behavior ratings on the ECBI slightly increased, and his mother reported continued problems with noncompliance, unless he is given a reward. She reported he recently started kindergarten and there were no reports of behavioral concerns yet. Leo did not require a diaper and had wet himself only once at school. His mother reported that Leo continued seeing an occupational therapist to work on his fine motor skills and toileting. During the check-in, Leo engaged in appropriate play and showed fewer than typical instances of disruptive behavior, including interrupting and rough play. He did not engage in any aggressive or destructive behavior. His mother initially attended to these behaviors, but was responsive to coaching to use planned ignoring paired with labeled praise of positive opposite behaviors (e.g., patient waiting). She was also coached to use direct commands when Leo ran out of the playroom and when he stood on the time-out chair, with which he complied and she gave him a token.

Leo's mother was coded and briefly coached in CDI-CU. She showed an increase in reflections and a decrease in questions, although she also increased commands and decreased labeled praise, favoring unlabeled praise. Eye contact and reciprocal play were good, and she showed moderate warmth (e.g., laughing, gently patting the child's back). CDI-CU coaching goals included increasing labeled praise and reducing commands. The mother was coached in PDI-CU to deliver effective play-based, real-life (e.g., "stand beside me"), and cleanup commands. Leo complied with 10 out of 10 effective commands and did not require a time-out warning or the chair. She was receptive to CDI-CU and PDI-CU coaching, increasing her use of labeled praise often by converting unlabeled praises to be more specific and focused on positive opposite behaviors when prompted (e.g., "Thank you for sitting on the floor" in response to Leo sitting on the time-out chair and then sitting down near her to play with the toys). During PDI-CU coaching, she increased her use of direct commands and effectively converted indirect commands to be direct when prompted. She also improved in her ability to stay silent after issuing a command and instead used nonverbal pointing gestures to clarify her request (e.g., pointing to the toy and then to its container during cleanup commands). She struggled to praise Leo's targeted "listening" behavior when he complied, often praising him for the specific behavior instead (e.g., "Thank you for putting the car in the box"). During coaching, Leo was engaged and receptive in play with his mother, was interested and excited about earning tokens, and only displayed a few disruptive behaviors, including whining and sitting on the time-out chair instead of playing. His mother was coached to use a mixture of planned ignoring and effective commands in response, with which Leo immediately complied.

During the debrief, the therapist discussed the importance of consistent home practice of CDI-CU and PDI-CU skills and problem solved barriers to homework completion. Leo's mother reported a renewed commitment to daily practice of PCIT-CU skills. She was instructed to focus on increasing behavior descriptions and reducing questions in CDI-CU practice. For daily PDI-CU homework practice, she was instructed to practice using effective cleanup commands, as well as two to four carefully planned effective everyday commands (e.g., cleaning up toys, brushing hair), when there is time to follow through if time-out is needed.

PDI-CU Coach Session 3

The goals of this treatment session are to

- review the effect of treatment on the child's behavior,
- continue strengthening the caregiver's CDI-CU and PDI-CU skills, and
- focus on generalizing PDI-CU skills beyond the formal coaching situation.

Leo's mother reported practicing CDI-CU 5 days and PDI-CU 4 days out of the 7 days since the last session, with no instances of using the time-out room or chair for noncompliance. However, she reported that Leo tended to wait until the last minute to comply with her command. A discussion with the therapist determined that the mother had been counting the 5 seconds allowance for him to comply out loud. The therapist provided the rationale for staying silent after issuing an effective command to encourage quick listening. Leo earned 12 tokens for compliance over the previous week, which he traded in for rewards. The warmth of play was rated between 2 (*somewhat*) and 3 (*very*). A key goal of this session was to focus on generalizing PDI-CU skills beyond the formal coaching period. The mother reported continued improvements in Leo's behavior over the past week with few instances of yelling, swearing, or hitting, which tended to be exclusively directed toward his sister, describing Leo as "calmer." She also reported he was more interested in academic tasks such as writing. She explained that he was transitioning to school better than she expected, with no reports from the school about behavioral concerns or instances of aggression toward peers. His mother also reported that she will be using a sticker chart assigned by his occupational therapist to improve toileting. The therapist asked Leo's mother to sign a release of information consent form to enable communication with the occupational therapist, with an eye toward integrating the family's existing token economy system into their toileting intervention plan.

During the check-in, Leo behaved appropriately and engaged in independent play. When playing with the therapist while his mother completed the ECBI, Leo showed turn-taking and sharing behaviors. His mother was coded and briefly coached in CDI-CU, increasing her use of do skills, and decreasing her questions and commands with no negative talk. Because of her increased use of unlabeled praise, coaching focused on converting these to labeled praise and decreasing commands. She showed appropriate eye contact, reciprocal play, and a moderate level of warmth (i.e., smiling, laughter). During PDI-CU coding, only one of the mother's six commands were effective (17%), which she followed through correctly with labeled praise for listening and a token. She had insight into her frequent use of ineffective commands (e.g., "Can you please . . .?"), explaining that she intentionally did not follow through with labeled praise plus token. Coaching successfully focused on increasing the mother's independent generation of effective commands. Leo's mother improved in her ability to stay silent and use only nonverbal gestures for clarification after issuing a command. Leo complied with six of seven effective commands issued by his mother, for which she independently gave labeled praise for listening plus token. Leo did not comply with one effective cleanup command to put magnet tiles back in their box, instead ignoring the command and continuing to stack them. During this single time-out episode, Leo sat on the chair seven times because he refused to comply with the original command; however, he did not go to the time-out room, as he remained sitting on the chair for the full 3 minutes and 5 quiet seconds. His mother initially had difficulty bringing Leo to the time-out chair, which resolved. While on the time-out chair, Leo yelled, swore, kicked, and took off and threw his shoes, which his mother successfully ignored. Leo was otherwise mostly engaged and receptive in play, was interested and excited to earn tokens, and only displayed a few disruptive behaviors, including whining and sitting on the time-out chair instead of playing. His mother was coached to use a mixture of redirection, planned ignoring, and effective commands in response, with which Leo immediately complied.

Although Leo calmed down after time-out and returned to calm CDI-CU play with his mother, during the debrief, he resumed engaging in several aggressive and destructive behaviors including throwing toys, moving the furniture, attempting to leave the playroom, and hitting his mother. The therapist attributed these behaviors to Leo being upset about going to time-out during coaching. Leo later reported to his mother that he was upset because he wanted to first stack all the tiles together before packing them away in their container. Due to time constraints, the therapist prompted Leo's mother to use planned ignoring of these disruptive behaviors, with labeled praise for positive opposite behaviors instead of using commands. The therapist also provided the rationale for following through with time-out despite Leo's reported intention to put the tiles away after first stacking them all, to assist him with learning quick compliance. She engaged Leo's mother in a discussion about how to increase the effectiveness of her commands by tailoring them to Leo's level of understanding and to make them as specific as possible to encourage quality compliance (e.g., "Please put the tiles in the box gently" to address his rough throwing of tiles in the container when he eventually complied with original command). The therapist also discussed expanding use of the token system to shape other positive behaviors beyond listening. Using the "Target Behavior List" handout, the therapist asked the mother to write down any remaining difficult-to-manage problem behaviors to help identify positive opposite target behaviors to reinforce with tokens. The positive opposite behaviors included being gentle, keeping his hands and feet to himself, and talking politely, to replace problem behaviors of slamming the car door, hitting or kicking, and swearing, respectively. Leo's mother was assigned daily CDI and using PDI throughout the day when needed (e.g., getting dressed, brushing teeth). The reward chart was reviewed to ensure rewards were still motivating to Leo and that he could achieve the number of tokens required to earn them.

PDI-CU Coach Session 4

The goals for this treatment session are to

- provide intensive coaching of CDI-CU and PDI-CU skills to achieve mastery criteria, and

- identify remaining issues needing to be addressed using the house rules variation of the PDI-CU procedure.

Leo's mother reported practicing 4 of the 7 days since her last session because Leo was sick on 2 days. She denied any difficulties during home practice and she rated their special time as somewhat warm across all days. She described Leo as being highly reward-motivated, reporting he earned 12 tokens during the week and did not require time-out for noncompliance. She explained that Leo enjoys his current list of possible rewards. She reported continued improvement in Leo's behavior at home, with no instances of hitting her and fewer instances of yelling and swearing, which tended to be directed at other family members. She denied any feedback from the school about his misbehavior over the past week. Leo's mother reported Leo began speech therapy in the past week.

During the check-in, Leo mostly engaged in appropriate behavior except for attempting to leave the playroom a few times. His mother was coached to use effective commands to return him to the playroom, with which he quickly complied. On one occasion, his mother got hold of Leo to return him to the playroom. She was effectively coached in CDI-CU to increase her use of labeled praise and decrease her use of commands. She often used labeled praise for positive opposite behaviors of calm play and sitting quietly. Leo was observed to be more hyperactive and disruptive than usual, engaging in rough play, running against walls, and disengaging from play by sitting in the time-out chair. During PDI-CU coaching, Leo's mother was effectively coached to increase her use of effective direct commands with correct follow-through. She was observed to consistently independently generate effective commands but was coached to increase their specificity by using qualifying words such as "quickly" or "gently." She experienced some difficulty staying silent after issuing an effective command, evidenced by giving additional verbal explanations or clarification along with pointing gestures. Leo complied with five of seven of her effective commands. When Leo was compliant, his mother mostly followed through correctly, although she struggled to consistently give labeled praise paired with a token for "listening," instead using a mixture of unlabeled praise, not issuing a token, and praising the specific behavior requested. On occasion, she struggled to move Leo to the time-out chair or room and she used negative talk. The two times he did not comply, Leo went to the time-out chair five times and the time-out room three times, with the second time-out episode being about one third of the total length of the first. While in time-out, Leo yelled, swore, kicked walls, spat, and threw items. After complying with the final command, he calmed down following several minutes of special play with his mother.

During the debrief, Leo threw toys, moved furniture, and hit his mother. Because of time constraints, his mother was coached to use planned ignoring with labeled praise for positive opposite behaviors instead of commands. The therapist reviewed the difference between indirect and direct commands and provided the rationale for using effective direct commands only when necessary and based on an assessment of Leo's current capacity to comply (e.g., using fewer in the early morning and immediately after school when he is tired). The therapist also discussed the importance of consistently implementing PDI-CU for noncompliance to support Leo in learning boundaries and quick compliance. She explained the house rules time-out procedure and discussed suitable remaining problem behaviors with which to use it. For example, one of the house rules was "no hurting others" to target Leo's hitting and spitting behavior at home. The therapist discussed using this procedure in tandem with expanding the token economy system to increase desired positive opposite behaviors listed on the "Target Behavior List" handout. Leo's mother was assigned daily CDI-CU focusing on increasing labeled praise and decreasing questions, as well as PDI-CU practice throughout the day when needed.

PDI-CU Coach Session 5

The goals for this treatment session are to

- continue coaching PDI-CU toward mastery criteria,
- add another house rule if indicated,
- introduce the public behavior PDI-CU procedure, and
- begin preparing the family for graduation.

Leo's mother reported practicing 5 of the 7 days since her last session and denied any difficulties during home practice. She rated their special time as somewhat warm across all days. Leo received 16 tokens over the week for compliance with cleanup and real-life commands and there were no instances of time-out for noncompliance or for violation of the "no hurting" house rule. She reported often forgetting to give Leo his token until he reminds her. Leo chose to trade in his tokens for shopping for a toy over the weekend. His mother reported no longer counting out loud after issuing commands and observing quicker compliance from Leo in the past week. Although she reported a reduction in him slamming car doors and that there were no instances of spitting or hitting in the past week, she denied giving tokens for positive opposite behaviors or using the house rules time-out procedure. She reported continued improvement in his behavior at home and school, explaining that Leo's teacher told her he is calmer and no longer reacts aggressively when provoked by peers. However, she reported continued aggression and swearing toward his sister, for which she did not implement the house rules time-out procedure because she felt Leo's sister provoked him.

During the check-in, Leo mostly engaged in appropriate play but threw toys into the time-out room. His mother issued a direct command to stay in the playroom. The house rule of "no hurting" was introduced to Leo before coding and coaching his mother in CDI-CU and PDI-CU. During CDI-CU coding, Leo's mother increased her use of labeled praise and decreased her use of commands but worsened on other do and don't skills. CDI-CU coaching effectively focused on increasing behavior descriptions and reflections, with some prompting required (e.g., "What's he doing with his hands?"/"Can you repeat that?"). The mother provided labeled praise for positive opposite calm play behavior. During PDI-CU coding, she issued two effective, specific commands out of four total commands, with which she correctly followed through with labeled praise for listening plus a token. PDI-CU coaching focused on increasing the specificity of direct commands. She improved in staying silent and using nonverbal pointing gesture reminders after issuing a command and used correct follow-through, except for occasional negative talk. Leo did not comply with one of two effective commands and went to the time-out chair four times and the time-out room three times. His mother sometimes struggled to quickly move Leo to the time-out chair and room but effectively used planned ignoring of his yelling and kicking the walls while in time-out. The intensity of these behaviors was less than in previous sessions (i.e., no spitting or hitting, and less swearing). After complying with the final command, he calmed down following some special play.

During the debrief, Leo engaged in some disruptive behaviors, but these were notably reduced relative to previous sessions and he did not hit his mother. Due to time constraints, Leo's mother was coached in using planned ignoring with labeled praise for positive opposite behaviors. The therapist reviewed the house rules time-out procedure, including using it for aggressive behavior the mother perceives as being provoked by Leo's sister, and encouraged the mother's use of PDI-CU throughout the day as needed. The therapist discussed the rationale for Leo's mother always keeping tokens with her to enable immediate tangible reinforcement for Leo's compliance and other desirable target behaviors. She explained how to use PDI-CU in public, although the mother reported limited instances of disruptive public behavior. Leo's mother was assigned daily CDI-CU focused on increasing behavior descriptions and reflections. She was also assigned PDI-CU home practice throughout the day as needed, and for violation of house rules of "no hurting" and a newly introduced "no swearing" house rule. The therapist encouraged Leo's mother to generously give tokens for Leo's desirable target behaviors of "being gentle with items" (e.g., closing car doors gently) and "keeping hands and feet to self."

PDI-CU Coach Session 6

The goals for this treatment session are to

- focus on coaching CDI-CU and PDI-CU skills that remain deficient toward achieving mastery criteria;
- add another house rule, if indicated;
- practice the public behavior procedure, if indicated; and
- continue preparing the family for graduation.

Leo's mother reported practicing 4 of the 7 days since her last session and denied any difficulties. She rated their special time as somewhat warm across all days. Leo received 12 tokens over the week, and his mother denied any instances of time-out for noncompliance or violation of house rules. She reported no instances of Leo spitting, slamming car doors, hitting, and less swearing over the past week, although she intended to implement the house rules time-out procedure if needed. She reported continued forgetting to give Leo tokens for target behaviors. She reported continued improvement in his behavior at home and school, explaining that he did not engage in physical aggression or spitting, reduced his swearing during arguments with his sister, and was gentler when closing the car door. Session goals included improving CDI-CU and PDI-CU skills through coaching, adding a new house rule, and practicing PDI-CU in public.

During the check-in, Leo mostly engaged in appropriate play but was rough with the toys, attempted to leave the playroom, and refused to return the bug-in-ear device, for which his mother issued a direct command. The therapist reminded Leo of the "no hurting" and "no swearing" house rules before coding and coaching the mother in CDI-CU and PDI-CU. During CDI-CU coding, Leo's mother increased her use of behavior descriptions but decreased reflections and increased questions and commands. During PDI-CU coding, she issued two effective commands out of five total commands but did not correctly follow through on either. Instead, she issued either unlabeled praise or praised the specific action requested instead of the target listening behavior. Leo's mother was coached to use CDI-CU and PDI-CU during a public behavior outing, for which she provided clear, positively stated behavioral expectations of Leo prior. During the outing around his school, his mother was coached to give labeled praise and tokens for Leo showing target behaviors of staying close to her and being quiet and calm. She was successfully coached in PDI-CU, using six effective commands with which Leo was 100% compliant, staying silent after issuing the command, and correctly following through with labeled praise for listening plus a token. Consequently, Leo did not require time-out during the public outing coaching.

During the debrief, Leo engaged in several disruptive behaviors, including throwing out toys he had cleaned up and upending furniture. Due to time constraints, Leo's mother was coached in using planned ignoring. The therapist engaged the mother in a discussion of her high endorsement of dawdling behavior on the ECBI, which she attributed to her dressing Leo instead of requiring him to dress himself because they have limited time in the mornings. The therapist encouraged Leo's mother to practice using PDI-CU for Leo getting himself dressed on the weekends when they were less busy and she had the time to follow through for noncompliance, which she agreed to try. The therapist encouraged the mother to continue using the house rules time-out procedure for violating "no hurting" and "no swearing" house rules, while also rewarding desirable positive opposite behaviors with tokens. Leo's mother raised that Leo insisted on wearing diapers to school, and the therapist encouraged use of tokens to reinforce wearing underwear at home for increasingly longer time periods until the target equivalent school length is achieved, before applying this approach in the school setting. The therapist reiterated the importance of Leo's mother always keeping tokens on her to enable immediate tangible reinforcement for Leo's compliance and other desirable target behaviors. She was assigned daily CDI-CU focused on increasing labeled praise and reducing questions and commands. She was also assigned PDI-CU home practice throughout the day as needed, and for violation of "no hurting" and "no swearing" house rules. The therapist advised Leo's mother to come to the next treatment session without Leo, as they would be transitioning to the final treatment phase that begins with a caregiver-only teach session.

The Coaching and Rewarding Emotional Skills Phase

The third phase of PCIT-CU is the CARES module. It is a unique phase to PCIT-CU that is not included in the standard PCIT approach. The CARES module lasts seven sessions, starting with a caregiver-only teaching session, followed by six coaching sessions with both caregiver and child to improve the child's socio-emotional competence and emotional literacy, focusing on those skills that research has shown to need strengthening in children with the LPE specifier.

CARES Session 1: The Teach Session

Leo's mother canceled two sessions prior to attending this session. The ICU rating scale was readministered to her before beginning the session. Her total ICU score was 45, which falls in the clinically significant range. Session goals were to

- explain the importance of teaching emotional literacy skills for children with the LPE specifier,
- provide an overview of the CARES program,
- explain how caregivers can help children improve their skills for recognizing and responding to others' emotions by labeling emotions and modeling how to use other forms of "feelings talk" and respond prosocially to others' distress, and
- discuss how to apply the child's existing token economy system to reward their compliance with CARES activities and increase other target behaviors.

Leo's mother reported practicing CDI and PDI only twice in the past week with warmth ratings of *somewhat* (2 out of 4), but she explained she played board games (e.g., matching game, Jenga) with him one on one. She reported giving him nine tokens and denied any instances of time-out in the past week. She did not complete her homework sheets for the prior 2 weeks and reportedly forgot what home practice she completed. She described Leo as more "mature" and "calmer," explaining that he infrequently displays behavioral difficulties at home anymore, except for when his sister frustrates him. She further explained that he now only tends to get angry with her when she does not understand or hear him. She denied any significant concerns with home compliance. She explained he is putting forward greater effort at school and better engaging in classroom activities. However, she reported some anxiety when separating from her or his sister's father when going to school.

The mother was engaged throughout the CARES teach session and she endorsed the family's need for the CARES module to improve Leo's ability to empathize with others and regulate his emotions. She reflected that she is unemotional herself and the family rarely talks about feelings, except for her telling Leo it is okay to cry or be upset. She also reflected that Leo may have learned callous behaviors, such as laughing at people who are hurt, from his sister. At the end of the teach session, Leo's mother was assigned homework including daily labeling of emotions, playing a feelings flashcard game with Leo, and reading emotional literacy–focused books. The therapist provided her with a YouTube playlist with example books read aloud (Kimonis, n.d.-d). She further explained the importance of Leo's mother maintaining her CDI and PDI skills while in CARES, instructing her to continue daily CDI practice and PDI practice throughout the day as needed and for broken house rules of "no hurting" and "no swearing." Leo's mother was also encouraged to use tokens paired with labeled praise for Leo's compliance with effective commands and for prosocial behaviors including using words to explain his preferences and feelings and for greeting others, which she identified as a social skill she wanted to encourage. The therapist explained how to use emotion coaching at appropriate times by first validating Leo's feelings and identifying their triggers (e.g., "You're feeling angry because I said you couldn't have ice cream") before either planned ignoring of minor misbehavior or following through with a consequence for a broken house rule. She also explained how to "strike when the iron is cold" by talking about emotions afterward when Leo is in a calm state and receptive to such a discussion.

CARES Session 2: Learning to Recognize Others' Emotions

The following week, mother and Leo attended the session together. Session goals include the following:

- explaining the token economy system to the child for completing CARES in-clinic session activities,
- teaching the caregiver and the child how to identify and label basic feelings using microexpression training, and
- explaining to the caregiver how to reinforce child compliance with CARES learning activities using a combination of tokens and labeled praise.

Leo's mother reported that since her last session, Leo had been assessed by a pediatrician and received a diagnosis of ASD. She noted that Leo had been on a waitlist for this local Aboriginal health service since the CDI phase of PCIT. At that time, both the PCIT clinician and the school had recommended that she seek a referral from her general practitioner to explore the potential need for medication management, given Leo's high levels of inattention and hyperactivity observed in treatment sessions. According to the pediatrician's report, the ASD diagnosis was made based on clinical observations and developmental history rather than any formal testing, however. The pediatrician's report did not indicate any consideration of the LPE specifier.

Leo's mother reported practicing CDI on 4 days and PDI on 3 days in the past week but denied completing any CARES homework activities due to lack of time. She rated warmth as "2" (*somewhat*). She reported giving Leo 19 tokens over the past week and denied any instances of time-out. She reported continued improvement in Leo's behaviors at home, including compliance and no instances of swearing. She reported the only time Leo is aggressive is when he gets frustrated while in the car with his sister, leading him to swear at her and pull her hair. The therapist advised her to apply PDI for the broken "no hurting" house rules after returning home from car rides. Leo's mother reported Leo's continued unhappiness over separating from her when going to school.

Leo was difficult to engage in CARES activities, often disengaging, refusing to respond, becoming distracted (e.g., leaving his chair to look around the room or play with toys), and demanding tokens. He required constant redirection, prompting to stay on task and engage with the activities, and close-ended questions to elicit a response. During microexpression training, Leo was generally good at identifying happy, sad, angry, and surprised emotions, but he had difficulty recognizing fear. He was able to learn microexpressions associated with each macroemotion but required significant prompting to respond throughout the activity. Leo generated the following set of microexpressions during the training: happy (smiling, mouth goes up at the sides; eyes get smaller); sad (mouth goes down at the sides; eyebrows go up in the middle and down on the sides); angry (eyebrows go down in the middle; sometimes, the mouth is open in a yell); afraid (mouth opens straight to the sides; eyes get bigger; eyebrows go up); and surprise (mouth opens down in a circle, eyes get bigger, eyebrows go up). His mother was attentive and engaged throughout CARES activities, actively participating in each with the therapist and helping to engage Leo by reminding him to pay attention and prompting him to respond.

During the debrief, Leo's mother was encouraged to continue helping Leo to identify microexpressions linked with different emotions and to label emotions. The therapist assigned the mother daily CDI and PDI throughout the day and for house rules of "no hurting" and "no swearing." Also, for homework, she was assigned the emotions collage activity (i.e., caregiver and child create a collage of emotional faces grouped by emotion type by cutting them out of printed media or drawings, pasting them onto poster board, and labeling relevant microexpressions), daily feelings flash card games, and advised to use tokens to reward Leo's compliance with these activities and use of other prosocial behaviors, including feelings talk. Since he refused to engage in the "emotions photoshoot" by acting out various emotional expressions, his mother was asked to complete this at home and send these images to therapist.

CARES Session 3: Learning to Recognize Caregiver–Child Emotions

Leo's mother canceled two sessions due to school holidays. Session goals include:

- continue teaching emotion recognition skills, focusing on the caregiver and the child labeling their own and others' emotions.

The mother reported completing CDI every day (rated "somewhat" warm each day) and PDI on 4 days in the past week. She denied completing any CARES homework activities because she reportedly forgot. She noted continued improvements in Leo's behavior, including few instances of hitting or swearing and less sibling conflict than usual. However, she reported an increase in Leo's disruptive behavior and disengagement during his appointments with other allied health professionals, such as with his speech and occupational therapists.

Leo was very difficult to engage in CARES activities, often disengaging, refusing to respond or responding without effort, and leaving his chair to play with other objects in the room. He required close-ended questions and constant prompting (e.g., first–then statements about the number of faces that he needed to complete before getting a token) to facilitate his attention and engagement. During the microexpression training review, Leo was inconsistently able to accurately identify microexpressions associated with happy, sad, angry, and surprised facial expression stimuli, and he continued to have difficulty with fear expressions. During the blank face activity, Leo's accuracy at using clipped eyes, noses, and mouths depicting various emotions to construct various emotional expressions increased across trials. During the feelings flash card game, Leo accurately identified emotions on the flashcards and his mother's and therapist's facial emotional expressions. He refused to mimic emotional expressions himself and instead used the facial feature clippings to mimic flashcard expressions. His mother was attentive and engaged throughout CARES activities, actively participating and reminding Leo to pay attention and respond. She sometimes used negative talk but was receptive to the therapist's prompts to use effective direct commands or planned ignoring to manage misbehavior.

During the debrief, the mother was encouraged to use PDI for broken house rules and noncompliance, and to continue daily practice of CDI. The therapist reiterated the importance of home practice of CARES activities to support Leo's learning of emotional literacy skills. For homework, the mother was assigned daily emotion labeling, feelings flash card activity, and reading emotional literacy books. Leo refused to engage in the home emotions photoshoot and, so, generic pictures were used for social stories instead of personalizing them.

CARES Session 4: Linking Emotions With Context

Goals for this session include:

- continuing to teach emotion recognition skills, focusing on situation-based emotions (i.e., understanding the link between emotions and context), and

- teaching the child to predict how someone is likely to feel in different situations.

Leo's mother reported practicing CDI every day (warmth rated between 2 [*somewhat*] and 3 [*very*]), PDI five times (assigning 26 tokens and no with instances of time-out), and completing CARES homework on 4 days in the week since her last session. She attributed her increase in homework completion to the family staying at her daughter's father's house over the past couple of weeks, where they have less access to distractions such as TV. She misunderstood how to complete the labeling activity by writing down emotions experienced by her and Leo instead of verbally labeling them. She denied reading feelings books or doing flash card activities, attributing the former to Leo's dislike of reading. She reported ongoing difficulties with Leo's school refusal and disruptive and disengaged behavior during his other allied health appointments.

Leo continued to be difficult to engage in CARES activities, often disengaging and leaving his chair to play with objects in the room, requiring close-ended questions to elicit a response and constant prompting for him to attend and engage, including reminders about how many items he needed to complete to earn a token and select a reward from the surprise box. During the blank face activity, Leo was able to create accurate emotional faces using clippings of individual facial feature expressions. During the emotions game on the tablet, Leo was engaged and mostly accurate in identifying emotional expressions, even for more complex emotions like frustration. The therapist was unable to effectively engage Leo in identifying microexpressions during this activity, as he advanced to the next item too quickly and refused to respond to questions. However, he wanted to persist with additional items before moving on to the next activity. During the situations-based emotions vignette activity, involving showing Leo images of emotional scenarios and asking him what the protagonist is feeling and why, he was able to generate realistic examples of emotions in particular scenarios. After prompting, he was able to understand how multiple emotions could be experienced in a single scenario (e.g., feeling both sad and scared when lost). He sometimes persisted with repeating a description of the scenario when asked why someone might experience a given emotion in that situation, to which the therapist provided the rationale for experiencing the emotion.

During the feelings flash card game, Leo was mostly accurate at identifying emotional expressions and was willing and able to use his own facial expressions to mimic an angry face. With some assistance from his mother, he could generate basic examples of situations where he might experience the emotion depicted on the flash card (e.g., feeling angry when mother leaves him at school when the bell rings, feeling frightened when bitten by the family dog). His mother also effectively expressed a time when she felt angry because Leo did not listen to her. She was attentive and engaged throughout CARES activities, actively participating and reminding Leo to pay attention and respond. When she used negative talk ("Stop that!") to respond to his misbehavior, she was prompted to use planned ignoring or effective commands instead. For homework, his mother was assigned daily emotion labeling, social stories, feelings flash card game, and tablet emotions game, the latter of which she reported a high level of motivation to use based on Leo's in-session engagement with the activity. She was also encouraged to continue daily CDI and PDI for compliance and house rules.

CARES Session 5: Coping With Negative Emotions

Session goals include:

- reviewing emotion recognition skills, and
- teaching the stop–breathe–think sequence for coping with negative emotions (e.g., anger, frustration).

Leo's mother reported completing 5 days each of CDI, PDI, and CARES homework in the week since her last session. She rated CDI as somewhat warm, gave Leo 23 tokens, and denied any instances of time-out. She reported moderate completion of each of the CARES homework activities except for labeling feelings displayed by characters in children's books, TV, or movies and she read half of the "I Want to Play" social story on 1 day. She reported that Leo was more internally motivated to comply with her commands and to engage in prosocial behaviors (e.g., volunteering to help clean up at his speech pathologist appointment), reflecting a shift from his more external motivation by responding to her commands by asking "What do I get out of it?" or demanding a token. She also reported less swearing, aggression, and sibling conflict (e.g., hair pulling) than usual. She partly attributed sibling-related improvements to her setting new boundaries in the car by allowing the children to pick the music at designated times of day (e.g., sister in the mornings and Leo in the afternoons). She also reported newly initiating a visual schedule at home to help address Leo's difficulties with changes to the routine. Leo was more engaged in several of the CARES activities relative to previous weeks, but continued to sometimes be disengaged and distracted, and required constant prompting and reminders about the tokens and prize box, with which his mother assisted. During the tablet-based emotions game, Leo mostly accurately identified emotional expressions throughout. During the feelings flash card game, he accurately identified and mimicked some emotions (e.g., anger, shock) and was able to generate appropriate examples of situations when he felt a given emotion (e.g., feeling happy when he does not need to go to school, sad when he cannot play outside when he is sick). However, he struggled for sadness, stating, "I never feel sad." He was able to generate examples of when his mother or the therapist felt particular emotions (e.g., feeling sad when sick, scared when finding a snake in the room), giving an example discussed in the previous session (i.e., his mother feeling sad when paying her bills). When discussing the stop–breathe–think strategy, Leo chose to call this "special breathing" when asked by the therapist. The therapist read the stop–breathe–think social story to Leo, with which he partially initially engaged. During the stop–breathe–think vignettes activity, he struggled to generate examples of "okay" and "not okay" choices. The therapist engaged Leo in a role-play example of feeling angry when he does not want to go to school, modeling to Leo how to use the stop–breathe–think technique and explaining that it helps to calm him down when he is feeling angry.

Leo's mother was assigned daily completion of CARES activities including emotional labeling, social stories, feelings flash card game, and tablet-based emotions game. The therapist discussed continuing to reinforce compliance and prosocial behaviors with tokens plus labeled praise and to extend the token system to reinforce Leo's use of stop–breathe–think over the week. She was encouraged to continue daily CDI and PDI practice.

CARES Session 6: Recognizing and Responding to Signs of Distress
Sessions goals include:

- teaching recognition of early physiological and mental signs of distress, and
- teaching emotion regulation strategies.

Leo's mother completed CDI, PDI, and CARES homework every day in the week since her last session, which she again attributed to staying at her daughter's father's house that is relatively free of distractions. She rated warmth in CDI between "2" (*somewhat*) and "3" (*very*) and assigned 35 tokens with no instances of time-out. She labeled her own and Leo's feelings daily, read feelings books on 2 days, and labeled feelings displayed in children's books, TV, or movie characters on 1 day of the week. She denied playing the feelings flash card game. She also denied practicing "special breathing," Leo's chosen name for the stop–breathe–think technique, attributing this to him being calm during the past week. She explained that Leo is going to bed earlier (around 10 p.m.) and is less angry than usual. She reported continued improvements in Leo's behavior with no instances of aggression or swearing, stating that Leo's uncle also commented on his improved behavior. She stated that Leo is initiating appropriate play with others at home (e.g., card games), is more open to trying new foods, and is often immediately compliant with her commands, even without receiving a token reward. His mother also noted calmer behavior at school, evidenced by his compliance with lining up in the mornings, less defiance around going to school, and wanting to engage with schoolwork and activities (e.g., reading a library book, coloring). Leo notably received an award for mathematics at his school assembly. His mother reported increased engagement from Leo at his speech and occupational therapy appointments, which she attributed to the therapist recently using rewards to motivate him.

Leo was difficult to engage in CARES activities, disengaging, throwing items, drawing on the table, and requiring close-ended questions to respond, constant prompting, and reminders about the tokens and prize box, with which his mother assisted. During the volcano activity, Leo demonstrated a basic understanding of using "special breathing" with therapist prompting. During the anger warning signs component, he was able to identify and generate different bodily cues related to increasing intensities of anger (e.g., body feeling hot, clenched hands, gritted teeth, angry face). During discussion of the cool down toolbox, Leo was able to identify and select to include in his toolbox some realistic "cool down" strategies to use when feeling frustrated or angry. These included drawing or coloring, riding his bike, counting to 20, blowing bubbles, playing with toys or a game, listening to music, and talking to his mother. He engaged in a role-play of a situation that makes him feel frustrated (i.e., when his sister takes or hides his belongings), but struggled somewhat to consistently role-play using stop–breathe–think as a cool down strategy. During the debrief, the therapist discussed the importance of timing emotion coaching and using different emotion regulation strategies according to Leo's intensity of emotion, linking this to the volcano analogy (e.g., validate and redirect at early stages, calm down corner at later stages). His mother was assigned daily CARES homework, including emotion labeling, social stories, and the feelings flash card game. She was encouraged to continue with daily home practice of CDI and PDI, maintaining house rules of "no hurting" and "no swearing."

CARES Session 7: Review and Graduation

Session goals include:

- discussing and reviewing all previously completed CARES activities,
- reviewing treatment program successes, and
- planning for future maintenance of treatment gains.

Leo's mother reported completing CDI, PDI, and CARES homework activities each day in the week since her last session. She mostly rated her CDI as "somewhat" warm, except for 1 day when they played cars, which she rated as "very" warm. She gave Leo 30 tokens, averaging four per day, and denied any instances of time-out for noncompliance or for breaking the "no hurting" active house rule. She reported labeling her own and Leo's emotions daily, mostly as "happy," but denied practicing other CARES homework activities. She reported being unable to practice "special breathing" or using the cool down toolbox because Leo was calm this past week. The therapist praised Leo's mother for her consistent practice of PCIT-CU skills and linked this to Leo's continued calm behavior. The mother noted continuous improvements in Leo's openness to trying new things (e.g., putting his face underwater during swimming lessons, reading library books), more engaged behavior during speech and occupational therapy, proactive cleaning up without requiring commands, and earlier bedtimes than before. His mother explained that her friend who was visiting the family home with a younger child and had not seen Leo in some time commented on his improved and more prosocial behavior (i.e., waiting for the younger child to stop playing with a toy rather than snatching it from her). She reflected on finding the feelings talk with Leo personally helpful. She also reported some success in managing his unwillingness to attend school by arriving early to give him more time to settle into class before other students arrive.

Leo was moderately difficult to engage in CARES activities, as evidenced by him disengaging, moving around and playing with objects in the room, and requiring close-ended questions to elicit responses, constant prompting, and reminders about the token system and prize box to reengage him. His mother was attentive and engaged and supported the therapist to keep Leo on task. During the emotion recognition activities review, Leo was consistently accurate at identifying microexpressions in happy, sad, angry, scared, and surprised faces with prompting. During the vignette activity review, Leo was able to generate realistic examples of emotions experienced by characters in each vignette and provide basic reasons for these emotions, although he often simply described the scenario as the reason. During a review of stop–breathe–think, Leo was able to independently name each step of the technique and he practiced the steps with prompting. For the "think" component, however, he was unable to label his feelings or identify "okay" behaviors in various scenarios. During the discussion about the cool down toolbox, Leo proactively practiced the "counting to 20" cool down strategy while looking at his visual toolbox. His mother expressed her belief that Leo "knows about feelings but does not care." The therapist discussed the importance of continuing consistent reinforcement of his use of CARES skills and prosocial behaviors with CDI do skills, particularly labeled praise and tokens. She reviewed the "Phasing Out the Token System" handout to explain how to gradually phase it out and reinstate it if problematic behaviors reemerge or when teaching new skills or replacement behaviors. The therapist discussed the importance of continued regular home practice of PCIT and CARES strategies after treatment ends to support Leo's maintenance of behavioral and emotional improvements.

TREATMENT OUTCOMES

The family was reassessed 1 and 2 weeks after completing CARES and they returned to complete a follow-up assessment three months after treatment ended. ECBI intensity T-scores across treatment are depicted in Figure 9.3, demonstrating a significant reduction in the frequency of Leo's conduct problems across treatment to within normal limits by posttreatment. He showed a slight increase in conduct problems at the 3-month follow-up, but they remained within normal limits. CBCL scores for the mother and teacher are reported in Table 9.1.

Posttreatment Assessment

During the clinical interview, the mother described Leo's behavior as a "100% flip" from before treatment with PCIT-CU began and his teacher stated, "I'm very proud of [Leo]; he is a new boy!" His mother reflected that others also noticed his improvement, including a family friend and Leo's uncle. Improvements included increased and faster compliance with his mother's and teacher's requests, which was reflected in a change from 11% compliance

FIGURE 9.3. Intensity of Conduct Problems Reported by the Mother and the Teacher Across PCIT-CU Treatment and at 3-Month Follow-Up Assessment

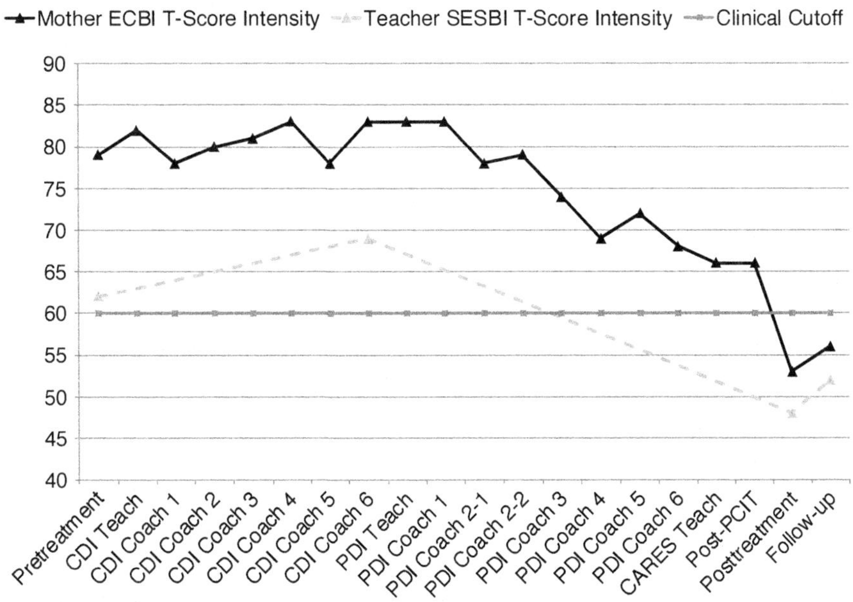

Note. The intensity of conduct problems (T-scores) was measured for the mother on the ECBI and for the teacher on the SESBI. CARES = Coaching and Rewarding Emotional Skills; CDI = child-directed interaction; ECBI = Eyberg Child Behavior Inventory; SESBI = Sutter-Eyberg Student Behavior Inventory; PCIT-CU = Parent–Child Interaction Therapy: Callous-Unemotional version; PDI = parent-directed interaction.

TABLE 9.1. Mother and Teacher T-scores on Child Behavior Checklist (CBCL) *DSM*-Oriented and Composite Scales at Pre- and Posttreatment and 3-Month Follow-Up

	Pretreatment		Posttreatment		Follow-up	
Scale	Mother	Teacher	Mother	Teacher	Mother	Teacher
Depressive problems	63	**95-C**	*68-B*	54	63	54
Anxiety problems	63	**93-C**	**85-C**	**76-C**	51	64
Autism spectrum problems	64	**82-C**	—	—	—	—
ADHD problems	52	*68-B*	56	51	51	52
ODD problems	**73-C**	**80-C**	55	54	52	60
Conduct problems	—	—	**74-C**	61	63	*66-B*
Internalizing composite	**65-C**	**91-C**	**72-C**	**70-C**	52	**68-C**
Externalizing composite	*62-B*	**75-C**	**66-C**	59	56	*63-B*
Total problems	*63-B*	**91-C**	**71-C**	*60-B*	55	*62-B*

Note. Bold text with -C indicates clinically significant score, and italicized text with -B indicates borderline clinical range. Preschool version (1.5–5 years) completed at pretreatment and school-age version completed at posttreatment according to child's current age. A conduct problems scale is not available in preschool version, and an autism spectrum scale is not available in the school-age version. Due to a change in grade, a different teacher completed the pretreatment questionnaire from posttreatment and follow-up measures. ADHD = attention-deficit/hyperactivity disorder; *DSM* = *Diagnostic and Statistical Manual of Mental Disorders*; ODD = oppositional defiant disorder.

with his mother's effective commands at pretreatment to 67% compliance at posttreatment. Leo's mother denied having to use time-out warnings or time-out with Leo in recent weeks because of his high level of compliance. She reported a significant reduction in his verbal and physical aggression, explaining that he no longer swears in public, at teachers, family members, or at her, and only rarely swears when angry about something his sister did or when his mother misunderstands him. She reported he no longer hits and recently stopped pulling his sister's hair while in the car, which she attributed in part to her use of prevention strategies. The teacher described him as well behaved in the classroom. His mother noted a reduction in other disruptive and hyperactive behavior, most notably less interrupting and more patient waiting (e.g., sitting quietly beside mother while she talks to a friend). On the DISCAP completed with his mother, Leo did not meet diagnostic criteria for ODD or CD. His mother did not endorse any ODD symptoms and endorsed only the lying symptom for CD. She reported that his last use of a weapon to injure another person was over 6 months ago.

Leo's mother reported continued use of CDI-CU and PDI-CU strategies, including the token economy system, but reported relatively less use of CARES strategies. She explained that Leo asks for special play and engages in it well. She also reported that Leo spontaneously engages in positive behaviors without being told, such as cleaning up toys and independently arranging his room neatly. She reported using the token system with his occupational therapist to support his toileting. She estimated that Leo earns around five tokens a day for compliance but admitted she does not always follow through with giving him tokens because he asks for them less. She explained that Leo also demands tokens less and instead often complies without needing tokens. His mother explained that she found CARES strategies more difficult to use with Leo because she believes he knows and understands emotions (e.g., able to accurately identify microexpressions) but does not care enough to respond prosocially. She also reflected that her family of origin and her own family were not emotional, describing CARES as a learning process for herself and Leo.

Leo's mother was observed again during three structured play situations—child-led play, parent-led play, and cleanup—and coded using the DPICS. Her play was reciprocal with appropriate levels of eye contact, warmth, and enthusiasm and Leo readily engaged in play with her. As shown in Figures 9.1 and 9.2 earlier in the chapter, his mother's CDI do skills deteriorated since posttreatment, but she maintained a low level of don't skills. She was able to effectively ignore Leo's minor misbehavior. During parent-led play, Leo's mother increased her use of questions to eight (e.g., math questions) and used four indirect commands, none of which provided opportunity for Leo to comply (e.g., "We can share, can't we?"). In the cleanup observation, Leo complied with 67% of his mother's six effective commands, which she described as typical of his behavior at home. She did not use labeled praise for quick listening (instead praising the activity; e.g., "Good work packing that away") or tokens to reward compliance. When Leo was not compliant, she occasionally attempted to reason with him or repeat the command or warning, with which he complied.

His mother reported that Leo is much more affectionate with her, staying close to her, cuddling her more, and holding her hand in public, which he did not do before treatment started. On the CAPE 1.1, which was rated on the basis of a clinical interview with his mother and other clinical data obtained from his mother, teacher, and session observations, Leo continued to meet LPE diagnostic criteria with three of four items endorsed as highly descriptive of him: lack of remorse or guilt, callous–lack of empathy, and shallow or deficient affect. Leo was described as not caring, denying wrongdoing and instead blaming others, and not apologizing if he intentionally or accidentally hurts others; showing no reaction to others' emotions and little interest in doing something nice for others; and hiding his emotions, except for anger. However, his mother described instances of Leo drawing a picture for his teacher and picking a flower to give to his mother, which he reportedly would not have done prior to treatment. Also, the unconcerned about performance item was rated as only moderately descriptive of Leo, with contrary evidence including his care and pride over achievements and awards; wanting to do homework, correct any errors, and return it to his teacher on time; and answering questions in class. His teacher stated, "He works well when praised and treated in a gentle and caring manner. He loves to help me in the classroom." However, Leo was also described as rushing through schoolwork and not trying his hardest, and sometimes blaming others when it was not done properly (e.g., "You made me rush"). His teacher also reported that when he gets into fights with peers, Leo tends to blame others for "starting it." On a paper emotion recognition task, Leo had 62.5% correct responses with 25% of fear items and 75% of sad facial expressions correctly identified.

His mother reported her remaining areas of concern being his anxiety when separated from her, in crowded places, or new situations, and his continued wearing of diapers due to enuresis. However, his mother and teacher also reported improvements in his anxious behaviors, such as recently getting up in front of other students at a school assembly to accept a mathematics award and more easily separating from caregivers at school drop-off.

Leo's mother's satisfaction with the treatment process and outcomes was 4.4 out of 5 on the Therapy Attitude Inventory (Eyberg & Johnson, 1974). She perceived that the PCIT-CU treatment was effective for improving Leo's behavior, particularly the token system, which she attributed to his reward-motivated nature. She expressed positive feelings about the program's influence on her warmth and responsiveness to Leo and her setting up of clear routines and boundaries, reflecting the goals of PCIT-CU to increase warm, firm, but fair parenting. She further reported improved daily routines, including Leo going to bed earlier (by 10:30 p.m.) after moving forward the family's dinner time, and waking earlier (by 8 a.m.), being in a happier mood, and being generally compliant with her instructions to get ready for school so he can arrive earlier than the other students to help settle in. His mother reported the main barriers to treatment that occurred sometimes included conflicts with other scheduled activities, family member sickness, her mother's serious illness, life stress, moving house, and limited available time to complete homework. On the CGAS (Shaffer et al., 1983), the therapist scored the family at 50 (obvious problems).

Three-Month Follow-Up Assessment

Leo's mother used the phrase "night and day" to describe the change and improvements in Leo's behavior since participating in PCIT-CU. She reported a maintenance of his increased compliance, explaining that he typically immediately does what he is told even when not receiving tokens for listening, except when intensively engaged in a solo activity. On these occasions, Leo will ask politely if he can have extra time to complete the activity before completing the command. She denied needing to use time-out chair warnings or time-out and explained that Leo no longer demands tokens or rewards from her for listening. His mother also reported that he will voluntarily clean up his toys without being asked. She also stated that there was a maintained reduction in Leo's verbal and physical aggression, denying that he hits her or his sister or pulls his sister's hair, and noting that he rarely swears or uses his middle finger at home, and never at school. She explained that Leo and his sister occasionally engage in verbal "nitpicking" arguments, but that this is often due to his sister provoking him. She otherwise reported an improved sibling relationship, sharing that on a recent family fishing trip, she observed the siblings talking nicely to each other. However, around the transition time of returning to school from vacation and while Leo's usual teacher was on leave, she reported a temporary increase in Leo's yelling and aggression toward her daughter's father and with peers at school when he is frustrated or he does not get his way. She explained this usually occurred when he was provoked, describing an instance of reactive aggression where Leo hit a peer with a stick after the peer punched him in the stomach. She also reported that, on other occasions, he told a teacher when he was having a problem with a peer. His mother was advised to return to using the "no hurting" house rule with time-out to address any continued aggressive behaviors occurring at home or school. On the DISCAP interview with his mother, Leo did not meet diagnostic criteria for ODD or CD. She did not endorse any ODD symptoms. She endorsed two CD symptoms of using a weapon to injure another person, for the incident detailed earlier, and lying or stealing. She explained that Leo hides items (e.g., the occupational therapist's keys, his sister's AirPods) as a "game" and refuses to say where he put them.

Leo's mother reported an increase in Leo's prosocial behaviors. She explained that Leo is more helpful, such as volunteering to get groceries or find lost items, and he recently began helping his sister when asked (e.g., getting her a cup of water). She attributed these changes to their participation in PCIT-CU, and in particular its effect on reducing tension and anger in their relationships. The mother reported increased turn taking, such as winning at board games.

When describing the instance of peer aggression, she explained that although Leo does not verbally express remorse at the time, he does now admit to the wrongdoing and appears to be upset by his actions (e.g., signs of embarrassment, freezing, or crying). Leo's mother reported further reductions in his level of CU traits on the ICU (see Table 9.2). On the CAPE 1.1. interview with the mother and using other clinical data obtained from the assessment, Leo continued to meet LPE diagnostic criteria with two of four items endorsed as highly descriptive of him: lack of remorse or guilt and callous–lack of empathy. She explained that he rarely admits to wrongdoing or apologizes and blames others (per the teacher's report), but reported some improvement in his level of remorse, as evidenced by Leo appearing embarrassed, feeling bad, and staying silent instead of arguing or blaming others as he did previously. She also explained that he briefly attends to but does not appear to care or express concern if someone is hurt, although she reported he is caring toward animals, voluntarily helps others, and is more affectionate (e.g., holding hands, playing cooperatively with peers) since starting PCIT-CU. His mother reported that Leo no longer appears "cold and callous" as he did previously. She did not endorse the unconcerned about performance symptom, explaining that Leo is proud of school achievements (i.e., school athletics and merit awards), tries his best and works hard at activities at school and in therapy, and enjoys doing homework and coloring but does not mind if it is messy. The shallow or deficient affect symptom was rated as only moderately descriptive of Leo, with his mother stating that he more openly and genuinely expresses happiness, anger, and fear, both verbally and behaviorally, but will not express sadness and is not upset when something bad happens to someone else. Leo inconsistently engaged with the paper-based emotion recognition task. He was often distracted, looking away from the screen, at the tokens, or toward his mother, and requiring frequent prompting, redirecting, and breaks to complete the tasks. On the emotion recognition task, Leo had 58.3% correct responses with 75% of fear items and 50% of sad facial expressions correctly identified.

Leo's mother reported continuing to use CDI-CU and PDI-CU strategies, but less use of CARES and the token economy system. She reported completing special time on more days than not, describing Leo's preferred activities as coloring and board games. She also said that Leo enjoys special time and continued to use PDI but explained that the token system is no longer necessary to motivate his compliance. She said that she continues to "pick and choose

TABLE 9.2. Mother and Teacher Raw Total Scores on Inventory of Callous-Unemotional Traits (ICU) at Pre- and Posttreatment and 3-Month Follow-Up

	Pretreatment		Posttreatment		Follow-up	
Scale	Mother	Teacher	Mother	Teacher	Mother	Teacher
ICU total score	51	57	47	28	43	26

Note. Due to a change in grade, a different teacher completed the pretreatment questionnaire from posttreatment and follow-up measures.

battles" when deciding whether to use PDI for important situations. In less important situations, she reported giving him choices. The therapist discussed ways the mother can continue to support Leo's development of emotion regulation skills and prosocial behaviors using CARES strategies (e.g., stop–breathe–think, cool down toolbox).

Leo's mother was observed during three structured play situations: child-led play, parent-led play, and cleanup, and coded using the DPICS. During child-led play, Leo was engaged, interested, and took part in reciprocal play with his mother. He was observed to initiate some eye contact and engage in sharing and helping behaviors. His mother was observed to display moderate to high levels of enthusiasm and warmth (i.e., smiling, positive eye contact, sitting or standing close to and facing Leo), engage in reciprocal play, and generally follow his lead. As shown in Figure 9.1, his mother's CDI do skills reduced and her don't skills increased, except for increased reflections and maintaining no negative talk. Her 16 questions were a mixture of tip ups, question tags, and information questions. She was observed to effectively ignore minor misbehaviors, such as Leo trying to shake the time-out chair. His mother somewhat increased her use of labeled praise and behavior descriptions and reduced questions during parent-led play and cleanup observations. Leo was mostly immediately compliant with his mother's play-based effective commands (75% compliant) and suggestions during parent-led play. During the cleanup observation, Leo complied with 86% of his mother's six effective commands. His mother inconsistently used labeled praise and did not give any tokens to reward compliance, which led to Leo demanding tokens from her. When Leo did not comply, his mother was observed to repeat the command rather than follow through with the PDI-CU sequence, and she struggled to stay silent between issuing a command and waiting for him to comply.

In other areas, his mother reported reduced interrupting and improved patient waiting, explaining that Leo will typically quietly wait for her to finish a conversation. She reported continued concerns about Leo's anxiety and social skills but described these problems as more manageable. She explained that Leo dislikes when other children look at him, which she addresses by bringing him to school early or requesting for his teacher to bring him into the classroom when he is late. She reported that Leo has a few friends at school, but they often engage in bickering and competitive behaviors, such as arguing over who came first or sharing toys. His mother reported that Leo has a teacher's aide to support him with reading and writing since he is behind his peers in these areas. On the CGAS, the therapist scored the family at 50 (obvious problems) based on his continued social skills deficits and high levels of hyperactivity or impulsivity.

His mother's satisfaction with the treatment process and outcomes was 4.3 out of 5 on the Therapy Attitude Inventory. Items rated 5 out of 5 centered around improvements in child behavior, compliance, general personal or family problems, and the type of program used. The remaining items were rated 4 out of 5, except for a rating of 3 out of 5 for learning "a few new [rather than several '4' or many very useful '5'] techniques" for teaching child new skills.

CHAPTER SUMMARY

This case example illustrates how challenging, but also how rewarding, it can be to work with children with the LPE specifier and their caregivers. Leo made significant gains across multiple domains. His prosocial behaviors increased and his conduct problems, including noncompliance, aggression, and swearing, reduced to within normal limits. These behavioral improvements enabled Leo to better participate in school and have more effective relationships with his peers. Perhaps most notably, there was a marked improvement in the warmth and connection between Leo and his mother, which had been severely strained due to his persistent negative behavior.

However, Leo's case also highlights important limitations of PCIT-CU. Despite receiving intensive, tailored intervention, he continued to experience impairments in social, behavioral, and academic functioning. His CU traits, while somewhat reduced, still met the threshold for the LPE specifier diagnosis. This underscores a key point: Even evidence-based tailored treatments such as PCIT-CU may require further adaptation and extension for more severe cases. One likely limited factor in Leo's treatment was the fixed session format, of the research trial in which the family participated, which did not allow for continued treatment until the family met CDI-CU and PDI-CU skill mastery criteria. It is possible that children with more severe presentations, like Leo, require more extended treatment to achieve mastery. It is plausible that Leo's engagement with the CARES emotion training phase, and his development of associated emotional literacy skills and prosocial emotions, might have improved with better PDI-CU mastery and greater child compliance.

Leo's limited treatment response may also reflect the presence of elevated internalizing problems, which suggest he falls into the "secondary CU traits" subtype. As discussed further in Chapter 11, our research has found that children with secondary CU traits tend to show less sustained improvement in dysregulated behaviors after PCIT-CU, compared with those with primary CU traits (who do not show elevated internalizing problems). This distinction has meaningful treatment implications. It may point to the need for addressing additional parenting factors, such as high stress and negative attributions about the child, to sustain gains and prevent posttreatment deterioration in PRIDE skills, as seen in Leo's case. In situations involving significant deterioration in caregiver's PRIDE skills or child conduct problems after treatment ends, PCIT-CU booster sessions can be offered. We deliberately selected Leo's case over one with more obvious improvements to highlight these nuanced challenges and the need for future refinement. While PCIT-CU has demonstrated significant short-term benefits for many children with the LPE specifier, ongoing clinical research should investigate ways to improve outcomes, particularly for children with more severe and complex clinical presentations.

10

Expanding the Reach of Treatments for Children and Adolescents With Limited Prosocial Emotions

Parent–Child Interaction Therapy: Callous–Unemotional version (PCIT-CU) is emerging as a promising tailored treatment for children with conduct problems and limited prosocial emotions. However, like most evidence-based interventions for childhood mental disorders, it is not accessible to most affected children within their communities. This chapter discusses our clinical research to address barriers to accessing PCIT-CU and to expand its reach. Specifically, we discuss internet-delivered PCIT-CU (iPCIT-CU) treatment using a telehealth platform, including a consideration of ethical and practical issues for practitioners. Another approach we have pursued to expand the reach of PCIT-CU is to deliver it in schools. This chapter discusses a school adaptation of Parent–Child Interaction Therapy (PCIT) and PCIT-CU that involves teachers and paraprofessionals (i.e., teaching/educational/classroom/learning support assistants or aides, student learning support officers) in the treatment process together with caregivers on school grounds. This school PCIT-CU adaptation has shown potential to enhance generalization of improvements to classroom settings, addressing a key limitation of parent management training (PMT) programs that improvements reported by parents at home often do not extend to the school setting. Further, this chapter provides a template for developing and testing enhancements to other evidence-based treatments for serious conduct problems to be more effective for youth with elevated CU traits, as guided by our development of PCIT-CU. This includes discussing how a similar approach can be used to tailor other evidence-based treatments for people with limited

https://doi.org/10.1037/0000500-011
A Clinical Guide to Working With Youth With Conduct Disorders and Limited Prosocial Emotions, by P. J. Frick and E. R. Kimonis

prosocial emotions in older age groups. This chapter concludes with a discussion on future directions in treating children and adolescents with the limited prosocial emotions (LPE) specifier.

BARRIERS TO EVIDENCE-BASED INTERVENTIONS

Despite the availability of well-established, effective interventions for child conduct problems (Eyberg et al., 2008; Kaminski & Claussen, 2017) and progress in adapting these treatments for children with the LPE specifier, most children who need these interventions do not receive them. This limit in the reach of these treatments is largely due to a significant gap between the availability of treatments like PCIT-CU tested in experimental university settings and those available in the community. This gap is a result of several significant barriers limiting children's access to evidence-based psychological treatments, including

- limited availability (e.g., long waitlists to access services, shortages in trained workforce),
- limited accessibility (e.g., treatment cost, scheduling, transportation, childcare obstacles), and
- limited acceptability (e.g., fear of stigmatization, privacy concerns, cultural beliefs) of services (Comer et al., 2015; Hansen et al., 2019; Sanders et al., 2022).

For example, one survey found that over half of parents saw service costs as a major obstacle to seeking treatment, and more than one third identified not knowing where to seek help and experiencing long waiting times to access treatment as barriers (Tully et al., 2017). Together, these barriers contribute to the high rates of unmet need for children with serious conduct problems, including those with the LPE specifier (Johnson et al., 2018; Lawrence et al., 2015).

For families living in rural, remote, and impoverished communities, geographic disparities in children's mental health care further exacerbate problems with access to effective treatment. For example, where we practice, in Australia, where the University of New South Wales (UNSW) Parent–Child Research Clinic is located, 72% of psychological services are concentrated in metropolitan areas, leaving rural regions with far fewer options (Kavanagh et al., 2023). In Louisiana in the southern United States, with a higher percentage of rural areas, the Health Resources and Services Administration considers 97% (i.e., 62 of 64) of the parishes in the state as being mental health professional shortage areas (Louisiana Department of Health, 2025).

Because of a lack of psychologists, psychiatrists, or social workers, rural and remote towns often attempt to fill this gap with general practitioners, school counselors, and pediatricians, who tend to have neither specialized training in managing serious or complex conduct problems, nor adequate time to provide the intensive and individualized services required to treat children with serious conduct problems. One review of large studies ($N \geq 1,000$) conducted with children and adolescents in the United States, Canada, Great Britain, Australia, and New Zealand found that only one quarter of families with a child with a clinical diagnosis accessed specialist mental health services (Waddell et al., 2002). Many of these families experienced long delays in accessing treatment, with 4 years being the median delay experienced following the onset of oppositional defiant disorder (ODD). Once families accessed services, they often received treatments that were not evidence-based. One explanation for this trend is that regional and remote clinicians often have limited access to resources and fewer opportunities for professional development in evidence-based treatments, exacerbating the disparity in care between rural and metropolitan areas.

INTERNET ADAPTATIONS OF PARENT MANAGEMENT TRAINING

The emergence of *telehealth*—defined as the use of electronic media for real-time interactions that would traditionally occur in person (Comer et al., 2017)—offered an innovative solution to addressing geographic disparities in access to mental health care as well as other traditional barriers (Comer et al., 2015; Doss et al., 2017). Teleconferencing technology enables real-time, remote delivery of interventions traditionally provided in person, regardless of a family's geographic location and proximity to a clinic. These technological advances transformed health care delivery and reshaped mental health services by expanding the reach of evidence-based treatments like PCIT to be more widely accessible to families, particularly those living in underserved areas. Telehealth treatments overcome logistical barriers to treatment, such as transportation and scheduling challenges, while also reducing the stigma involved in attending a mental health clinic by allowing families to receive care in their homes. By delivering treatments directly to families in their natural settings, telehealth also extends the ecological validity of these interventions, applying them in the very contexts where the child's behavior problems occur. Thus, telehealth helped to bridge the gap between research-supported treatments and real-world accessibility, while also offering a cost-effective alternative to in-person care by reducing costs by up to one third (Comer et al., 2017; Day & Sanders, 2018). The COVID-19 pandemic was a catalyst for more widespread global dissemination of telehealth treatments, which have been integrated into routine care in many U.S. and other Global North countries, with high client satisfaction and promising outcomes (Comer et al., 2017; Dadds, Thai, et al., 2019).

Online adaptations of PMT specifically have demonstrated efficacy for treating child conduct problems across diverse settings, including rural populations who face limited access to care (Baumel et al., 2017; Corralejo & Rodríguez, 2018, Dadds, Thai, et al., 2019; Fleming et al., 2017). Like the clinic-based PMT programs, online PMT programs range in delivery format and intensity, from low-intensity, self-guided modules (Enebrink et al., 2012) to high-intensity interventions involving real-time, therapist-guided coaching via video teleconferencing (VTC; Comer et al., 2017). Like in-person interventions, engagement and retention outcomes are better for programs combining self-guided content with VTC-enabled therapist support. For example, the online version of the Triple P Positive Parenting Program (TPOL; Turner & Sanders, 2011) is a low-intensity, self-guided intervention with eight modules found to be effective in reducing conduct problems in 2- to 9-year-old Australian children (Sanders et al., 2012). Adding therapist support to TPOL by using telephone calls increased its impact (Day & Sanders, 2018). However, the overall utility of both online versions was limited by poor engagement. That is, only 47% of parents completed the telephone-supported version of TPOL and only 23% completed standard TPOL. However, other studies of VTC-enhanced PMT have reported more promising results. In a study of 22 families of 3- to 12-year-old children with oppositional defiant disorder (ODD) or conduct disorder (CD), results of VTC-enhanced PMT were similar to a matched sample of 25 families who had received in-person PMT, with both groups showing 90% or higher retention rates (Kirkman et al., 2016). Also, VTC-based PMT has been shown to be effective in both urban and rural settings, as demonstrated by studies in the United States and Australia (Dadds, Thai, et al., 2019; Kirkman et al., 2016).

Most research on online PMT comes from controlled research environments, and few studies have evaluated its effectiveness in real-world settings. One study conducted in Sweden on the online iCOMET program found lower effectiveness for the online version of PMT in reducing posttreatment conduct problems and higher dropout rates (47%) compared with the in-person Family Check-Up program (33%; Ghaderi et al., 2018). In contrast, a randomized trial conducted in rural Australia, comparing in-person and VTC-enhanced PMT, found no significant differences in clinician- or caregiver-rated conduct problems between the two formats, and both groups yielded high caregiver satisfaction ratings (Dadds, Thai, et al., 2019). Overall, the effectiveness of online PMT programs is influenced by the intensity of the program, in terms of the level of therapist involvement, dosage, and whether the child is involved in treatment with the caregiver. Thus, PCIT that offers a high level of intensity with parent and child involved together in treatment is particularly well-suited for online, face-to-face delivery.

INTERNET-DELIVERED PARENT–CHILD INTERACTION THERAPY AND CALLOUS–UNEMOTIONAL VERSION

Compared with many other internet PMT programs that are delivered using an online modular format, in iPCIT, a therapist meets face to face with clients via VTC to provide live, real-time coaching during caregiver–child interactions. PCIT and its adaptation for children with callous–unemotional (CU) traits (PCIT-CU) are particularly amenable to this interactive web setup given their delivery format involving therapists observing from behind a one-way mirror and live coaching parents via a caregiver-worn wireless bug-in-the-ear device. iPCIT mimics traditional in-clinic PCIT by allowing therapists to observe the caregiver–child dyad in their natural setting using VTC and provide parents with instantaneous feedback during in-home caregiver–child interactions using a wireless earphone (see Figure 10.1). Thus, this format maintains the same level of therapist contact as in-person PCIT.

Research supports the effectiveness of iPCIT in treating child conduct problems across different settings. For example, a randomized trial comparing iPCIT with in-clinic PCIT in U.S. metropolitan areas found that both formats were equally effective in reducing the conduct problems of 3- to 5-year-old children, with both groups showing adequate retention rates (70%) and high caregiver satisfaction ratings. Families assigned to iPCIT also reported fewer barriers to treatment and clinicians rated them as showing higher rates of "excellent treatment responder" status (45% for iPCIT vs. 15% for in-clinic PCIT; Comer et al., 2017). The authors attributed the enhanced treatment response with iPCIT to its improved ecological validity in treating child behavior in the same home setting where it is occurring (Comer et al., 2015, 2017).

In a study we conducted with 27 families in rural Australia, Fleming et al. (2021) evaluated iPCIT delivered from a community-based clinic miles away.

FIGURE 10.1. Demonstration of Live Coaching Online

Note. The therapist, Dr. Georgette Fleming, provides live coaching for a caregiver (actor) to implement child-directed interaction skills with their child (actor) using internet-delivered Parent-Child Interaction Therapy (iPCIT). Photo by Georgette Fleming. Used with permission.

Mothers reported significant improvements in child behavior and showed improved parenting practices, with effect sizes ranging from "small" to "very large" ($d = 0.3–1.4$). Treatment retention was at 63%, and caregivers expressed high treatment satisfaction and were compliant with homework activities. These findings demonstrate the real-world potential of iPCIT to bridge the research-to-practice gap. It also led the community-based clinic involved in the treatment trial to integrate iPCIT into its routine care. Thus, iPCIT offers a promising solution for expanding access to evidence-based treatments for childhood conduct problems, especially in underserved communities. By delivering treatment in naturalistic settings and reducing logistical barriers, these technological innovations have the potential to narrow the research-to-practice gap and improve outcomes for more children and families in need.

Internet-Delivered Parent–Child Interaction Therapy With Children With the Limited Prosocial Emotions Specifier

Efforts to overcome access-to-care barriers using online interventions are promising, but they are only effective if families complete and benefit from the treatment. As detailed in Chapter 7, children with elevated CU traits show a more severe and stable pattern of conduct problems that are less likely to normalize with treatment, even those producing large effect sizes like PCIT. Developments in targeted treatment of children with CU traits have for the most part occurred independently from efforts to improve the accessibility of PMT through online delivery. This disconnect is problematic given that children who fail to respond to online PMT, particularly those living in rural areas, may have limited alternatives (Jones et al., 2013). The reliance of the most widely available online PMT programs on low-intensity, self-guided modules with minimal therapist involvement (Baumel et al., 2017) is unlikely to adequately address the complex needs of children with the LPE specifier. For example, in one of the only studies to compare children with high versus low CU traits on outcomes following online PMT (self-guided iCOMET), those with elevated CU traits had significantly greater posttreatment conduct problems than those with lower CU traits (Högström et al., 2013). This finding suggests that low-intensity online interventions with limited to no therapist contact are likely to be insufficient for children with the LPE specifier.

When treating children with the LPE specifier, iPCIT's supposed improved ecological validity (Comer et al., 2015) might aid in mitigating the detrimental effects of CU traits on treatment by enabling therapists and parents to tailor interventions more effectively. At the same time, the remote delivery format of iPCIT reduces environmental control for therapists, which may complicate treatment efforts for children with CU traits who typically show more severe and aggressive conduct problems (Fleming et al., 2017). We tested whether CU traits moderated the efficacy of iPCIT compared to clinic-based PCIT in a study of 40 families with 3- to 5-year-old children diagnosed with ODD or CD (83.5% boys; Fleming et al., 2020). Families were randomized to receive either iPCIT or clinic-based PCIT. Findings showed that the negative influence of CU traits on outcomes was more pronounced for children treated with iPCIT relative to in-clinic PCIT. Parents of children with CU traits reported less treatment satisfaction, with this effect being greater for iPCIT than in-clinic PCIT, although dropout rates did not differ between delivery formats. However, the presence of CU traits did not moderate differences in posttreatment conduct problem severity or overall treatment response between the two PCIT formats, suggesting some potential for iPCIT.

Only one study to date has tested engagement outcomes and preliminary efficacy of iPCIT-CU in a small sample of young children. In 3- to 5-year-old children with conduct problems and the LPE specifier in Australia ($N = 10$), Fleming (2019) used a quasi-experimental design to compare those receiving iPCIT-CU from their homes ($n = 5$) with a matched control group who received in-clinic PCIT-CU ($n = 5$). Families were matched according to (a) child age, (b) initial conduct problem severity, and (c) treatment conducted during the same time period. Both groups received the same number of individual iPCIT-CU treatment sessions—seven weekly, 1-hour sessions each of CDI-CU, PDI-CU, and CARES—covering identical content. Results showed that both groups showed significant and large improvements in caregiver-rated and observed child conduct problems and positive parenting with treatment, which did not differ between PCIT-CU formats. For both groups, treatment retention was high (100% in PCIT-CU vs. 90% in iPCIT-CU), parents reported high treatment satisfaction (mean posttreatment TAI = 4.66 [$SD = 0.43$] for iPCIT-CU and 4.65 [$SD = 0.57$] for in-clinic PCIT-CU out of 5), and rates of missed or canceled sessions or homework completion across phases did not differ between PCIT-CU formats. Using reliable and clinically significant change indicators, we further found that iPCIT-CU was equivalent to in-clinic iPCIT-CU for improving child conduct problems: 3 months after treatment ended 80 to 100% of children in both groups showed reliable improvement on all conduct problem measures and up to 80% of children in both groups scored below clinical cutoffs on at least one conduct problem measure (Fleming, 2019). While these results need to be replicated in a larger sample using a more rigorous experimental design, they provide at least promising support that iPCIT-CU is a feasible and promising intervention for improving outcomes in children with CU traits, particularly those living in rural or underserved communities where alternative treatment options are limited.

Taken together, these findings suggest that VTC-enabled online PMT, as in the case of iPCIT-CU, may be a viable option for treating childhood conduct problems presenting with elevated CU traits, particularly when access to traditional in-clinic care is limited. iPCIT-CU has potential to improve outcomes for children with the LPE specifier who receive less benefit and show less global improvement in child functioning from standard online PMT interventions relative to other children with conduct problems. Importantly, online PMT involving direct therapist support produced better outcomes for children with elevated CU traits than self-guided PMT interventions. Thus, including more intensive, individualized, therapist-guided elements when delivering online

PMT appears to be crucial for addressing the specific and complex needs of children with CU traits.

Internet-Delivered Parent-Child Interaction Therapy: Callous-Unemotional Version Treatment Protocol

iPCIT for children with CU traits (iPCIT-CU) is an internet-delivered format of PCIT-CU that uses using widely available videoconferencing platforms such as Zoom, Microsoft Teams, or Cisco Webex (at the time of writing) to deliver real-time, face-to-face sessions online. Like all telehealth services, iPCIT-CU providers must take reasonable steps to ensure the confidentiality, privacy, and security of clients' personal information and put in safeguards against its unauthorized access and misuse (Kramer et al., 2015). In line with guidelines established by the developer of iPCIT, it is recommended that, before starting treatment, therapists discuss issues related to technology-based breaches of confidentiality and security with families (Comer et al., 2015).

While its delivery method differs from traditional in-clinic PCIT-CU, iPCIT-CU's content remains mostly consistent with the PCIT-CU protocol. The only exception is the recommended addition of an initial session, as is recommended for iPCIT (Comer et al., 2015), for the purpose of introducing parents to the technological aspects of treatment. Adequately familiarizing the family with the technology empowers them to quickly and effectively address technological difficulties that occur during treatment sessions. In this initial session, the therapist instructs caregivers to treat the iPCIT-CU appointment in the same way that they would an in-office session—by setting phones to silent mode and minimizing distractions (e.g., media turned off, securing pets in another room, organizing caregiving for siblings as required)—to ensure a focused and controlled in-home environment. Other iPCIT-CU–related considerations may be addressed either in this introductory meeting or, if more appropriate, in the subsequent caregiver-only CDI-CU teaching session. These include topics such as the following (Fleming, 2019):

- preparing the physical space (e.g., choosing an appropriate room for play therapy, arranging furniture and technology, selecting toys),
- ensuring adequate lighting (so that both caregiver–child interactions and therapist observations are clear),
- maintaining privacy and confidentiality (e.g., reducing interruptions from other household members or visitors), and
- promoting safety and backup communication (e.g., identifying alternative methods of contact in case of technical difficulties).

For example, in iPCIT-CU, it is important for therapists to work with caregivers to identify a suitable location for placing their computer, tablet, or phone so the therapist has a good view of the play area, while also keeping the device out of the reach of the child with LPE who can be destructive with property. The therapist may also advise the caregiver to remove any valuable objects from the room, particularly when entering the PDI-CU discipline phase of treatment.

During iPCIT-CU sessions, the treating therapist should be positioned in a private space equipped with reliable and speedy internet access and a computer with webcam and microphone. This will reduce the number of interruptions caused by technological mishaps or failures (Fleming et al., 2017). This technological setup allows for caregiver–child interactions from the predesignated room in the family's home to be streamed live to the therapist's computer or tablet at a remote site via secure, encrypted video. During the check-in and debrief components of iPCIT-CU coaching sessions, it is recommended that the audio settings are adjusted to output sound via the family's computer speaker to enable concurrent communication with the caregiver and/or child, where appropriate. This will require the therapist and parent to be familiar with computer audio settings in order to toggle back and forth. In some cases, when families struggle with technology, therapists may request control access of their computing device to change settings for the caregiver where the VTC software enables this functionality. During the coaching portion of treatment sessions, the audio settings will need to be adjusted to transmit sound to the wireless earpiece connected to the VTC software. This setup allows the observing therapist to provide real-time coaching and feedback to the caregiver while they engage freely with their child in play. This format parallels traditional PCIT, where therapists use a wireless bug-in-ear device to provide live guidance to the caregiver from behind a one-way mirror. If required and feasible, therapists can equip families with any necessary technology, such as webcams or wireless earphones, as part of the iPCIT-CU participation kit.

In iPCIT-CU, the therapist coaches the caregiver in the same core skills of PCIT-CU, including use of PRIDE skills, differential attention, and effective discipline strategies, with adjustments to accommodate the needs of children with the LPE specifier. Session materials, which are traditionally provided in-person during in-clinic PCIT-CU, are made available digitally in iPCIT-CU. Progression through treatment follows the same criteria as in-clinic PCIT-CU. Caregivers advance from one PCIT-CU phase to the next based on mastery of skills and the child's normalization of behavior, as measured using standardized assessment tools such as the Eyberg Child Behavior Inventory (ECBI), which can be set up to be administered via online survey software. Despite the transition to digital delivery, iPCIT-CU maintains all essential elements of PCIT-CU, providing structured, evidence-based intervention while making treatment more accessible by using modern technology to deliver care directly to families in their homes.

When conducting iPCIT-CU sessions, therapists must consider and plan for issues related to family safety that can arise when conducting treatment over the internet. This is because therapists have less control over the clinical environment. For example, in our case study describing iPCIT-CU treatment of a 5-year-old boy, Matthew, this reduced environmental control manifested as significant in-session disruptions for various reasons, including the child escaping the designated intervention room, introducing PCIT-inappropriate toys and activities, and engaging in severe disruptive behavior during the check-in and debrief discussion components surrounding coaching periods (Fleming et al., 2017). While similar disruptions occur with in-clinic treatment, as illustrated in the PCIT-CU case example in Chapter 9, the limited control over the treatment session adds another layer of challenges. Challenges around caregiver and child safety are likely to increase during the PDI phase of treatment when children often escalate their aggression with the introduction of time-out (McNeil & Hembree-Kigin, 2011). A useful and recommended approach is to collaboratively develop a safety plan with caregivers in the initial technological set-up. This includes confirming and recording accurate contact details for caregivers and key family members, along with discussing the limits of confidentiality (e.g., situations where there is reasonable concern for the safety of the child or others; Kramer et al., 2015). For providers who are geographically distant from families, it is also advisable to establish links with local health professionals or community services to ensure that immediate support is available should clinical emergencies or high-risk circumstances arise (Kramer et al., 2015). With these considerations in mind, tailored internet-delivered treatment offers a viable option for delivering psychological services to children with CU traits who do not have access to specialized intervention in their communities.

ADDRESSING ACCESSIBILITY AND GENERALIZATION TO SCHOOL SETTINGS

In this section, we discuss another approach we have pursued to expand the reach of PCIT-CU. This approach involves delivering treatment in schools and involving educators in treatment sessions alongside caregivers. This program of clinical research is also aimed at addressing a major limitation of PMT programs generally, which is their limited generalization of behavioral improvements seen at home to the classroom setting. Schools worldwide face the increasing challenge of disruptive, aggressive, and unsafe student behavior. These problems were exacerbated by the COVID-19 pandemic, particularly within economically disadvantaged communities. The pandemic amplified existing stressors, such as economic instability, family conflict, dysfunctional parenting practices, and mental health issues, further burdening already overstretched support services in vulnerable communities (Brown et al., 2020; Penner et al., 2022; Westrupp et al., 2023).

Consequently, many children with serious conduct problems were left for educators to manage, as schools are where children spend a large majority of their waking hours. School problems are greatest for the subset of children with conduct problems who also show the LPE specifier. A meta-analytic review of 37 empirical studies found that school-aged children with CU traits in the

United States showed poorer academic performance (i.e., lower grades, test scores), worse peer and teacher relationships (i.e., fewer positive peer interactions, lower-quality student–teacher relationships), and greater conduct problems and aggression at school than children low on CU traits (Levine et al., 2023). The strained relationships between children with elevated CU traits and their teachers parallels dysfunctional caregiver–child interactions in the home setting and support the need to deliver tailored PMT programs with an intensive relationship enhancement component to teachers.

Increasing calls have been made to equip schools and teachers with the skills to manage increasing disruptive and aggressive student behaviors. For decades, advocates have pressed for implementing evidence-based psychological interventions in everyday settings like schools to improve their accessibility and consumer uptake. School delivery has potential to overcome many of the barriers impacting availability, accessibility, and acceptability of evidence-based psychological interventions for children and families (Atkins et al., 2017; Sanchez et al., 2018). This is because school-based interventions are particularly effective in overcoming barriers such as stigma and service scarcity, which often limit access to mental health support (Sanchez et al., 2018). Unlike services delivered through the mental health system, which can be hindered by long waitlists, practical obstacles, high costs, and restrictive inclusion criteria, school-embedded interventions are more readily accessible to families. For example, school-based interventions can be delivered

- to families at a close and familiar location (i.e., their child's school),
- at a convenient time (i.e., before, during, or after school hours), and
- usually at low to no cost to families.

School counselors can offer only limited support as they are often overburdened and lack specialized expertise in treating complex behavior problems, further highlighting the need for interventions like PCIT-CU to be delivered in schools.

Beyond issues of accessibility, a major limitation to evidence-based interventions for young children with conduct problems is that improvements seen at home often do not transfer to the school setting, where disruptive behaviors persist and continue to negatively impact both student and teacher interactions and well-being (Waschbusch et al., 2019). Current estimates suggest that around 75% of children who show behavioral improvements at home with a typical PMT intervention continue to struggle in school settings, especially after extended follow-up periods (Drugli & Larsson, 2006). This finding is likely due in large part to the most efficacious PMT interventions rarely involving teachers in treatment in a standardized way. When it comes to managing student disruptive behaviors, teachers self-report a lack of skills (McKenzie et al., 2014). Results of surveys have shown that teachers often feel underqualified to manage classroom behavior problems and lack mental health literacy and access to referral options (Walter et al., 2006; Webster-Stratton et al., 2004). Our own research with 390 preschool and elementary school educators specifically found low rates of knowledge (57% correct responses on a knowledge test) of the characteristics and effective behavior management of children with conduct problems, including those with the LPE specifier, which did not differ by years of teaching experience or accreditation status (Fleming et al., 2024). Notably, knowledge was lowest for paraprofessional staff. These findings support the critical need to deliver universal mental health literacy training focused on the characteristics of students with the LPE specifier to educators.

Another critical benefit of educating teachers on the characteristics of students with the LPE specifier is that teachers spend a large proportion of the day with children and are often the first to notice when a child is struggling relative to their peers. This places them in the optimal position to refer children with emerging serious conduct problems and poorly developing prosocial emotions as early as possible for intervention. Teachers also play a pivotal role in shaping students' behavior, but they cannot effectively do this unless they receive adequate training in evidence-based behavior management strategies. Even when their students and their families are receiving efficacious treatments like PMT, it is common that their teachers will not be involved in this treatment. This represents a missed opportunity to align the implementation of behavior management strategies between home and school, which can yield the fastest and longest lasting improvements in student behavior.

Consequently, we formed a partnership with several schools in our area to coproduce a school adaptation of PCIT and PCIT-CU as a solution to overcome what we saw as three of the major limitations to evidence-based treatment for child conduct problems:

- most children who need treatment are unable to access it,
- conduct problems do not normalize with treatment for children with the LPE specifier necessitating delivery of tailored treatments such as PCIT-CU, and
- improvements in child conduct problems reported by parents at home following PMT often do not extend to the school or classroom settings.

These challenges represent our key motivators for developing "school PCIT" and "school PCIT-CU," which we describe in greater detail in the next section.

School Parent-Child Interaction Therapy and School Parent-Child Interaction Therapy: Callous-Unemotional Version

From a school interventions context, school PCIT and school PCIT-CU were designed as Tier 3-indicated individual interventions implemented by specialists to students with conduct problems, within a multitiered system and continuum of positive behavior interventions and supports (PBIS; Lee & Gage, 2020). Addressing a major criticism of most tier systems used by schools, that they often neglect parent involvement in intervention (Garbacz et al., 2015), school PCIT and school PCIT-CU were designed as accessible, school-based PMT early interventions for students with severe or complex disruptive behavior that integrate parents into school-based interventions, as supported by robust empirical evidence of the caregiver's influence on children's behavioral, academic, and social outcomes at school, and by findings of enhanced school-based intervention effects with active family engagement (Sanders et al., 2017; Weist et al., 2017).

School PCIT and school PCIT-CU were coproduced over a 3-year period, involving working with leadership and educators from a network of six public primary schools and one preschool located in South West Sydney, which is in the largest Australian state of New South Wales. The key goal of this coproduction process was to enhance the interventions' effectiveness, acceptability, sustainability, and scalability by involving these educational stakeholders in all stages of the clinical research and tailoring the school-based PCIT or PCIT-CU interventions to the needs of their students with conduct problems and their families and teachers. Using a coproduction framework, the research progressed through three phases—evidence, development, and testing—over six distinct steps (for an extended description, see Fleming, Kershaw, et al., in press).

To test this school adaptation, a specialized clinic "hub" space with technological infrastructure required to deliver PCIT was built on the grounds of the lead participating school. The technological setup required included vandal-proof cameras to capture sessions, microphones for clear audio input, a transmitter–receiver system, a speaker for playback, recording and storage equipment, a digital mixer to balance sound, and a computer equipped with video management software. A later iteration of this clinic space for a regional setting also included a system for providing remote live supervision to clinicians in the delivery of school PCIT or PCIT-CU using VTC technology with access to clinic video and audio streams. Using a hub and spoke delivery model, therapists delivered the interventions from this school clinic hub to nominated students from across the participating school network. Families and teachers of students from nonhub schools, which were all located less than 10 miles from the hub school, traveled to the hub school clinic to receive treatment. Students were recruited into the clinical trial via one of three referral pathways, determined using stakeholder feedback:

- children attending preschools in the transition-to-school program,
- a grade-wide screening of kindergarten to second grade students enrolled in the participating schools, or
- teacher referral.

Eligible students were offered treatment when parents and/or teachers rated them in the clinically significant range on a measure of child conduct problems. Thus, these children had varying levels of CU traits. As in in-clinic PCIT or PCIT-CU, following a comprehensive pretreatment assessment, caregivers participated in weekly, 1-hour treatment sessions that were provided at no cost to the family. All caregivers were encouraged to participate, given enhanced treatment outcomes with father involvement (Piotrowska et al., 2020).

We began by testing the feasibility and preliminary efficacy of PCIT or PCIT-CU delivered at school. Data obtained from our first cohort of 27 students (*M* age = 6.48 years, *SD* = 1.07, range: 3.47–7.97; 70% boys) with clinically significant conduct problems who participated in PCIT/PCIT-CU with their primary caregiver demonstrated the feasibility of PCIT or PCIT-CU delivered on school grounds. The dropout rate of 33% was comparable or less than other community-delivered PCIT services, and treatment completers reported a high degree of satisfaction with PCIT or PCIT-CU, with an overall satisfaction score on the TAI of 4.72 out of 5 (*SD* = 0.30). For the families for whom ECBI scores were available, 82% showed clinical and reliable improvement at post-treatment and 81% at a 3-month follow-up assessment. However, according to the teacher report on the SESBI, only 56% at posttreatment and 44% at follow-up showed reliable improvement at school. These results indicated that PCIT or PCIT-CU delivered at school was a feasible intervention that meaningfully improved conduct problems in the home setting. However, implementing PCIT or PCIT-CU at school was insufficient to meaningfully impact conduct problems in the school setting, according to educators. Such findings are consistent with prior results of PMT trials finding limited generalization to the school setting (Helander et al., 2024).

Following this initial pilot testing, we elicited feedback on these results from our educational stakeholders and this feedback heavily emphasized the need for PCIT or PCIT-CU delivered at school to build educator capacity for addressing conduct problems occurring at school. We worked with our stakeholders to comodify the school PCIT and PCIT-CU research protocol to include both a universal and targeted teacher training component. For the universal component, we developed a series of active-learning workshops (8-hour equivalent) to deliver to all school staff working with students in preschool through second grade to improve their mental health literacy regarding

- the characteristics of conduct problems and CU traits,
- evidence-based theory and principles of behavior management, and
- evidence-based behavior management strategies from PCIT/PCIT-CU frameworks.

For the targeted teacher training component, we invited school staff working with the target child to participate in individual intervention sessions alongside students and their caregivers, with their consent to do so. These educators participated by observing caregiver coaching from behind the one-way mirror as well as by receiving real-time in-clinic coaching in school PCIT or PCIT-CU skills from a clinician via a bug-in-ear device while they interacted with their student. Specifically, school PCIT or PCIT-CU integrates educators into at least four in-clinic coaching sessions with both caregiver and child, two in the CDI phase and two in the PDI phase, with the option for additional sessions if requested and/or necessary (for an extended description, see Fleming,

Kershaw, et al., in press). This approach aims to enhance caregiver–teacher collaboration and home–school communication, and to promote joint and consistent behavior management across settings. This is expected to produce greater and sustained changes in child, caregiver, and teacher behavior across both home and school settings.

The next step in our research involved testing the acceptability and efficacy of these modified school PCIT and PCIT-CU interventions (with enhanced educator involvement), in a second cohort of students from the same school network. Results from a sample of 42 students (*M* age = 6.05 years, *SD* = 0.69, range: 5.02–7.87; 71% boys) with clinically significant conduct problems who participated in school PCIT or PCIT-CU with their primary caregiver, which ran during the COVID-19 pandemic and necessitated our quick pivoting to iPCIT or iPCIT-CU, revealed a higher dropout rate of 59% relative to our initial pilot test; however, when we examined ECBI Intensity scores for families who started but dropped out of treatment, we saw that most of these children (86%) scored in the normal range of functioning at their last PCIT session before dropping out. These findings indicated that these children did receive clinical benefit from their partial participation in school PCIT or PCIT-CU. Similarly, other research has found that completing at least four sessions of standard in-clinic PCIT was associated with a medium to large improvement in ECBI intensity scores ($d = 0.70$), prompting calls to reconceptualize treatment dropout from PCIT (Lieneman et al., 2019). Regarding treatment satisfaction, caregivers in our school PCIT–PCIT-CU trial reported an overall high average level of satisfaction with this enhanced educator involvement version (TAI score of 4.32 out of 5, *SD* = 0.55). Regarding efficacy, 87% and 90% of children showed clinical and/or reliable improvement in caregiver-rated conduct problems at posttreatment and 3-month follow-up, respectively. For teacher-rated conduct problems, 75% and 64% of children showed clinical and/or reliable improvement at posttreatment and follow-up, respectively. These findings support that substantially involving educators in school PCIT and PCIT-CU intervention sessions using a combination of universal and targeted strategies enhances the generalization of treatment gains to the school setting, although these findings need replication in a more rigorous randomized clinical trial, which is underway at the time of writing.

Importantly, school PCIT and PCIT-CU extend existing approaches to treating children with conduct problems in three key ways. First, they systematically involve teachers and paraprofessional school support staff directly in the treatment process with parents by providing these educators with universal and targeted training that includes intensive in vivo coaching in the application of relationship enhancement and behavior management skills. This ensures that these strategies are consistently applied across home and school settings, which is crucial for the long-term success of early interventions and generalization of improvements to the classroom. Second, it embeds specialist child mental health support directly in the learning environments of children with severe or complex conduct problems. This approach also makes treatment more accessible to those who need it. Third, it tailors treatment to the needs of children presenting with the LPE specifier, enabling matching of treatment to the individual needs of this group of students with conduct problems. That is, children with the LPE specifier can be provided PCIT-CU, ensuring that treatment outcomes are maximized. All educators learn about the important differences between children with conduct problems with and without the LPE specifier to better facilitate their tailoring of behavior management strategies. Results from our randomized controlled trial testing a self-guided online version of our universal teacher training workshop with 275 educators found that those randomized to immediately access the intervention showed greater postintervention knowledge of complex conduct problems, self-efficacy in classroom management, and rated their nominated student with conduct problems as showing lower CU traits than a waitlist control group of educators (Boulton et al., in press). In conclusion, school PCIT and PCIT-CU represent a promising approach to extending intervention reach and addressing major gaps in current services.

APPLYING THE PARENT-CHILD INTERACTION THERAPY: CALLOUS-UNEMOTIONAL VERSION MODEL TO TAILOR OTHER TREATMENT PROGRAMS FOR CHILDREN AND ADOLESCENTS WITH THE LIMITED PROSOCIAL EMOTIONS SPECIFIER

We have described our PCIT-CU model in depth in this book to illustrate how research on children and adolescents with CU traits can be used to enhance interventions that have proven to reduce conduct problems to be more effective for these youth. We feel that this approach can guide adaptations to other evidence-based treatments for children and adolescents with the LPE specifier, particularly those targeting older children outside the 2- to 7-year-old PCIT age range and adolescents. In Exhibit 10.1, we summarize what we feel are key considerations in treating children and adolescents with the LPE specifier that apply to our PCIT-CU intervention and can be extended to other treatments.

We recognize that these recommendations for enhancing other approaches to treatment have not been directly tested to determine if they make these interventions more effective for children and adolescents with the LPE specifier, as we have done for PCIT-CU. Such outcome tests are clearly needed in future research. However, we feel that, based on our success with PCIT-CU, these recommendations are justified until such research is conducted. To aid clinicians in making such modifications to other treatments, we provide an example of how another PMT program that was developed for older children and adolescents could be modified according to these principles.

Illustrative Example: Modifying Kazdin's (2005) Parent Management Training Program

Kazdin's (2005) PMT program is designed for treating children and adolescents aged 7 to 14 years with conduct problems and it has proven to be efficacious

EXHIBIT 10.1

Overview of Key Considerations and Practical Recommendations for Working With Children and Adolescents With Conduct Problems and the Limited Prosocial Emotions Specifier

Risk/causal factors

- A minority of children (25% to 35%) with childhood-onset conduct problems show elevated callous-unemotional (CU) traits and would meet diagnostic criteria for the limited prosocial emotions (LPE) specifier.
- Children and adolescents with conduct problems and the LPE specifier differ from other youth with conduct problems on several emotional, cognitive, social, and behavioral characteristics.
- A key emotional difference is that they are inaccurate in identifying others' emotional expressions, particularly recognizing signs of distress such as sadness or fear. This emotional deficit is thought to originate from a temperament characterized by emotional underreactivity, as well as atypical patterns of attentional orienting to people, faces and their salient features during emotional expressions. They are also emotionally underreactive to punishing or threatening stimuli.
- A key cognitive difference is that they expect that engaging in antisocial behavior will result in rewarding outcomes, and they value these outcomes more so than avoiding punishment. They also struggle to learn changes in contingencies, specifically to stop doing a behavior that was previously rewarded but is now punished.
- A key social difference is that children and adolescents with the LPE specifier experience lower levels of warm and responsive parenting, and this drives their increasing conduct problems. The callous and unemotional style of these children also increases parental stress and makes it difficult for parents to use the warm and responsive parenting that these children need. Also, youth with the LPE specifier tend to form friendships with other deviant peers, which, although short in duration and lacking in closeness, are more likely to lead to, or instigate these peers to engage in, antisocial, bullying, or criminal behavior.
- A key behavioral difference is that children and adolescents with the LPE specifier begin showing serious conduct problems and criminal behavior earlier in development, on average before age 8, which includes aggression and violence that is more likely to harm its victims, bullying, risky sexual behaviors, harmful substance use, and criminal behavior that continues during and after incarceration. The behavior problems of youth with the LPE specifier are more often motivated by spitefulness or vindictiveness, or the desire to obtain a goal (e.g., a tangible item, dominance over smaller or weaker others), in addition to being in response to real or perceived provocation by others.
- The causal processes that lead children and adolescents with LPE to develop conduct problems, involving these and other risk factors, differ from other youth with serious conduct problems.

Assessment

- Assess a wide range of conduct problems and determine if the number of problems, duration, and impairment across settings meet oppositional defiant disorder (ODD) and/or conduct disorder diagnostic criteria.
- Assess for comorbidities, including attention-deficit/hyperactivity disorder (ADHD), anxiety, depression (including suicidal ideation), harmful substance use, and adjustment problems in social, academic, or occupational domains, which are more common among some youth with the LPE specifier relative to youth without this specifier.
- Within the context of a broader assessment for conduct problems, routinely assess all children for the LPE specifier using current diagnostic classification criteria, especially when their behavior problems onset before age 10.
- Use a comprehensive rating scale that assesses all LPE specifier criteria (i.e., Inventory of Callous Unemotional Traits [ICU]).
- Use multirater assessment to determine that LPE symptoms present across relationships and settings and across time (12 months or more). Interpret discrepancies across informants by considering the most valid reporters for the child's age (e.g., as outlined for the ICU in Chapter 5, Table 5.3).

(continues)

EXHIBIT 10.1

Overview of Key Considerations and Practical Recommendations for Working With Children and Adolescents With Conduct Problems and the Limited Prosocial Emotions Specifier (*Continued*)

- Consider using a tiered approach to assessing the LPE specifier by first using the ICU as a screening tool to identify children at risk. Second, administer the Clinical Assessment of Prosocial Emotions only to those who score above ICU cutoffs (Chapter 5, Table 5.2) to determine if a diagnosis is warranted.

Treatment

- Children and adolescents with the LPE specifier typically end evidence-based treatments for conduct problems with significant levels of behavior problems that often still meet diagnostic criteria for ODD and/or conduct disorder (CD).
- Treat children and adolescents with conduct problems and the LPE specifier using a base intervention that is
  - efficacious for treating conduct problems, including (a) parent management training (PMT); (b) cognitive behavior therapy (CBT) that includes a PMT component; or (c) a multimodal treatment that uses various modalities, including PMT to target multiple risk factors (e.g., functional family therapy [FFT]), and
  - adapted or modified to target the distinct needs of individuals with the LPE specifier based on the most current available research (i.e., Parent–Child Interaction Therapy: Callous–Unemotional version [PCIT-CU]).
- For children under age 12, when selecting the base intervention deliver PMT as the recommended first-line treatment; for children aged 12 and older, deliver either a combination of PMT and CBT that targets dysfunctional cognitive biases seen in CU traits, or intensive and individualized multimodal treatment (i.e., FFT).
- Include the child or adolescent in treatment sessions with the caregivers.
- Use a PMT program that integrates an intensive relationship enhancement component aimed at fostering a warm and responsive caregiver–child relationship that the child experiences as rewarding and is developmentally appropriate, before delivering behavior management strategies.
- Within PMT, emphasize reward-based behavior management strategies (i.e., social reinforcers, tangible reinforcers, preferred activities and privileges, personalized token economy system) for increasing desirable and prosocial child behaviors over punishment-based strategies, and continually refresh rewards to match the child's self-interests to maintain child motivation and engagement with the token system.
- Within PMT, use in vivo coaching of caregivers to support highly consistent and timely implementation of behavior management strategies for minor misbehavior (i.e., planned ignoring paired with labeled praise of positive opposite behaviors) and for serious misbehavior that cannot be ignored including escalation in response to planned ignoring (i.e., ages 7 and under: time-out from reinforcement with a backup procedure to teach the child to remain in the time-out chair, wherever possible; ages 8 to 10: variant of time-out involving privilege removal to teach the child to remain seated quietly in the time-out chair; ages 11 and up: privilege removal, assigning low-rate chores).
- Deliver adjunctive emotion recognition training to the youth and the parent, where possible (e.g., Coaching and Rewarding Emotional Skills [CARES] module for younger children, Mindreading program or alternatives for older children and adolescents).
- Administer parent-focused intervention strategies aimed at reducing parenting stress and continually monitor and problem solve barriers to their implementation across treatment.
- Use higher intensity treatments (20 or more treatment sessions), striving to maintain a regular weekly frequency of sessions to support parental consistency in implementing strategies.
- For a child or adolescent with comorbid ADHD and dysregulated, impulsive, or aggressive behaviors that undermine treatment progress, refer them for a medical evaluation to determine whether a combination of psychosocial treatment and stimulant medication is medically indicated.

in reducing the behavior problems in this age group across multiple studies (Beelmann et al., 2023; Comer et al., 2013; van Aar et al., 2017). It typically consists of at least 12 one-hour weekly sessions delivered to parents alone, with skill rehearsal via therapist-led role-plays. To tailor this program for youth with the LPE specifier, the following modifications could be made, similar to those that we made to create PCIT-CU.

Enhancing the Caregiver–Child Relationship

Before beginning PMT behavior management sessions, an extended relationship enhancement component to increase parental warmth and responsiveness could be added to the standard intervention. Strategies can be drawn from the emerging adaptation of PCIT for older children between 7 and 10 years old (Gibson et al., 2021; Parent–Child Interaction Therapy Adapted for Older Children [PCIT-OC], n.d.). In PCIT-OC, parents and their child engage in therapeutic play- or activity-based interactions. During these interactions, parents practice the relationship-building PRIDE skills (praise, reflect, imitate, describe, and enjoy in standard PCIT or emotional expression in PCIT-CU), adapted to be developmentally appropriate for older children:

- **Praise:** Encourage a mix of labeled, unlabeled, and nonverbal praise (e.g., physical affection, actions), emphasizing sincerity.
- **Reflections:** Teach caregivers to summarize or paraphrase their child's statements instead of repeating them verbatim. For children and adolescents with the LPE specifier, these active listening skills can be further adapted to encourage emotion validation skills taught in CDI-CU (e.g., "It sounds like you felt really sad and left out when your friends didn't invite you along").
- **Imitation:** Encourage caregivers to join, show interest or approval for, or be inspired by the child's activities instead of directly copying, mimicking, or "outdoing" their child's behaviors. For children and adolescents with the LPE specifier, CDI-CU "E" skills can be integrated by having caregivers mirror their child's appropriate body language and vocal tone.
- **Descriptions:** Encourage caregivers to describe both the child's and their own behaviors, thoughts and feelings. Similarly, the "E" skill of CDI-CU emphasizes feelings talk.
- **Enjoy:** Beyond expressing genuine enthusiasm during therapeutic parent-child interactions, emotional expression ("E") skills from CDI-CU remain age-appropriate to use with older children and adolescents with limited prosocial emotions. These skills include making appropriate eye contact, using genuinely enthusiastic and positive tone/pitch of voice, using warm body language, and verbally expressing affection (e.g., saying "I love you").

With older children, it is important to use developmentally appropriate toys or activities that facilitate caregivers' practice of PRIDE skills (e.g., arts and crafts, hobbies, advanced construction toys, painting nails), while not promoting violent or rough play (e.g., play weapons, bats, balls), competitive activities (e.g., games where one side must win or lose), games with complex or rigid rules that can create conflict if not followed, or those that prevent caregiver–child interaction (e.g., tablets, books, skateboards). Older children and adolescents can collaborate with caregivers and therapists to identify preferred and suitable activities for these special interactions at home, including more lengthy or complex activities (e.g., complex Lego building kits) that are reserved for therapeutic use only and can be carried over from one day to the next. Home practice is extended to 10 minutes daily (compared with 5 minutes in standard PCIT/PCIT-CU) and can be adjusted upward for adolescents.

As noted earlier, Kazdin's (2005) program is designed to be implemented with caregivers only. From our work in the development of PCIT-CU, we feel that it is important to include the child or adolescent in the intervention. However, for older children and adolescents, it is important that therapists build rapport with them through check-ins to ensure their treatment buy-in as an active member of the treatment team (e.g., asking about home practice, explaining coaching and PRIDE skills, focusing on a child's skill of the day such as "accepting no," using CDI skills with the child or adolescent). Attending and planned ignoring skills (taught in Session 4 of Kazdin's program) can be introduced earlier than in the standard PMT manual, and during this relationship enhancement phase, with therapist-supported coaching to ensure correct application.

Enhancing Behavior Management Strategies

Kazdin's PMT sessions that focus on reinforcement and consistent use of a range of punishment procedures tailored to the child's age (e.g., time-out, loss of privileges, extra chores) are critical for the program effectiveness for all youth with conduct problems, including those with the LPE specifier. However, the key recommendations for enhancing this part of treatment specifically for youth with the LPE specifier is that, when focusing on use of positive reinforcement, it is important to emphasize shaping prosocial behavior using both social reinforcers and tangible reinforcers (i.e., point incentive chart). The use of token economies (i.e., systems for earning points or some form of "token" that can be exchanged for prizes or privileges) should specifically target underdeveloped prosocial and emotional literacy skills.

Emotion Recognition Training

Like most PMT programs, Kazdin's approach does not include emotion recognition training and should be supplemented, similar to what we did with adding the "CARES" module in PCIT-CU. We feel that the components of our CARES approach can be modified to be appropriate for older children and adolescents. However, there are also other options available for use in older samples.

- **Mindreading program (Baron-Cohen et al., 2004):** An intervention designed to teach children and adults emotion recognition, which has proven to enhance the effectiveness of PMT in 6- to 16-year-old youths high on CU traits (Dadds, Cauchi, et al., 2012).

- **Faces intervention (Neumann et al., 2015):** A computerized nine-session emotion recognition intervention proven to reduce conduct problems in 12- to 18-year-old adolescents who had committed criminal acts (Hubble et al., 2015).

In addition to these two options for emotion recognition training that have some data to support their efficacy, there are other promising approaches being developed.

- **Facial Affect Sensitivity Training (FAST; White et al., 2022):** A computerized 11-session emotion recognition training under development for children and adolescents with the LPE specifier.
- **Impact Virtual Reality (VR) program (Thomson et al., 2025):** Four 20-minute intervention modules codesigned with youth to teach emotion recognition and regulation skills to 10- to 17-year-olds, using a gamified interaction that is explicitly designed to combat low rates of treatment engagement in treating youth with the LPE specifier.

CHAPTER SUMMARY

This chapter provides an overview of two examples of promising approaches to extending the reach of PCIT-CU for children with the LPE specifier, iPCIT-CU and school PCIT-CU, and offers recommendations for extending what we learned from the PCIT-CU model to adapt other treatments for older children and adolescents with the LPE specifier. The iPCIT-CU and school PCIT-CU adaptations were developed to increase the availability of and access to specialist psychological services within the community for children with conduct problems and varying levels of CU traits. Integrating psychological interventions into everyday contexts, such as the family home using iPCIT-CU or the child's school using school PCIT-CU, offers potentially sustainable and scalable solutions to the challenges facing traditional psychological interventions for children with serious conduct problems, including those who show the LPE specifier (Chacko et al., 2016). Clinicians are encouraged to consider these alternative treatment delivery formats to enhance treatment access and engagement for families experiencing major barriers to accessing specialist care.

While iPCIT-CU was adapted to enable remote delivery and has shown promise in initial studies, research evaluations of it currently remain limited to controlled research environments. Thus, there is a pressing need for its evaluation under real-world conditions to determine its true effectiveness and applicability to a broader and more diverse population within community settings. Also, to date, school PCIT-CU has been tested in only two school clusters, with a third regional site underway, using an open-trial design in disadvantaged, culturally and linguistically diverse communities within New South Wales, Australia's most populous state. Further rigorous research using randomized controlled designs and larger samples is urgently needed to test these alternative delivery models. This will enable testing of whether the educator enhancements of school PCIT or PCIT-CU are superior to PCIT or PCIT-CU or school treatment as usual for improving cross-setting conduct problems and CU traits. Additionally, through our consultations during the coproduction process our stakeholders identified a need for in-classroom coaching of teachers to implement school PCIT or PCIT-CU strategies, constituting a valuable future research direction that we are currently piloting.

Other future directions for this line of clinical research are to test whether iPCIT-CU and school PCIT-CU can be delivered at scale to improve proximal child and family outcomes, as well as more distal outcomes, such as peer and teacher well-being and alleviation of teacher workforce shortages plaguing many school districts. Research on the school-based adaptation in other jurisdictions is needed to understand whether it represents a viable model for school districts within other communities and countries that diverge in their educational structure and quality, policies, and cultural beliefs and values. Promisingly, standard PCIT has demonstrated acceptability and efficacy across many countries and cultures across the globe. In order to refine these treatment adaptations and optimize outcomes across diverse populations, we need research testing mechanisms of change, such as

- the educator's observed and self-reported use of student–teacher relationship enhancement and behavior management strategies,
- consistency in strategy use between home and school settings, and
- improved student–teacher relationship quality and warmth.

A greater understanding of the mechanisms that drive change is important for clarifying how and why the PCIT-CU treatment model produces meaningful and sustained improvements in children's antisocial and prosocial behaviors.

Finally, we developed PCIT-CU in a way that can guide modifications to other treatments to be more effective in treating children and adolescents with the LPE specifier, particularly those targeting older children outside the 2- to 7-year-old PCIT age range and adolescents. We recognize that these recommendations for enhancing other approaches to treatment have not been directly tested to determine if they make these interventions more effective for youth with the LPE specifier, as we have done for PCIT-CU. Such outcome tests are clearly an important need for future research. However, we feel that, based on our success with PCIT-CU, these recommendations are a useful clinical guide, until such research is conducted.

IV

FUTURE DIRECTIONS FOR RESEARCH AND PRACTICE

11

A Road Map for the Future of Assessing and Treating Children and Adolescents With Limited Prosocial Emotions

As outlined in the previous three chapters, we adapted Parent–Child Interaction Therapy (PCIT), an evidence-based treatment for children with serious conduct problems, to better address the needs of children with elevated callous–unemotional (CU) traits. This adaptation, called Parent–Child Interaction Therapy: Callous–Unemotional version (PCIT-CU), was further modified for use in settings beyond traditional mental health clinics. To improve accessibility for families of children with the limited prosocial emotions (LPE) specifier facing significant barriers to specialized mental health services in their communities, we developed an internet-delivered version (iPCIT-CU) for use in the home and school PCIT-CU for use at school. By involving teachers in treatment alongside caregivers in school PCIT-CU, we saw those improvements in children's conduct problems seen at home better generalized to the classroom setting with teachers. Important future research directions are to evaluate PCIT-CU and its modifications in larger scale randomized controlled trials with diverse populations and under real-world conditions.

We believe that our approach to modifying an established treatment for children with serious conduct problems, based on research on the characteristics of children with the LPE specifier, provides a practical road map for clinicians treating children and adolescents with the LPE specifier beyond the use of PCIT-CU. We feel that these strategies provide a helpful template for enhancing other treatments that have proven efficacious in reducing conduct problems to be even more effective for children and adolescents with

https://doi.org/10.1037/0000500-012
A Clinical Guide to Working With Youth With Conduct Disorders and Limited Prosocial Emotions, by P. J. Frick and E. R. Kimonis

the LPE specifier. However, we want to recognize that such modifications have not been extensively tested and it will be important to evaluate them in randomized controlled trials with diverse populations and under real-world conditions.

This final chapter concludes with a discussion of other areas for further research and future frontiers in the treatment of children and adolescents with the LPE specifier. This section is by no means exhaustive but instead intends to highlight several opportunities for contributing to the evolving understanding of limited prosocial emotions in youth and to develop interventions that can transform their lives and futures.

FUTURE DIRECTIONS

As a field, scholars have made considerable progress in understanding what factors differentiate children with conduct problems who are at greatest risk for initiating these problems earlier in life; persisting and worsening in these problems over time, across settings, and in multiple relationships; and responding less well to existing evidence-based treatments for child conduct problems, namely, in understanding the importance of CU traits. We have developed tools for reliably and validly identifying LPE across the lifespan from preschool age to adulthood, which researchers must continue to refine to optimize assessment as they generate new research findings. There is a growing understanding of those risk factors that lead children with the LPE specifier to develop and maintain serious, chronic problem behaviors that violate others' rights and societal norms. This understanding is continually being advanced with new insights generated from basic science research. Scholars have begun to translate this knowledge into treatments that are more effective at sustaining improvements in outcomes, and have conducted research into extending their reach, but there is a lot more work for this field to do toward alleviating the societal burden of CU traits.

Advancing Understanding of Risk Factors for Callous-Unemotional Traits

First, more basic science research on risk factors for CU traits, particularly those that are potentially modifiable, is needed. For example, much time has been dedicated to understanding the nature of parental warmth and what role it plays in the development of CU traits. Through an iterative theoretically and empirically driven process, we developed an observational coding tool called the Warmth and Affection Coding System (WACS-II) to operationalize and monitor treatment-related changes in parental warmth (Prasad et al., 2023). We conducted research to refine this tool and create a parent self-report version, which led us to reconceptualize warmth as a unitary construct comprising both verbal and nonverbal caregiver behaviors (Koh et al., 2024). In parallel, we analyzed what caregivers seeking treatment at our clinic said about their children with conduct problems within 5-minute speech samples, providing valuable insights into how caregivers think and feel differently about their children with CU traits (Kaouar et al., 2024). This ongoing research program improved our understanding of how parental warmth differs for children with higher CU traits. That is, we now understand that caregivers of children with the LPE specifier report less often

- complimenting their child;
- telling their child they love them;
- hugging, kissing, smiling, and laughing with their child;
- looking at, facing, and sitting close to their child when interacting;
- using emotional language ("feelings talk");
- using facial expressions that communicate care and approval;
- having warm attributions about their child; and
- attributing their child's prosocial behaviors to altruistic intentions.

In short, the lack of warmth between caregivers and their children with the LPE specifier is expressed in several different nuanced caregiver behaviors and verbalizations during caregiver–child interactions and appears to be underpinned by more negative thoughts about the child.

This research program has been instrumental in refining how therapists target parental warmth in PCIT-CU treatment. With this understanding, therapists are better able to coach families on how to increase warmth in their interactions with their child with CU traits. Our findings have clarified the importance of addressing caregivers' problematic cognitions about their child during coaching sessions. Critically, mothers with more negative attributions about their child at pretreatment experienced less improvement with PCIT treatment (Fleming, Sawrikar, et al., 2025). Applying this knowledge, during live coaching in PCIT-CU therapists use higher-order coaching statements that are aimed at reframing the child's behaviors in a more positive light for the caregiver. For example, caregivers with particularly negative and hostile views of their child can be helped to see in the moment how their child's behavior is aimed at seeking connection with the caregiver rather than having a more sinister ulterior motive. Our research with teachers suggests they experience similar negative attributions about their students with CU traits, pointing to the value of targeting these cognitions within school PCIT-CU as well (Fleming, Boulton, et al., 2025). These topics are the focus of our research program that is underway as of this writing. An important future direction for this work is to advance understanding of cultural differences in the expressive displays that drive human perceptions of warmth. This research is important for improving our measurement of the warmth construct and monitoring treatment outcomes (e.g., improvements in parental warmth) using tools whose scores are reliable and valid for culturally and linguistically diverse children and families. Conducting this sort of basic and applied research is also critical to optimizing treatments for children with the LPE specifier by refining existing and identifying new treatment targets.

Identifying Predictors and Moderators of Treatment Outcomes and Adherence

A second critical future clinical research direction is to better understand for whom treatments work better or worse. This involves examining predictors and moderators of PCIT-CU treatment response and adherence. We have only conducted one published study on this question to date, which tested whether child anxiety moderated PCIT-CU outcomes (Fleming et al., 2023). We chose to focus on anxiety because a substantial and growing literature finds that individuals with the LPE specifier who show comorbid anxiety present with a particularly severe and complex clinical and behavioral profile involving greater symptoms of posttraumatic stress disorder (PTSD), attention-deficit/hyperactivity disorder (ADHD), substance-related disorders, borderline personality disorder (BPD), more severe and impulsive aggression, and greater risk for suicide and self-harm than children with conduct problems alone or children with conduct problems and the LPE specifier who do not have comorbid anxiety (for a review, see Craig et al., 2021; Kimonis, 2023). These children and adolescents with co-occurring conduct problems, CU traits, and anxiety are described as having "secondary CU traits."

Secondary CU traits are thought to develop via a distinct developmental pathway from primary CU traits (presenting in the absence of anxiety and the predominant focus of this book) and from conduct problems without CU traits. Specifically, the Emotionally Sensitive Child–Adverse Parenting Experiences–Allostatic Overload (ESCAPE-ALL; Kimonis, 2023) model for the development of secondary CU traits posits that from infancy these children show temperaments characterized by heightened emotional sensitivity (e.g., difficult to soothe and settle in infancy, angry or irritable from toddlerhood, negative affectivity and general heightened physiological reactivity across development) that make them more challenging to parent and to form healthy and secure attachments with, especially for their vulnerable caregivers with mental health problems like depression, anxiety, and a history of trauma. From early in the child's life, these caregivers and children are mismatched, as evidenced in their poorly synced behavior, affect, and communication (i.e., aspects of mutually responsive orientation), and this mismatch contributes to insecure caregiver–child attachment. Additionally, their home environments are marred by chaos, dysfunction, and conflict, and this and the caregiver relationship are sources of chronic stress for the child. These chronic stressful experiences of the child are inadequately buffered by the caregiver because of the insecure, often disorganized, caregiver–child attachment. Over time, this chronic stress produces persistently elevated levels of stress hormones, damaging the child's developing stress response system through an allostatic overload process (i.e., stress overwhelms the body's coping ability—imagine repeatedly stretching a rubber band, whereby it bounces back initially but, over time, gets weaker and snaps). The consequence of this developmental process is a complex clinical presentation in the child involving callousness and overmodulation of emotion, alongside negative affectivity and impulsive aggression.

Our treatment research with 45 families with a 3- to 7-year-old child with conduct problems and the LPE specifier found that those children classified with secondary CU traits deteriorated in their defiant and dysregulated behaviors after PCIT-CU treatment ended, relative to children with primary CU traits who maintained their treatment gains (Fleming et al., 2023). Similarly, in their sample of clinic-referred adolescents with conduct problems treated with either functional family therapy (FFT) or an active control treatment, Thøgersen et al. (2022) found that those with high-anxious secondary CU traits showed significantly less improvement in rule-breaking behaviors at an 18-month follow-up than those with primary CU traits or conduct problems alone. Together, these important findings highlight the critical need for further basic science and clinical research to identify those risk factors that are unique to the development of secondary CU traits, and which can be targeted within personalized treatments.

We have begun to uncover differences in the parenting experiences of children with secondary relative to primary CU traits. Consistent with the ESCAPE-ALL model, our research has clarified that the parenting experiences of clinic-referred children with secondary CU traits are more dysfunctional than those of children with primary CU traits. For example, in a series of studies with our clinical samples of 3- to 7-year-old children with conduct problems, we found that children classified with secondary CU traits had mothers who reported a more negative relationship with their child that was characterized by feelings of anger or hostility, active avoidance of the child, and/or a desire to harm their child relative to mothers of children with primary CU traits (Kaouar et al., 2024). Other research (Milner, 2003) found that these types of parental cognitions contribute to increased child maltreatment. Caregivers of children with secondary CU traits also reported experiencing the greatest levels of parenting stress, particularly around the child's level of difficulty (e.g., frequent crying, moody and easily upset, overly reactive) and the dysfunctional nature of the caregiver–child relationship (e.g., lack of close and warm feelings, limited positive affect between the dyad; Kaouar et al., 2024). Observations of caregiver–child dyads also revealed that dyads of children with secondary CU traits did not visibly enjoy one another's company, expressed little positive affect together, and back-and-forth communication between them was minimal or poorly synchronized, relative to nonanxious children with the LPE specifier (primary CU) and children with conduct problems alone (Kaouar et al., 2025). As we explain previously, this new knowledge provides insights into how we can refine treatments for children with secondary CU traits, such as by addressing negative parental cognitions that get in the way of relationship building, and also teaching other emotion regulation skills and strategies to caregivers to encourage calmer responses to bothersome child behaviors (e.g., excessive child negative affectivity). The more limited verbal and nonverbal inputs these children receive and send are likely to negatively impact their socio-emotional development and attachments. Similarly, our findings supporting emotional sensitivity in children and adolescents with secondary CU traits, as opposed to emotional underreactivity that is seen in primary CU traits, highlight that CARES treatment components may need modification for children with secondary CU traits to place less emphasis on increasing their attention to distressed facial microexpressions and greater emphasis on teaching them emotion regulation strategies (Kimonis, 2023). Importantly, to date, there are no targeted treatments developed specifically for children with secondary CU traits, although they are in dire need of intervention since they have the greatest societal impact and burden.

Relating to the CARES phase of PCIT-CU, another important research direction is to better understand how the emotional processing patterns of children with the LPE specifier differ from typically developing children. This knowledge is needed to refine how intervention modules like CARES teach children with the LPE specifier to improve their recognition of others' emotions, such as by attending to salient facial or situational cues. Most understanding about facial emotional processing in people with CU traits originates from research using static eye-tracking paradigms to examine eye gaze patterns while people view static photographic images of actors expressing various emotions. For example, using a community sample of 5- to 10-year-old children, Demetriou and Fanti (2022) compared 31 children selected for high CU traits to 28 children selected for low CU traits on their eye gaze patterns while viewing photographs of adult and child actors expressing different emotions. They found that children with the LPE specifier fixated less on the eye region and more to the mouth region across all emotions (fear, sadness, anger, happiness), replicating prior findings from Dadds et al. (2007) using an older sample of 100 8- to 15-year-old private school boys. Those boys high on CU traits who automatically first fixated on the eyes of emotional faces and fixated for longer were significantly more accurate at recognizing fearful facial expressions (Dadds et al., 2007). Others have found that atypical gaze patterns in children with the LPE specifier are specific to fearful (Leno et al., 2021), surprised (Martin-Key et al., 2018), or sad (Billeci et al., 2019) facial expression stimuli. While these research findings have been useful for understanding how the eye gaze patterns of children and adolescents with the LPE specifier differ from typically developing youth—by focusing on facial cues that are perhaps less helpful than others for deciphering emotion, it is unknown whether this pattern extends to real-world interactions that play a key role in shaping children's emotional, social, and moral development. Our ongoing research extends on this prior work by using wearable eye-tracking technology (i.e., child-worn glasses) during caregiver–child interactions involving manipulations of a caregiver's emotional expression, to advance understanding of whether and how children with the LPE specifier differ from healthy children and children with conduct problems alone in their eye gaze patterns to more complex real-life caregiver emotions. A key goal of this emerging research program is to uncover insights that could refine interventions focused on addressing the emotional processing deficits seen in children with CU traits.

Disseminating Treatments Tailored for Children and Adolescents With the Limited Prosocial Emotions Specifier

The next frontier for research on PCIT-CU and its adaptations, and other tailored treatments, is their dissemination. Tailored treatments like PCIT-CU will have only limited impact if they are not effectively and broadly disseminated. The effective dissemination of treatment adaptations for children and adolescents with the LPE specifier should be guided by empirically supported dissemination models for other evidence-based manualized child and family mental health treatments (Fixsen et al., 2005; Southam-Gerow et al., 2008), as well as successful models for disseminating and scaling standard PCIT (Beveridge et al., 2015; Herschell et al., 2018). Fortunately, the nesting of PCIT-CU within an established PMT treatment, PCIT, which is relatively well established in the United States and several other countries around the world, facilitates its dissemination through targeting existing PCIT practitioner communities. This is a strategic starting point since training in standard PCIT is a prerequisite for delivering PCIT-CU. Comprehensive training manuals, videos, and digital resources for delivering PCIT-CU and CARES, as well as professional learning workshops, have been developed and iteratively refined with feedback from clinician end users. The protocols include fidelity checklists and trainings that discuss the importance of adhering to the PCIT-CU model, to support clinicians in delivering treatment with integrity.

We are also beginning to expand the workforce of PCIT-CU trainers, toward ensuring the model's scalability. Important next steps are to build more partnerships with key organizations, health- and education-focused governmental agencies, and independent educational systems to promote PCIT-CU and identify potential sites to implement it, as we have done with our pilot trials of iPCIT in an Australian community mental health setting (Fleming et al., 2021) and school PCIT or PCIT-CU in a governmental primary school setting (Fleming, Kershaw, et al., in press). At the time of writing, we received Australian federal funding in partnership with three school networks to extend school PCIT and PCIT-CU to a regional community in which we will administer a cluster randomized controlled trial together with our metropolitan sites to determine whether school PCIT or PCIT-CU is more effective and cost-effective than standard school services for disruptive behavior in diverse students. These data will be important for selling policymakers and stakeholders on the value of investing in scaling this early intervention, which is essential to its widespread adoption. We have also learned that it is imperative to have stakeholder champions to help promote and support uptake. Furthermore, we continually use the data we gather from our clinical trials to refine our treatments, training materials, and dissemination strategies.

A major barrier to scaling tailored treatments like PCIT-CU and its adaptations is the limited trained workforce and high workforce attrition rates. In vivo coaching is a cornerstone of PCIT that partly underpins its superior efficacy relative to other parent management training (PMT) programs (Kaminski et al., 2008), but most trained therapists have not had prior experience with in vivo coaching and learning how to do it effectively with diverse clientele requires extensive training, experience, and clinical mentorship. As of this writing, the PCIT certification process (a prerequisite for delivering PCIT-CU) requires that training clinicians complete at least 1 full year of ongoing clinical supervision with at least two cases to completion (i.e., achieving PCIT graduation criteria), after completing 40 hours of face-to-face training with a PCIT-certified trainer, as a key prerequisite for certification to be granted by the accrediting body, PCIT International (n.d.). The benefits of such a comprehensive training process are that new PCIT trainees show high levels of fidelity to the program (Travis & Brestan-Knight, 2013) and their initial clients show significant pre- to posttreatment improvements in conduct problems and parenting behaviors (Pearl et al., 2012). However, one study of 143 PCIT trainees also found that three quarters of new trainees did not complete all training requirements necessary for PCIT certification, pointing to the need for further research into reducing barriers for training clinicians (Beveridge et al., 2015). Contemporary research into PCIT training models has focused on identifying the most efficient and effective ways of training clinicians to deliver and train others to deliver PCIT, toward improving its scalability and sustainability (Niec, 2018; Niec et al., 2023)—an area ripe for research on PCIT-CU and its delivery adaptations. For example, Todd and Niec (2025) compared 108 clinicians randomly allocated to one of three PCIT training formats: online synchronous (4-hour live training with 7–12 trainees), online asynchronous (2–3-hour self-guided video modules with embedded quizzes and automated feedback), and written materials only (2-hour self-guided). They found that of the 69 participants who completed all study elements, those in synchronous or asynchronous online trainings showed significantly greater CDI skills, DPICS coding accuracy, and satisfaction with training than trainees who only received written materials, although the synchronous training group was more likely to complete training (77%) than the asynchronous (45%) and written materials (48%) groups. These findings highlight the need for further research investigating factors influencing trainee retention, and research into the utility of blended models incorporating both asynchronous and synchronous training components. The findings support the promise of addressing shortages in PCIT-trained clinicians via online training methods that increase clinician access to PCIT training at a reduced delivery cost.

This workforce problem is not unique to PCIT, as it plagues the delivery of all mental health services, particularly those targeted at youth populations. There is some evidence that the limited workforce for treating antisocial clients, including children, may stem in part from gaps in graduate education and training. That is, Hyatt and colleagues (2025) explored the clinical experiences, training exposure, and self-efficacy of graduate students enrolled in clinical psychology programs across the United States in working with patients exhibiting antagonism (i.e., conduct disorders, CU traits, antisocial personality, psychopathy), compared with working with clients with internalizing problems (i.e., anxiety, depression). Their survey of about 20% of U.S.-based trainees revealed a significant discrepancy in training in working with these different client populations; specifically, students received considerably less coursework, less practical experience, and less supervision in treating both child and adult patients with antagonism-related problems. As a result, these students felt less competent in treating antagonistic individuals, required more supervision, and perceived their interventions as being less effective. These findings prompted calls to urgently enhance the training and resources available to clinical psychology trainees and practitioners working with clients exhibiting the LPE specifier and to allocate more funding to their treatment, given their significant global burden (Kimonis & Gooi, 2025). It has been suggested that the underfunding of conduct and other antisocial disorders may be partly because of the lack of recognition of these conditions as legitimate mental health disorders (Burt et al., 2018; Hawes et al., 2023). This is especially problematic given that conduct disorders are a leading cause of disability among children aged 0 to 14 years, as shown in the Global Burden of Disease Study (GBD 2019 Mental Disorders Collaborators, 2022). To reduce this societal burden, funding should be directed toward graduate and professional clinician training, prevention and intervention, as well as continued translational psychological and neuroscience research to inform the development of effective targeted treatments that address the root causes of CU traits.

CONCLUSION

Children with conduct problems and the LPE specifier engage in behaviors that are extremely challenging and often seriously harmful to those around them. They typically begin showing oppositional, antagonistic, aggressive, and destructive behaviors very early in life and persist in them as they age. Without effective management, these behaviors worsen over time, cause conflict with important people in their lives, and damage foundational relationships in ways that can detrimentally affect the child's ability to form meaningful bonds and caring relationships over their lifetime. These social impairments often extend to other important life domains, impacting on educational attainment, occupational success, financial stability, quality of life, and mental and physical health and well-being. Over their lifetimes, individuals with the LPE specifier place tremendous strain on societal educational, health, and justice resources, producing significant economic burden. However, providing children with the LPE specifier with timely and effective intervention has demonstrated potential to transform their lives, as we observed in our trials and illustrated in our case example of Leo.

Critically, clinicians can play a key role in shaping the futures of children with serious conduct problems. Our hope is that this book empowers practitioners globally to maximize the benefits of their work with these children and families by considering the presence of the LPE specifier for all children who present with conduct problems, using evidence-based assessment methods and tools to screen, assess, and diagnose LPE, and administering evidence-based treatment that is tailored to their unique needs. We provide a road map for how to achieve this, based on our decades of research and clinical work, which we hope inspires more researchers and clinicians to contribute to this critically important, incredibly challenging, yet immensely rewarding, line of work.

APPENDIX

QR Codes for Accessing Various Assessment Tools, Treatment Manuals, and Other Resources

QR Code to Access Various Versions of the Inventory for Callous-Unemotional Traits (ICU) and Supporting Material

Note. From *Inventory of Callous-Unemotional Traits*, by P. J. Frick, 2004, LSU, Developmental Psychopathology Lab (https://faculty.lsu.edu/pfricklab/cape.php). Copyright 2004 by Paul J. Frick.

QR Code to Access the Clinical Assessment of Prosocial Emotions (CAPE) and Supporting Material

Note. Adapted from *Clinical Assessment of Prosocial Emotions: Version 1.1* (CAPE Version 1.1), by P. J. Frick, 2013, LSU, Developmental Psychopathology Lab (https://faculty.lsu.edu/pfricklab/cape.php). Copyright 2013 by Paul J. Frick.

QR Code to Access the *Parent–Child Interaction Therapy: Callous–Unemotional Version Treatment Manual* (PCIT-CU, Version 2.2)

Note. From *Parent–Child Interaction Therapy: Callous–Unemotional Version Treatment Manual* (PCIT-CU, Version 2.2), by E. R. Kimonis, 2024, Lulu Press (https://www.lulu.com/shop/eva-kimonis/parent-child-interaction-therapy-callous-unemotional-version-treatment-manual-pcit-cu-version-22/paperback/product-2mjrj9n.html?q=Parent-Child+Interaction+Therapy+Callous-Unemotional+Version+Treatment+Manual). Copyright 2024 by Eva R. Kimonis.

QR Code to Access the *Coaching and Rewarding Emotional Skills Treatment Manual* (CARES Module; Version 5.1)

Note. From *Coaching and Rewarding Emotional Skills (CARES) Treatment Manual* (CARES Module; Version 5.1), by E. R. Kimonis, 2024, Lulu Press (https://www.lulu.com/shop/eva-kimonis/coaching-and-rewarding-emotional-skills-cares-treatment-manual-cares-module-version-51/paperback/product-7kqjpym.html?q=Parent-Child+Interaction+Therapy+Callous-Unemotional+Version+Treatment+Manual). Copyright 2024 by Eva R. Kimonis.

QR Code to Access a Request Form for Various Digital Treatment Resources, Including Training Videos

Note. Webform to request access to Parent–Child Interaction Therapy: Callous–Unemotional version (PCIT-CU) digital resources, Qualtrics Survey (https://unswpsy.au1.qualtrics.com/jfe/form/SV_enXzhWPEkz80NPU).

REFERENCES

Abidin, R. R. (1995). *Parenting stress index: Professional manual* (3rd ed.). Psychological Assessment Resources.

Achenbach, T. M., & Rescorla, L. A. (2001). *Manual for the ASEBA school-age forms and profiles*. University of Vermont, Research Center for Children, Youth, & Families.

Adolphs, R., Gosselin, F., Buchanan, T. W., Tranel, D., Schyns, P., & Damasio, A. R. (2005). A mechanism for impaired fear recognition after amygdala damage. *Nature, 433*(7021), 68–72. https://doi.org/10.1038/nature03086

Agazzi, H., Childres, J., & Armstrong, K. (2017). *Helping our toddlers, developing our children's skills: Trainer's manual* (3rd ed.). University of South Florida.

Agazzi, H., Knap, K., & Kimonis, E. R. (2020). Parent–child interaction therapy-callous unemotional adaptation for a preschool boy with conduct problems. *Clinical Case Studies, 19*(5), 370–385. https://doi.org/10.1177/1534650120950524

Alexander, J. F., Waldron, H. B., Robbins, M. S., & Neeb, A. A. (2013). *Functional family therapy for adolescent behavior problems*. American Psychological Association. https://doi.org/10.1037/14139-000

American Psychiatric Association. (1980). *Diagnostic and statistical manual of mental disorders* (3rd ed.).

American Psychiatric Association. (1987). *Diagnostic and statistical manual of mental disorders* (3rd ed., rev.).

American Psychiatric Association. (1994). *Diagnostic and statistical manual of mental disorders* (4th ed.).

American Psychiatric Association. (2013). *Diagnostic and statistical manual of mental disorders* (5th ed.). https://doi.org/10.1176/appi.books.9780890425596

American Psychiatric Association. (2022). *Diagnostic and statistical manual of mental disorders* (5th ed., text rev.). https://doi.org/10.1176/appi.books.9780890425787

Armstrong, K., Lilly, C., & Curtiss, H. (2006). *Helping our toddlers, developing our children's skills*. University of South Florida, Department of Pediatrics, Division of Child Development.

Atkins, M. S., Cappella, E., Shernoff, E. S., Mehta, T. G., & Gustafson, E. L. (2017). Schooling and children's mental health: Realigning resources to reduce disparities and advance public health. *Annual Review of Clinical Psychology, 13*(1), 123–147. https://doi.org/10.1146/annurev-clinpsy-032816-045234

Augimeri, L. K., Farrington, D. P., Koegl, C. J., & Day, D. M. (2007). The SNAP™ Under 12 Outreach Project: Effects of a community based program for children with conduct problems. *Journal of Child and Family Studies, 16*(6), 799–807. https://doi.org/10.1007/s10826-006-9126-x

Autism Centre of Excellence at Cambridge. (n.d.). *Mindreading all level bundle.* https://resources.autismcentreofexcellence.org/p/mindreading-all-level-bundle

Bagner, D. M., & Eyberg, S. M. (2007). Parent–child interaction therapy for disruptive behavior in children with mental retardation: A randomized controlled trial. *Journal of Clinical Child and Adolescent Psychology, 36*(3), 418–429. https://doi.org/10.1080/15374410701448448

Bagner, D. M., Sheinkopf, S. J., Vohr, B. R., & Lester, B. M. (2010). Parenting intervention for externalizing behavior problems in children born premature: An initial examination. *Journal of Developmental & Behavioral Pediatrics, 31*(3), 209–216. https://doi.org/10.1097/dbp.0b013e3181d5a294

Bansal, P. S., Haas, S. M., Willoughby, M. T., Coles, E. K., Pelham, W. E., Jr., & Waschbusch, D. A. (2020). A pilot study of emotional response to time-out in children with conduct problems and callous-unemotional traits. *Psychological Reports, 123*(5), 2017–2037. https://doi.org/10.1177/0033294119884014

Bansal, P. S., Waschbusch, D. A., Haas, S. M., Babinski, D. E., King, S., Andrade, B. F., & Willoughby, M. T. (2019). Effects of intensive behavioral treatment for children with varying levels of conduct problems and callous-unemotional traits. *Behavior Therapy, 50*(1), 1–14. https://doi.org/10.1016/j.beth.2018.03.003

Barker, J. M., & Hawes, D. J. (2024). Practitioner review: A core competencies perspective on the evidence-based treatment of child conduct problems. *Journal of Child Psychology and Psychiatry, 65*(2), 124–136. https://doi.org/10.1111/jcpp.13882

Barkley, R. A. (2013). *Defiant children: A clinician's manual for assessment and parent training* (3rd ed.). Guilford Press. https://doi.org/10.1111/camh.12073_4

Baron-Cohen, S., Golan, O., Wheelwright, S., & Hill, J. J. (2004). *Mindreading: The interactive guide to emotions.* Jessica Kingsley Limited.

Barry, C. T., Frick, P. J., DeShazo, T. M., McCoy, M., Ellis, M., & Loney, B. R. (2000). The importance of callous-unemotional traits for extending the concept of psychopathy to children. *Journal of Abnormal Psychology, 109*(2), 335–340. https://doi.org/10.1037/0021-843X.109.2.335

Baumel, A., Mathur, N., Pawar, A., & Muench, F. (2021). Psychosocial interventions for children with externalized behavior problems: An updated meta-analysis of moderator effects. *Journal of Child and Family Studies, 30*(1), 65–86. https://doi.org/10.1007/s10826-020-01863-6

Baumel, A., Pawar, A., Mathur, N., Kane, J. M., & Correll, C. U. (2017). Technology-assisted parent training programs for children and adolescents with disruptive behaviors: A systematic review. *The Journal of Clinical Psychiatry, 78*(8), e957–e969. https://doi.org/10.4088/JCP.16r11063

Beauchaine, T. P., Webster-Stratton, C., & Reid, M. J. (2005). Mediators, moderators, and predictors of 1-year outcomes among children treated for early-onset conduct problems: A latent growth curve analysis. *Journal of Consulting and Clinical Psychology, 73*(3), 371–388. https://doi.org/10.1037/0022-006X.73.3.371

Bedford, R., Pickles, A., Sharp, H., Wright, N., & Hill, J. (2015). Reduced face preference in infancy: A developmental precursor to callous-unemotional traits? *Biological Psychiatry, 78*(2), 144–150. https://doi.org/10.1016/j.biopsych.2014.09.022

Beelmann, A., Arnold, L. S., & Hercher, J. (2023). Parent training programs for preventing and treating antisocial behavior in children and adolescents: A comprehensive meta-analysis of international studies. *Aggression and Violent Behavior, 68,* 101798. https://doi.org/10.1016/j.avb.2022.101798

Berkovits, M. D., O'Brien, K. A., Carter, C. G., & Eyberg, S. M. (2010). Early identification and intervention for behavior problems in primary care: A comparison of two abbreviated versions of parent–child interaction therapy. *Behavior Therapy, 41*(3), 375–387. https://doi.org/10.1016/j.beth.2009.11.002

Berryessa, C. M., & Wohlstetter, B. (2019). The psychopathic "label" and effects on punishment outcomes: A meta-analysis. *Law and Human Behavior, 43*(1), 9–25. https://doi.org/10.1037/lhb0000317

Beveridge, R. M., Fowles, T. R., Masse, J. J., McGoron, L., Smith, M. A., Parrish, B. P., Circo, G., & Widdoes, N. (2015). State-wide dissemination and implementation of parent–child interaction therapy (PCIT): Application of theory. *Children and Youth Services Review, 48,* 38–48. https://doi.org/10.1016/j.childyouth.2014.11.013

Billeci, L., Muratori, P., Calderoni, S., Chericoni, N., Levantini, V., Milone, A., Nocentini, A., Papini, M., Ruglioni, L., & Dadds, M. (2019). Emotional processing deficits in Italian children with disruptive behavior disorder: The role of callous unemotional traits. *Behaviour Research and Therapy, 113,* 32–38. https://doi.org/10.1016/j.brat.2018.12.011

Bjørnebekk, G., & Kjøbli, J. (2017). Observed callousness as a predictor of treatment outcomes in parent management training. *Clinical Child Psychology and Psychiatry, 22*(1), 59–73. https://doi.org/10.1177/1359104515621961

Bjørseth, Å., & Wichstrøm, L. (2016). Effectiveness of parent–child interaction therapy (PCIT) in the treatment of young children's behavior problems. A randomized controlled study. *PLOS One, 11*(9), e0159845. https://doi.org/10.1371/journal.pone.0159845

Blader, J. C., Pliszka, S. R., Kafantaris, V., Foley, C. A., Crowell, J. A., Carlson, G. A., Sauder, C. L., Margulies, D. M., Sinha, C., Sverd, J., Matthews, T. L., Bailey, B. Y., & Daviss, W. B. (2013). Callous-unemotional traits, proactive aggression, and treatment outcomes of aggressive children with attention-deficit/hyperactivity disorder. *Journal of the American Academy of Child & Adolescent Psychiatry, 52*(12), 1281–1293. https://doi.org/10.1016/j.jaac.2013.08.024

Blair, R. J. R. (2003). Facial expressions, their communicatory functions and neuro–cognitive substrates. *Philosophical Transactions of the Royal Society of London. Series B: Biological Sciences, 358*(1431), 561–572. https://doi.org/10.1098/rstb.2002.1220

Blizzard, A. M., Barroso, N. E., Ramos, F. G., Graziano, P. A., & Bagner, D. M. (2018). Behavioral parent training in infancy: What about the parent–infant relationship? *Journal of Clinical Child & Adolescent Psychology, 47*(Suppl. 1), S341–S353. https://doi.org/10.1080/15374416.2017.1310045

Boccaccini, M. T., Murrie, D. C., Clark, J. W., & Cornell, D. G. (2008). Describing, diagnosing, and naming psychopathy: How do youth psychopathy labels influence jurors? *Behavioral Sciences and the Law, 26*(4), 487–510. https://doi.org/10.1002/bsl.821

Boulton, A. L., Fleming, G. E., Prasad, A. H., Kershaw, K. A., & Kimonis, E. R. (in press). Testing the acceptability, feasibility, and preliminary efficacy of an internet-delivered positive classroom management training (iPCMT) for elementary school educators. *Research in Child and Adolescent Psychopathology.*

Brown, S. M., Doom, J. R., Lechuga-Peña, S., Watamura, S. E., & Koppels, T. (2020). Stress and parenting during the global COVID-19 pandemic. *Child Abuse & Neglect, 110*(Pt. 2), 104699. https://doi.org/10.1016/j.chiabu.2020.104699

Budd, K. S. (2018). Teacher-child interaction training. In L. N. Niec (Ed.), *Handbook of parent–child interaction therapy: Innovations and applications for research and practice* (pp. 215–231). Springer. https://doi.org/10.1007/978-3-319-97698-3

Burt, S. A., Hyde, L. W., Frick, P. J., Jaffee, S. R., Shaw, D. S., & Tremblay, R. (2018). Commentary: Childhood conduct problems are a public health crisis and requires resources: A commentary on Rivenbark et al. (2018). *Journal of Child Psychology and Psychiatry, 59*(6), 711–713. https://doi.org/10.1111/jcpp.12930

Byrd, A. L., Loeber, R., & Pardini, D. A. (2014). Antisocial behavior, psychopathic features, and abnormalities in reward and punishment processing in youth. *Clinical Child and Family Psychology Review, 17*(2), 125–156. https://doi.org/10.1007/s10567-013-0159-6

Caldwell, M., Skeem, J., Salekin, R., & Van Rybroek, G. (2006). Treatment response of adolescent offenders with psychopathy features: A 2-year follow-up. *Criminal Justice and Behavior, 33*(5), 571–596. https://doi.org/10.1177/0093854806288176

Caldwell, M. F., & Van Rybroek, G. J. (2001). Efficacy of a decompression treatment model in the clinical management of violent juvenile offenders. *International Journal of Offender Therapy and Comparative Criminology, 45*(4), 469–477. https://doi.org/10.1177/0306624X01454006

Canino, G., Polanczyk, G., Bauermeister, J. J., Rohde, L. A., & Frick, P. J. (2010). Does the prevalence of CD and ODD vary across cultures? *Journal of Social Psychiatry and Psychiatric Epidemiology, 45*(7), 695–704. https://doi.org/10.1007/s00127-010-0242-y

Cardinale, E. M., & Marsh, A. A. (2020). The reliability and validity of the Inventory of Callous Unemotional Traits: A meta-analytic review. *Assessment, 27*(1), 57–71. https://doi.org/10.1177/1073191117747392

Carlson, J. M., & Reinke, K. S. (2014). Attending to the fear in your eyes: Facilitated orienting and delayed disengagement. *Cognition and Emotion, 28*(8), 1398–1406. https://doi.org/10.1080/02699931.2014.885410

Cauffman, E., Beardslee, J., Fine, A., Frick, P. J., & Steinberg, L. (2021). Crossroads in juvenile justice: The impact of initial processing decision on youth 5 years after first arrest. *Development and Psychopathology, 33*(2), 700–713. https://doi.org/10.1017/S095457942000200X

Center on the Social and Emotional Foundations for Early Learning. (n.d.). *Resources: PreSchool training modules.* https://csefel.vanderbilt.edu/resources/training_preschool.html

Chacko, A., Jensen, S. A., Lowry, L. S., Cornwell, M., Chimklis, A., Chan, E., Lee, D., & Pulgarin, B. (2016). Engagement in behavioral parent training: Review of the literature and implications for practice. *Clinical Child and Family Psychology Review, 19*(3), 204–215. https://doi.org/10.1007/s10567-016-0205-2

Chan, A. B., Fleming, G. E., Kaouar, S., & Kimonis, E. R. (2023). The measure of empathy in early childhood: Testing the reliability, validity, and clinical utility of scores in early childhood. *Psychological Assessment, 35*(9), 791–803. https://doi.org/10.1037/pas0001257

Christian, R. E., Frick, P. J., Hill, N. L., Tyler, L., & Frazer, D. R. (1997). Psychopathy and conduct problems in children: II. Implications for subtyping children with conduct problems. *Journal of the American Academy of Child and Adolescent Psychiatry, 36*(2), 233–241. https://doi.org/10.1097/00004583-199702000-00014

Chronis-Tuscano, A., Lewis-Morrarty, E., Woods, K. E., O'Brien, K. A., Mazursky-Horowitz, H., & Thomas, S. R. (2016). Parent–child interaction therapy with emotion coaching for preschoolers with attention-deficit/hyperactivity disorder. *Cognitive and Behavioral Practice, 23*(1), 62–78. https://doi.org/10.1016/j.cbpra.2014.11.001

Ciucci, E., Baroncelli, A., Facci, C., Righi, S., & Frick, P. J. (2024). Callous-unemotional traits and emotion perception accuracy and bias in youths. *Children, 11*(4), 419. https://doi.org/10.3390/children11040419

Cleckley, H. (1976). *The mask of sanity*. Mosby. (Original work published 1941)

Colins, O. F., Andershed, H., Frogner, L., Lopez-Romero, L., Veen, V., & Andershed, A. K. (2014). A new measure to assess psychopathic personality in children: The Child Problematic Traits Inventory. *Journal of Psychopathology and Behavioral Assessment, 36*(1), 4–21. https://doi.org/10.1007/s10862-013-9385-y

Colins, O. F., Van Damme, L., Hendriks, A. M., & Georgiou, G. (2020). The *DSM-5* with limited prosocial emotions specifier for conduct disorder: A systematic literature review. *Journal of Psychopathology and Behavioral Assessment, 42*(2), 248–258. https://doi.org/10.1007/s10862-020-09799-3

Comer, J. S., Chow, C., Chan, P. T., Cooper-Vince, C., & Wilson, L. A. (2013). Psychosocial treatment efficacy for disruptive behavior problems in very young children: A meta-analytic examination. *Journal of the American Academy of Child & Adolescent Psychiatry, 52*(1), 26–36. https://doi.org/10.1016/j.jaac.2012.10.001

Comer, J. S., del Busto, C., Dick, A. S., Furr, J. M., & Puliafico, A. C. (2018). Adapting PCIT to treat anxiety in young children: The PCIT CALM program. In L. N. Niec (Ed.), *Handbook of parent–child interaction therapy: Innovations and applications for research and practice* (pp. 129–147). Springer. https://doi.org/10.1007/978-3-319-97698-3

Comer, J. S., Furr, J. M., Cooper-Vince, C., Madigan, R. J., Chow, C., Chan, P. T., Idrobo, F., Chase, R. M., McNeil, C. B., & Eyberg, S. M. (2015). Rationale and considerations for the internet-based delivery of parent–child interaction therapy. *Cognitive and Behavioral Practice, 22*(3), 302–316. https://doi.org/10.1016/j.cbpra.2014.07.003

Comer, J. S., Furr, J. M., Miguel, E. M., Cooper-Vince, C. E., Carpenter, A. L., Elkins, R. M., Kerns, C. E., Cornacchio, D., Chou, T., Coxe, S., DeSerisy, M., Sanchez, A. L., Golik, A., Martin, J., Myers, K. M., & Chase, R. (2017). Remotely delivering real-time parent training to the home: An initial randomized trial of internet-delivered parent–child interaction therapy (I-PCIT). *Journal of Consulting and Clinical Psychology, 85*(9), 909–917. https://doi.org/10.1037/ccp0000230

Conners, C. K., Epstein, J. N., March, J. S., Angold, A., Wells, K. C., Klaric, J., Swanson, J. M., Arnold, L. E., Abikoff, H. B., Elliott, G. R., Greenhill, L. L., Hechtman, L., Hinshaw, S. P., Hoza, B., Jensen, P. S., Kraemer, H. C., Newcorn, J. H., Pelham, W. E., Severe, J. B., & Wigal, T. (2001). Multimodal treatment of ADHD in the MTA: An alternative outcome analysis. *Journal of the American Academy of Child & Adolescent Psychiatry, 40*(2), 159–167. https://doi.org/10.1097/00004583-200102000-00010

Corralejo, S. M., & Domenech Rodríguez, M. M. (2018). Technology in parenting programs: A systematic review of existing interventions. *Journal of Child and Family Studies, 27*(9), 2717–2731. https://doi.org/10.1007/s10826-018-1117-1

Cotter, A., Todd, M., & Brestan-Knight, E. (2018). Parent–child interaction therapy for children with selective mutism (PCIT-SM). In L. N. Niec (Ed.), *Handbook of parent–child interaction therapy: Innovations and applications for research and practice* (pp. 113–128). Springer. https://doi.org/10.1007/978-3-319-97698-3

Craig, S. G., Goulter, N., & Moretti, M. M. (2021). A systematic review of primary and secondary callous-unemotional traits and psychopathy variants in youth. *Clinical Child and Family Psychology Review, 24*(1), 65–91. https://doi.org/10.1007/s10567-020-00329-x

Crapanzano, A. M., Frick, P. J., Childs, K., & Terranova, A. M. (2011). Gender differences in the assessment, stability, and correlates to bullying roles in middle school children. *Behavioral Sciences & the Law, 29*(5), 677–694. https://doi.org/10.1002/bsl.1000

Curtis, N. M., Ronan, K. R., & Borduin, C. M. (2004). Multisystemic treatment: A meta-analysis of outcome studies. *Journal of Family Psychology, 18*(3), 411–419. https://doi.org/10.1037/0893-3200.18.3.411

Dadds, M., & Hawes, D. (2006). *Integrated family intervention for child conduct problems: A behaviour-attachment-systems intervention for parents.* Australian Academic Press.

Dadds, M. R., Allen, J. L., McGregor, K., Woolgar, M., Viding, E., & Scott, S. (2014). Callous-unemotional traits in children and mechanisms of impaired eye contact during expressions of love: A treatment target? *Journal of Child Psychology and Psychiatry, 55*(7), 771–780. https://doi.org/10.1111/jcpp.12155

Dadds, M. R., Allen, J. L., Oliver, B. R., Faulkner, N., Legge, K., Moul, C., Woolgar, M., & Scott, S. (2012). Love, eye contact and the developmental origins of empathy v. psychopathy. *The British Journal of Psychiatry, 200*(3), 191–196. https://doi.org/10.1192/bjp.bp.110.085720

Dadds, M. R., Cauchi, A. J., Wimalaweera, S., Hawes, D. J., & Brennan, J. (2012). Outcomes, moderators, and mediators of empathic-emotion recognition training for complex conduct problems in childhood. *Psychiatry Research, 199*(3), 201–207. https://doi.org/10.1016/j.psychres.2012.04.033

Dadds, M. R., English, T., Wimalaweera, S., Schollar-Root, O., & Hawes, D. J. (2019). Can reciprocated parent–child eye gaze and emotional engagement enhance treatment for children with conduct problems and callous-unemotional traits: A proof-of-concept trial. *Journal of Child Psychology and Psychiatry, 60*(6), 676–685. https://doi.org/10.1111/jcpp.13023

Dadds, M. R., Jambrak, J., Pasalich, D., Hawes, D. J., & Brennan, J. (2011). Impaired attention to the eyes of attachment figures and the developmental origins of psychopathy. *Journal of Child Psychology and Psychiatry, 52*(3), 238–245. https://doi.org/10.1111/j.1469-7610.2010.02323.x

Dadds, M. R., El Masry, Y., Wimalaweera, S., & Guastella, A. J. (2007). Reduced eye-gaze explains "fear blindness" in childhood psychopathic traits. *Journal of the American Academy of Child & Adolescent Psychiatry, 47*(4), 455–463. https://doi.org/10.1097/CHI.0b013e31816407f1

Dadds, M. R., Perry, Y., Hawes, D. J., Merz, S., Riddell, A. C., Haines, D. J., Solak, E., & Abeygunawardane, A. I. (2006). Attention to the eyes and fear-recognition deficits in child psychopathy. *The British Journal of Psychiatry, 189*(3), 280–281. https://doi.org/10.1192/bjp.bp.105.018150

Dadds, M. R., & Rhodes, T. (2008). Aggression in young children with concurrent callous–unemotional traits: Can the neurosciences inform progress and innovation in treatment approaches? *Philosophical Transactions of the Royal Society of London. Series B: Biological Sciences, 363*(1503), 2567–2576. https://doi.org/10.1098/rstb.2008.0029

Dadds, M. R., & Salmon, K. (2003). Punishment insensitivity and parenting: Temperament and learning as interacting risks for antisocial behavior. *Clinical Child and Family Psychology Review, 6*(2), 69–86. https://doi.org/10.1023/a:1023762009877

Dadds, M. R., Thai, C., Mendoza Diaz, A., Broderick, J., Moul, C., Tully, L. A., Hawes, D. J., Davies, S., Burchfield, K., & Cane, L. (2019). Therapist-assisted online treatment for child conduct problems in rural and urban families: Two randomized controlled trials. *Journal of Consulting and Clinical Psychology, 87*(8), 706–719. https://doi.org/10.1037/ccp0000419

Dandreaux, D. M., & Frick, P. J. (2009). Developmental pathways to conduct problems: A further test of the childhood and adolescent-onset distinction. *Journal of Abnormal Child Psychology, 37*(3), 375–385. https://doi.org/10.1007/s10802-008-9261-5

Datyner, A., Kimonis, E. R., Hunt, E., & Armstrong, K. (2016). Using a novel emotional skills module to enhance empathic responding for a child with conduct disorder with limited prosocial emotions. *Clinical Case Studies, 15*(1), 35–52. https://doi.org/10.1177/1534650115588978

Davis, M., & Whalen, P. J. (2001). The amygdala: Vigilance and emotion. *Molecular Psychiatry, 6*(1), 13–34. https://doi.org/10.1038/sj.mp.4000812

Dawel, A., O'Kearney, R., McKone, E., & Palermo, R. (2012). Not just fear and sadness: Meta-analytic evidence of pervasive emotion recognition deficits for facial and vocal expressions in psychopathy. *Neuroscience & Biobehavioral Reviews, 36*(10), 2288–2304. https://doi.org/10.1016/j.neubiorev.2012.08.006

Day, J. J., & Sanders, M. R. (2018). Do parents benefit from help when completing a self-guided parenting program online? A randomized controlled trial comparing Triple P Online with and without telephone support. *Behavior Therapy, 49*(6), 1020–1038. https://doi.org/10.1016/j.beth.2018.03.002

De Brito, S. A., Forth, A. E., Baskin-Sommers, A. R., Brazil, I. A., Kimonis, E. R., Pardini, D., Frick, P. J., Blair, R. J. R., & Viding, E. (2021). Psychopathy. *Nature Reviews Disease Primers*, 7(1), 49. https://doi.org/10.1038/s41572-021-00282-1

De Los Reyes, A. (2024). *Discrepant results in mental health research: What they mean, why they matter, and how they inform scientific practices*. Oxford University Press. https://doi.org/10.1093/oso/9780197686607.001.0001

De Los Reyes, A., Augenstein, T. M., Wang, M., Thomas, S. A., Drabick, D. A. G., Burgers, D. E., & Rabinowitz, J. (2015). The validity of the multi-informant approach to assessing child and adolescent mental health. *Psychological Bulletin, 141*(4), 858–900. https://doi.org/10.1037/a0038498

Dedousis-Wallace, A., Drysdale, S. A., McAloon, J., & Ollendick, T. H. (2021). Parental and familial predictors and moderators of parent management treatment programs for conduct problems in youth. *Clinical Child and Family Psychology Review, 24*(1), 92–119. https://doi.org/10.1007/s10567-020-00330-4

Demetriou, C. A., & Fanti, K. A. (2022). Are children high on callous-unemotional traits emotionally blind? Testing eye-gaze differences. *Child Psychiatry & Human Development, 53*(4), 623–634. https://doi.org/10.1007/s10578-021-01152-3

Deng, J., Wang, M. C., Zhang, X., Shou, Y., Gao, Y., & Luo, J. (2019). The Inventory of Callous Unemotional Traits: A reliability generalization meta-analysis. *Psychological Assessment, 31*(6), 765–780. https://doi.org/10.1037/pas0000698

Domitrovich, C. E., Greenberg, M. T., Kusche, C., & Cortes, R. (2005). *The preschool PATHS curriculum*. Channing Bete.

Doss, B. D., Feinberg, L. K., Rothman, K., Roddy, M. K., & Comer, J. S. (2017). Using technology to enhance and expand interventions for couples and families: Conceptual and methodological considerations. *Journal of Family Psychology, 31*(8), 983–993. https://doi.org/10.1037/fam0000349

Drislane, L. E., Patrick, C. J., & Arsal, G. (2014). Clarifying the content coverage of differing psychopathy inventories through reference to the triarchic psychopathy measure. *Psychological Assessment, 26*(2), 350–362. https://doi.org/10.1037/a0035152

Drugli, M. B., & Larsson, B. (2006). Children aged 4–8 years treated with parent training and child therapy because of conduct problems: Generalisation effects to day-care and school settings. *European Child & Adolescent Psychiatry, 15*(7), 392–399. https://doi.org/10.1007/s00787-006-0546-3

Dudgeon, P., Bray, A., D'costa, B., & Walker, R. (2017). Decolonising psychology: Validating social and emotional wellbeing. *Australian Psychologist, 52*(4), 316–325. https://doi.org/10.1111/ap.12294

Edens, J. F., Mowle, E. N., Clark, J. W., & Magyar, M. S. (2017). "A psychopath by any other name?": Juror perceptions of the *DSM-5* "limited prosocial emotions" specifier. *Journal of Personality Disorders, 31*(1), 90–109. https://doi.org/10.1521/pedi_2016_30_239

Eisenberg, N., & Morris, A. S. (2002). Children's emotion-related regulation. In R. Kail (Ed.), *Advances in child development and behavior* (Vol. 30, pp. 189–229). Academic Press. https://doi.org/10.1016/s0065-2407(02)80042-8

Eisenstadt, T. H., Eyberg, S., McNeil, C. B., Newcomb, K., & Funderburk, B. (1993). Parent–child interaction therapy with behavior problem children: Relative effectiveness of two stages and overall treatment outcome. *Journal of Clinical Child Psychology, 22*(1), 42–51. https://doi.org/10.1207/s15374424jccp2201_4

Ekman, P. (1993). Facial expression and emotion. *American Psychologist, 48*(4), 384–392. https://doi.org/10.1037/0003-066X.48.4.384

Ekman, P., & Friesen, W. V. (1975). *Unmasking the face: A guide to recognizing emotions from facial clues*. Malor Books.

Elizur, Y., Somech, L. Y., & Vinokur, A. D. (2017). Effects of parent training on callous-unemotional traits, effortful control, and conduct problems: Mediation by parenting. *Journal of Abnormal Child Psychology, 45*(1), 15–26. https://doi.org/10.1007/s10802-016-0163-7

Enebrink, P., Högström, J., Forster, M., & Ghaderi, A. (2012). Internet-based parent management training: A randomized controlled study. *Behaviour Research and Therapy, 50*(4), 240–249. https://doi.org/10.1016/j.brat.2012.01.006

Engelhardt, L. E., Mann, F. D., Briley, D. A., Church, J. A., Harden, K. P., & Tucker-Drob, E. M. (2016). Strong genetic overlap between executive functions and intelligence. *Journal of Experimental Psychology: General, 145*(9), 1141–1159. https://doi.org/10.1037/xge0000195

Eyberg, S., & Pincus, D. (1999). *Eyberg Child Behavior Inventory & Sutter-Eyberg Student Behavior Inventory-Revised: Professional manual*. Psychological Assessment Resources.

Eyberg, S. M., & Funderburk, B. W. (2011). *Parent–child interaction therapy protocol.* PCIT International.

Eyberg, S. M., & Johnson, S. M. (1974). *Therapy Attitude Inventory (TAI).* APA PsycTests. https://doi.org/10.1037/t16794-000

Eyberg, S. M., Nelson, M. M., & Boggs, S. R. (2008). Evidence-based psychosocial treatments for children and adolescents with disruptive behavior. *Journal of Clinical Child & Adolescent Psychology, 37*(1), 215–237. https://doi.org/10.1080/15374410701820117

Eyberg, S. M., Nelson, M. M., Ginn, N. C., Bhuiyan, N., & Boggs, S. R. (2013). *Dyadic parent-child interaction coding system (DPICS): Comprehensive manual for research and training* (4th ed.). PCIT International.

Ezpeleta, L., de la Osa, N., Granero, R., Penelo, E., & Domenech, J. M. (2013). Inventory of Callous-Unemotional Traits in a community sample of preschoolers. *Journal of Clinical Child and Adolescent Psychology, 42*(1), 91–105. https://doi.org/10.1080/15374416.2012.734221

Fagan, A. A., & Benedini, K. M. (2016). How do family-focused prevention programs work? A review of mediating mechanisms associated with reductions in youth antisocial behaviors. *Clinical Child and Family Psychology Review, 19*(4), 285–309. https://doi.org/10.1007/s10567-016-0207-0

Fanti, K. A. (2018). Understanding heterogeneity in conduct disorder: A review of psychophysiological studies. *Neuroscience & Biobehavioral Reviews, 91,* 4–20. https://doi.org/10.1016/j.neubiorev.2016.09.022

Fanti, K. A., Demetriou, C. A., & Kimonis, E. R. (2013). Variants of callous–unemotional conduct problems in a community sample of adolescents. *Journal of Youth and Adolescence, 42*(7), 964–979. https://doi.org/10.1007/s10964-013-9958-9

Fanti, K. A., & Kimonis, E. R. (2012). Bullying and victimization: The role of conduct problems and psychopathic traits. *Journal of Research on Adolescence, 22*(4), 617–631. https://doi.org/10.1111/j.1532-7795.2012.00809.x

Fanti, K. A., & Kimonis, E. R. (2013). Dimensions of juvenile psychopathy distinguish "bullies," "bully-victims," and "victims." *Psychology of Violence, 3*(4), 396–409. https://doi.org/10.1037/a0033951

Fanti, K. A., Panayiotou, G., Lazarou, C., Michael, R., & Georgiou, G. (2016). The better of two evils? Evidence that children exhibiting continuous problems high or low on callous-unemotional traits score on opposite directions on physiological and behavioral measures of fear. *Development and Psychopathology, 28*(1), 185–198. https://doi.org/10.1017/S0954579415000371

Farrington, D. P., Gallagher, B., Morley, L., St Ledger, R. J. S., & West, D. J. (1988). Are there any successful men from criminogenic backgrounds? *Psychiatry: Interpersonal and Biological Processes, 51*(2), 116–130. https://doi.org/10.1080/00332747.1988.11024387

Fixsen, D. L., Naoom, S. F., Blasé, K. A., Friedman, R. M., & Wallace, F. (2005). *Implementation research: A synthesis of the literature.* University of South Florida, Louis de la Parte Florida Mental Health Research Institute, the National Implementation Research Network.

Fleming, G. (2019). *Internet-delivered parent training for young Australian children with conduct problems: Adapting treatment for non-responders* [Doctoral dissertation, UNSW Sydney]. UNSWorks. https://hdl.handle.net/1959.4/62698

Fleming, G. E., Boulton, A. L., Kershaw, K. A., Prasad, A. H., & Kimonis, E. R. (2025). "The student will always be a problem": Callous-unemotional traits are associated with specific dimensions of teacher attributions. *Teaching and Teacher Education, 155,* 104912. https://doi.org/10.1016/j.tate.2024.104912

Fleming, G. E., Boulton, A. L., Prasad, A. H., Kershaw, K. A., & Kimonis, E. R. (2024). Educator knowledge of childhood conduct problems and callous-unemotional traits. *Research on Child and Adolescent Psychopathology, 52*(11), 1693–1706. https://doi.org/10.1007/s10802-024-01230-9

Fleming, G. E., Kershaw, K. A., Lam, A., Lee, Y. T., Clark-Whitney, E., Beem, L., Prasad, A. H., Frick, P. J., & Kimonis, E. R. (in press). Parent–child interaction therapy (PCIT) delivered in the school setting with teacher involvement: A co-produced intervention for students with conduct problems. *Australian Psychologist.*

Fleming, G. E., & Kimonis, E. R. (2018). PCIT for children with callous-unemotional traits. In L. N. Niec (Ed.), *Handbook of parent–child interaction therapy: Innovations and applications for research and practice* (pp. 19–34). Springer. https://doi.org/10.1007/978-3-319-97698-3

Fleming, G. E., Kimonis, E. R., Datyner, A., & Comer, J. S. (2017). Adapting internet-delivered parent–child interaction therapy to treat co-occurring disruptive behavior and callous-unemotional traits: A case study. *Clinical Case Studies, 16*(5), 370–387. https://doi.org/10.1177/1534650117699471

Fleming, G. E., Kimonis, E. R., Furr, J. M., & Comer, J. S. (2020). Internet-delivered parent training for preschoolers with conduct problems: Do callous-unemotional traits moderate efficacy and engagement? *Journal of Abnormal Child Psychology, 48*(9), 1169–1182. https://doi.org/10.1007/s10802-020-00660-5

Fleming, G. E., Kohlhoff, J., Morgan, S., Turnell, A., Maiuolo, M., & Kimonis, E. R. (2021). An effectiveness open trial of internet-delivered parent training for young children with conduct problems living in regional and rural Australia. *Behavior Therapy, 52*(1), 110–123. https://doi.org/10.1016/j.beth.2020.03.001

Fleming, G. E., Neo, B., Briggs, N. E., Kaouar, S., Frick, P. J., & Kimonis, E. R. (2022). Parent training adapted to the needs of children with callous–unemotional traits: A randomized controlled trial. *Behavior Therapy, 53*(6), 1265–1281. https://doi.org/10.1016/j.beth.2022.07.001

Fleming, G. E., Neo, B., Kaouar, S., & Kimonis, E. R. (2023). Treatment outcomes of children with primary versus secondary callous-unemotional traits. *Research on Child and Adolescent Psychopathology, 51*(11), 1581–1594. https://doi.org/10.1007/s10802-023-01112-6

Fleming, G. E., Sawrikar, V., Kaouar, S., Neo, B., McDonogh, C., & Kimonis, E. R. (2025). The impact of parental cognitions on outcomes of behavioral parent training for children with conduct problems. *Behavior Therapy, 56*(5), 917–934. https://doi.org/10.1016/j.beth.2025.02.004

Florean, I. S., Dobrean, A., Păsărelu, C. R., Georgescu, R. D., & Milea, I. (2020). The efficacy of internet-based parenting programs for children and adolescents with behavior problems: A meta-analysis of randomized clinical trials. *Clinical Child and Family Psychology Review, 23*(4), 510–528. https://doi.org/10.1007/s10567-020-00326-0

Forehand, R., Lafko, N., Parent, J., & Burt, K. B. (2014). Is parenting the mediator of change in behavioral parent training for externalizing problems of youth? *Clinical Psychology Review, 34*(8), 608–619. https://doi.org/10.1016/j.cpr.2014.10.001

Forgatch, M. S., & DeGarmo, D. S. (1999). Parenting through change: An effective prevention program for single mothers. *Journal of Consulting and Clinical Psychology, 67*(5), 711–724. https://doi.org/10.1037/0022-006X.67.5.711

Forth, A. E., Bergstrom, H., & Clark, H. J. (2015). Psychopathic traits in adolescence: Assessment and implications. In C. B. Gacono (Ed.), *The clinical and forensic assessment of psychopathy: A practitioner's guide* (pp. 115–136). Routledge. https://doi.org/10.4324/9781315764474

Forth, A. E., Kosson, D. S., & Hare, R. D. (2003). *The Psychopathy Checklist: Youth Version manual*. Multi-Health Systems.

Fox, E., & Damjanovic, L. (2006). The eyes are sufficient to produce a threat superiority effect. *Emotion, 6*(3), 534–539. https://doi.org/10.1037/1528-3542.6.3.534

Frick, P. J. (2004). *Inventory of callous-unemotional traits*. LSU, Developmental Psychopathology Lab. https://faculty.lsu.edu/pfricklab/icu.php

Frick, P. J. (2012). Developmental pathways to conduct disorder: Implications for future directions in research, assessment, and treatment. *Journal of Clinical Child & Adolescent Psychology, 41*(3), 378–389. https://doi.org/10.1080/15374416.2012.664815

Frick, P. J. (2013). *CAPE Version 1.1*. LSU, Developmental Psychopathology Lab. https://faculty.lsu.edu/pfricklab/cape.php

Frick, P. J. (2021). Is a rose really just as sweet? Editorial: On becoming "Research on Child and Adolescent Psychopathology." *Research on Child and Adolescent Psychopathology, 49*(1), 1–4. https://doi.org/10.1007/s10802-020-00718-4

Frick, P. J. (2022). Some critical considerations in applying the construct of psychopathy to research and classification of childhood disruptive behavior disorders. *Clinical Psychology Review, 96*, 102188. https://doi.org/10.1016/j.cpr.2022.102188

Frick, P. J., Barry, C. T., & Kamphaus, R. W. (2020). *Clinical assessment of children's personality and behavior* (4th ed.). Springer. https://doi.org/10.1007/978-3-030-35695-8

Frick, P. J., Bodin, S. D., & Barry, C. T. (2000). Psychopathic traits and conduct problems in community and clinic-referred samples of children: Further development of the Psychopathy Screening Device. *Psychological Assessment, 12*(4), 382–393. https://doi.org/10.1037/1040-3590.12.4.382

Frick, P. J., Cornell, A. H., Barry, C. T., Bodin, S. D., & Dane, H. A. (2003). Callous-unemotional traits and conduct problems in the prediction of conduct problem severity, aggression, and self-report of delinquency. *Journal of Abnormal Child Psychology, 31*(4), 457–470. https://doi.org/10.1023/a:1023899703866

Frick, P. J., & Hare, R. D. (2001). *The antisocial process screening device*. Multi-Health Systems.

Frick, P. J., & Kemp, E. C. (2021). Conduct disorders and empathy development. *Annual Review in Clinical Psychology, 17*(1), 391–416. https://doi.org/10.1146/annurev-clinpsy-081219-105809

Frick, P. J., Lahey, B. B., Loeber, R., Tannenbaum, L. E., Van Horn, Y., Christ, M. A. G., Hart, E. A., & Hansen, K. (1993). Oppositional defiant disorder and conduct disorder: A meta-analytic review of factor analyses and cross-validation in a clinic sample. *Clinical Psychology Review, 13*(4), 319–340. https://doi.org/10.1016/0272-7358(93)90016-f

Frick, P. J., & McMahon, R. J. (2018). Child and adolescent conduct problems. In J. Hunsley & E. J. Mash (Eds.), *A guide to assessments that work* (2nd ed., pp. 71–96). Oxford University. https://doi.org/10.1093/med-psych/9780190492243.003.0005

Frick, P. J., & Morris, A. S. (2004). Temperament and developmental pathways to severe conduct problems. *Journal of Clinical Child and Adolescent Psychology, 33*(1), 54–68. https://doi.org/10.1207/S15374424JCCP3301_6

Frick, P. J., & Nigg, J. T. (2012). Current issues in the diagnosis of attention-deficit hyperactivity disorder, oppositional defiant disorder, and conduct disorder. *Annual Review of Clinical Psychology, 8*(1), 77–107. https://doi.org/10.1146/annurev-clinpsy-032511-143150

Frick, P. J., O'Brien, B. S., Wootton, J. M., & McBurnett, K. (1994). Psychopathy and conduct problems in children. *Journal of Abnormal Psychology, 103*(4), 700–707. https://doi.org/10.1037/0021-843X.103.4.700

Frick, P. J., Ray, J. V., Thornton, L. C., & Kahn, R. E. (2014a). Annual research review: A developmental psychopathology approach to understanding callous-unemotional traits in children and adolescents with serious conduct problems. *Journal of Child Psychology and Psychiatry, 55*(6), 532–548. https://doi.org/10.1111/jcpp.12152

Frick, P. J., Ray, J. V., Thornton, L. C., & Kahn, R. E. (2014b). Can callous-unemotional traits enhance the understanding, diagnosis, and treatment of serious conduct problems in children and adolescents? A comprehensive review. *Psychological Bulletin, 140*(1), 1–57. https://doi.org/10.1037/a0033076

Frick, P. J., Stickle, T. R., Dandreaux, D. M., Farrell, J. M., & Kimonis, E. R. (2005). Callous-unemotional traits in predicting the severity and stability of conduct problems and delinquency. *Journal of Abnormal Child Psychology, 33*(4), 471–487. https://doi.org/10.1007/s10648-005-5728-9

Frick, P. J., & Viding, E. M. (2009). Antisocial behavior from a developmental psychopathology perspective. *Development and Psychopathology, 21*(4), 1111–1131. https://doi.org/10.1017/S0954579409990071

Gagne, J., Liew, J., & Nwadinobi, O. K. (2021). How does the broader construct of self-regulation relate to emotional regulation in young children? *Developmental Review, 60,* 100965. https://doi.org/10.1016/j.dr.2021.100965

Gajos, J. M., & Beaver, K. M. (2016). The effect of omega-3 fatty acids on aggression: A meta-analysis. *Neuroscience & Biobehavioral Reviews, 69,* 147–158. https://doi.org/10.1016/j.neubiorev.2016.07.017

Garbacz, S. A., McIntosh, K., Eagle, J. W., Dowd-Eagle, S. E., Hirano, K. A., & Ruppert, T. (2015). Family engagement within schoolwide positive behavioral interventions and supports. *Preventing School Failure: Alternative Education for Children and Youth, 60*(1), 60–69. https://doi.org/10.1080/1045988x.2014.976809

Garcia, A. M., Graziano, P. A., & Hart, K. C. (2018). Response to time-out among preschoolers with externalizing behavior problems: The role of callous-unemotional traits. *Child Psychiatry & Human Development, 49*(5), 699–708. https://doi.org/10.1007/s10578-018-0788-6

GBD 2019 Mental Disorders Collaborators. (2022). Global, regional, and national burden of 12 mental disorders in 204 countries and territories, 1990–2019: A systematic analysis for the Global Burden of Disease Study 2019. *Lancet Psychiatry, 9*(2), 137–150. https://doi.org/10.1016/S2215-0366(21)00395-3

Ghaderi, A., Kadesjö, C., Björnsdotter, A., & Enebrink, P. (2018). Randomized effectiveness trial of the family check-up versus internet-delivered parent training (iComet) for families of children with conduct problems. *Scientific Reports, 8*(1), 11486. https://doi.org/10.1038/s41598-018-29550-z

Gibson, K., Motzenbecker, T., Harvey, C., Han, R., & McNeil, C. (2021). *Parent–child interaction therapy (PCIT) adapted for older children: A research development manual.*

https://www.amazon.com/Parent-Child-Interaction-Therapy-Adapted-Children/dp/B09DJ56QHS/ref=sr_1_3?crid=14VJS6C3YGC9R&keywords=pcit+adapted+for+older+children&qid=1644530174&sprefix=pcit+adapted+for+older+children%2Caps%2C44&sr=8-3

Goetz, C. M., Frick, P. J., Thornton, L., Ray, J. V., Meyers, T. W., Steinberg, L., & Cauffman, E. (2025). Effects of neighborhood disadvantage and peer deviance on adolescent antisocial behavior: Testing potential interactions with age-of-onset. *Development & Psychopathology, 37*(1), 164–175. https://doi.org/10.1017/S0954579423001499

Goetz, C. M., Miller, T. A., & Frick, P. J. (2024). The Clinical Assessment of Prosocial Emotions (CAPE): Initial tests of reliability and validity in a clinic-referred sample of children and adolescents. *Psychological Assessment, 36*(8), 452–461. https://doi.org/10.1037/pas0001320

Golmaryami, F. N., Vaughan, E. P., & Frick, P. J. (2021). Callous-unemotional traits and romantic relationships. *Personality and Individual Differences, 168*, Article 110408. https://doi.org/10.1016/j.paid.2020.110408

Gözüm, A. I. C., & Aktulun, O. U. (2021). Relationship between pre-schoolers self-regulation, language, and early academic skills: The mediating role of self-regulation and moderating role of gender. *Current Psychology, 40*(10), 4718–4740. https://doi.org/10.1007/s12144-021-01699-3

Gray, C. (2000). *The new social story book*. Future Horizons.

Grieve, R., & Mahar, D. (2010). The emotional manipulation–psychopathy nexus: Relationships with emotional intelligence, alexithymia and ethical position. *Personality and Individual Differences, 48*(8), 945–950. https://doi.org/10.1016/j.paid.2010.02.028

Grolnick, W. S., Bridges, L. J., & Connell, J. P. (1996). Emotion regulation in two-year-olds: Strategies and emotional expression in four contexts. *Child Development, 67*(3), 928–941. https://doi.org/10.1111/j.1467-8624.1996.tb01774.x

Haas, S. M., Becker, S. P., Epstein, J. N., & Frick, P. J. (2018). Callous-unemotional traits are uniquely associated with poorer peer functioning in school-aged children. *Journal of Abnormal Child Psychology, 46*(4), 781–793. https://doi.org/10.1007/s10802-017-0330-5

Haas, S. M., & Waschbusch, D. A. (2012). Callous-unemotional traits and their relevance to ADHD. *The ADHD Report, 20*(3), 5–9. https://doi.org/10.1521/adhd.2012.20.3.5

Haas, S. M., Waschbusch, D. A., Pelham, W. E., King, S., Andrade, B. F., & Carrey, N. J. (2011). Treatment response in CP/ADHD children with callous/unemotional traits. *Journal of Abnormal Child Psychology, 39*(4), 541–552. https://doi.org/10.1007/s10802-010-9480-4

Hanf, C. (1969, April). *A two-stage program for modifying maternal controlling during mother-child (MC) interaction* [Paper presentation]. Meeting of the Western Psychological Association, Vancouver, BC, Canada.

Hansen, A., Broomfield, G., & Yap, M. B. (2019). A systematic review of technology-assisted parenting programs for mental health problems in youth aged 0–18 years: Applicability to underserved Australian communities. *Australian Journal of Psychology, 71*(4), 433–462. https://doi.org/10.1111/ajpy.12250

Hare, R. D. (1980). A research scale for the assessment of psychopathy in criminal populations. *Personality and Individual Differences, 1*(2), 111–119. https://doi.org/10.1016/0191-8869(80)90028-8

Hare, R. D. (1999). *Without conscience: The disturbing world of the psychopaths among us.* Guilford Press.

Harpur, T. J., Hare, R. D., & Hakstian, A. R. (1989). Two-factor conceptualization of psychopathy: Construct validity and assessment implications. *Journal of Consulting and Clinical Psychology, 1*(1), 6–17. https://doi.org/10.1037/1040-3590.1.1.6

Hawes, D. J., & Dadds, M. R. (2005). The treatment of conduct problems in children with callous-unemotional traits. *Journal of Consulting and Clinical Psychology, 73*(4), 737–741. https://doi.org/10.1037/0022-006X.73.4.737

Hawes, D. J., & Dadds, M. R. (2007). Stability and malleability of callous-unemotional traits during treatment for childhood conduct problems. *Journal of Clinical Child and Adolescent Psychology, 36*(3), 347–355. https://doi.org/10.1080/15374410701444298

Hawes, D. J., Dadds, M. R., Brennan, J., Rhodes, T., & Cauchi, A. (2013). Revisiting the treatment of conduct problems in children with callous-unemotional traits. *Australian & New Zealand Journal of Psychiatry, 47*(7), 646–653. https://doi.org/10.1177/0004867413484092

Hawes, D. J., Gardner, F., Dadds, M. R., Frick, P. J., Kimonis, E. R., Burke, J. D., & Fairchild, G. (2023). Oppositional defiant disorder. *Nature Reviews Disease Primers, 9*(1), 31. https://doi.org/10.1038/s41572-023-00441-6

Hawes, D. J., Kimonis, E. R., Mendoza Diaz, A., Frick, P. J., & Dadds, M. R. (2020). The Clinical Assessment of Prosocial Emotions (CAPE 1.1): A multi-informant validation study. *Psychological Assessment, 32*(4), 348–357. https://doi.org/10.1037/pas0000792

Hawes, S. W., Byrd, A. L., Henderson, C. E., Gazda, R. L., Burke, J. D., Loeber, R., & Pardini, D. A. (2014). Refining the parent-reported Inventory of Callous–Unemotional Traits in boys with conduct problems. *Psychological Assessment, 26*(1), 256–266. https://doi.org/10.1037/a0034718

Helander, M., Asperholm, M., Wetterborg, D., Öst, L. G., Hellner, C., Herlitz, A., & Enebrink, P. (2024). The efficacy of parent management training with or without involving the child in the treatment among children with clinical levels of disruptive behavior: A meta-analysis. *Child Psychiatry & Human Development, 55*(1), 164–181. https://doi.org/10.1007/s10578-022-01367-y

Henery, J., Fleming, G. E., Neo, B., Kaouar, S., & Kimonis, E. R. (2025). *Validation of the Parental Affection/Warmth Scale (PAWS) in parents of young children with varying levels of conduct problems and callous-unemotional traits* [Unpublished manuscript]. School of Psychology, University of New South Wales.

Henggeler, S. W. (2011). Efficacy studies to large-scale transport: The development and validation of multisystemic therapy programs. *Annual Review of Clinical Psychology, 7*(1), 351–381. https://doi.org/10.1146/annurev-clinpsy-032210-104615

Herschell, A. D., Schaffner, K. F., Taber-Thomas, S., & Scudder, A. T. (2018). Getting parent–child interaction therapy to scale. In L. N. Niec (Ed.), *Handbook of parent–child interaction therapy: Innovations and applications for research and practice* (pp. 391–405). Springer. https://doi.org/10.1007/978-3-319-97698-3

Högström, J., Enebrink, P., & Ghaderi, A. (2013). The moderating role of child callous-unemotional traits in an internet-based parent-management training program. *Journal of Family Psychology, 27*(2), 314–323. https://doi.org/10.1037/a0031883

Hubble, K., Bowen, K. L., Moore, S. C., & Van Goozen, S. H. (2015). Improving negative emotion recognition in young offenders reduces subsequent crime. *PLOS One, 10*(6), e0132035. https://doi.org/10.1371/journal.pone.0132035

Hyatt, C. S., Phillips, N. L., Sleep, C. E., Lynam, D. R., & Miller, J. D. (2025). Graduate student perspectives on training and clinical experiences with antagonism treatment. *Personality Disorders: Theory, Research, and Treatment, 16*(4), 299–304. https://doi.org/10.1037/per0000688

Hyde, L. W., & Dotterer, H. L. (2022). The nature and nurture of callous-unemotional traits. *Current Directions in Psychological Science, 31*(6), 546–555. https://doi.org/10.1177/09637214221121302

Hyde, L. W., Waller, R., Trentacosta, C. J., Shaw, D. S., Neiderhiser, J. M., Ganiban, J., Reiss, D., & Leve, L. D. (2016). Heritable and nonheritable pathways to early callous-unemotional behaviors. *The American Journal of Psychiatry, 173*(9), 903–910. https://doi.org/10.1176/appi.ajp.2016.15111381

Insel, T. R. (2015). The NIMH experimental medicine initiative. *World Psychiatry, 14*(2), 151–153. https://doi.org/10.1002/wps.20227

Jean-Richard-dit-Bressel, P., Lee, J. C., Liew, S. X., Weidemann, G., Lovibond, P. F., & McNally, G. P. (2023). A cognitive pathway to punishment insensitivity. *Proceedings of the National Academy of Sciences of the United States of America, 120*(15), e2221634120. https://doi.org/10.1073/pnas.2221634120

Jensen, P. S., Hinshaw, S. P., Swanson, J. M., Greenhill, L. L., Conners, C. K., Arnold, L. E., Abikoff, H. B., Elliott, G., Hechtman, L., Hoza, B., March, J. S., Newcorn, J. H., Severe, J. B., Vitiello, B., Wells, K., & Wigal, T. (2001). Findings from the NIMH Multimodal Treatment Study of ADHD (MTA): Implications and applications for primary care providers. *Journal of Developmental & Behavioral Pediatrics, 22*(1), 60–73. https://doi.org/10.1097/00004703-200102000-00008

Johnson, S. E., Lawrence, D., Sawyer, M., & Zubrick, S. R. (2018). Mental disorders in Australian 4- to 17-year olds: Parent-reported need for help. *Australian & New Zealand Journal of Psychiatry, 52*(2), 149–162. https://doi.org/10.1177/0004867417706032

Jones, D. J., Forehand, R., Cuellar, J., Kincaid, C., Parent, J., Fenton, N., & Goodrum, N. (2013). Harnessing innovative technologies to advance children's mental health: Behavioral parent training as an example. *Clinical Psychology Review, 33*(2), 241–252. https://doi.org/10.1016/j.cpr.2012.11.003

Jones, S., & Cauffman, E. (2008). Juvenile psychopathy and judicial decision making: An empirical analysis of an ethical dilemma. *Behavioral Sciences & the Law, 26*(2), 151–165. https://doi.org/10.1002/bsl.792

Jouriles, E. N., McDonald, R., Spiller, L., Norwood, W. D., Swank, P. R., Stephens, N., Ware, H., & Buzy, W. M. (2001). Reducing conduct problems among children of battered women. *Journal of Consulting and Clinical Psychology, 69*(5), 774–785. https://doi.org/10.1037//0022-006x.69.5.774

Kahn, R. E., Frick, P. J., Golmaryami, F. N., & Marsee, M. A. (2017). The moderating role of anxiety in the associations of callous-unemotional traits with self-report and laboratory measures of affective and cognitive empathy. *Journal of Abnormal Child Psychology, 45*, 583–596. https://doi.org/10.1007/s10802-016-0179-z

Kahn, R. E., Frick, P. J., Youngstrom, E., Findling, R. L., & Youngstrom, J. K. (2012). The effects of including a callous–unemotional specifier for the diagnosis of conduct disorder. *Journal of Child Psychology and Psychiatry, 53*(3), 271–282. https://doi.org/10.1111/j.1469-7610.2011.02463.x

Kahn, R. E., Frick, P. J., Youngstrom, E. A., Youngstrom, J. K., Feeny, K. C., & Findling, R. L. (2013). Distinguishing primary and secondary variants of callous-unemotional traits among adolescents in a clinic-referred sample. *Psychological Assessment, 25*(3), 966–978. https://doi.org/10.1037/a0032880

Kaminski, J. W., & Claussen, A. H. (2017). Evidence base update for psychosocial treatments for disruptive behaviors in children. *Journal of Clinical Child & Adolescent Psychology, 46*(4), 477–499. https://doi.org/10.1080/15374416.2017.1310044

Kaminski, J. W., Valle, L. A., Filene, J. H., & Boyle, C. L. (2008). A meta-analytic review of components associated with parent training program effectiveness. *Journal of Abnormal Child Psychology, 36*(4), 567–589. https://doi.org/10.1007/s10802-007-9201-9

Kaouar, S. (2025). *Investigating parental and dyadic mechanisms in the development and maintenance of heterogeneous conduct problems for young clinic-referred children* [Unpublished doctoral dissertation]. The University of New South Wales.

Kaouar, S., Fleming, G. E., Neo, B., Hawes, D. J., Eapen, V., & Kimonis, E. R. (2024). Dimensions of warm parenting attributions differentiate conduct problem subtypes in young children. *Research on Child and Adolescent Psychopathology, 52*(2), 223–236. https://doi.org/10.1007/s10802-023-01111-7

Kaouar, S., Fleming, G.E., Neo, B., McDonogh, C., Koh, L., Chan, A.B., Chen, L., Forrest, S., Hawes, D.J., Eapen, V. & Kimonis, E.R. (2025). *Out of sync: Parent-child behavioral synchrony in conduct problem subgroups* [Manuscript submitted for publication]. School of Psychology, University of New South Wales.

Kavanagh, B. E., Corney, K. B., Beks, H., Williams, L. J., Quirk, S. E., & Versace, V. L. (2023). A scoping review of the barriers and facilitators to accessing and utilising mental health services across regional, rural, and remote Australia. *BMC Health Services Research, 23*(1), 1060. https://doi.org/10.1186/s12913-023-10034-4

Kazdin, A. E. (2005). *Parent management training: Treatment for oppositional, aggressive, and antisocial behavior in children and adolescents*. Oxford University Press.

Kazdin, A. E., Bass, D., Siegel, T., & Thomas, C. (1989). Cognitive-behavioral therapy and relationship therapy in the treatment of children referred for antisocial behavior. *Journal of Consulting and Clinical Psychology, 57*(4), 522–535. https://doi.org/10.1037//0022-006x.57.4.522

Kemp, E. C., Frick, P. J., Matlasz, T. M., Clark, J. E., Robertson, E. L., Ray, J. V., Thornton, L. C., Myers, T. D. W., Steinberg, L., & Cauffman, E. (2023). Developing cut-off scores for the Inventory of Callous-Unemotional Traits (ICU) in justice-involved and community samples. *Journal of Clinical Child and Adolescent Psychology, 52*(4), 519–532. https://doi.org/10.1080/15374416.2021.1955371

Kemp, E. C., Miller, T., Speck, J. S., & Frick, P. J. (2025). *Emotional reactivity and recognition deficits in individuals with callous-unemotional (CU) traits: Evidence from two multilevel meta-analyses* [Manuscript submitted for publication]. Department of Psychology, Louisiana State University.

Kemp, E. C., Picou, P., Vaughan, E. P., Robertson, E. L., Walker, T. M., Frick, P. J., Hill, R., & de Back, J. (in press). The moderating role of callous-unemotional (CU) traits on risk factors for suicide in a psychiatric inpatient adolescent sample. *Journal of Applied Research on Children*.

Kemp, E. C., Ray, J. V., Frick, P. J., Robertson, E. L., Fanti, K. A., Essau, C. A., Baroncelli, A., Ciucci, E., & Bijttebier, P. (2024). Inventory of Callous-Unemotional Traits (ICU) factor structure and measurement invariance in an adolescent multinational sample. *Journal of Clinical Child and Adolescent Psychology, 53*(4), 595–606. https://doi.org/10.1080/15374416.2022.2148531

Kemp, E. C., Ray, J. V., Frick, P. J., Speck, J. S., Thornton, L. C., Myers, T. D. W., Robertson, E. L., Steinberg, L., & Cauffman, E. (2024). The Inventory of Callous-Unemotional Traits (ICU) self-report version: Factor structure, measurement invariance, and predictive validity in justice-involved male adolescents. *Psychological Assessment, 36*(9), 562–571. https://doi.org/10.1037/pas0001322

Kennedy, H., Ball, K., & Barlow, J. (2017). How does video interaction guidance contribute to infant and parental mental health and well-being? *Clinical Child Psychology and Psychiatry, 22*(3), 500–517. https://doi.org/10.1177/1359104517704026

Kennedy, S. C., Kim, J. S., Tripodi, S. J., Brown, S. M., & Gowdy, G. (2016). Does parent–child interaction therapy reduce future physical abuse? A meta-analysis. *Research on Social Work Practice, 26*(2), 147–156. https://doi.org/10.1177/1049731514543024

Kerr, M., Van Zalk, M., & Stattin, H. (2012). Psychopathic traits moderate peer influence on adolescent delinquency. *Journal of Child Psychology and Psychiatry, 53*(8), 826–835. https://doi.org/10.1111/j.1469-7610.2011.02492.x

Kimonis, E. R. (n.d.-a). *Coaching and rewarding emotional skills (CARES) treatment manual (CARES module; Version 5.1)*. Lulu Press.

Kimonis, E. R. (n.d.-b). *Parent–child interaction therapy callous-unemotional version treatment manual (PCIT-CU, Version 2.2)*. Lulu Press.

Kimonis, E. R. (n.d.-c). *Webform to request access to PCIT-CU digital resources*. Qualtrics. https://unswpsy.au1.qualtrics.com/jfe/form/SV_enXzhWPEkz80NPU

Kimonis, E. [pcitcu]. (n.d.-d). *CARES* [Video playlist]. YouTube. https://www.youtube.com/playlist?list=PLxI4P74xkKQrifBH6q3Mu6oDAe3O_Tjro

Kimonis, E. [School PCIT Clinic]. (n.d.-e.). *2D animation for teaching time out with Mr. Bear (CU PCIT)* [Video]. YouTube. https://youtu.be/AX2QQH9ARdk

Kimonis, E. R. (2023). The emotionally sensitive child-adverse parenting experiences-allostatic (over) load (ESCAPE-AL) model for the development of secondary psychopathic traits. *Clinical Child and Family Psychology Review, 26*(4), 1097–1114. https://doi.org/10.1007/s10567-023-00455-2

Kimonis, E. R. (2024). *Parent–child interaction therapy callous–unemotional version treatment manual (PCIT-CU, Version 2.2)*. Lulu Press. https://www.lulu.com/shop/eva-kimonis/parent-child-interaction-therapy-callous-unemotional-version-treatment-manual-pcit-cu-version-22/paperback/product-2mjrj9n.html

Kimonis, E. R., & Armstrong, K. (2012). Adapting parent–child interaction therapy to treat severe conduct problems with callous-unemotional traits: A case study. *Clinical Case Studies, 11*(3), 234–252. https://doi.org/10.1177/1534650112448835

Kimonis, E. R., Bagner, D. M., Linares, D., Blake, C. A., & Rodriguez, G. (2014). Parent training outcomes among young children with callous–unemotional conduct problems with or at risk for developmental delay. *Journal of Child and Family Studies, 23*(2), 437–448. https://doi.org/10.1007/s10826-013-9756-8

Kimonis, E. R., Cooper, F., Neo, B., Fleming, G. E., Chan, M. E., McDonogh, C., & Bressel, P. J. R. D. (2024). Affective and behavioral responses to time-out in preschool children with conduct problems and varying levels of callous-unemotional traits. *Behavior Therapy, 56*(2), 422–437. https://doi.org/10.1016/j.beth.2024.07.005

Kimonis, E. R., Cross, B., Howard, A., & Donoghue, K. (2013). Maternal care, maltreatment and callous-unemotional traits among urban male juvenile offenders.

Journal of Youth and Adolescence, 42(2), 165–177. https://doi.org/10.1007/s10964-012-9820-5

Kimonis, E. R., Fanti, K. A., Anastassiou-Hadjicharalambous, X., Mertan, B., Goulter, N., & Katsimicha, E. (2016). Can callous-unemotional traits be reliably measured in preschoolers? *Journal of Abnormal Child Psychology, 44*(4), 625–638. https://doi.org/10.1007/s10802-015-0075-y

Kimonis, E. R., Fanti, K. A., Frick, P. J., Moffitt, T. E., Essau, C., Bijjtebier, P., & Marsee, M. A. (2015). Using self-reported callous-unemotional traits to cross-nationally assess the *DSM-5* "With Limited Prosocial Emotions" specifier. *Journal of Child Psychology and Psychiatry, 56*(11), 1249–1261. https://doi.org/10.1111/jcpp.12357

Kimonis, E. R., Fanti, K. A., Goulter, N., & Hall, J. (2017). Affective startle potentiation differentiates primary and secondary variants of juvenile psychopathy. *Developmental Psychopathology, 29*(4), 1149–1160. https://doi.org/10.1017/S0954579416001206

Kimonis, E. R., Fanti, K. A., Isoma, Z., & Donoghue, K. (2013). Maltreatment profiles among incarcerated boys with callous-unemotional traits. *Child Maltreatment, 18*(2), 108–121. https://doi.org/10.1177/1077559513483002

Kimonis, E. R., Fleming, G., Briggs, N., Brouwer-French, L., Frick, P. J., Hawes, D. J., Bagner, D. M., Thomas, R., & Dadds, M. (2019). Parent–child interaction therapy adapted for preschoolers with callous-unemotional traits: An open trial pilot study. *Journal of Clinical Child & Adolescent Psychology, 48*(Suppl. 1), S347–S361. https://doi.org/10.1080/15374416.2018.1479966

Kimonis, E. R., Frick, P. J., & Barry, C. T. (2004). Callous-unemotional traits and delinquent peer affiliation. *Journal of Consulting and Clinical Psychology, 72*(6), 956–966. https://doi.org/10.1037/0022-006X.72.6.956

Kimonis, E. R., Frick, P. J., Boris, N. W., Smyke, A. T., Zeanah, C. H., Cornell, A. H., & Farrell, J. M. (2006). Callous-unemotional traits, behavioral inhibition, and parenting: Independent predictors of aggression in a high-risk preschool sample. *Journal of Child and Family Studies, 15*(6), 745–756. https://doi.org/10.1007/s10826-006-9047-8

Kimonis, E. R., Frick, P. J., Skeem, J., Marsee, M. A., Cruise, K., Muñoz, L. C., Aucoin, K. J., & Morris, A. S. (2008). Assessing callous–unemotional traits in adolescent offenders: Validation of the Inventory of Callous–Unemotional Traits. *Journal of the International Association of Psychiatry and Law, 31*(3), 241–252. https://doi.org/10.1016/j.ijlp.2008.04.002

Kimonis, E. R., & Gooi, C. H. (2025). Commentary: Treating populations with antagonistic traits—Reflections on Hyatt, Phillips, et al. (2025) and considerations for clinical psychology training programs. *Personality Disorders: Theory, Research, and Treatment, 16*(4), 310–314. https://doi.org/10.1037/per0000719

Kimonis, E. R., Kennealy, P. J., & Goulter, N. (2016). Does the self-report Inventory of Callous-Unemotional Traits predict recidivism? *Psychological Assessment, 28*(12), 1616–1624. https://doi.org/10.1037/pas0000292

Kimonis, E. R., Kidd, J., Most, S. B., Krynen, A., & Liu, C. (2020). An elusive deficit: Psychopathic personality traits and aberrant attention to emotional stimuli. *Emotion, 20*(6), 951–964. https://doi.org/10.1037/emo0000601

Kimonis, E. R., Le, B., Fleming, G. E., Kyranides, M. N., Demetriou, C. A., Fanti, K. A., Neo, B., Prasad, A. H., Chan, A., Hawes, D. J., & Eapen, V. (2023). Facial reactions to emotional films in young children with conduct problems and varying levels of callous-unemotional traits. *Journal of Child Psychology and Psychiatry, 64*(3), 357–366. https://doi.org/10.1111/jcpp.13701

Kimonis, E. R., Skeem, J. L., Cauffman, E., & Dmitrieva, J. (2011). Are secondary variants of juvenile psychopathy more reactively violent and less psychosocially mature than primary variants? *Law and Human Behavior, 35*(5), 381–391. https://doi.org/10.1007/s10979-010-9243-3

Kimonis, E. R., Tatar, J. R., & Cauffman, E. (2012). Substance-related disorders among juvenile offenders: What role do psychopathic traits play? *Psychology of Addictive Behaviors, 26*(2), 212–225. https://doi.org/10.1037/a0028047

Kirkman, J. J., Hawes, D. J., & Dadds, M. R. (2016). An open trial for an e-health treatment for child behavior disorders I: Social acceptability, engagement, and therapeutic process. *Evidence-Based Practice in Child and Adolescent Mental Health, 1*(4), 196–212. https://doi.org/10.1080/23794925.2016.1230481

Kjøbli, J., Zachrisson, H. D., & Bjørnebekk, G. (2018). Three randomized effectiveness trials—One question: Can callous-unemotional traits in children be altered? *Journal of Clinical Child & Adolescent Psychology, 47*(3), 436–443. https://doi.org/10.1080/15374416.2016.1178123

Kochanska, G. (1995). Children's temperament, mother's discipline, and security of attachment: Multiple pathways to emerging internalization. *Child Development, 66*(3), 597–615. https://doi.org/10.1111/j.1467-8624.1995.tb00892.x

Kochanska, G. (1997). Multiple pathways to conscience for children with different temperaments: From toddlerhood to age 5. *Developmental Psychology, 33*(2), 228–240. https://doi.org/10.1037/0012-1649.33.2.228

Kochanska, G., Boldt, L. J., Kim, S., Yoon, J. E., & Philibert, R. A. (2015). Developmental interplay between children's biobehavioral risk and the parenting environment from toddler to early school age: Prediction of socialization outcomes in preadolescence. *Development and Psychopathology, 27*(3), 775–790. https://doi.org/10.1017/S0954579414000777

Kochanska, G., Kim, S., Boldt, L. J., & Yoon, J. E. (2013). Children's callous-unemotional traits moderate links between their positive relationships with parents at preschool age and externalizing behavior problems at early school age. *Journal of Child Psychology and Psychiatry, 54*(11), 1251–1260. https://doi.org/10.1111/jcpp.12084

Kochanska, G., Koenig, J. L., Barry, R. A., Kim, S., & Yoon, J. E. (2010). Children's conscience during toddler and preschool years, moral self, and a competent, adaptive developmental trajectory. *Developmental Psychology, 46*(5), 1320–1332. https://doi.org/10.1037/a0020381

Kochanska, G., & Thompson, R. A. (1997). The emergence and development of conscience in toddlerhood and early childhood. In J. E. Grusec & L. Kuczynski (Eds.), *Parenting and children's internalization of values* (pp. 53–77). Wiley.

Koh, L., Neo, B., Fleming, G. E., Kaouar, S., Henery, J., Briggs, N., & Kimonis, E. R. (2024). Development and validation of the Parental Affection/Warmth Scale (PAWS) in a sample of parents of 2- to 8-year-olds. *Psychological Assessment, 36*(12), 722–734. https://doi.org/10.1037/pas0001343

Kolko, D. J., Dorn, L. D., Bukstein, O. G., Pardini, D., Holden, E. A., & Hart, J. (2009). Community vs. clinic-based modular treatment of children with early-onset ODD or CD: A clinical trial with 3-year follow-up. *Journal of Abnormal Child Psychology, 37*(5), 591–609. https://doi.org/10.1007/s10802-009-9303-7

Kraemer, H. C., Wilson, G. T., Fairburn, C. G., & Agras, W. S. (2002). Mediators and moderators of treatment effects in randomized clinical trials. *Archives of General Psychiatry, 59*(10), 877–883. https://doi.org/10.1001/archpsyc.59.10.877

Kramer, G. M., Kinn, J. T., & Mishkind, M. C. (2015). Legal, regulatory, and risk management issues in the use of technology to deliver mental health care.

Cognitive and Behavioral Practice, 22(3), 258–268. https://doi.org/10.1016/j.cbpra.2014.04.008

Kurtz, S., McNeil, C., Funderburk, B., Brestan-Knight, E., Nelson, M., & Chavez, F. (2024, September 3–6). *PCIT greatest hits: Looking back to inform our future* [Panel presentation]. PCIT International Convention 2024, Knoxville, Tennessee, United States. https://www.pcit.org/2024-convention.html

Kusche, C. A., & Greenberg, M. T. (1994). *The PATHS curriculum.* Developmental Research and Programs.

Kyranides, M. N., Fanti, K. A., Petridou, M., & Kimonis, E. R. (2020). In the eyes of the beholder: Investigating the effect of visual probing on accuracy and gaze fixations when attending to facial expressions among primary and secondary callous-unemotional variants. *European Child & Adolescent Psychiatry, 29*(10), 1441–1451. https://doi.org/10.1007/s00787-019-01452-z

Larson, J., & Lochman, J. E. (2010). *Helping schoolchildren cope with anger: A cognitive-behavioral intervention.* Guilford Press.

Lavigne, J. V., LeBailly, S. A., Gouze, K. R., Cicchetti, C., Jessup, B. W., Arend, R., Pochyly, J., & Binns, H. J. (2008). Predictor and moderator effects in the treatment of oppositional defiant disorder in pediatric primary care. *Journal of Pediatric Psychology, 33*(5), 462–472. https://doi.org/10.1093/jpepsy/jsm075

Lawing, K., Frick, P. J., & Cruise, K. R. (2010). Differences in offending patterns between adolescent sex offenders high or low in callous-unemotional traits. *Psychological Assessment, 22*(2), 298–305. https://doi.org/10.1037/a0018707

Lawrence, D., Johnson, S., Hafekost, J., Boterhoven De Haan, K., Sawyer, M. G., Ainley, J., & Zubrick, S. R. (2015). *The mental health of children and adolescents: Report on the second Australian child and adolescent survey of mental health and wellbeing.* Department of Health. https://www.health.gov.au/sites/default/files/documents/2020/11/the-mental-health-of-children-and-adolescents_0.pdf

Lee, A., & Gage, N. A. (2020). Updating and expanding systematic reviews and meta-analyses on the effects of school-wide positive behavior interventions and supports. *Psychology in the Schools, 57*(5), 783–804. https://doi.org/10.1002/pits.22336

Leijten, P., Gardner, F., Melendez-Torres, G. J., van Aar, J., Hutchings, J., Schultz, S., Knerr, W., & Overbeek, G. (2019). Meta-analyses: Key parenting program components for disruptive child behavior. *Journal of the American Academy of Child & Adolescent Psychiatry, 58*(2), 180–190. https://doi.org/10.1016/j.jaac.2018.07.900

Leijten, P., Melendez-Torres, G. J., Gardner, F., van Aar, J., Schulz, S., & Overbeek, G. (2018). Are relationship enhancement and behavior management "the golden couple" for disruptive child behavior? Two meta-analyses. *Child Development, 89*(6), 1970–1982. https://doi.org/10.1111/cdev.13051

Leno, V. C., Bedford, R., Chandler, S., White, P., Yorke, I., Charman, T., Pickles, A., & Simonoff, E. (2021). Callous-unemotional traits in youth with autism spectrum disorder (ASD): Replication of prevalence estimates and associations with gaze patterns when viewing fearful faces. *Development and Psychopathology, 33*(4), 1220–1228. https://doi.org/10.1017/s0954579420000449

Lesack, R., Bearss, K., Celano, M., & Sharp, W. G. (2014). Parent–child interaction therapy and autism spectrum disorder: Adaptations with a child with severe developmental delays. *Clinical Practice in Pediatric Psychology, 2*(1), 68–82. https://doi.org/10.1037/cpp0000047

Levantini, V., Muratori, P., Bertacchi, I., Crilli, V., Marzono, A., Masi, G., Milone, A., & Kimonis, E. R. (2024). The "measure of empathy in early childhood": Psychometric properties and associations with externalizing problems and callous unemotional traits. *Child Psychiatry and Human Development*. Advance online publication. https://doi.org/10.1007/s10578-024-01673-7

Levine, R. S., Smith, K., & Wagner, N. J. (2023). The impact of callous-unemotional traits on achievement, behaviors, and relationships in school: A systematic review. *Child Psychiatry & Human Development, 54*(6), 1546–1566. https://doi.org/10.1007/s10578-022-01344-5

Lieneman, C. C., Quetsch, L. B., Theodorou, L. L., Newton, K. A., & McNeil, C. B. (2019). Reconceptualizing attrition in parent–child interaction therapy: "Dropouts" demonstrate impressive improvements. *Psychology Research and Behavior Management, 12*, 543–555. https://doi.org/10.2147/prbm.s207370

Liu, J., Raine, A., Venables, P. H., & Mednick, S. A. (2004). Malnutrition at age 3 years and externalizing behavior problems at ages 8, 11, and 17 years. *American Journal of Psychiatry, 161*(11), 2005–2013. https://doi.org/10.1176/appi.ajp.161.11.2005

Lochman, J. E., Baden, R. E., Boxmeyer, C. L., Powell, N. P., Qu, L., Salekin, K. L., & Windle, M. (2014). Does a booster intervention augment the preventive effects of an abbreviated version of the coping power program for aggressive children? *Journal of Abnormal Child Psychology, 42*(3), 367–381. https://doi.org/10.1007/s10802-013-9727-y

Lochman, J. E., Boxmeyer, C., Powell, N., Qu, L., Wells, K., & Windle, M. (2009). Dissemination of the Coping Power program: Importance of intensity of counselor training. *Journal of Consulting and Clinical Psychology, 77*(3), 397–409. https://doi.org/10.1037/a0014514

Lochman, J. E., Powell, N. P., & Jones, S. (2022). The Coping Power program for children with aggressive behavior problems. In P. C. Kendall (Ed.), *Flexibility within fidelity: Breathing life into a psychological treatment manual* (pp. 211–230). Oxford University Press. https://doi.org/10.1093/med-psych/9780197552155.003.0012

Lochman, J. E., & Wells, K. C. (2002a). Contextual social–cognitive mediators and child outcome: A test of the theoretical model in the Coping Power program. *Development and psychopathology, 14*(4), 945–967. https://doi.org/10.1017/s0954579402004157

Lochman, J. E., & Wells, K. C. (2002b). The Coping Power program at the middle-school transition: Universal and indicated prevention effects. *Psychology of Addictive Behaviors, 16*(4S), S40–S54. https://doi.org/10.1037/0893-164x.16.4s.s40

Lochman, J. E., & Wells, K. C. (2003). Effectiveness of the coping power program and of classroom intervention with aggressive children: Outcomes at a 1-year follow-up. *Behavior Therapy, 34*(4), 493–515. https://doi.org/10.1016/s0005-7894(03)80032-1

Lochman, J. E., & Wells, K. C. (2004). The coping power program for preadolescent aggressive boys and their parents: Outcome effects at the 1-year follow-up. *Journal of Consulting and Clinical Psychology, 72*(4), 571–578. https://doi.org/10.1037/0022-006x.72.4.571

Lochman, J. E., Wells, K. C., Qu, L., & Chen, L. (2013). Three year follow-up of Coping Power intervention effects: Evidence of neighborhood moderation? *Prevention Science, 14*(4), 364–376. https://doi.org/10.1007/s11121-012-0295-0

Loney, B. R., Frick, P. J., Ellis, M., & McCoy, M. G. (1998). Intelligence, psychopathy, and antisocial behavior. *Journal of Psychopathology and Behavioral Assessment, 20*(3), 231–247. https://doi.org/10.1023/a:1023015318156

Louisiana Department of Health. (2025, January). *Health professional shortage areas*. https://wellaheadla.com/healthcare-access/health-professional-shortage-areas/

Lynam, D. R. (1996). The early identification of chronic offenders: Who is the fledgling psychopath? *Psychological Bulletin, 120*(2), 209–234. https://doi.org/10.1037/0033-2909.120.2.209

Lynam, D. R., Caspi, A., Moffitt, T. E., Loever, R., & Stouthamer-Loeber, M. (2007). Longitudinal evidence that psychopathy scores in early adolescence predict adult psychopathy. *Journal of Abnormal Psychology, 116*(1), 155–165. https://doi.org/10.1037/0021-843x.116.1.155

Manders, W. A., Deković, M., Asscher, J. J., van der Laan, P. H., & Prins, P. J. M. (2013). Psychopathy as predictor and moderator of multisystemic therapy outcomes among adolescents treated for antisocial behavior. *Journal of Abnormal Child Psychology, 41*(7), 1121–1132. https://doi.org/10.1007/s10802-013-9749-5

Marsee, M. A., Frick, P. J., Barry, C. T., Kimonis, E. R., Munoz-Centifanti, L. C., & Aucoin, K. J. (2014). Profiles of the forms and functions of self-reported aggression in three adolescent samples. *Development and Psychopathology, 26*(3), 705–720. https://doi.org/10.1017/s0954579414000339

Marsh, A. A., & Ambady, N. (2007). The influence of the fear facial expression on prosocial responding. *Cognition and Emotion, 21*(2), 225–247. https://doi.org/10.1080/02699930600652234

Marsh, A. A., & Blair, R. J. R. (2008). Deficits in facial affect recognition among antisocial populations: A meta-analysis. *Neuroscience & Biobehavioral Reviews, 32*(3), 454–465. https://doi.org/10.1016/j.neubiorev.2007.08.003

Martin-Key N. A., Graf, E. W., Adams, W. J., & Fairchild, G. (2018). Facial emotion recognition and eye movement behaviour in conduct disorder. *Journal of Child Psychology and Psychiatry, 59*(3), 247–257. https://doi.org/10.1111/jcpp.12795

Masi, G., Fantozzi, P., Muratori, P., Bertolucci, G., Tacchi, A., Villafranca, A., Pfanner, C., & Cortese, S. (2020). Emotional dysregulation and callous unemotional traits as possible predictors of short-term response to methylphenidate monotherapy in drug-naïve youth with ADHD. *Comprehensive Psychiatry, 100*, 152178. https://doi.org/10.1016/j.comppsych.2020.152178

Matlasz, T. M., Frick, P. J., & Clark, J. E. (2022). Understanding the social relationships of youth with callous-unemotional traits using peer nominations. *Journal of Clinical Child and Adolescent Psychology, 51*(4), 530–542. https://doi.org/10.1080/15374416.2020.1823847

Matlasz, T. M., Frick, P. J., & Clark, J. E. (2023). A comparison of parent, teacher, and youth ratings on the Inventory of Callous-Unemotional Traits. *Assessment, 30*(1), 210–224. https://doi.org/10.1177/10731911211047893

Matos, M., Torres, R., Santiago, R., Jurado, M., & Rodríguez, I. X. A. (2006). Adaptation of parent–child interaction therapy for Puerto Rican families: A preliminary study. *Family Process, 45*(2), 205–222. https://doi.org/10.1111/j.1545-5300.2006.00091.x

McCart, M. R., Priester, P. E., Davies, W. H., & Azen, R. (2006). Differential effectiveness of behavioral parent-training and cognitive-behavioral therapy for antisocial youth: A meta-analysis. *Journal of Abnormal Child Psychology, 34*(4), 525–541. https://doi.org/10.1007/s10802-006-9031-1

McCart, M. R., & Sheidow, A. J. (2016). Evidence-based psychosocial treatments for adolescents with disruptive behavior. *Journal of Clinical Child & Adolescent Psychology, 45*(5), 529–563. https://doi.org/10.1080/15374416.2016.1146990

McCauley, K. L., Shadur, J. M., Hoffman, E. M., MacPherson, L., & Lejuez, C. W. (2016). Adolescent callous-unemotional traits and parental knowledge as predictors of unprotected sex among youth. *Behavior Modification, 40*(1–2), 70–96. https://doi.org/10.1177/0145445515615355

McDonald, R., Dodson, M. C., Rosenfield, D., & Jouriles, E. N. (2011). Effects of a parenting intervention on features of psychopathy in children. *Journal of Abnormal Child Psychology, 39*(7), 1013–1023. https://doi.org/10.1007/s10802-011-9512-8

McKenzie, P., Weldon, P. R., Rowley, G., Murphy, M., & McMillan, J. (2014). *Staff in Australia's schools 2013: Main report on the survey*. Department of Education. https://nla.gov.au/nla.obj-3063860471/view

McMahon, R. J., & Forehand, R. L. (2019). Helping the noncompliant child. In J. L. Lebow, A. L. Chambers, & D. C. Breunlin (Eds.), *Encyclopedia of couple and family therapy* (pp. 1359–1364). Springer International Publishing. https://doi.org/10.1007/978-3-319-49425-8_382

McMahon, R. J., & Frick, P. J. (2019). Conduct and oppositional disorders. In M. J. Prinstein, E. A. Youngstrom, E. J. Mash, & R. A. Barkley (Eds.), *Treatment of childhood disorders* (4th ed., pp. 102–174). Guilford Press.

McMahon, R. J., Witkiewitz, K., Kotler, J. S., & the Conduct Problems Prevention Research Group. (2010). Predictive validity of callous-unemotional traits measures in early adolescence with respect to multiple antisocial outcomes. *Journal of Abnormal Psychology, 119*(4), 52–763. https://doi.org/10.1037/a0020796

McNeil, C. B., & Hembree-Kigin, T. L. (2011). *Parent child interaction therapy* (2nd ed.). Springer.

McNeil, C. B., Quetsch, L. B., & Anderson, C. M. (Eds.). (2019). *Handbook of parent–child interaction therapy for children on the autism spectrum*. Springer. https://doi.org/10.1007/978-3-030-03213-5

Meehan, A. J., Maughan, B., Cecil, C. A. M., & Barker, E. (2017). Interpersonal callousness, and co-occurring anxiety: Developmental validity of an adolescent taxonomy. *Journal of Abnormal Psychology, 126*(2), 225–236. https://doi.org/10.1037/abn0000235

Mestre, J. M., Taubner, S., Mota, C. P., Rangel Henriques, M., Saliba, A., Heinonen, E., Ramos, S., Moreno-Peral, P., Volkert, J., Adler, A., Barkauskiene, R., Conejo-Cerón, S., Di Giacomo, D., Ioannou, Y., Mucha Vieira, F., Røssberg, J. I., Sales, C. M. D., Schmidt, S. J., Stepisnik Perdih, T., . . . Protić, S. (2022). Theories of change and mediators of psychotherapy effectiveness in adolescents with externalising behaviours: A systematic review. *Frontiers in Psychiatry, 12*, 730921. https://doi.org/10.3389/fpsyt.2021.730921

Miller, N. V., Haas, S. M., Waschbusch, D. A., Willoughby, M. T., Helseth, S. A., Crum, K. I., Coles, E. K., & Pelham, W. E., Jr. (2014). Behavior therapy and callous-unemotional traits: Effects of a pilot study examining modified behavioral contingencies on child behavior. *Behavior Therapy, 45*(5), 606–618. https://doi.org/10.1016/j.beth.2013.10.006

Milner, J. S. (2003). Social information processing in high-risk and physically abusive parents. *Child Abuse & Neglect, 27*(1), 7–20. https://doi.org/10.1016/S0145-2134(02)00506-9

Moffitt, T. E. (2018). Male antisocial behaviour in adolescence and beyond. *Nature Human Behaviour, 2*(3), 177–186. https://doi.org/10.1038/s41562-018-0309-4

Moffitt, T. E., Arseneault, L., Jaffee, S. R., Kim-Cohen, J., Koenen, K. C., Odgers, C. L., Slutske, W. S., & Viding, E. (2008). Research review: *DSM-V* conduct disorder: Research needs for an evidence base. *Journal of Child Psychology and Psychiatry, 49*(1), 3–33. https://doi.org/10.1111/j.1469-7610.2007.01823.x

Moffitt, T. E., Caspi, A., Harrington, H., & Milne, B. J. (2002). Males on the life-course-persistent and adolescence-limited antisocial pathways: Follow-up at age 26 years. *Development and Psychopathology, 14*(1), 179–207. https://doi.org/10.1017/s0954579402001104

Molinuevo, B., Martínez-Membrives, E., Pera-Guardiola, V., Requena, A., Torrent, N., Bonillo, A., Batalla, I., Torrubia, R., & Frick, P. J. (2020). Psychometric properties of the Clinical Assessment of Prosocial Emotions: Version 1.1 (CAPE 1.1) in young males who were incarcerated. *Criminal Justice and Behavior, 47*(5), 547–563. https://doi.org/10.1177/0093854819892931

Moore, A. A., Carney, D., Moroney, E., Machlin, L., Towbin, K., Brotman, M. A., Pine, D. S., Leibenluft, E., Roberson-Nay, R., & Hettema, J. M. (2017). The Inventory of Callous-Unemotional Traits (ICU) in children: Reliability and heritability. *Behavior Genetics, 47*(2), 141–151. https://doi.org/10.1007/s10519-016-9831-1

Moul, C., Robinson, O. J., & Livesey, E. J. (2021). Antisocial learning: Using learning window width to model callous-unemotional traits? *Computational Psychiatry, 5*(1), 54–59. https://doi.org/10.5334/cpsy.68

Muñoz, L. C., Kerr, M., & Besic, N. (2008). The peer relationships of youths with psychopathic personality traits: A matter of perspective. *Criminal Justice and Behavior, 35*(2), 212–227. https://doi.org/10.1177/0093854807310159

Muratori, P., Bertacchi, I., Masi, G., Milone, A., Nocentini, A., Powell, N. P., Lochman, J. E., Jones, S., Kassing, F., & Romero, D. (2019). Effects of a universal prevention program on externalizing behaviors: Exploring the generalizability of findings across school and home settings. *Journal of School Psychology, 77*, 13–23. https://doi.org/10.1016/j.jsp.2019.09.002

Muratori, P., Milone, A., Levantini, V., Ruglioni, L., Lambruschi, F., Pisano, S., Masi, G., & Lochman, J. E. (2019). Six-year outcome for children with ODD or CD treated with the coping power program. *Psychiatry Research, 271*, 454–458. https://doi.org/10.1016/j.psychres.2018.12.018

Muratori, P., Milone, A., Manfredi, A., Polidori, L., Ruglioni, L., Lambruschi, F., Masi, G., & Lochman, J. E. (2017). Evaluation of improvement in externalizing behaviors and callous-unemotional traits in children with disruptive behavior disorder: A 1-year follow up clinic-based study. *Administration and Policy in Mental Health and Mental Health Services Research, 44*(4), 452–462. https://doi.org/10.1007/s10488-015-0660-y

Murrie, D. C., Boccaccini, M. T., McCoy, W., & Cornell, D. G. (2007). Diagnostic labeling in juvenile court: How do descriptions of psychopathy and conduct disorder influence judges? *Journal of Clinical Child and Adolescent Psychology, 36*(2), 228–241. https://doi.org/10.1080/15374410701279602

Musser, E. D., Galloway-Long, H. S., Frick, P. J., & Nigg, J. T. (2013). Emotional regulation and heterogeneity in attention deficit hyperactivity disorder. *Journal of the American Academy of Child and Adolescent Psychiatry, 52*(2), 163–171. https://doi.org/10.1016/j.jaac.2012.11.009

National Institute for Health and Care Excellence. (2017). *Antisocial behaviour and conduct disorders in children and young people: Recognition and management* (Clinical guideline 158). https://www.nice.org.uk/guidance/cg158

Neo, B., Fleming, G. E., Kaouar, S., Chan, M. E., Huang, N. N., Hawes, D. J., Eapen, V., Briggs, N., & Kimonis, E. R. (2023). Clinical utility of diagnosing limited prosocial emotions in young children using the Clinical Assessment of Prosocial Emotions (CAPE). *Psychological Assessment, 35*(12), 1085–1097. https://doi.org/10.1037/pas0001279

Neo, B., & Kimonis, E. R. (2021). Callous–unemotional traits linked to earlier onset of self-reported and official delinquency in incarcerated boys. *Law and Human Behavior, 45*(6), 554–565. https://doi.org/10.1037/lhb0000472

Neumann, D., Babbage, D. R., Zupan, B., & Willer, B. (2015). A randomized controlled trial of emotion recognition training after traumatic brain injury. *The Journal of Head Trauma Rehabilitation, 30*(3), E12–E23. https://doi.org/10.1097/HTR.0000000000000054

Niec, L. N. (2018). Parent–child interaction therapy: A transdiagnostic intervention to enhance family functioning. In L. N. Niec (Ed.), *Handbook of parent–child interaction therapy: Innovations and applications for research and practice* (pp. 3–15). Springer. https://doi.org/10.1007/978-3-319-97698-3

Niec, L. N., Barnett, M. L., Prewett, M. S., & Shanley Chatham, J. R. (2016). Group parent–child interaction therapy: A randomized control trial for the treatment of conduct problems in young children. *Journal of Consulting and Clinical Psychology, 84*(8), 682–698. https://doi.org/10.1037/a0040218

Niec, L. N., Brodd, I., & Schoonover, C. E. (2023). Searching for the standard: The impact of level of training on in vivo coaching in parent–child interaction therapy. *Behavior Modification, 47*(1), 93–112. https://doi.org/10.1177/01454455221099647

Niec, L. N., Todd, M., Brodd, I., & Domoff, S. E. (2022). PCIT-health: Preventing childhood obesity by strengthening the parent–child relationship. *Cognitive and Behavioral Practice, 29*(2), 335–347. https://doi.org/10.1016/j.cbpra.2020.07.001

Nigg, J. T. (2000). On inhibition/disinhibition in developmental psychopathology: Views from cognitive and personality psychology and a working inhibition taxonomy. *Psychological Bulletin, 126*(2), 220–246. https://doi.org/10.1037/0033-2909.126.2.220

Odgers, C. L., Caspi, A., Broadbent, J. M., Dickson, N., Hancox, R. J., Harrington, H., Poulton, R., Sears, M. R., Thomson, W. M., & Moffitt, T. E. (2007). Prediction of differential adult health burden by conduct problem subtypes in males. *Archives of General Psychiatry, 64*(4), 476–484. https://doi.org/10.1001/archpsyc.64.4.476

Odgers, C. L., Moffitt, T. E., Broadbent, J. M., Dickson, N., Hancox, R. J., Harrington, H., Poulton, R., Sears, M. R., Thomson, W. M., & Caspi, A. (2008). Female and male antisocial trajectories: From childhood origins to adult outcomes. *Development and Psychopathology, 20*(2), 673–716. https://doi.org/10.1017/s0954579408000333

Ogden, T., Forgatch, M. S., Askeland, E., Patterson, G. R., & Bullock, B. M. (2005). Implementation of parent management training at the national level: The case of Norway. *Journal of Social Work Practice, 19*(3), 317–329. https://doi.org/10.1080/02650530500291518

Ospina, M. B., Krebs Seida, J., Clark, B., Karkhaneh, M., Hartling, L., Tjosvold, L., Vandermeer, B., & Smith, V. (2008). Behavioural and developmental interventions for autism spectrum disorder: A clinical systematic review. *PLOS One, 3*(11), e3755. https://doi.org/10.1371/journal.pone.0003755

Oxford, M., Cavell, T. A., & Hughes, J. N. (2003). Callous/unemotional traits moderate the relation between ineffective parenting and child externalizing problems: A partial replication and extension. *Journal of Clinical Child and Adolescent Psychology, 32*(4), 577–585. https://doi.org/10.1207/s15374424jccp3204_10

Pardini, D. A., Byrd, A. L., Hawes, S. W., & Docherty, M. (2018). Unique dispositional precursors to early-onset conduct problems and criminal offending in adulthood. *Journal of the American Academy of Child & Adolescent Psychiatry, 57*(8), 583–592. https://doi.org/10.1016/j.jaac.2018.04.013

Pardini, D. A., Lochman, J. E., & Frick, P. J. (2003). Callous/unemotional traits and social-cognitive processes in adjudicated youths. *Journal of the American Academy of Child and Adolescent Psychiatry, 42*(3), 364–371. https://doi.org/10.1097/00004583-200303000-00018

Pardini, D. A., Obradovic, J., & Loeber, R. (2006). Interpersonal callousness, hyperactivity/impulsivity, inattention, and conduct problems as precursors to delinquency persistence in boys: A comparison of three grade-based cohorts. *Journal of Clinical Child and Adolescent Psychology, 35*(1), 46–59. https://doi.org/10.1207/s15374424jccp3501_5

Parent, J., Jones, D. J., DiMarzio, K., Yang, Y., Wright, K. L., Sullivan, A. D., & Forehand, R. (2023). The effects of young children's callous-unemotional traits on behaviorally observed outcomes in standard and technology-enhanced behavioral parent training. *Research on Child and Adolescent Psychopathology, 51*(2), 165–175. https://doi.org/10.1007/s10802-022-00979-1

Pasalich, D. S., Dadds, M. R., Hawes, D. J., & Brennan, J. (2012). Do callous-unemotional traits moderate the relative importance of parental coercion versus warmth in child conduct problems? An observational study. *Journal of Child Psychology and Psychiatry, 52*(12), 1308–1315. https://doi.org/10.1111/j.1469-7610.2011.02435.x

Pasalich, D. S., Witkiewitz, K., McMahon, R. J., Pinderhughes, E. E., & The Conduct Problems Prevention Research Group. (2016). Indirect effects of the Fast Track intervention on conduct disorder symptoms and callous-unemotional traits: Distinct pathways involving discipline and warmth. *Journal of Abnormal Child Psychology, 44*(3), 587–597. https://doi.org/10.1007/s10802-015-0059-y

Patrick, C. J. (2022). Psychopathy: Current knowledge and future directions. *Annual Review of Clinical Psychology, 18*(1), 387–415. https://doi.org/10.1146/annurev-clinpsy-072720-012851

Patterson, G. R. (1982). *A social learning approach: III. Coercive family process.* Castalia.

Patterson, G. R. (2016). Coercion theory: The study of change. In T. J. Dishion & J. J. Snyder (Eds.), *The Oxford handbook of coercive relationship dynamics* (pp. 7–22). Oxford University Press. https://doi.org/10.1093/oxfordhb/9780199324552.001.0001

Paul Ekman Group. (n.d.). *Micro expressions training tools.* https://www.paulekman.com/micro-expressions-training-tools/

PCIT for Older Children. (n.d.). *PCIT adapted for older children.* https://pcitforolderchildren.com/

PCIT International. (n.d.). *PCIT certified therapist requirements.* https://www.pcit.org/therapist-requirements.html

Pearl, E., Thieken, L., Olafson, E., Boat, B., Connelly, L., Barnes, J., & Putnam, F. (2012). Effectiveness of community dissemination of parent–child interaction therapy. *Psychological Trauma: Theory, Research, Practice, and Policy, 4*(2), 204–213. https://doi.org/10.1037/a0022948

Pelham, W. E. Jr., & Fabiano, G. A. (2008). Evidence-based psychosocial treatments for attention-deficit/hyperactivity disorder. *Journal of Clinical Child & Adolescent Psychology, 37*(1), 184–214. https://doi.org/10.1080/15374410701818681

Pelham, W. E., Jr., & Hoza, B. (1996). Intensive treatment: A summer treatment program for children with ADHD. In E. D. Hibbs & P. S. Jensen (Eds.), *Psychosocial treatments for child and adolescent disorders: Empirically based strategies for clinical practice* (pp. 311–340). American Psychological Association. https://doi.org/10.1037/10196-013

Penner, F., Elzaki, Y., Contreras, H. T., Santos, R. P., & Sarver, D. E. (2022). Behavioral, affective, and cognitive parenting mechanisms of child internalizing and externalizing problems during the COVID-19 pandemic. *Research on Child and Adolescent Psychopathology, 50*(9), 1121–1138. https://doi.org/10.1007/s10802-022-00920-6

Perlstein, S., Fair, M., Hong, E., & Waller, R. (2023). Treatment of childhood disruptive behavior disorders and callous-unemotional traits: A systematic review and two multilevel meta-analyses. *Journal of Child Psychology and Psychiatry, 64*(9), 1372–1387. https://doi.org/10.1111/jcpp.13774

Phillips, S., & Mychailyszyn, M. (2021). A review of parent–child interaction therapy (PCIT): Applications for youth anxiety. *Children and Youth Services Review, 125*, 105986. https://doi.org/10.1016/j.childyouth.2021.105986

Phillips, S. T., & Mychailyszyn, M. P. (2023). Parent–child interaction therapy for preschool aged youth: A meta-analysis of developmental specificity. *Child & Youth Care Forum, 52*(2), 267–284. https://doi.org/10.1007/s10566-022-09694-w

Pincus, D. B., Santucci, L. C., Ehrenreich, J. T., & Eyberg, S. M. (2008). The implementation of modified parent–child interaction therapy for youth with separation anxiety disorder. *Cognitive and Behavioral Practice, 15*(2), 118–125. https://doi.org/10.1016/j.cbpra.2007.08.002

Piotrowska, P. J., Tully, L. A., Collins, D. A., Sawrikar, V., Hawes, D., Kimonis, E. R., Lenroot, R. K., Moul, C., Anderson, V., Frick, P. J., & Dadds, M. R. (2020). ParentWorks: Evaluation of an online, father-inclusive, universal parenting intervention to reduce child conduct problems. *Child Psychiatry & Human Development, 51*(4), 503–513. https://doi.org/10.1007/s10578-019-00934-0

Prasad, A. H., Keevers, Y., Kaouar, S., & Kimonis, E. R. (2023). Conception and development of the Warmth/Affection Coding System (WACS): A novel hybrid behavioral observational tool for assessing parent-to-child warmth. *Research on Child and Adolescent Psychopathology, 51*(9), 1357–1369. https://doi.org/10.1007/s10802-023-01055-y

Prasad, A. H., & Kimonis, E. R. (2018). Effects of the "limited prosocial emotions" specifier for conduct disorder on juror perceptions of juvenile offenders. *Criminal Justice & Behavior, 45*(10), 1547–1564. https://doi.org/10.1177/0093854818774381

Pringsheim, T., Hirsch, L., Gardner, D., & Gorman, D. A. (2015). The pharmacological management of oppositional behaviour, conduct problems, and aggression in children and adolescents with attention-deficit hyperactivity disorder, oppositional defiant disorder, and conduct disorder: A systematic review and meta-analysis. Part 1: Psychostimulants, alpha-2 agonists, and atomoxetine. *The Canadian Journal of Psychiatry, 60*(2), 42–51. https://doi.org/10.1177/070674371506000202

Quay, H. C. (1987). Patterns of delinquent behavior. In H. C. Quay (Ed.), *Handbook of juvenile delinquency* (pp. 118–138). Wiley. https://doi.org/10.1016/S0140-1971(88)80040-x

Raine, A., Cheney, R. A., Ho, R., Portnoy, J., Liu, J., Soyfer, L., Hibbeln, J., & Richmond, T. S. (2016). Nutritional supplementation to reduce child aggression: A randomized, stratified, single-blind, factorial trial. *Journal of Child Psychology and Psychiatry, 57*(9), 1038–1046. https://doi.org/10.1111/jcpp.12565

Raine, A., Fung, A. L. C., Gao, Y., & Lee, T. M. (2021). Omega-3 supplementation, child antisocial behavior, and psychopathic personality: A randomized, double-blind, placebo-controlled, stratified, parallel group trial. *European Child & Adolescent Psychiatry, 30*(2), 303–312. https://doi.org/10.1007/s00787-020-01513-8

Raine, A., Leung, C. C., Singh, M., & Kaur, J. (2020). Omega-3 supplementation in young offenders: A randomized, stratified, double-blind, placebo-controlled, parallel-group trial. *Journal of Experimental Criminology, 16*(3), 389–405. https://doi.org/10.1007/s11292-019-09394-x

Ray, J. V., & Frick, P. J. (2020). Assessing callous-unemotional traits using the total score from the Inventory of Callous-Unemotional Traits: A meta-analysis. *Journal of Clinical Child and Adolescent Psychology, 49,* 190–199. https://doi.org/10.1080/15374416.2018.1504297

Ray, J. V., Frick, P. J., Thornton, L. C., Myers, T. D. M., Steinberg, L., & Cauffman, E. (2019). Estimating and predicting the course of callous-unemotional traits in first-time adolescent offenders. *Child Development, 55*(8), 1709–1719. https://doi.org/10.1037/dev0000748

Ray, J. V., Frick, P. J., Thornton, L. C., Steinberg, L., & Cauffman, E. (2016a). Impulse control and callous-unemotional traits distinguish patterns of delinquency and substance use in justice involved adolescents: Examining the moderating role of neighborhood context. *Journal of Abnormal Child Psychology, 44*(3), 599–611. https://doi.org/10.1007/s10802-015-0057-0

Ray, J. V., Frick, P. J., Thornton, L. C., Steinberg, L., & Cauffman, E. (2016b). Positive and negative item wording and its influence on the assessment of callous-unemotional traits. *Psychological Assessment, 28*(4), 394–404. https://doi.org/10.1037/pas0000183

Rivenbark, J. G., Odgers, C. L., Caspi, A., Harrington, H., Hogan, S., Houts, R. M., Poulton, R., & Moffitt, T. E. (2018). The high societal costs of childhood conduct problems: Evidence from administrative records up to age 38 in a longitudinal birth cohort. *Journal of Child Psychology and Psychiatry, 59*(6), 703–710. https://doi.org/10.1111/jcpp.12850

Robbins, M. S., Alexander, J. F., Turner, C. W., & Hollimon, A. (2016). Evolution of functional family therapy as an evidence-based practice for adolescents with disruptive behavior problems. *Family Process, 55*(3), 543–557. https://doi.org/10.1111/famp.12230

Robertson, E. L., Frick, P. J., Ray, J. V., Thornton, L. C., Wall Myers, T. D., Steinberg, L., & Cauffman, E. (2021). Do callous–unemotional traits moderate the effects of the juvenile justice system on later offending behavior? *Journal of Child Psychology and Psychiatry, 62*(2), 212–222. https://doi.org/10.1111/jcpp.13266

Robertson, E. L., Frick, P. J., Walker, T. M., Kemp, E. C., Ray, J. V., Thornton, L. C., Myers, T. D. W., Steinberg, L., & Cauffman, E. (2020). Callous-unemotional traits and risk of gun carrying and use during crime. *American Journal of Psychiatry, 117*(9), 827–833. https://doi.org/10.1176/appi.ajp.2020.19080861

Rowe, R., Maughan, B., Moran, P., Ford, T., Briskman, J., & Goodman, R. (2010). The role of callous unemotional traits in the diagnosis of conduct disorder. *Journal of Child Psychology and Psychiatry, 51*(6), 688–695. https://doi.org/10.1111/j.1469-7610.2009.02199.x

Rowe, R., Maughan, B., Pickles, A., Costello, E. J., & Angold, A. (2002). The relationship between *DSM-IV* oppositional defiant disorder and conduct disorder: Findings from the Great Smoky Mountains Study. *Journal of Child Psychology and Psychiatry, 43*(3), 365–373. https://doi.org/10.1111/1469-7610.00027

Sakki, H., Clair, M. S., Hwang, S., & Allen, J. L. (2023). The association between callous-unemotional traits and substance use in childhood and adolescence: A systematic review and meta-analysis. *Journal of Affective Disorders, 338*, 502–517. https://doi.org/10.1016/j.jad.2023.06.051

Salekin, R. T., & Hare, R. D. (2016). *Proposed Specifiers for Conduct Disorder (PSCD) scale* [Unpublished test].

Sanchez, A. L., Cornacchio, D., Poznanski, B., Golik, A. M., Chou, T., & Comer, J. S. (2018). The effectiveness of school-based mental health services for elementary-aged children: A meta-analysis. *Journal of the American Academy of Child & Adolescent Psychiatry, 57*(3), 153–165. https://doi.org/10.1016/j.jaac.2017.11.022

Sanders, M. R. (1999). Triple P-Positive Parenting Program: Towards an empirically validated multilevel parenting and family support strategy for the prevention of behavior and emotional problems in children. *Clinical Child and Family Psychology Review, 2*(2), 71–90. https://doi.org/10.1023/a:1021843613840

Sanders, M. R., Baker, S., & Turner, K. M. (2012). A randomized controlled trial evaluating the efficacy of Triple P Online with parents of children with early-onset conduct problems. *Behaviour Research and Therapy, 50*(11), 675–684. https://doi.org/10.1016/j.brat.2012.07.004

Sanders, M. R., Divan, G., Singhal, M., Turner, K. M., Velleman, R., Michelson, D., & Patel, V. (2022). Scaling up parenting interventions is critical for attaining the sustainable development goals. *Child Psychiatry & Human Development, 53*(5), 941–952. https://doi.org/10.1007/s10578-021-01171-0

Sanders, M. R., Healy, K. L., Grice, C., & Del Vecchio, T. (2017). Evidence-based parenting programs: Integrating science into school-based practice. In M. Thielsking & M. D. Terjesen (Eds.), *Handbook of Australian school psychology: Bridging the gaps in international research, practice, and policy* (pp. 537–551). Springer. https://doi.org/10.1007/978-3-319-45166-4_27

Satodiya, R., Bied, A., Shah, K., Parikh, T., & Ash, P. (2024). A systematic review of multisystemic therapy in adolescent sex offenders. *The Journal of the American Academy of Psychiatry and the Law, 52*(1), 51–60. https://www.psycnet.org/record/2025-19551-006

Schwenck, C., Mergenthaler, J., Keller, K., Zech, J., Salehi, S., Taurines, R., Romanos, M., Schecklmann, M., Schneider, W., Warnke, A., & Freitag, C. M. (2012). Empathy in children with autism and conduct disorder: Group specific profiles and developmental aspects. *Journal of Child Psychology and Psychiatry, 53*(6), 651–659. https://doi.org/10.1111/j.1469-7610.2011.02499.x

Scott, S., Knapp, M., Henderson, J., & Maughan, B. (2001). Financial cost of social exclusion: Follow-up study of antisocial children into adulthood. *BMJ, 323*(7306), 191. https://doi.org/10.1136/bmj.323.7306.191

Shaffer, D., Gould, M. S., Brasic, J., Ambrosini, P., Fisher, P., Bird, H., & Aluwahlia, S. (1983). A children's global assessment scale (CGAS). *Archives of General Psychiatry, 40*(11), 1228–1231.

Sharp, C., & Kine, S. (2008). The assessment of juvenile psychopathy: Strengths and weaknesses of currently used questionnaire measures. *Child and Adolescent Mental Health, 13*(2), 85–95. https://doi.org/10.1111/j.1475-3588.2008.00483.x

Sheidow, A. J., McCart, M. R., & Drazdowski, T. K. (2022). Family-based treatments for disruptive behavior problems in children and adolescents: An updated review of rigorous studies (2014–April 2020). *Journal of Marital and Family Therapy, 48*(1), 56–82. https://doi.org/10.1111/jmft.12567

Sheldrick, R. C., Kendall, P. C., & Heimberg, R. G. (2001). The clinical significance of treatments: A comparison of three treatments for conduct disordered children. *Clinical Psychology: Science and Practice, 8*(4), 418–430. https://doi.org/10.1093/clipsy.8.4.418

Silverthorn, P., Frick, P. J., & Reynolds, R. (2001). Timing of onset ad correlates of severe conduct problems in adjudicated girls and boys. *Journal of Psychopathology and Behavioral Assessment, 23*(3), 171–181. https://doi.org/10.1023/A:1010917304587

Skeem, J. L., Polaschek, D. L. L., Patrick, C. J., & Lilienfeld, S. O. (2013). Psychopathic personality: Bridging the gap between scientific evidence and public policy. *Psychological Science in the Public Interest, 12*(3), 95–162. https://doi.org/10.1177/1529100611426706

Skuse, D. (2003). Fear recognition and the neural basis of social cognition. *Child and Adolescent Mental Health, 8*(2), 50–60. https://doi.org/10.1111/1475-3588.00047

Somech, L. Y., & Elizur, Y. (2012). Promoting self-regulation and cooperation in pre-kindergarten children with conduct problems: A randomized controlled trial. *Journal of the American Academy of Child & Adolescent Psychiatry, 51*(4), 412–422. https://doi.org/10.1016/j.jaac.2012.01.019

Sourander, A., Jensen, P., Ronning, J. A., Niemela, S., Helenius, H., Sillanmaki, L., Kumpulainen, K., Piha, J., Tamminen, T., Moilanen, I., & Albqvist, F. (2007). What is the early adulthood outcome of boys who bully or who are bullied in childhood? The Finnish "From a Boy to a Man" study. *Pediatrics, 120*(2), 397–404. https://doi.org/10.1542/peds.2006-2704

Southam-Gerow, M. A., Marder, A. M., & Austin, A. A. (2008). Dissemination of evidence-based manualized treatments for children and families in practice settings. In R. G. Steele, T. D. Elkin, & M. C. Roberts (Eds.), *Handbook of evidence-based therapies for children and adolescents: Bridging science and practice* (pp. 447–469). Springer Science. https://doi.org/10.1007/978-0-387-73691-4_25

Spinrad, T. L., Morris, A. S., & Luthar, S. S. (2020). Introduction to the special issue: Socialization of emotion and self-regulation: Understanding processes and application. *Developmental Psychology, 56*(3), 385–389. https://doi.org/10.1037/dev0000904

Storch, E. A., Masia-Warner, C., Crisp, H., & Stein, R. G. (2005). Peer victimization and social anxiety in adolescence: A prospective study. *Aggressive Behavior, 31*(5), 437–452. https://doi.org/10.1002/ab.20093

Thøgersen, D. M., Elmose, M., Viding, E., McCrory, E., & Bjørnebekk, G. (2022). Behavioral improvements but limited change in callous-unemotional traits in adolescents treated for conduct problems. *Journal of Child and Family Studies, 31*(12), 3342–3358. https://doi.org/10.1007/s10826-022-02435-6

Thomas, R., Abell, B., Webb, H. J., Avdagic, E., & Zimmer-Gembeck, M. J. (2017). Parent–child interaction therapy: A meta-analysis. *Pediatrics, 140*(3), e20170352. https://doi.org/10.1542/peds.2017-0352

Thomas, R., & Zimmer-Gembeck, M. J. (2007). Behavioral outcomes of parent–child interaction therapy and Triple P—Positive Parenting Program: A review and meta-analysis. *Journal of Abnormal Child Psychology, 35*(3), 475–495. https://doi.org/10.1007/s10802-007-9104-9

Thomas, R., & Zimmer-Gembeck, M. J. (2012). Parent–child interaction therapy: An evidence-based treatment for child maltreatment. *Child Maltreatment, 17*(3), 253–266. https://doi.org/10.1177/1077559512459555

Thomson, N. D., Kevorkian, S. S., Hazlett, L., Perera, R., & Vrana, S. (2025). A new treatment approach to conduct disorder and callous-unemotional traits: An assessment of the acceptability, appropriateness, and feasibility of Impact VR. *Frontiers in Psychiatry, 16*, 1484938. https://doi.org/10.3389/fpsyt.2025.1484938

Thornton, L. C., Frick, P. J., Crapanzano, A. M., & Terranova, A. M. (2013). The incremental utility of callous-unemotional traits in predicting aggression and bullying in a community sample of boys and girls. *Psychological Assessment, 31*(2), 256–270. https://doi.org/10.1037/a0031153

Thornton, L. C., Frick, P. J., Ray, J. V., Wall Myers, T. D., Steinberg, L., & Cauffman, E. (2019). Risky sex, drugs, sensation seeking, and callous unemotional traits in justice-involved male adolescents. *Journal of Clinical Child and Adolescent Psychology, 48*(1), 68–79. https://doi.org/10.1080/15374416.2017.1399398

Thornton, L. C., Frick, P. J., Shulman, E. P., Ray, J. V., Steinberg, L., & Cauffman, E. (2015). Callous-unemotional traits and adolescents' role in group crime. *Law and Human Behavior, 39*(4), 368–377. https://doi.org/10.1037/lhb0000124

Tissue, A. D., Hawes, D. J., Lechowicz, M. E., & Dadds, M. R. (2022). Reliability and validity of the *DSM-5* Diagnostic Interview Schedule for Children, Adolescents, and Parents-5 in externalizing disorders and common comorbidities. *Clinical Child Psychology and Psychiatry, 27*(3), 870–881. https://doi.org/10.1177/13591045211061800

Todd, M., & Niec, L. N. (2025). The efficacy of online training in parent–child interaction therapy: Synchronous, asynchronous, and written formats. *Professional Psychology: Research and Practice, 56*(3), 201–210. https://doi.org/10.1037/pro0000621

Travis, J. K., & Brestan-Knight, E. (2013). A pilot study examining trainee treatment session fidelity when parent–child interaction therapy (PCIT) is implemented in community settings. *The Journal of Behavioral Health Services & Research, 40*(3), 342–354. https://doi.org/10.1007/s11414-013-9326-2

Tully, L. A., Piotrowska, P. J., Collins, D. A., Mairet, K. S., Black, N., Kimonis, E. R., Hawes, D. J., Moul, C., Lenroot, R. K., Frick, P. J., Anderson, V., & Dadds, M. R. (2017). Optimising child outcomes from parenting interventions: Fathers' experiences, preferences and barriers to participation. *BMC Public Health, 17*(1), 1–14. https://doi.org/10.1186/s12889-017-4426-1

Turner, K. M. T., & Sanders, M. R. (2011). *Triple P Online* [Interactive internet program]. Triple P International. https://www.triplep-parenting.net.au/au/parenting-courses/triple-p-online-under-12/

Valcan, D. S., Davis, H., & Pino-Pasternak, D. (2018). Parental behaviours predicting early childhood executive functions: A meta-analysis. *Educational Psychology Review, 30*(3), 607–649. https://doi.org/10.1007/s10648-017-9411-9

van Aar, J., Leijten, P., de Castro, B. O., & Overbeek, G. (2017). Sustained, fade-out or sleeper effects? A systematic review and meta-analysis of parenting interventions for disruptive child behavior. *Clinical Psychology Review, 51*, 153–163. https://doi.org/10.1016/j.cpr.2016.11.006

van der Stouwe, T., Asscher, J. J., Stams, G. J. J., Deković, M., & van der Laan, P. H. (2014). The effectiveness of multisystemic therapy (MST): A meta-analysis. *Clinical Psychology Review, 34*(6), 468–481. https://doi.org/10.1016/j.cpr.2014.06.006

Vaughan, E. P., Frick, P. J., Robertson, E. L., Ray, J. V., Thornton, L. C., Myers, T. D. W., Steinberg, L., & Cauffman, E. (2023). Interpersonal relationships and callous-unemotional traits during adolescence and young adulthood: An investigation of bidirectional effects in parent, peer, and romantic relationships. *Clinical Psychological Science, 11*(3), 391–408. https://doi.org/10.1177/21677026221101070

Viding, E. (2020). *Psychopathy: A very short introduction*. Oxford University Press. https://doi.org/10.1093/actrade/9780198802266.001.0001

Viding, E., Blair, R. J. R., Moffitt, T. E., & Plomin, R. (2005). Evidence for substantial genetic risk for psychopathy in 7-year-olds. *Journal of Child Psychology & Psychiatry, 46*(6), 592–597. https://doi.org/10.1111/j.1469-7610.2004.00393.x

Viding, E., Jones, A. P., Frick, P. J., Moffitt, T. E., & Plomin, R. (2008). Heritability of antisocial behaviour at nine-years: Do callous-unemotional traits matter? *Developmental Science, 11*(1), 17–22. https://doi.org/10.1111/j.1467-7687.2007.00648.x

Viding, E., & McCrory, E. (2019). Towards understanding atypical social affiliation in psychopathy. *The Lancet Psychiatry, 6*(5), 437–444. https://doi.org/10.1016/S2215-0366(19)30049-5

Viding, E., Sebastian, C. L., Dadds, M. R., Lockwood, P. L., Cecil, C. A., De Brito, S. A., & McCrory, E. J. (2012). Amygdala response to preattentive masked fear in children with conduct problems: The role of callous-unemotional traits. *American Journal of Psychiatry, 169*(10), 1109–1116. https://doi.org/10.1176/appi.ajp.2012.12020191

Waddell, C., Offord, D. R., Shepherd, C. A., Hua, J. M., & McEwan, K. (2002). Child psychiatric epidemiology and Canadian public policy-making: The state of the science and the art of the possible. *The Canadian Journal of Psychiatry, 47*(9), 825–832. https://doi.org/10.1177/070674370204700903

Wagner, N., Mills-Koonce, R., Willoughby, M., Propper, C., Rehder, P., & Guerone-Sela, N. (2017). Respiratory sinus arrhythmia and heart period in infancy as correlates of later oppositional defiant and callous-unemotional behaviors. *International Journal of Behavioral Development, 41*(1), 127–135. https://doi.org/10.1177/0165025415605391

Walker, T. M., Frick, P. J., Matlasz, T. M., Robertson, E. L., Mikolajewski, A. J., Mitchell, C., Lopez-Duran, N., Monk, C., & Hyde, L. W. (2021). Psychometric properties of a semistructured interview to assess limited prosocial emotions. *Assessment, 28*(7), 1755–1764. https://doi.org/10.1177/1073191120947796

Waller, R., Baskin-Sommers, A. R., & Hyde, L. W. (2018). Examining predictors of callous unemotional traits trajectories across adolescence among high-risk males. *Journal of Clinical Child and Adolescent Psychology, 47*(3), 444–457. https://doi.org/10.1080/15374416.2015.1102070

Waller, R., Gardner, F., & Hyde, L. W. (2013). What are the associations between parenting, callous–unemotional traits, and antisocial behavior in youth? A systematic review of evidence. *Clinical Psychology Review, 33*(4), 593–608. https://doi.org/10.1016/j.cpr.2013.03.001

Waller, R., Gardner, F., Viding, E., Shaw, D. S., Dishion, T. J., Wilson, M. N., & Hyde, L. W. (2014). Bidirectional associations between parental warmth, callous unemotional behavior, and behavior problems in high-risk preschoolers. *Journal of Abnormal Child Psychology, 42*(8), 1275–1285. https://doi.org/10.1007/s10802-014-9871-z

Waller, R., & Hyde, L. W. (2017). Callous–unemotional behaviors in early childhood: Measurement, meaning, and the influence of parenting. *Child Development Perspectives, 11*(2), 120–126. https://doi.org/10.1111/cdep.12222

Waller, R., & Wagner, N. (2019). The Sensitivity to Threat and Affiliative Reward (STAR) model and the development of callous-unemotional traits. *Neuroscience and Biobehavioral Reviews, 107*, 656–671. https://doi.org/10.1016/j.neubiorev.2019.10.005

Waller, R., Wagner, N. J., Barstead, M. G., Subar, A., Petersen, J. L., Hyde, J. S., & Hyde, L. W. (2020). A meta-analysis of the associations between callous-unemotional traits and empathy, prosociality, and guilt. *Clinical Psychology Review, 75*, 101809. https://doi.org/10.1016/j.cpr.2019.101809

Walter, H. J., Gouze, K., & Lim, K. G. (2006). Teachers' beliefs about mental health needs in inner city elementary schools. *Journal of the American Academy of Child & Adolescent Psychiatry, 45*(1), 61–68. https://doi.org/10.1097/01.chi.0000187243.17824.6c

Ward, M. A., Theule, J., & Cheung, K. (2016). Parent–child interaction therapy for child disruptive behaviour disorders: A meta-analysis. *Child & Youth Care Forum, 45*(5), 675–690. https://doi.org/10.1007/s10566-016-9350-5

Warren, J. M., Halpin, S. A., Hanstock, T. L., Hood, C., & Hunt, S. A. (2022). Outcomes of parent–child interaction therapy (PCIT) for families presenting with child maltreatment: A systematic review. *Child Abuse & Neglect, 134*, 105942. https://doi.org/10.1016/j.chiabu.2022.105942

Waschbusch, D. A., Breaux, R. P., & Babinski, D. E. (2019). School-based interventions for aggression and defiance in youth: A framework for evidence-based practice. *School Mental Health, 11*(1), 92–105. https://doi.org/10.1007/s12310-018-9269-0

Waschbusch, D. A., Carrey, N. J., Willoughby, M. T., King, S., & Andrade, B. F. (2007). Effects of methylphenidate and behavior modification on the social and academic behavior of children with disruptive behavior disorders: The moderating role of callous/unemotional traits. *Journal of Clinical Child and Adolescent Psychology, 36*(4), 629–644. https://doi.org/10.1080/15374410701662766

Waschbusch, D. A., Walsh, T. M., Andrade, B. F., King, S., & Carrey, N. J. (2007). Social problem solving, conduct problems, and callous-unemotional traits in children. *Child Psychiatry and Human Development, 37*(4), 293–305. https://doi.org/10.1007/s10578-006-0033-6

Waschbusch, D. A., Willoughby, M. T., Haas, S. M., Ridenour, T., Helseth, S., Crum, K. I., Altszuler, A. R., Ross, J. M., Coles, E. K., & Pelham, W. E. (2020). Effects of behavioral treatment modified to fit children with conduct problems and callous-unemotional (CU) traits. *Journal of Clinical Child & Adolescent Psychology, 49*(5), 639–650. https://doi.org/10.1080/15374416.2019.1614000

Waschbusch, D. A. (2002). A meta-analytic examination of comorbid hyperactive-impulsive-attention problems. *Psychological Bulletin, 128*(1), 118–150. https://doi.org/10.1037/0033-2909.128.1.118

Webster-Stratton, C. (2011). *The Incredible Years parents, teachers, and children's training series: Program content, methods, research and dissemination 1980–2011*. Incredible Years Inc.

Webster-Stratton, C., Reid, M. J., & Hammond, M. (2004). Treating children with early-onset conduct problems: Intervention outcomes for parent, child, and teacher training. *Journal of Clinical Child and Adolescent Psychology, 33*(1), 105–124. https://doi.org/10.1207/S15374424JCCP3301_11

Weist, M. D., Garbacz, S. A., Lane, K. L., & Kincaid, D. (2017). *Aligning and integrating family engagement in Positive Behavioral Interventions and Supports (PBIS): Concepts and strategies for families and schools in key contexts.* University of Oregon Press.

Westrupp, E. M., Bennett, C., Berkowitz, T., Youssef, G. J., Toumbourou, J. W., Tucker, R., Andrews, F. J., Evans, S., Teague, S. J., Karantzas, G. C., Melvin, G. M., Olsson, C., Macdonald, J. A., Greenwood, C. J., Mikocka-Walus, A., Hutchinson, D., Fuller-Tyszkiewicz, M., Stokes, M. A., Olive, L., . . . & Sciberras, E. (2023). Child, parent, and family mental health and functioning in Australia during COVID-19: Comparison to pre-pandemic data. *European Child & Adolescent Psychiatry, 32*(2), 317–330. https://doi.org/10.1007/s00787-021-01861-z

White, B. A., Dede, B., Heilman, M., Revilla, R., Lochman, J., Hudac, C. M., Bui, C., & White, S. W. (2022). Facial affect sensitivity training for young children with emerging CU traits: An experimental therapeutics approach. *Journal of Clinical Child & Adolescent Psychology, 51*(3), 264–276. https://doi.org/10.1080/15374416.2022.2056895

White, S. F., Frick, P. J., Lawing, K., & Bauer, D. (2013). Callous–unemotional traits and response to functional family therapy in adolescent offenders. *Behavioral Sciences & the Law, 31*(2), 271–285. https://doi.org/10.1002/bsl.2041

Wolraich, M. L., Hagan, J. F., Allan, C., Chan, E., Davison, D., Earls, M., Evans, S. W., Flinn, S. K., Froehlich, T., Frost, J., Holbrook, J. R., Lehmann, C. U., Lessin, H. R., Okechukwu, K., Pierce, K. L., Winner, J., & Zurhellen, W. (2019). Clinical practice guideline for the diagnosis, evaluation, and treatment of attention-deficit/hyperactivity disorder in children and adolescents. *Pediatrics, 144*(4), e20192528. https://doi.org/10.1542/peds.2019-2528

Wootton, J. M., Frick, P. J., Shelton, K. K., & Silverthorn, P. (1997). Ineffective parenting and childhood conduct problems: The moderating role of callous-unemotional traits. *Journal of Consulting and Clinical Psychology, 65*(2), 301–308. https://doi.org/10.1037/0022-006X.65.2.292.b

World Health Organization. (1992). *The ICD-10 classification of mental and behavioural disorders: Clinical descriptions and diagnostic guidelines.* https://www.who.int/publications/i/item/9241544228

World Health Organization. (2018). *International statistical classification of diseases and related health problems* (11th ed.). https://icd.who.int/

Zhang, H., Wang, W., & Li, Z. (2024). Effectiveness of parent–child interaction therapy for maltreated families: A meta-analysis of randomized controlled trials. *Trauma, Violence, & Abuse, 25*(4), 2689–2702. https://doi.org/10.1177/15248380231222041

INDEX

A

ADHD. *See* Attention-deficit/hyperactivity disorder
Adherence to treatment, 120, 148–149, 186, 266–268
Adjustment problems, 32–34, 50, 60, 63, 255
Affect, shallow or deficient, 15–17, 23, 80, 107–109, 149
Affection, parental. *See* Parental warmth and affection
Aggression, severe, 15, 26, 28–31, 61, 64–66, 85, 139, 168, 183–184, 255
  proactive, premedicated, or instrumental, 30–31, 64
  reactive, 30, 51
  relational, 65
Alexander, J. F., 132–133
American Psychiatric Association
  DSM-III, 16
  DSM-III-R, 17
  DSM-IV, 17
  DSM-5, 75, 21–23, 59–60
  DSM-5-TR, 59–60, 63–64, 71
Amygdala, 41, 136
Anger Coping program, 131
Antisocial behavior, 14–16, 20, 30
  risk for, 28–30
Antisocial personality disorder (ASPD), 15–16, 26, 28, 270
Antisocial Process Screening Device (APSD), 71–72
Anxiety, 17, 61, 66–67, 143, 194, 255, 266
Armstrong, K., 181, 202
ASD. *See* Autism spectrum disorder
ASPD (antisocial personality disorder). *See* Antisocial personality disorder (ASPD)
Assessment. *See also* Conduct disorders assessment
  in case study, 192–195
  callous–unemotional traits, 71–73
  common causal pathways, 70–71
  common comorbidities, 65–69
  guidelines for general considerations in, 59–65, 255–256
Attention-deficit/hyperactivity disorder (ADHD), 18–19, 27, 61, 66, 110, 123, 128–129, 143, 194, 255
Australia, 93, 119–120, 192, 196, 240, 242–243, 245, 251, 260, 269
Autism spectrum disorder (ASD), 69, 120, 135, 143, 178, 194, 223–224

B

Barriers to treatment, 240–241
Behavior management, reward-based, 125–126, 138
Behavior management strategy enhancement, 258
Behavior(s)
  antisocial, 28–30
  criminal, 31–32
  risky sexual, 26, 33–34, 68, 255
  suicidal, 26, 34, 61, 67, 266

Blader, J. C., 110, 129
Boredom susceptibility, 124, 187
Bullying, 26, 31–33, 61–62, 65, 255

C

Callous-lack of empathy trait, 54–55, 103–105
Callous–unemotional (CU) traits
- assessment of, 71, 111, 255–256
- future directions for research, 264–265
- secondary CU traits, 67, 237, 266–268
- stability and later psychopathic traits, 28–29

CAPE. *See* Clinical Assessment of Prosocial Emotions (CAPE)
Cardinale, E. M., 83, 84
Caregiver–child emotions, learning to recognize, 42–43, 171–173, 223–225
Caregiver-child relationship enhancement, 138, 143–144, 182, 249, 253, 256–258
CARES (Coaching and Rewarding Emotional Skills) module. *See* Coaching and Rewarding Emotional Skills (CARES) module
Carrey, N. J., 125, 129, 130
Case study, 191–237
- assessment pretreatment, 192–195
- CARES treatment phase, 222–230
- CDI-CU treatment phase, 196–208
- cultural adaptation, 196
- PDI-CU treatment phase, 208–222
- treatment outcomes, 230–236

Cauchi, A. J., 119, 135–136, 259
Causal pathways to serious conduct problems, 47–56
- adolescent-onset conduct problems, 49–51
- childhood-onset conduct problems with LPE specifier, 39, 53–55
- childhood-onset conduct problems without LPE specifier, 38, 51–53

CBCL (Child Behavior Checklist), 194, 230–231
CBT (Cognitive-behavior therapy), 130–133, 139–140, 180, 256
CD (conduct disorder), 194
CDI-CU. *See* Child-directed interaction for children and adolescents with callous–unemotional traits (CDI-CU) phase of treatment
CDI (child-directed interaction) phase of treatment, 143–152
Center on the Social and Emotional Foundations for Early Learning, 178
CGAS (Children's Global Assessment Scale), 194
Child Behavior Checklist (CBCL). *See* CBCL (Child Behavior Checklist)
Child–caregiver relationship enhancement. *See* Caregiver–child relationship enhancement
Child-directed interaction for children and adolescents with callous–unemotional traits (CDI-CU) phase of treatment, 151–152, 156–163, 167–168, 183–184, 196–208
- challenges and strategies, 182–184
- coaching sessions, 198–208
- Do/Don't skills, 199–200
- goals and materials, 151–155
- teaching session, 197–198

Child-directed interaction (CDI) phase of treatment, 143–144, 147–150
- mastery criteria, 144, 149

Child-led play, 127, 194–195, 199, 232, 236
Child maltreatment risk, 143
Child Problematic Traits Inventory (CPTI), 71
Child punishment insensitivity, addressing in PDI, 149, 163–170
Children's Global Assessment Scale (CGAS), 194
Cleckley, H., 14–15
Clinical Assessment of Prosocial Emotions (CAPE), 91–97, 194
- administration of, 94–95
- development, 92
- integrating into broader assessment of conduct problems, 109–110
- reliability and validity, 93–94
- semi-structured interviews, 95–97
- training requirements, 93

Clinical Assessment of Prosocial Emotions (CAPE) scoring
- callous-lack of empathy, 103–105
- general considerations, 98–100
- guidelines for integrating information, 98
- lack of remorse or guilt, 100–102
- shallow or deficient affect, 107–109
- unconcerned about performance, 105–107

Coaching and Rewarding Emotional Skills (CARES) module, 149, 170–181, 187–188, 222–230
- cool down toolbox, 180–181
- coping with negative emotions, 227–228
- "I Want to Play" social story, 179
- learning to recognize caregiver–child emotions, 225
- learning to recognize others' emotions, 223–224
- linking emotions with context, 225–227
- microexpression training, 172, 177–178, 223–24
- recognizing and responding to signs of distress, 228–229
- review and graduation, 229–230

social stories, 178
staircase to success, 175
stop–breathe–think, 179
teaching session, 222–223
Coercive cycle, parent-child, 117
Cognitive-behavior therapy (CBT), 130–132
Cognitive bias, 131, 256
Common causal pathways assessment, 70–71
Common comorbidities assessment, 65–69
Conduct disorder (CD), 22, 59, 63, 194
adolescent-onset, 17–18, 38, 49–51, 69–71
childhood-onset, 17–18, 27, 38–39, 51–55, 71
solitary aggressive, 17
undersocialized, 16–18
Conduct disorders assessment, 61–74
callous–unemotional traits, 71–74
common comorbidities, 65–69
general guidelines for, 61–62
key indicators of common causal pathways, 70–71
multiple risk factors, 69–70
number and severity of conduct problems, 63–65
Conduct problems, 38, 49–51, 109–110
Conduct Problems Prevention Research Group, 27
Conscience, 13, 54–55
Consistency. *See* Parental Consistency
Contagious crying, 42
Cool Down Toolbox, 180–181
Coping Power program, 131–132
COVID-19 pandemic, 241, 248
CPTI (Child Problematic Traits Inventory), 71
Criminal behavior, 31–32, 68
Crying, contagious, 42
CU traits. *See* Callous–unemotional traits

D

Dadds, M., 120, 122, 135–137, 268
Datyner, A., 181
Defiant Children program, 118
Deng, J., 83
Depression, 66, 194
Developmental delay, 120, 143
Diagnostic and Statistical Manual of Mental Disorders, Fifth Edition (DSM-5; American Psychiatric Association), 21–23
Diagnostic and Statistical Manual of Mental Disorders, Fifth Edition, Text Revision (DSM-5-TR; American Psychiatric Association), 59–60, 63–64, 71
Diagnostic and Statistical Manual of Mental Disorders, third edition (DSM-III; American Psychiatric Association), 16
Diagnostic Interview Schedule for Children, Adolescents, and Parents (DISCAP), 194
DPICS. *See* Dyadic parent-child interaction coding system
DSM. See Diagnostic and Statistical Manual of Mental Disorders
Dudgeon, P., 196
Dyadic parent–child interaction coding system (DPICS), 143–144, 160, 194–195
Dysfunctional parent–child interactions, 122

E

ECBI. *See* Eyberg Child Behavior Inventory
ECBI talk, 163
Edens, J. F., 75
Eight rules for giving effective commands, 144–145
Emotional, cognitive, and social characteristics, 37–56
deficits in emotional reactivity and emotion recognition, 40–44
parenting factors, 45–47
punishment insensitivity, 44–45
Emotional engagement intervention, 137
Emotional reactivity deficits, 40–42
Emotion recognition, 43–44, 136, 170–171, 223–225, 258
Emotion recognition training, 258–259
Emotion regulation, 51–52, 170–171
Emotions, linking with context, 225–229
Empathy, 13–14, 28, 55, 136, 170–171. *See also* Callous-lack of empathy trait; Callous–unemotional traits
English, T., 136–137
Evidence-based interventions, barriers to, 240–241
Experimental therapeutics, 135, 137
Eyberg Child Behavior Inventory (ECBI), 159, 162–163, 183, 194
Ezpeleta, L., 85, 119

F

Faces intervention, 259
Facial Affect Sensitivity Training (FAST), 137, 259
Fear blindness, 136
Fleming, G. E., 182, 243, 245
Friendships, 33
Functional family therapy (FFT), 132–134, 139, 267

G

Gang activity, 32
Genetics, 40
Goetz, C. M., 94, 111
Guilt, 13–14, 28, 55, 100–102

H

Hanf, C., 118–119
Hare, R. D., 15
Harsh parenting, 51, 122
Hawes, D. J., 83–84, 94, 119, 120, 122
Helping Our Toddlers, Developing Our Children's Skills intervention, 202
Helping the Noncompliant Child, 118–119, 124
Home reward possibilities, 164–165
Hyatt, C. S., 270

I

ICD-10. See International Classification of Diseases (ICD-10; World Health Organization)
Identity development, 50
Impact Virtual Reality (VR) program, 259
Impulsivity, 18–19, 72
Incredible Years, 118
Informants, use of different, 86–89
Informational frame, 125
Intellectual disability, 143
International Classification of Diseases (ICD-10; World Health Organization), 17, 22–23, 59
Internet adaptations of parent management training. *See* Parent management training, Internet adaptations
Internet-delivered Parent–Child Interaction Therapy (iPCIT), 242–248
Internet-delivered programs, 241–248
Inventory of Callous–Unemotional Traits (ICU), 79–90
  cutoff scores, 84–86
  development of, 73
  factor analyses, 82–83
  items, 80
  item wording, 81–82
  preschool, 81, 85
  translations, 81
  reliability, 83–84
  treatment monitoring, 89–90
  use as a screener, 86
  use of different informants, 86–89
  validity, 84

K

Kazdin, A. E., 116, 118, 126, 131, 254, 257–258
Kimonis, E. R., 181–182
Kochanska, G., 54–55, 127, 156

L

Learning window, 124
Limited prosocial emotions (LPE) specifier
  and childhood-onset conduct problems, 51–55
  and criminal behavior, 31–32
  diagnostic research on, 20–23
  disseminating treatments tailored for, 269–271
  future directions for, 263–271
  key considerations for children with, 255–256
  and other adjustment problems, 33–34
  PCIT-CU for, 141–189, 254–259
  and problems in social relationships, 32–33
  and risk for antisocial behavior, 28–30
  scoring, 103–105
  specific treatments for, 135–138
  and violence and severe aggression, 28–30
Limited prosocial emotions (LPE) specifier, diagnostic research, 13–24
  on construct of psychopathology, 14–18
  on extension of construct of psychopathology to youth, 18–20
  on LPE specifier, 20–23
Louisiana, 240

M

Marsh, A. A., 83–84
The Mask of Sanity (Cleckley), 14
Materials, for PCIT-CU, 151–155
McDonald, R., 121
Medication, stimulant. *See* Stimulant medication
Mendota Juvenile Treatment Center (MJTC), 134–135
Methylphenidate. *See* Stimulant medication
Microexpression training. *See* Coaching and Rewarding Emotional Skills (CARES) module, microexpression training
Miller, N. V., 125
Mindreading, 135–136, 178, 258–259
MJTC (Mendota Juvenile Treatment Center), 134–135
Mobile app, 124
Moore, A. A., 83
Multimodal interventions, 132–135, 139
Multisystemic therapy (MST), 132, 134
Mutism, selective, 143

N

Narcissistic traits, 19
National Institute of Mental Health (NIMH), 135

Negative reinforcement, 118
Neo, B., 94
New Zealand, 4, 17
Nutritional supplements. *See* Omega-3 nutritional supplements

O

Obesity, 143
ODD (oppositional-defiant disorder), 59, 64, 194
Omega-3 nutritional supplements, 129–130
Online programs, 241–248
Oregon Social Learning Center, 118

P

Parental warmth and affection, 45–47, 126–128, 150, 156–157, 159
Parent–child coercive cycle, 117
Parent–Child Interaction Therapy (PCIT)
  adaptations for callous–unemotional traits, 141–189
  overview of, 142–148
  training in, 269–271
  in school setting, 248–254
Parent–Child Interaction Therapy adapted for callous–unemotional traits (PCIT-CU), 141–189. *See also* Child-directed interaction for children and adolescents with callous–unemotional traits (CDI-CU) phase of treatment; Coaching and Rewarding Emotional Skills (CARES) module; Parent-directed interaction for children and adolescents with callous–unemotional traits (PDI-CU), phase of treatment
  adaptation for school settings, 248–254
  addressing child punishment insensitivity and reward dominance in PDI, 149, 163–170
  applying the model to tailor other treatments, 254–259
  barriers to evidence-based interventions, 240–241
  Coaching and Rewarding Emotional Skills (CARES) module, 149, 171–181, 187–188
  common challenges and strategies in implementation, 182–183
  expanding reach of, 240–259
  feasibility, 182
  fixed-session format, 149
  goals and materials, 151–155
  home reward possibilities, 165
  house rules, 168–169
  internet adaptations, 241–246
  internet-delivered, 242–248
  internet-delivered PCIT, 242–248
  iPCIT-CU treatment protocol, 246–248
  and other programs for those with LPE, 254–259
  open trial, 182
  overview of PCIT, 142–148
  parental cognitions, 160, 183, 186, 265
  parental warmth and affection, 45–46, 148, 156–157
  PCIT, adapted for, 181–188
  PDI-CU, 184–187
  public behavior, 169
  randomized controlled trial, 182
  in school setting, 250–254
  "Showing You Care" social story, 160–161
  specific adaptations to CDI, 156, 158–160, 162–163
  stress relief strategies, 162
  structure of sessions, 159
  supporting research, 181–182
  time-out procedure, 122–125, 145–148, 166
Parent–child relationship, 119, 126–127
Parental consistency, 121, 125–126
Parental stress, 162
Parent-directed interaction for children and adolescents with callous–unemotional traits (PDI-CU), phase of treatment, 164, 166–170, 184–187, 208–222
Parent-directed interaction (PDI) phase of treatment, 143–150
  addressing child punishment insensitivity and reward dominance, 163–165
  coaching session, 210–222
  mastery criteria, 147, 170
  teaching session, 208–210
Parenting Stress Index–Short Form (PSI-SF), 202
Parent management training, 116–128
  combined with stimulant medication, 128–129
  internet adaptations of, 241–242
  parental warmth, 126–128
  parent–child coercive cycle, 117
  reward-based behavior management, 125–126, 138
  time-out, 122–125, 145–147, 163, 166, 184–186
Parent Management Training-Oregon Model (PMTO), 118, 120
Pasalich, D. S., 45
PATHS (Promoting Alternative Thinking Strategies) curriculum, 131, 179
Patterson, G. R., 117–118
PAWS (Parental Affection/Warmth Scale), 158–159
PCL (Psychopathy Checklist), 15
PDI (parent-directed interactions). *See* Parent-directed interaction (PDI) phase of treatment

PDI-CU. *See* Parent-directed interaction for children and adolescents with callous–unemotional traits (PDI-CU), phase of treatment
Peer relationships, 33, 68
meanness, 32, 105
rejection, 31
Perlstein, S., 132
Planned ignoring, 126, 139, 144, 160, 180, 183, 197, 199–201, 203–211, 214–215, 217, 218, 220, 221, 223, 225, 227, 256, 258
PMT. *See* Parent management training
PMTO (Parent Management Training-Oregon Model), 118, 120
Points system, 126
Positive opposite behaviors, 126, 144, 151, 168–169, 187, 199–200, 201, 203–207, 212, 215, 217–221, 256
Positive Parenting Program, Triple P (TPOL), 118, 242
Premature birth, 120
Preschool Training Module 2, 178
PRIDE (praise, speech reflections, behavior imitation and description, expression of enjoyment) skills, 143–144, 156, 160
Problem-solving skills training (PSST), 131
"Project Support" parenting intervention, 121
Promoting Alternative Thinking Strategies (PATHS), 131, 179
Proposed Specifiers for Conduct Disorder (PSCD), 71
Prosocial behaviors, 29
PSI-SF (Parenting Stress Index–Short Form). *See* Parenting Stress Index–Short Form (PSI-SF)
PSST (problem-solving skills training), 131
Psychopathology, 14–20
Psychopathy, 14–16
Psychopathy Checklist: Youth Version (PCL-YV), 73
Punishment insensitivity, 44–45, 122
Punishment insensitivity, addressing in PDI, 149, 163–170
Punishment learning, 124

Q

QR codes for accessing resources, 273–274
Quay, H. C., 16

R

Raine, A., 130
Rebelliousness, 50
Relationship enhancement, caregiver–child, 127, 138, 257–258
Relationships, peer, 68
Relationships, social, 32–33
Reliability
of CAPE, 93–94
of Inventory of Callous–Unemotional Traits (ICU), 83–84
Remorse, 100–102
Research, 263–271
and LPE specifier, 269–271
and risk factors for callous–unemotional traits, 264–265
and treatment outcomes and adherence, 266–268
Reward-based behavior management, 125–126, 138
Reward dominance, addressing in PDI, 149, 163–170
Rewards at home, 165
Risk(s)
in adolescent- vs. child-onset conduct problem groups, 49–53
for antisocial behavior, 28–30
assessment of multiple, 69–70
behaviors, sexual, 33–34
for child maltreatment, 143
and conduct disorders, 47–49, 63
for CU traits, future directions for research, 264–265
long-term outcomes of conduct disorders, 4, 6
of suicidal behavior, 67
Ritalin. *See* Stimulant medication
Rowe, R., 60

S

School settings, 248–254
Schwenck, C., 69
Scoring CAPE. *See* Clinical Assessment of Prosocial Emotions (CAPE) scoring
Selective attention, 126
Selective mutism, 143
Separation anxiety, 143
SEWB (social and emotional well-being) model, 196
Sex offending, 30
Sexual behaviors, risky, 33–34
Shallow or deficient affect, 107–109
"Showing You Care" social story, 160–161
Silent cognitive retraining, 137
SNAP (Stop-Now-And-Plan), 131
Social and emotional well-being (SEWB) model, 196
Social Interaction Learning framework, 118
Social relationship problems, 32–33
Social stories, 160, 178
Special education services, 76
Special play. *See* Parent management training
Stigma, minimizing, 13, 16, 74–77

Stimulant medication, 110, 128–130, 139
Stop-Now-And-Plan (SNAP). *See* SNAP (Stop-Now-And-Plan)
STP. *See* Summer treatment programs
Substance use, 33, 67–68
Suicidal behavior, 34, 67
Summer treatment programs (STPs), 123, 125–126, 129
Sweden, 242

T

TAI (Therapy Attitude Inventory), 181
Target Behavior List, 168
Technology-enhanced, 124
Telehealth, 241
Therapy Attitude Inventory (TAI), 181
Thøgersen, D. M., 134, 267
Thornton, L. C., 34
Time-in, 127–128
Time-outs, 122–125, 145–147, 163, 166, 184–186
Time-out room, 147–148
Token economy, 138, 149, 152–153, 155, 163–167, 170, 172–176, 181, 186–188, 208, 210–219, 222–223, 256
Tokens, 126
TPOL (Triple P Positive Parenting Program), 242
Trauma and abuse, 9, 67, 110
Treatment outcomes, 230–236
  callous–unemotional traits, 120
  dose, 121
  dropout, 119, 148
  future directions for research, 266–268
  posttreatment assessment, 230–234
  three-month follow-up assessment, 234–236
Triarchic Psychopathy Measure (TriPM), 72
Triple P Positive Parenting Program, 242

U

Unconcerned about performance trait, 105–107
Undersocialized (term), 17
University of New South Wales (UNSW) Parent–Child Research Clinic, 240

V

Validity, of CAPE, 93–94
Video teleconferencing (VTC), 242–243, 245, 247, 251
Viding, E., 40
Violence, 28–30, 66–67

W

Warmth, parental. *See* Parental warmth and affection
Warmth/Affection Coding System (WACS-II), 158–160, 264
Warmth and affection handout, 157
Waschbusch, D. A., 125–126, 129–130
World Health Organization, 17, 22–23, 59

ABOUT THE AUTHORS

Paul J. Frick, PhD, is a licensed clinical psychologist and the Roy Crumpler memorial chair and director of clinical training in the Department of Psychology at the Louisiana State University. Dr. Frick's continuing line of research focuses on how children develop serious behavior problems and aggression and on the implications of this knowledge for assessment, treatment, and public policy. Dr. Frick's research publications are highly cited, and he has developed a number of measures to aid in the assessment and diagnosis of youth with emotional or behavioral problems. These measures have been widely used in research and clinical practice worldwide. Dr. Frick has received a number of awards for his research. He was awarded the 2015 Robert D. Hare Lifetime Achievement Award from the Society for the Scientific Study of Psychopathy. In 2020 he received the award for Contributions in Psychological Science from the Louisiana Psychological Association. In 2021, he was awarded the Bob Smith, Excellence in Psychological Assessment Award from the Society for Clinical Child and Adolescent Psychology (SCCAP), Division 53 of the American Psychological Association. In 2023, he was named a distinguished research master by the Louisiana State University Office Research and Economic Development.

Dr. Frick was the editor of the *Journal of Clinical Child and Adolescent Psychology* (2007–2011), the official journal of Division 53, and the editor of *Research on Child and Adolescent Psychopathology* (2018–2022), the official journal of the International Society for Research on Child and Adolescent Psychopathology. He was a member of the American Psychiatric Association's *DSM-5* Workgroup for ADHD and the Disruptive Behavior Disorders (2007–2012) and was the section editor (2018–2021) of the "Disruptive, Impulse-Control, and Conduct Disorders" chapter for the *DSM-5-TR*.

Eva R. Kimonis, MS, PhD, is a clinical psychologist and professor of psychology at the University of New South Wales (UNSW). She founded and is director of the UNSW Parent–Child Research Clinic that specializes in providing state-of-the-art assessment and treatment for children with conduct problems. Dr. Kimonis is an international authority on the development, assessment, and treatment of childhood conduct disorders and psychopathic traits. She served as associate editor for the journal *Research on Child and Adolescent Psychopathology* and president of the Society for the Scientific Study of Psychopathy. Dr. Kimonis is a recipient of the Eric Taylor Translational Research into Practice Award (2023) from the Association for Child and Adolescent Mental Health (ACAMH) and a prestigious Fulbright Award from the J. William Fulbright Foreign Scholarship Board (2012–2013). She is a certified therapist and Australia-wide trainer of Parent–Child Interaction Therapy (PCIT), which she adapted to target the unique needs of children with conduct problems and limited prosocial emotions, and for delivery in school settings with educator involvement.